# Ethnography and Schools

**Immigration and the Transnational Experience**
Series Editor: Enrique (Henry) T. Trueba, Pedro Reyes, and Yali Zou

# Ethnography and Schools

*Qualitative Approaches to
the Study of Education*

Yali Zou
and
Enrique (Henry) T. Trueba

ROWMAN & LITTLEFIELD PUBLISHERS, INC.
Lanham • Boulder • New York • Oxford

ROWMAN & LITTLEFIELD PUBLISHERS, INC.

Published in the United States of America
by Rowman & Littlefield Publishers, Inc.
4720 Boston Way, Lanham, Maryland 20706
www.rowmanlittlefield.com

12 Hid's Copse Road
Cumnor Hill, Oxford OX2 9JJ, England

British Library Cataloguing in Publication Information Available

**Library of Congress Cataloging-in-Publication Data**

Ethnography and schools : qualitative approaches to the study of education / [edited by]
Yali Zou and Enrique (Henry) T. Trueba.
    p.   cm.—(Immigration and the transnational experience)
    Includes bibliographical references and index.
    ISBN 0-7425-1736-5 (alk. paper)—ISBN 0-7425-1737-3 (pbk. : alk. paper).
    1. Educational anthropology.   2. Immigrants—Education—United States.
    I. Zou, Yali.   II. Trueba, Enrique T., 1931–   III. Series.
    LB45 .E8394   2002
    306.43—dc21                                                    2001057856

Printed in the United States of America

∞ ™ The paper used in this publication meets the minimum requirements of American
National Standard for Information Sciences—Permanence of Paper for Printed Library
Materials, ANSI/NISO Z39.48-1992.

# Contents

# Acknowledgments

In February 2000 a group of scholars from around the country gathered at the University of Houston to discuss the current status of educational ethnography and the most current research. Faculty and students from numerous universities, including Harvard University, Stanford University, and the University of Texas–Austin, attended and responded with enthusiasm to some of the ideas presented. That conference was organized with funds from the Spencer Foundation. It was in this conference that a number of current research reports (including reports on a study conducted in Houston with Spencer Foundation monies) and the idea of this volume were generated. Portions of the research reported in this book were made possible (in part) by a grant from the Spencer Foundation. We want to thank the Spencer Foundation for its generous support. As expected, we also want to make clear that the work and the conclusions reached in the various chapters and the positions stated by the authors are solely the responsibility of the authors.

We want to take this opportunity to recognize the staff of the Asian American Studies Center and the team of graduate students who assisted us in the organization of this volume. We wish to express our gratitude to Dean Birkenkamp, Christine Gatliffe, and Alison Sullenburg for the guidance, support, and excellent suggestions that enhanced the implementation of this volume.

~

# Dedication

This volume is dedicated to David Martin Smith, a dear colleague, friend, and superb ethnographer committed to social justice and educational equity. He was a genuine inspiration for the contributors and editors of this volume. Born on January 23, 1935, on a family farm in upstate New York, he attended Nyack College, graduating in 1956. An ordained minister, he completed a master's degree in linguistics in 1965 at the Hartford Seminary Foundation and worked as both a missionary linguist and a Fulbright-Hayes Scholar in West Africa. He received a doctorate in anthropological linguistics from Michigan State University in 1969. David was married to Perry Gilmore and worked with her in numerous projects in Alaska, Pennsylvania, Australia, New Zealand, and Russia. David was an associate director, with Dell Hymes, Erving Goffman, and John Szwed, of the Center for Urban Ethnography at the University of Pennsylvania; the creator of the Penn Forum for Ethnography and Education; and president of the Council on Anthropology and Education. He published significant papers in both linguistic and educational anthropology. He was a professor of anthropology, linguistics, and education at four major universities: Georgetown, Temple, University of Pennsylvania, and University of Alaska, Fairbanks, where he was founder and two-term president of the faculty senate. He was a visiting scholar at Stanford University, Curtin University's Centre for Aboriginal Studies in Australia, and the Navajo Nation's Dine College. Finally, he was Professor Emeritus of anthropology and linguistics at the University of Alaska, Fairbanks, and affiliate senior researcher at the Bureau of Applied Research in Anthropology at the University of Arizona. A soft-spoken and gentle man with a zest for life, he was recognized by his colleagues as a relentless defender and ally of disenfranchised populations around the globe and a fierce advocate for student and faculty rights. David died in Tucson, Arizona, on December 9, 2000, after suffering a sudden and massive stroke. He will be remembered as a visionary pioneer in the field of ethnography and education.

# Introduction: Historical Perspectives on the Ethnography of Schools

*Enrique (Henry) T. Trueba and Yali Zou*

Immigrants are the first to be blamed when the economy is doing poorly and the last to be praised when the economy is doing well. They are the most convenient scapegoats when crime statistics are on the rise or when Aptitude Test scores are counted. (P. McLaren 2000:1)

To place in its appropriate context the discussion of recent advances in educational ethnography, one needs to document historically its continued progress through the last century, its conspicuous struggles through the crises of a modern world, changed drastically by hatred and destruction, religious and secular philosophies, technological revolutionary trends in the media (instant visual global communication), politically and economically supported terrorism against "capitalist" societies, and an ever-increasing flow of immigrants seeking jobs and freedom, blinded by dreams of prosperity and romantic misperception of the affluent Western societies. The events of September 11, 2001, have forced all of us to restructure our concept of modern America in a global struggle for a democratic way of life, a tolerant coexistence with interracial, interethnic, and multilingual societies around the world. The realization that life is precious and even the most powerful nations are vulnerable today brings us back to education as the foundation of our prosperity and our democracy. Schools and teachers have suddenly acquired a new significance and demand additional support to prepare a new generation of Americans from highly diversified ethnic, racial, cultural, and

1

linguistic backgrounds. We are more eager to study schools and to assist them in their difficult tasks of educating a multiracial society for a new world and a new global society that protects itself not through conventional weapons and by purchasing with the almighty dollar the good will of other nations, but by our commitment to humanity and our respect for other cultures and ways of life.

The new awareness of the importance of schools and educational research brings us back to the contributions of this volume. More than ever we want to understand the best ways to educate children and to strengthen teacher preparation, the philosophical foundations of democratic organizations (schools, cities, churches, etc.) in a modern and highly diversified world, and in the microcosmos of that world that is our own American society. Social sciences, and certainly educational ethnography, must recognize the intrinsic difficulty in making sense of the world of other peoples whose languages and lifestyles are different from ours. Yet educational ethnography, with the help of anthropology and psychology, is venturing into methodological approaches that can best help us make sense of other worlds, and of children from those worlds in our own classrooms. Our classrooms are highly diversified primarily due to the rapid increase in immigration. The contributions of this volume go far beyond methodological insights to improve the practice of qualitative research in schools. This book presents important theoretical perspectives that have illuminated decades of work and have inspired many research projects resulting in a deeper understanding of cultural diversity. Research efforts have focused on what it means to be culturally different and to learn effectively in our classrooms. The discussion of historically important theoretical trends, the new reflections on the appropriate learning contexts in school and at home, the requirements for solid qualitative research, but most of all the new epistemologies brought by the work of ethnic scholars are turning educational ethnography into one of the most incisive and powerful research instruments in the exploration of new horizons and hopes for a better future. We are now exploring new ways to conduct qualitative research in schools with diverse student populations in order to pursue a new reform pedagogy based on principles of equity, justice, fairness, tolerance, and multiculturalism.

Immigration is not a new phenomenon. What is new about the rapid immigration and migration waves from developing countries to industrial societies, and within industrial societies? One answer is: their magnitude, their unique features, their resiliency, and their economic and social importance for our society. There are unexpected forces leading immigrants to adapt in new and creative ways. Simple assimilation is neither possible nor the most effective way to survive in the host country. Unlike the immigration of the last century from the European countries to the United States, the last four decades reveal drastic changes, according to Marcelo Suárez-Orozco:

> Immigration is the driving force behind a significant transformation of American society taking place at the end of the millennium. Few other social phenomena are likely to affect the future character of American culture and society as much as the ongoing wave of "new" immigration. . . . In 1945, just fifty years ago, the U.S. population was 87 percent white, 10 percent black, 2.5 percent Hispanic, and 0.5 percent Asian. Fifty years from now, in the year of 2050, demographic projections suggest a strikingly different population profile: 52.8 percent of the population will be white, 13.6 percent of the population will be black, 24.5 percent of the population will be Hispanic, and 8.2 percent of the population will be of Asian ancestry. (1998:5)

The economic and social mobility of ethnic populations and their increasing interethnic marriages as well as marriages with mainstream populations will soon make obsolete the current ethnic categories. In fact, the transnational character of immigrant groups (often dictated by economic constraints, employment patterns, and cultural needs) will change the ethos and cultural profile of America and its democratic institutions. Immigrants are concentrated in California, New York, Florida, Texas, and Illinois. In California, for example, about 20 percent of all school age children are immigrant. In New York City public schools today, 48 percent of all children come from immigrant households and speak hundreds of different languages. Overall, immigrants are not only culturally and racially diverse, economically and educationally stratified, but also view the United States in different ways. Consequently, the pattern of residence, the adaptive strategies, their mode of transnational lifestyle, and their role in this country's political and economic structure is multifaceted. Marcelo and Carola Suárez-Orozco observe that "among many immigrant groups today, length of residence in the United States seems associated with *declining* health, school achievement, and aspirations" and that "immigrant youth were healthier than their counterparts from nonimmigrant families" (2000:19–20).

If assimilation and acculturation models are in conflict with the reality of ethnic enclaves and the conspicuous multicultural, multilingual, and culturally diverse lifestyle of immigrant families, the question is: How do immigrants manage to function in different settings, and what happens to their ethnic identity? How do they manage to become effective participants in American society through the use of English and American cultural patterns, while at the same time they retain their home cultures and languages? Consequently, issues of identity and multiculturalism go together and seem to become functionally instrumental in the adaptation of newcomers to the United States.

Is the ability of immigrants to function effectively among members of mainstream society, to compete well with them in education and businesses, a new characteristic? Young generations of Asian Americans, Latinos, and other immigrants are genuinely proud to become mainstream Americans. Yet they remain active members of their respective ethnic groups with fluency in Mandarin, Spanish, Cantonese, Korean, or any other language spoken at home. Their ability to interact in interracial groups with African Americans, Latinos, Native Americans, and other "new" Americans from diverse origins and countries is considered one of the greatest assets of the most recent waves of immigrant youth. Obviously new immigrants see multiple memberships and the use of multiple linguistic codes as an asset. In fact, they often view their generation as gifted. As they learn the different communication styles and interactive patterns, they manage to mimic codes and patterns, and fit well in different groups without any penalties.

Would increasing miscegenation and intermarriage among ethnic and racial groups in modern society have stressed the need to interact meaningfully and effectively across ethnic, racial, and sociocultural groups? Many young people are increasingly multiracial and capable of working well across diverse groups. To assume that each person has only one and a fixed identity relatively unchanged across the cultural and social experiences that differentiate individuals is simplistic, reductionistic, and dysfunctional in modern society. George and Louise Spindler (Spindler and Spindler 2000:3–4) discuss the "enduring self," the "situated self," and the "endangered self" to pursue the changes in self-identity. These identities, however, are conceived as sequential and for the most part compatible and coherent in response to differential living environments. We feel that immigrants manage to acquire and maintain different identities that coexist and function without conflict in different context simultaneously. In fact, the brutal attack on America's citizens and the unexpected massive casualties and unspeakable carnage of September 11 brought together all Americans from every corner of the ethnic tapestry in eloquent and fervent demonstration of patriotism during the rescue operations in New York. Never before were Americans more united and more patriotic. In fact, they were proud to see workers from different ethnic groups searching for possible victims and helping along with other voluntary forces. The heroism of New Yorkers brought to all Americans pride and tears that inspired numerous spontaneous gatherings and generous efforts to send resources and funds to help New York and Washington, D.C., victims. Many of the organizers and participants in these meetings were clearly recent immigrants. The role of immigrants in the daily life of American society has brought a new type of unity and patriotism that cross-cuts factions and ethnic boundaries.

The adaptation of immigrants is not a simple path of unilinear acculturation or assimilation from the home culture to mainstream culture. In fact, American culture is undistinguishable from the culture of ethnic members in the same area. In Houston, Chinese Americans and mainstream Americans use the same restaurants, banks, and hospitals and frequent the same cinemas, churches, and recreation areas. In south Texas, the local culture of mainstream and of Mexican American families is shared in a number of ways. The way of life of immigrants in this part of the country would be dysfunctional and impossible if it was deprived of the ethnic cultural elements now accepted by all folks living here: cuisine, festive days, music, industry, churches, and so on. In fact, the success and resiliency of recent immigrants and their powerful influence in mainstream America are all the result of immigrants' creative ways of becoming "other" in different contexts. They must fit the expectations of employers and their own economic needs, and they must acquire communicative skills in another language and culture, without depriving themselves from their quintessential selves and security of the home culture. Practicing "other identities" is part of the adaptive process. See, for example, the work of Ricardo Ainslie (1998:283–300) among Mexicanos of Texas going to the "flea market" (or La Pulga, as they call it).

As times goes, if ethnic boundaries and former ethnic identities become less significant in American society, would multiple identities become commonplace? Would the general population in this country become multiracial, multicultural, and desegregated? If traditional groupings with oppositional political and cultural identities disappear, then racial, ethnic, and other categories should become useless and obsolete. What, if any, stratification will exist marking clearly the predominance of political and economic power groups across the multiracial and multicultural shades of citizens? One could speculate that the markers of new power hierarchies and distinctive identities will follow educational, socioeconomic, and technological lines.

Valencia describes some of the historical currents that have affected immigration policies in this country. The passing of the Immigration Act of 1924 followed years of debate and struggles to control European immigration currents from Italy, Russia, Poland, and Greece. The racial and ethnic biases of the act are generally accepted:

> The question remains, however, as the roles of mental testing, hereditarian psychologists and the eugenics movement influencing the passage of the statute. Several scholars have contended that hereditarianists and eugenicists—via intelligence test data—had profound influence in congressional debate and eventual passage of the Immigration Act of 1924. . . . These scholars, for the most part, point to Carl Brigham's 1923 book, A Study of American Intelligence, where he reanalyzed the Army intelligence data (WWI) by immigrant background and concluded the innate intellectual superiority of the Nordic-origin men over Army examinees whose ancestry could be traced to southern and eastern Europe. . . . Brigham's conclusions were far-reaching: In the sense of restrictive and selected immigration policy, the possibility of racial admixture looms large—which in turn will "allegedly" lead to the overall decline of American intelligence. (Valencia 1997:46)

One of the most effective ways of bringing equity in American society is to provide educational opportunities for all children, especially those from low-income homes and those excluded because they are from unwanted ethnic and racial backgrounds. Education not only for the excluded, but for the *excluding* will make a difference. In no uncertain ways, scholars have referred to the cultural capital of mainstream members of society as the critical factor for their success in schools. Because agents do not act in a vacuum but in specific contexts, Bourdieu conceived the notion of "field" (*champ*) as the concrete social situations, set of objective relations (to avoid deterministic analysis of behavior); social formations are structured by hierarchically organized series of fields, economic, political, educational, cultural, and so on, each with its own space and laws. Agents determine field structures, and a change in agents brings new field organization. Agents in any given field are in competition for control of resources and interests (not always material). In the cultural field, for example, competition over recognition and prestige, the symbolic capital in such a field (not of economic resources) is central. Cultural capital is in the crossing roads of a dialectic of "*connaissance*" and "*reconnaissance*" (knowledge and recognition). Bourdieu views cultural capital as a type of knowledge that allows persons to operate effectively in specific social settings, to understand and appreciate cultural values and symbolic systems, and consequently facilitate action. Having this knowledge, skills, and control of symbolic systems gives unique advantage to people. In academia the cultural capital required to succeed, to compete well, consists of intangibles (or "symbolic power" to use Bourdieu's term) such as knowledge and recognition, but beyond those of a set of symbolic systems acquired through family education since early childhood (see Bourdieu 1977, 1984, 1990, 1993). Cultural field is equivalent to "radical contextualization" because it takes into consideration not only the works or creation of intellectual products but also the specific agents in their complex relationships in a given field within a historical context. Bourdieu opposes simple internal analysis of texts in the absence of a historical context; internal analysis pursues explanations of discourse in the field of discourse itself; that is, this approach would be reductionistic because it would seek as the source of explanations and meaning of a cultural product, the product itself in isolation from the conditions of production and utilization without relating the space of the cultural product or discourse and the space of the positions used by those who create such product. Cultural production needs to take into consideration social class differences. The cultural field is subordinate to or dominated by other fields (political and economic). The control of symbolic forms of capital, such as knowledge and recognition in the academy, can be compatible with lack of economic power. In fact, most professors are not rich or politically powerful. For this reason Bourdieu views intellectuals as "subordinate" or "dominated" within the dominant class of professionals with lucrative careers. There is, however, a new source of academic capital coming from the experience and skills of members of ethnic groups. Historically, ethnic minorities have been marginal members of the academy. Recently, however, in selected disciplines (such as anthropology and sociology) they are beginning to take important roles in the development of new perspectives and approaches for research. Scholars have welcomed ethnic researchers as a means to renew theoretical and methodological instruments. Foley (1991, 1997, 1999) and Trueba (1988, 1999, 2002) have expressed their enthusiasm for the new developments in educational ethnography generated by ethnic anthropologists. According to these scholars, ethnic researchers bring about a different analytical approach and perspectives based on their personal experience and cultural capital.

This volume brings into perspective a number of currents in educational research. While the roots of our disciplines can be tracked down to the 1950s with the work by George Spindler in Stanford, the drastic changes occurring in educational ethnographic research are significant and at times disconcerting. This volume presents a number of chapters that extend to the span of theoretical and methodological preferences. Therefore, the reader should not look for a consensus or agreement in the selection of topics, methodologies, and theoretical premises. The book reflects the state of the art in educational ethnography, and its enormous and powerful differential developments.

In chapter 1 George Spindler brings concepts that until recently were unknown (cultural therapy, for example), yet were founded on research he and Louise, his late wife, conducted among the Menomini in the 1960s and 1970s. The message, however, is powerful and current. Chapter 2, by Harry F. Wolcott, offers the traditional criteria for the production of quality ethnographies. In the process, he shares his philosophy and epistemology that may seem to some modern ethnographers as inadequate to deal with equity issues. Hence the response by James J. Scheurich in chapter 3. This chapter is a critique of traditional ethnography that is not sensitive to equity issues, and assumes a neutral role in front of racial and ethic dilemmas. The insights from Scheurich clearly reflect a departure from previous scholarship in an attempt to resolve the conflict between modern methodological concerns and the earlier assumptions from ethnographers. We presented first the chapters laying the historical foundations for current and modern ethnographic methodologies as placed in their respective theoretical contexts. Chapter 4, by Phil F. Carspecken, is an in-depth discussion of both methodological and epistemological contrasts as faced by post-modern critical ethnographers. The subtle and philosophically sophisticated debates on data collection and interpretation are signals of the new times of clear consciousness about epistemology and equity in research. Chapter 5 by Joe Kincheloe and Peter McLaren enlighten us with a very erudite discussion of the origins of critical research and its relationship with critical theory through a series of reconceptualizations and adaptation in poststructural and postpsychoanalytical periods. This chapter is particularly important in providing a succinct summary of trends and ideologies related to qualitative educational research and specifically to modern ethnography. Their strong position is that "critical theory should not be treated as a universal grammar of revolutionary thought objectified and reduced to discrete formulaic pronouncements or strategies."

Chapter 6 by Douglas F. Foley, from the perspective of a traditional solid grounding of fieldwork and rigorous methodology, pursues similar lines of inquiry. He provides a broad anthropological canvas and clearly offers a new view of the role of ethnic researchers in educational ethnography. Foley, along with Spindler and Carspecken, make complementary and extremely valuable contributions that help the reader follow up the historical developments of ethnographic research focused on the cultural dimensions of behavior and focused on activities within schools and educational settings. What makes this volume substantial, challenging, and unique is its rich theoretical and methodological diversity illustrated by scholars such as Foley.

In chapter 7 David M. Smith discusses the nature and characteristics of urban ethnography. The transition from traditional anthropological field-work among exotic peoples in far away lands to our very close ethnic enclaves with unique sociocultural and linguistic characteristics is a quintessential feature of modern anthropology. The continuum between rural and urban within our own society is obvious since WWII. Rural communities, transient migrant populations, relocation of low-income blacks from rural areas in the South to urban ghettoes, the arrival of Latino immigrants to rural areas in Texas and California, and their subsequent move to urban areas, and other social and demographic phenomena speak eloquently to the relevance of urban ethnography. In chapter 8 Perry Gilmore discusses crucial adaptation of ethnographic research to indigenous people in Alaska. These "indigenous counter narratives" are one more significant development and adaptation of traditional sociolinguistic and anthropological research efforts to resolve the educational problems of neglected Aboriginal populations, and a new effort to decolonize American education in Alaska.

As we said earlier, this book is not a juxtaposition of theoretical and methodological statements on the foundations of qualitative or ethnographic research. It deals with the painful details of the findings of the most intimate fibers of educational leaders and teachers represented by the authors of this volume. In chapter 9, for example, Dr. Yali Zou presents a deeply touching account of her experiences as an immigrant and her transformation into a scholar between two cultures and languages. Her theoretical analysis and her candid description of events that occurred both in China and the United States are profoundly moving and inspiring. This chapter displays intellec-tual honesty, unusual insights into the minds of immigrants, and a very posi-tive outlook of the role of education in achieving equity. And chapter 10 by Peter Kiang, is another masterpiece of extraordinary narratives with serious reflections on the role of education. These two chapters, 9 and 10, constitute a significant contribution to our deeper understanding of the experiences of Asian Americans in the United States and the role of institutions working with them. Kiang focuses on the very pragmatic and realistic pedagogical challenges we face in working daily with Asian American students at the university.

Judy Radigan in chapter 11 offers a very interesting analysis of the "class clown" as means to sensitize us to the different epistemologies that ethnographers working with immigrant and culturally different children must take into consideration. The quality of her observations and her analysis are an excellent model to other researchers. She demonstrates a compassionate heart and deep understanding of the struggles immigrant students face in their attempt to belong in America and to succeed in high school. Portions of this chapter will be published elsewhere. Chapter 12 by Miguel A. and Francisco J. Guajardo offers a candid reaction to the entire volume from the perspective of community-based action research. What they want to do is to find the applicability (or lack thereof) of research methodologies that enhance the chances for a better education in schools populated predominantly by immigrant children. This chapter represents a refreshing analysis of where the entire discourse on educational research is going. It focuses on research based on critical pedagogy and critical ethnography, as well as on traditional and postmodern ethnographic approaches relative to their significance and relevance for pedagogical praxis. Rarely in the history of educational research do we see an encompassing discussion of the founders of a research field, and the most recent users of that field in community-based settings. Demystifying ethnographic research is no longer the work of the experts and esoteric scholars teaching at Harvard, Stanford, or Yale. It is now the prerogative of hard-working practitioners who have learned from their teachers in higher education without losing their identity as active members of ethnic communities.

# References

Ainslie, R. C., ed. "Cultural Mourning, Immigration, and Engagement: Vignettes from the Mexican Experience." Pp. 283–300 in M. M. Suárez-Orozco, ed., *Crossings*. Cambridge, Mass.: Harvard University Press and D. Rockefeller Center for Latin American Studies, 1998.

Bourdieu, P. *Distinction: A Social Critique of the Judgment of Taste*. Cambridge, Mass.: Harvard University Press, 1984.

Bourdieu, P. *The Logic of Practice*. Trans. R. Nice. Stanford, Calif.: Stanford University Press, 1990.

Bourdieu, P. *The Field of Cultural Production: Essays on Art and Literature*. New York: Columbia University Press, 1993.

Bourdieu, P. *Reproduction: In Education, Society and Culture*. Beverly Hills, Calif.: Sage, 1977.

Bourdieu, P. *An Invitation to Reflexive Sociology*. Cambridge, Mass.: Polity Press, 1992.

Foley, D. "Reconsidering Anthropological Explanations of Ethnic School Failure." *Anthropology and Education Quarterly*, 22 (1991): 60–86.

Foley, D. "Deficit Thinking Models Based on Culture: The Anthropological Protest." Pp. 113–131 in R. R. Valencia, ed., *The Evolution of Deficit Thinking: Educational Thought and Practice* London: Falmer Press, 1997.

Foley, D. "Reconceptualizing Ethnicity and School Achievement: The Rise of Ethnic Ethnographers." Unpublished manuscript, University of Texas–Austin, 1999.

McLaren, P. "Introduction. Democracy Sabotaged by Democracy: Immigration under Neoliberalism." Pp. 1–15 in H. Trueba and L. Bartolomé, ed., *Immigrant Voices: In Search of Educational Equity*. Lanham, Md.: Rowman & Littlefield, 2000.

Spindler, G., and L. Spindler. *Fifty Years of Anthropology and Education 1950–2000. A Spindler Anthology*. Mahwah, N.J.: Laurence Erlbaum Associates, 2000.

Suárez-Orozco, M. M. "Crossings: Mexican Immigration in Interdisciplinary Perspectives." Pp. 5–50 in M. M. Suárez-Orozco, ed., *Crossings*. Cambridge, Mass.: Harvard University Press and D. Rockefeller Center for Latin American Studies, 1998.

Suárez-Orozco, M. M., and C. Suárez-Orozco. "Some Conceptual Considerations in the Interdisciplinary Study of Immigrant Children" Pp. 17–35 in H. T. Trueba and L. Bartolomé, ed., *Immigrant Voices in Search of Pedagogical Reform*. Lanham, Md.: Rowman & Littlefield, 2000.

Trueba, H. T. "Culturally-Based Explanations of Minority Students' Academic Achievement." *Anthropology and Education Quarterly*, 19, 3 (1988): 270–87.

Trueba, H. T. *Latinos Unidos: From Cultural Diversity to the Politics of Solidarity*. Lanham, Md.: Rowman & Littlefield, 1999.

Trueba, H. T. "Multiple Ethnic, Racial, and Cultural Identities in Action: From Marginality to a New Cultural Capital in Modern Society." *Journal of Latinos and Education*, 1, 1 (2002): 7–28.

Trueba, H. T., and L. Bartolomé, ed. *Immigrant Voices: In Search of Educational Equity*. Lanham, Md.: Rowman & Littlefield, 2000.

Valencia, R. R. "Genetic Pathology Model of Deficit Thinking." Pp. 41–112 in R. R. Valencia, ed., *The Evolution of Deficit Thinking: Educational Thought and Practice*. London: Falmer Press, 1997.

# CHAPTER ONE

# The Collusion of Illusions and How to Get People to Tell You What They Don't Know

## George Spindler

I came to Stanford in the fall of 1950, after a full summer of research with the Menominee, to join a research team as an anthropologist. The team consisted of two professional educators, one sociologist, and a psychiatrist. Dr. Robert Bush, the director of the project, did not know exactly what an anthropologist should do in a study of schooling, but he wanted to try one out. The objective of the study, supported with Rosenberg money, was to do case studies of teachers in their classrooms, principals in their schools, and superintendents in their school systems. Our mode of operation was to go to a school, or a principal, or superintendent, explain what we wanted to do, and describe it as a way of "improving professional competence." This was apparently appealing to school faculties because every one we approached volunteered as subjects for study. Our promise was to do a thorough study of the situation, whatever it was, and provide feedback on the relevant parts, but violate no one's "privacy," and to improve the insight of the subject, whoever it was, into what s/he was doing and to what effect.

In the school, which I shall call Washington School, one of several we were working in, all of the faculty volunteered. We put their names on slips of paper and deposited them into a hat, from which we drew three names—one for the educator, one for the sociologist, and one for me. I met with my volunteer that same afternoon and explained who I was and what (I thought)

I would be doing. He turned out to be a healthy-looking white man of twenty-five years of age, with three years of teaching experience, from a local family of upper-middle-class origin whom I shall call Roger Harker. I started visiting his fifth-grade classroom the next day.

I wondered what I should observe and take notes on that first day and continued to wonder for the next few weeks. It was so boring! I had just come from the Menominee, where Louise and I had a most active summer, including my getting witched at a Medicine Lodge ceremony and landing the next day in a hospital with a high fever of "undiagnosed origin." I went to a shaman whom I had met who was a leader at the ceremony and asked him for something that would give me protection in similar circumstances. He expressed surprise that the sorcery would work on a white man, but acquiesced, telling me to return in four days and he would have an amulet prepared by then that would protect me. I came as scheduled, he "installed" the amulet with appropriate ritual, and I have carried it ever since. I am happy to say that I have not been subject to successful sorcery since that one time.

I knew I was doing anthropology. I wrote up the event, reinterviewed the shaman and numerous others, took further notes, and in general exploited my experience, and my feelings, to the fullest degree. But there was nothing to see, nothing to take notes on, in Roger Harker's classroom . . . I thought.

But one day, as I looked over the class of thirty-five fifth graders, I noticed that all of the good readers were on one side of the classroom and all of the poor readers were on the other side. (I had observed reading several times by then.) I further noticed that all of the good readers excepting two were white, quite middle class, and that all of the poor readers appeared to be members of minority groups and seemed to be of lower socioeconomic status. I devoted my next few visits to checking out this observation. I interviewed each child, consulted school records, and placed each one according to residential status. (The sociologist and I had assessed each residence according to a Lloyd Warner–type scale, and located it on a map. We canvassed the entire school district on foot.) My observations proved to be correct.

This started the ethnographic engine, and I set about preparing various situations in which his relations with these two types of children would be displayed, besides observing him behave as Roger Harker, fifth grade teacher. I also devised a questionnaire, using a Likert-type scale that I administered to him, to the principal and vice principal, and to various members of the superintendent's staff as well as the superintendent. The questionnaire contained sixteen statements about this teacher, such as "This teacher is accessible to children with problems: 'Much more so than most teachers,' 'somewhat more so than most teachers,' 'about as much so as most teachers,' 'less so than most teachers,' 'much less so than most teachers' '(check one).'" The "situations" I devised for him consisted of such things as a request that he write down the children whom he regarded as "best adjusted" (and define adjustment), and at different times, "most liked by their classmates," "most successful academically," "best liked by me (the teacher)," and so on. I also collected a sociogram for the class as a whole, which showed social preferences among the children, administered a questionnaire to the children somewhat similar to the one I had administered to him and the others who observed him, and interviewed each child about their relations with him. I had also interviewed each of the respondents to the questionnaire (principal, assistant principal, superintendent's staff, etc.).

The mass of data I had collected was almost too much. I had also collected a Rorschach and a Murray Thematic Apperception Test from him and did an expressive autobiographic interview with him (a technique Louise had used in her study of Menominee women).

But everything pointed in the same direction. He was very strongly biased on the side of the white middle-class and upper-middle-class children. He knew more information about them, he predicted success for them and failure for the lower socioeconomic status, he described their relations with each other in quite different terms, complimentary to the upper-status children. In all the dimensions Roger came down on the upper-status side. He wasn't mean or hostile to the lower-status children. He was a "nice" teacher. But he constructed a classroom that was conducive to learning for the upper-status children and discouraging to lower-status children. He constructed a mirror in which he, himself, was reflected (Spindler 1959; Spindler and Spindler 1990).

What was particularly impressive about all of this was that he was quite unaware that it was happening, and so were all of the "others" that rated him. He was uniformly regarded as one of their best young teachers, and he regarded himself, rating their perceptions of him on the same questionnaire, as one of the best. Only the children detected anything amiss.

The upper-status children rated him higher than the lower-status ones, but there were respondents from both groups that rated him low on "accessibility" and "easy to go to with problems." And there were numerous other indications of bias. Asked to describe the outstanding children in the sociogram of the classroom, including their standing with each other, he consistently described the upper-status children as highly popular with their classmates whereas the converse was more often true.

When I began to feed back these data to him, as my contract required, he became very upset, accusing me of skewing the data. But eventually he was won over to the truth of what I was telling him and began acquiring skills that would enable him to more effectively relate his teaching to the children that were being taught.

What impressed me most was that the whole educational situation in which Roger was imbedded was biased in the same way as he was. (I later did a study of the success or failure of Mexican American children in that community and discovered that the longer a child of that ethnicity attended school the lower his or her academic achievement score, and the lower the score on the mental maturity scale.) If I had not happened along just when I did Roger would have been promoted to administration and continued to compound his errors. He was promoted eventually anyhow, but after he had revised his construction of his classroom and teaching orientation.

This case, my first one, made a deep impression on me and influenced the next fifty years of professional development. My next one also impressed me deeply, for somewhat the same reasons, but with a difference (Spindler 1974).

We decided that we wanted to study someone whom the faculty of a school determined to be "adjusted" so we advanced this idea to one of the schools cooperating with us. The staff concurred enthusiastically. At the next faculty meeting they were ready. A well-dressed, brown-haired, ten-year-six-months-old girl, "one of the best students in the school," from a "good family," "well-liked by her classmates, in fact a leader among them," "pleasant and cooperative" had been selected. The criteria for "adjustment" were "academically successful, well organized, well liked by her peers, cooperative, gets along well with everyone." We shall call her Beth Anne. We started observing her the next day.

We began with the Thematic Apperception Test and the Rorschach. We took her academic standings and California Mental Maturity from school records. Both were at the high end of performance. To our surprise she exhibited some difficulties in her responses to the two projective techniques. She was quite emotionally constricted, unwilling or unable to let her imagination loose to help her solve problems posed by the stimuli of the two techniques. She appeared to be very anxious to please—concerned about whether she had given enough responses, whether they were like what others had produced, whether she had made them clear. If she dropped a Rorschach card two inches to the table she said, "Oh! Pardon me!"

Observations of her in her classroom group revealed other characteristics that did not fit the characterizations provided by the faculty. She seemed somewhat standoffish with her peers, relating well to only one other girl who appeared to be of the same social background (this was confirmed in an interview with the parents). She appeared worried about assignments, asking querulously about them when they were made. She was absent more often than the other fifth graders. A sociogram developed from responses to the question "Whom would you like to sit next to in this classroom?" showed her to be virtually isolated, only chosen second by her "best friend"!

A home visit revealed a very comfortable upper-middle-class domicile, with a somewhat worried looking woman, the child's mother (whom we shall call Beth Anne from now on) who assured me immediately that her husband would be home "any minute." He was, and we immediately started in on the interview, though the first question was asked by him. "What are you studying about Beth Anne and what have you found out?" I explained the reasons for studying her, the methods we used, and told them selectively what we had found out.

To make a long story short, the parents had noted some of the characteristics that we did and had, in a limited way, worried about them. Among other things the parents had noticed was an "abdominal tic" that she had exhibited in the past six months. The family doctor had said "not to worry about it" and that she would get over it "in due course." We discussed all of this and concluded that an effort should be made to relax some of the extraordinarily high expectations concerning her behavior and achievements.

When we took the report to the teachers we received a mixed reception. Some were openly skeptical about the significance of our observations and data. "She'll be fine." "She's a great reader." "There's nothing wrong with her imagination." "Her folks take her everywhere." "They went to Alaska last summer." "She will have an active social life, I am sure." "She'll belong to a sorority." Others began to see things that they had not mentioned when the choice of "best adjusted" was made. "I know you mentioned her little worried look, Mrs. ___"; "She was always friendly with me but I noticed that she seemed a little standoffish with the other children."

We obviously did not have a well-adjusted child as the focus of our study. She gave every evidence of a personality under siege. She was defending herself as best she could but it wasn't working. The question we were left with was: How could a whole faculty come to such a wrong conclusion? The answer, we decided, was that the teachers picked a child who conformed in every overt respect to their ideals, their projections of the good and desirable. She appeared to them to be what they would want their daughters to be.

In a way Beth Anne was like Roger Harker. Both of them represented idealizations projected from judges within the system. Neither of them fit the reality of the situation within which their (Beth and Roger) efficacy had to be evaluated. The illusions of the evaluators colluded to produce profoundly erroneous judgments. The students were too diverse to fit the unicultural mold that he, and the school system at that time, represented. The school, for Beth Anne, was likewise too diverse. She could not relate to her classmates because they mostly represented social statuses and ethnicity that were not hers, and her parents did not help her to see their value. But she was suffering from a general oppression that resulted from a concerted drive on the part of both teachers and parents to be all she could be—to fulfill their dreams.

These two cases, encountered so early in my career as educational anthropologist, influenced everything I did from that point on. The experience made me rediscover the old anthropological adage "Nothing is as it seems." The collusion of illusions is one of the reasons why this is so. The basic idea is that whole school systems (or social systems anywhere) may be centered on illusions about the nature of the situation they are dealing with, and responsible people will make decisions on the basis of them.

In the fall of 1959 we went to Germany to teach for Stanford at the Stanford overseas center in Beutelsbach, 14 kms SE from Stuttgart. The courses we were to teach were courses we had taught at Stanford, namely Anthropology 001 (Introd. Sociocultural), and American Culture (Anthro. 015). I started out the quarter doing pretty much what I had done at Stanford, but somehow it rang hollow. One day I stood on the rim of the Remstal (Rems Valley) looking at the five villages and the vineyards spread out before me and thought "Why are we studying Anthro 001, and American Culture 015 when we have these villages spread out before us in the valley below, all of them going through the pangs of adaptation to a changing world?" The next day I told the approximately eighty students in my classes, most of them sophomores, that the syllabi, directions for papers, and so on were null and void. We were going to study what was there in the valley before us. They were enthused, and that afternoon the first of what was a sixteen-year ethnographic field trip began. The results were so good that in 1973 I could publish a case study using a great deal of their work (G. Spindler and students 1973). Louise and I supervised their work and integrated their findings interpretively in our weekly class sessions. Of course there was a certain discontinuity over the years, since we were not at the Center more than three months at a time, and not every year. But the students learned so quickly that we were able to get going each new quarter without delay. Meanwhile our own interest in the Remstal as a research site grew and before the Center closed in 1975 we had started some projects of our own. Our Blood Indian research was winding down by then and we were looking for new territory. We went back to Germany in 1977 after the Center closed in 1975 to begin a follow-up of research I had begun in 1968. Louise entered into the school research full force at that time. Her presence made all the difference in the success of the project, both because she was another worker and a female, and because she was an especially sensitive one. We returned in 1981 and 1985. We had meanwhile returned in 1969, 1970, 1972, 1973, and 1975 to teach at Stanford in Germany. While we were teaching we did research ourselves, besides having sixty to eighty eager ethnographers pouring data into our files. I don't think anyone had ever had it so good in the field. My department objected to my being gone so much, but the university administration gave me the Dinkelspeil Award for Outstanding Service to Undergraduate Education for it, citing my using Beutelsbach as a "fresh window on the larger world." It is one of the prizes I have particularly enjoyed.

We started with a migration and assimilation model. We had thought that our focus should be on the mutual adaptation of the Einheimischen (natives) and the Fluchtlinge (those who fled from East Germany and homelands in Silesia, Russia, and Czechoslovakia) and other Zugezogenen (newcomers). Our first publication was *Burgbach: Urbanization and Identity in a German Village* (1973). As mentioned, this book was done with some 400 students whose ethnographic studies contributed directly to the publication. In it we tried to give a picture of the various kinds of people that lived in Beutelsbach (Burgbach) at that time and contrasted this diversity with the simple social structure of the pre–WWII period. During and since the war, the former village had swollen to well over twice its size with newcomers with a different religion (largely Catholic), including more urban dwellers, that were more educated, more often professional, speaking a different dialect than the Swabish spoken by the natives, and with quite different values. The ethnographic work, performed by students and by us, had been aimed at nailing down the cultural features of each group and their relationships with each other.

The role of the Grundschule in these relationships was of particular interest. We spent many hours in the school, observing, socializing, trying to understand how the school operated, what mission the teachers and principal felt they had, and how the school as a village entity related to the larger structure of education in Baden-Wurttemberg (the land, equivalent to province or state). We interacted with the staff. I went on hikes, watched ball games, ate lunch, and played with the children. Louise packed up to ten little girls into our Volkswagen before school and told jokes and riddles with them. I tried doing the work of the third-grade child to try to understand what it was like for them to be in school. They treated me like a big dumb kid, for my German was not quite up to the third-grade level at that time. And besides, third-grade German is remarkably different than adult Hoch Deutsch. I gave it up after a few weeks because I could not keep up with the work and do ethnography, but it was revealing and improved my rapport with the children.

"Schooling in Schoenhausen: A Study of Cultural Transmission and Instrumental Adaptation in an Urbanizing German Village" (G. Spindler 1974) examined these themes, with a focus on the Instrumental Activities Inventory (I.A.I.), which we had adapted to use in Germany and that was constructed so as to reveal the dynamics of changes from traditional to urbanized modern. (The I.A.I. consists of thirty-four line drawings of significant activities, possessions, or situations arranged from traditional to modern to which teachers, children, and parents respond.) Other publications followed: "Die Vermittlung von Kulturellen Werten und Spezifischen Anpassungsmechanismus in Einen Dorf mit Sunehmend stadtischen Geprage" (Spindler and Spindler 1978a); "Schooling in Schonhausen Revisited: A Restudy of Cultural Transmission and Instrumental Adaptation in an Urbanizing German Village, A Preliminary Report" (Spindler and Spindler 1978b); "Prospect for a Controlled Crosscultural Comparison of Schooling: Schonhausen and Roseville" (Spindler and Spindler 1987a); "Cultural Dialogue and Schooling in Schonhausen and Roseville: A Comparative Analysis" (Spindler and Spindler 1987b)"; "Schonhausen Revisited and the Rediscovery of Culture" (Spindler and Spindler 1987c). These latter titles represent a period of expansion in the German project. We concentrated solely on the German Grundschule in "Schonhausen" (pseudonym) through the 1981 visit, our purpose being to determine the role of the school in the massive changes taking place in the Remstal. We focused on the teachers as cultural transmitters and concluded they were a conservative influence, despite the fact that older teachers has been replaced by younger, recent graduates of the training institutions for teachers, that all of the curriculum had been changed, and the textbooks replaced in the sweeping reforms that the federal government had implemented. In fact the school appeared to act as a conservative factor of substantial proportions throughout the entire reform. To determine this we studied each teacher carefully, stressing advocacies, emphases, relations with state-sponsored projects and curricular content, and their responses to the I.A.I., which were uniformly on the culturally conservative side, making traditional instrumental choices.

We moved to a concept of self in our further analyses and defined an enduring self that we described as "romantic-idealistic" and a situated self that we described as "pragmatic." In these terms the enduring self was supported in the school's cultural transmission, with less enthusiasm devoted to the situated self. These two selves were represented in the transformative culture change overtaking the Remstal. This development was presented in various publications, particularly in "The Self and Instrumental Model in the Study of Culture Change" (Spindler and Spindler 1989).

In our 1981 field trip to the Remstal we had films we had taken in 1977 and 1981 of the teachers and the Schonhausen environs that we showed to teachers with the idea that we would use them as provocative stimuli for discussions. They did act in this way, and we found our studies of individual classrooms to be enhanced. But the interest of the teachers in their own behaviors and that of other teachers was so intense we could hardly get into the conversations and they ranged all over the place. The teachers were so invigorated by seeing themselves teach that they asked us to bring some similar films from a comparable school in the United States back with us when we came again.

That we did. We started work in a comparable school in "Roseville," Wisconsin, upon return to the United States and took films (later converted to videos) of classrooms in a school that was impressively like the German school. It was semirural, was of comparable size, used similar content for the curriculum, categorized in the same way into literature, grammar, mathematics, civics, or social studies, and was, of course, comparable in age and grade range.

We took films in the Roseville school that were virtual counterparts of the German films, showed the Roseville teachers their own films and the German films, and recorded their reactions, then returned to Germany to do the same with the Schonhausen teachers, children, and superintendent.

This move started a whole new phase of the German research that became transformed into a German/American comparative study. The most important publication issuing from this phase of the study is "Crosscultural, Comparative, Reflective Interviewing in Schonhausen and Roseville" (Spindler and Spindler 1993a).

Showing the films to the two audiences was an experience in itself. The Schulamptdirektor (superintendent), when he heard that we had taken films of an American school comparable to Schonhausen Grundschule (during our initial interview with him to ask for permission to carry out another period of research in one of his schools), insisted on seeing them immediately, for he was leaving on a trip the next day. So we gathered our films and our wits together (we had been in Germany only one day and our German was pretty rusty) and arrived at his office suite around 7:00 P.M. To our surprise, all of the Grundschule teachers and the principal were there.

Over excellent Remstal wine and fresh Kuchen we showed the films and discussed them. Everything was recorded. The superintendent spoke first:

> It is difficult for me to see whether these films are typical of either the school or of other schools in a broader area. If they are typical we come to a situation. I must say there is between the school in Roseville and that in Schonhausen a clear difference, a decisive difference. Our teachers, our understanding about school, are situated in a specific system. This system is influenced directly from above, from the school system viewpoint.

He went on to describe how there was a curricular plan formed from above that each teacher must follow, how the teacher brought all of the themes delineated in the plan together, and how everyone reached the same goal of instruction. He commented further on Roseville.

> If I am to take these pictures (of Roseville) that we have seen as typical, and you say they are, then it is very difficult for me to understand how instruction and progress can move together. There are many questions, many. For example, are the children able to reach, to proceed in similar steps towards learning goals? . . . How does the teacher handle the problem of having one group further along and the other hanging behind? I am not one to think there is only one way to get to Rome. But without doubt for us a goal is a goal and without doubt a goal is to be obtained. . . . Leistungsfahigkeit (productive efficiency) for the group is the purpose, not the purpose of the individual.

He had more to say but these quotes sum up his views and to a considerable degree those of the teachers, though there was some variation among them and they did not all take quite as hard a line as he did.

We showed the films separately again to the teachers and to all the grades in both the Schonhausen and Roseville schools. The reactions showed very clearly that each group within each school had somewhat differing perceptions of the differences between the two schools, but at the same time shared certain perceptions. This positionality revealed the nature of the culture of each school and showed how this culture was formed from both common features and differences.

Teachers revealed sentiments that they had never been able to enunciate in interviews concerning individualism, authority, control, achievement, responsibility, and so forth. And their own responses made visible to them their culturally determined biases, in the light of the biases of the "other." This experience acted as a form of "cultural therapy."

The problem with Roger Harker and with the faculty that selected Beth Anne as the best adjusted child in the school was that they were unaware of their own illusions They were operating with illusions about the reality that confronted them each day as they taught. These illusions stemmed directly from their own social experience, in their families of origin and in their social-professional experience. They were shared with their colleagues. Cultural therapy is the process of bringing those illusions to conscious realization, so that they can be dealt with in discussion and instructional experiences.

Cultural therapy first occurred to me when I worked with Roger Harker, and it is mentioned prominently in the first writing I did featuring his case study, "The Transmission of American Culture," the Third Burton Lecture in Elementary Education at Harvard University in 1957 (G. Spindler 1959). It lay more or less dormant through the years until the German and American studies brought it into focus again. In 1993 Louise and I formulated the concept further in "The Processes of Culture and Person: Cultural Therapy in Culturally Diverse Schools" (Spindler and Spindler 1993b), and "What Is Cultural Therapy?" in *Pathways to Cultural Awareness: Cultural Therapy with Teachers and Students* (Spindler and Spindler, 1994). This volume includes our presentation of the concept and ten chapters by others, many of them our former students, on their experiences with cultural therapy. My most recent attempt to explain the concept and its workings is "Three Categories of Cultural Knowledge Useful in Doing Cultural Therapy" (G. Spindler 1999), accompanied by a comment by Tom Schram "Cultural Therapy and the Explicitness of Our Intentions" (G. Spindler 1999).

In the context of this chapter, the easiest way to understand the concept of cultural therapy is to regard it as a process of eliminating the illusions one carries in a particular area of perception. This is not easy and false moves abound, but my experience leads me to feel that it is more attainable than we might think. Any successful educational experience is based in part on this process.

# Note

Our (George and Louise Spindler's) careers in anthropology and education
are the substance of *Fifty Years of Anthropology and Education: A Spindler Anthology,
1950–2000:* Mahwah, N.J.: Lawrence Erlbaum Associates, 2000.

# References

Spindler, George. "The Transmission of American Culture." In *Third Burton Lecture in
Elementary Education.* Cambridge, Mass.: School of Education, Harvard University,
1959.

Spindler, G. "Beth Anne: Teacher Perceptions of Adjustment." Pp. 139–53 in G. Spindler, ed., *Education and Cultural Process: Toward and Anthropology of Education.* New
York: Holt, Rinehart and Winston, 1974.

Spindler, G . "Three Categories of Cultural Knowledge Useful in Doing Cultural Therapy." *Anthropology and Education Quarterly,* 30, 4 (1999): 466–72.

Spindler, G., and students. *Burgbach: Urbanization and Identity in a German Village.* New
York: Holt, Rinehart and Winston, 1973.

Spindler, G., and L. Spindler. "Die Vermittlung von Kulturellen Werten und Spezifischen
Anpassungsmechanismus in Einen Dorf mit Sunehmend stadtischen Geprage."
Pp. 285–96 in M. Matter, ed., *Rheinisches Jahrbuch fur Volkskunde,* 27ed. Universitat
Bonn,. Max Matter.27 Jahrgang, 1978a.

Spindler, G., and L. Spindler. "Schooling in Schonhausen Revisited." *Anthropology and
Education Quarterly,* I (1978b): x, 3.

Spindler, G., and L. Spindler. "Prospect for a Controlled Crosscultural Comparison of
Schooling." In G. Spindler, ed., *Education and Cultural Process: Toward an Anthropology
of Education.* Prospect Heights: Waveland Press, 1987a.

Spindler, G., and L. Spindler. "Cultural Dialogue and Schooling in Schoenhausen and
Roseville." *Anthropology and Education Quarterly,* 19 (1987b): 3–16.

Spindler, G., and L. Spindler. "Schoenhausen Revisited and the Rediscovery of Culture."
In G. Spindler, ed., *Interpretive Ethnography of Education at Home and Abroad.* Hillsdale:
Erlbaum Press, 1987c.

Spindler, G., and L. Spindler. "The Self and the Instrumental Model in the Study of
Culture Change." Pp. 109–17 in *Proceedings of the Kroeber Anthropological Society.*
Berkeley: University of California Press, 1989.

Spindler, G., and L. Spindler. "Schooling in the American Cultural Dialogue." In G.
and L. Spindler, ed. (with Henry Trueba and Melvin Williams), *The American Cultural
Dialogue.* London: Falmer Press, 1990.

Spindler, G., and L. Spindler. "Crosscultural, Comparative, Reflective Interviewing in
Schoenhausen and Roseville." Pp. 53–92 in M. Schratz, ed., *Qualitative Voices in Educational Research.* Hillsdale, N.J.: Academic Press, 1993a.

Spindler, G., and L. Spindler. "The Processes of Culture and Person: Cultural Therapy in

Culturally Diverse Schools." Pp. 24–51 in P. Phelan and A. Davidson, ed., *Renegotiating Cultural Diversity in American Schools*. New York: Teachers College Press, 1993b.

Spindler, G., and L. Spindler. "What Is Cultural Therapy?" Pp. 1–34 in *Pathways to Cultural Awareness: Cultural Therapy with Teachers and Students*, G. and L. Spindler, ed. Thousand Oaks, Calif.: Corwin Press, 1994.

CHAPTER TWO

～

# Ethnography? Or Educational Travel Writing?

*Harry F. Wolcott*

"Whatever it is, it's *not* anthropology!"

With those words, unattributed at the time, I began a review of the literature in anthropology and education that I was invited to prepare for volume
37 of the *Review of Educational Research* (RER). Perhaps you have forgotten
my review, forgotten even that the "new" topic of anthropology and education was at one time regularly reviewed in that journal in a recurring three-
year cycle. More likely, you never knew any of this; volume 37 of *RER* was
published in 1967.

I note that the words I quoted, "Whatever it is, it's not anthropology!"
were unattributed at the time. Now, more than three decades later, full dis-
closure. They were spoken by George Spindler. And because they dealt
rather uncharitably with a then-recent publication that bore a telling title,
the specific work to which he was referring was not, and will not be, identified by name. I'll bet Spindler himself doesn't recall the publication that
prompted his comment. I remark on the incident to remind you—or to
inform you—that there has always been concern as to what warrants a legitimate claim to be hailed as "anthropology," or "ethnography," or "anthropology and education." It is still a concern, as noted in Henry Trueba's call for
the chapters assembled in this volume and his reflection on "the enormous
proliferation of ethnographic studies in the literature and their questionable
quality." It is this issue of "quality" that I address.

Memory fails on certain details, but I rather imagine the invitation to

27

prepare the review went originally to Spindler himself. Even in those early days he showed a talent for delegating tasks he was not interested in doing; I was dispatched as his substitute speaker at more than one local PTA while I was attending Stanford. Whatever the circumstances in this case, the invitation to prepare a review probably arrived late in 1965, well in advance of the issue of *RER* scheduled for February 1967. Spindler suggested that the assignment be given to me.

I had only recently completed my Ph.D. under Spindler's direction, with a major in education and a formal Ph.D. minor in cultural anthropology. I was beginning the second year of my appointment to the new R&D Center at the University of Oregon. Thanks to the Spindlers, things were going along hummingly for my dissertation to be transformed into *A Kwakiutl Village and School*, one of the monographs chosen to inaugurate a new series in education and culture to be launched by Holt Rinehart and Winston, also scheduled for release in 1967. It was Louise Spindler who had come up with the idea of a series parallel to their already highly successful *Case Studies in Cultural Anthropology*. Two of my fellow doctoral students at Stanford had recently completed dissertations that also fit the mold: John Singleton's *Nichu: A Japanese School* and Richard Warren's *Education in Rebhausen*. We were to be joined by two young fellows trying to invent cross-cultural psychology, Michael Cole and John Gay, with their monograph *The New Mathematics and an Old Culture*.[1]

In spite of having a major publication pending, I had published nothing at the time. In those days promotion and tenure decisions came quickly, not stretched over a seeming lifetime, as today, and I was constantly reminded of the "publish or perish" tradition in academia. (Today it's publish *and* perish.) I was pleased to be asked to do the review, in spite of the fact that I probably wasn't the person originally invited to write it. Still, I had no idea how to proceed. No doubt Spindler encouraged me and reminded me that preparing the review would give me an opportunity to mention (dare I say "advertise") the forthcoming new series, including my own monograph, something that a "less-thorough" reviewer might not be inclined to do. To be quite frank, Spindler didn't merely "suggest" I write the review, he told me to, so that was that.

Other than the attention I could draw to a set of forthcoming monographs that no one had yet seen or heard of, I wasn't sure there was enough "out there" to warrant a review. I had no idea how to proceed. Spindler helped me begin the roundup. And he wasn't sparing in his judgment that some of what was being promoted for its anthropological perspective showed little influence from anthropology.

As noted, "anthropology and education" had been plugged into a rotating cycle of topics reviewed every three years; 1967 marked its third time around. Meanwhile, those of us committed to this new field were watching what appeared to be the slow death of educational sociology, and we believed we knew what had sealed its fate. Rather than maintain strong ties with academic sociology, it had branched off to become an entity in itself, an educationist activity that literally beat the drum of social class, and of itself, to death. We did not want the same thing to happen to anthropology and education.

That is what I take to be the intent of Spindler's comment, voiced a decade after the appearance of his own *Education and Anthropology* (1955). Although that publication had anthropology and anthropologists rigorously and well represented, and in spite of what it became through successive iterations, beginning with *Education and Culture* in 1963, the original *Education and Anthropology* was little more than a report of conference proceedings. It was met with mixed reviews in spite of the brilliance of many of the papers themselves. Further, the new cohort of Stanford graduates, myself included, and a similarly trained cohort working with Solon T. Kimball at Teachers College, Columbia, were more likely perceived as part of the problem than part of the answer, for if our minds and hearts were in anthropology, our degrees were in education. We were hyphenated or "halfie" anthropologists, already "one step removed." (And get this: Initially, our collective applications to become Fellows of the American Anthropological Association were *categorically denied*, on the basis that our highest degrees were not in anthropology.)

I eventually drafted a fourteen-page review with fifty citations to lives and works you may not associate with that era, including the Anthropology Curriculum Project at Georgia, the Anthropology Curriculum Study Project of the AAA, Basil Bernstein's "elaborated and restricted code," Ted Brameld's "anthropotherapy" (shades of cultural therapy, eh?), Yehudi Cohen's "transition from childhood to adolescence," Elizabeth Eddy and Alexander Moore's studies for Project True (*Walk the White Line, Realities of the Urban Classroom*), Estelle Fuchs's *Pickets at the Gates*, Gumperz and Hymes's monograph on the ethnography of communication, Ruth Landes's *Culture in American Education*, Wax, Wax, and Dumont, "Formal Education in an American Indian Community," and Beatrice Whiting's one thousand-page collection, *Six Cultures: Studies of Child Rearing.*[2]

Spindler's offhand appraisal of one of the major works under scrutiny may have helped fine-tune not only the direction I took with the review but also the course I set for my professional life. No doubt meeting up with George Spindler was the major turning point in my academic career, but that dates back to 1959. By 1966 I had learned some anthropology, recognized its broad perspective in focusing on enculturation, successfully completed field-work—and among the Kwakiutl, with whom Franz Boas himself had begun working eighty years earlier—successfully written a dissertation, landed a position (the only one I ever needed), and begun fieldwork for a second major study, *The Man in the Principal's Office*. If all those events are more or less traceable to Spindler, his comment underscored a concern he had often expressed in the previous half-dozen years, a concern that by then I had taken up as a personal crusade. It was succinctly summarized in the words of another of Spindler's former students, Malcolm McFee: "If there is going to be an anthropology of education, there better be something recognizably anthropological about it."

Looking back (which is the only way to make sense of a career), I can attest that I have tried to do my part to ensure that the anthropology of edu-cation has maintained its anthropological orientation. Educational research is the area of education in which I happened to hunker down, and that is where I directed my energies. My efforts were drawn along the lines not only of cultural anthropology in general but specifically in the contributions to be made through its research arm: ethnography. *Educational researchers are methodologists*, and although that fact makes absolutely no sense to any anthropologist I have ever known, that is where I put my efforts. Somewhat ironically, I have come to be regarded as a methodologist.

Through the years, I have tried to help maintain standards for studies claiming to be ethnographic, yet to keep expectations realistic as to what ethnography can accomplish and when it is appropriate. As I have written elsewhere, I have tried to protect Fair Ethnography's name, at times appar-ently placing it just out of reach of those eager to claim the label but uncer-tain as to exactly what else is involved. On this single dimension (need I assure you?) my students once dubbed me Harry the Pure. If you weren't there to get that lesson in person, you can hardly miss the drift in the titles of some of my articles over the years:

Handle with Care: Necessary Precautions in the Anthropology of Schools (1971)
Criteria for an Ethnographic Approach to Research in Schools (1975)

How to Look Like an Anthropologist without Really Being One (1980)
Differing Styles of On-Site Research, Or, "If It Isn't Ethnography, What Is It?" (1982a)
On Ethnographic Intent (1988)
Making a Study "More Ethnographic" (1990a)
Posturing in Qualitative Inquiry (1992)

Method aside, my subject area interest has been the study of cultural acquisition and transmission, again attributed to Spindler, who was teaching a popular graduate course on cultural transmission as early as forty years ago. (Between cultural transmission and differential psychology, my parents wondered if my courses at Stanford were preparing me to be an auto mechanic.) I think culture acquisition is the bigger umbrella for work in anthropology and education, but that, too, is another story. Our concern here, as educational researchers, is with method, and thus with ethnography, and with ethnography in education.

As the field arm of cultural anthropology, "ethnography" can be substituted for "anthropology" in Spindler's caution. I have been ever ready to pounce and pronounce, "Whatever it is, it's not ethnography." In the decade just past, this effort has taken form in four publications.

For the first publication, I was invited by Mitch Allen to prepare a monograph on writing for the Sage series in qualitative research (see Wolcott 1990b). Writing about writing let me develop an idea already in mind after years of helping struggling scholars write their field studies: anticipating how you intend to *write up* your study is a great way to *begin* fieldwork, not a step that must wait till you complete it.

My next two books also addressed the interests of qualitative researchers more generally, rather than focus exclusively on ethnography: *Transforming Qualitative Data* (1994) and *The Art of Fieldwork* (1995). Both were heavily weighted toward ethnographic research, because they are based on my experience and understanding of research, but they were aimed at a broader audience, particularly at *educational* researchers. Mitch Allen was the editor in each case. By the time I was drafting the book on fieldwork, Mitch had his own imprimatur, AltaMira Press.

As I completed each of these books, Mitch immediately pressed me with the question, "What are you going to do for us next?" Writing about qualitative research in general had kept me from devoting attention exclusively to *ethnography*, and we agreed that for my next project I could, would, and should focus on that topic. That is the book I completed most recently, *Eth-*

*nography: A Way of Seeing*, published in July 1999. And that is the book, and story of a book, I turn to next.

## Writing *Ethnography: A Way of Seeing*

I have championed the cause, and taken as a sort of personal mantra, Spindler's comment intended for my ears alone, "Whatever it is, it's *not* anthropology." That provided me a comforting niche from which I could join in the academic pastime—to borrow Geertz's phrase—of "vexing" my colleagues. I have tried to proceed in a helpful and constructive way, underscoring what is unique about ethnography, what needs to be recognized as its special contribution, not simply telling people they weren't doing it. The titles I mentioned earlier reveal my efforts to respond positively, yet to state unequivocally, "If you want to do ethnography, here's what you can do and here's what you *must* do."

Although I got a lot of mileage out of such crusading, I felt I have never been able to supply a wholly satisfactory answer to the question, "What makes a study ethnographic?" I recognize ethnography most readily in its absence. Oh, I could whip up a definition or two, the simplest one examining word roots to come up with ethnos as "people," graph as "picture," and thus, ethnography as a picture of "people" or "other people." But I am not one to lean on simple or simplistic explanations of complex notions. My personal quest through these same years has been to try to discern ethnography's "essence," its critical attributes.

I felt that writing a book claiming "ethnography" for a title would not only allow me but would force me to tease out that elusive essence. And that might help establish some boundaries, so that researchers could no longer claim inadvertently to have "wandered into" ethnographic territory without realizing it. Qualitative researchers need a clear idea of how that territory looks and what one needs to traverse it. Although I did not have the answer at hand as to exactly what that ethnographic essence was, I assumed it would evolve as I wrote and pondered. That's what writing does for me. I would write a book somewhat autobiographically, the same style that I follow here, and let an ethnographic "essence" gradually reveal itself. I would tease out that essence in the course of writing about it.

Intending only to construct fences adequate to mark boundaries, along with allowing a glimpse of what was inside, I apparently overdid my zealousness. Instead of a fence, I built a wall. Of my first draft, editor Mitch Allen estimated that I had written a book of possible interest to "about 30 people, worldwide" in its appeal and narrow conception of what ethnography is and who is capable of doing it. As he noted—certainly from a publisher's standpoint, but from a reader's standpoint as well—the people who might be interested in what I had to say were not those "30 people, worldwide" (surely more than that!) but researchers in fields like educational research wanting to *learn more about ethnography*, not to be told they had neither the time nor talent to do it except perhaps for borrowing a fieldwork technique or two.

Back to the drawing boards, not to rewrite the book but to knock down the wall and replace it with something less formidable. That was mostly a matter of tone, changing from "If you aren't doing such-and-such, you'll never end up with ethnography" to "If you want to be able to claim that your study is ethnographic, here are some ways to go about it, some forms it can take." My search for the "essence" focused on identifying critical attributes.

And I found some. I didn't crisp them into a neat set of rules or laws or postulates; I just inventoried them as I went along. I figured I could sort out my collection of attributes later, hopefully in a brilliant culminating chapter in which I would collapse them into a few all-inclusive categories. In all, I identified a dozen attributes.

I was tempted to stop with only three, because I like to conceptualize things in sets of threes. And the three with which I began my inventory are compelling enough. It is often stated that anthropology is *holistic*, *cross-cultural*, and *comparative*. If ethnography is the field arm of the discipline, then ethnography should demonstrate those same traits.

But being holistic, cross-cultural, and comparative didn't seem enough. The list grew longer. Let me list the attributes I identified. I caution that if you are expecting some technical jargon or big intellectual breakthrough, you will be disappointed. This is pretty everyday stuff. After all, an approach that also goes by the name "participant observation" is hard to shroud in mystery!

## Attributes of Ethnography:
## A Tentative Inventory

As I believe I had successfully encapsulated it, ethnography can be characterized as being:

- Holistic
- Cross-cultural
- Comparative

- Based on firsthand experience
- The result of intimate, long-term acquaintance
- Conducted in natural settings
- Basically descriptive
- Nonevaluative
- Specific or "particular"
- Flexible and adaptive
- Idiosyncratic and individualistic
- Corroborative

The holistic attribute seemed especially important, since it points to the ethnographer's concern for *context*. That quality seemed destined to remain a key feature.

Cross-cultural comparison is but one dimension that comparison can take, so the two facets—cross-cultural, comparative—might conceivably be treated as one. But a cross-cultural perspective has been so central to the development of ethnography as the study of *the other* that I felt it warranted a separate category, a special kind of comparison.

Firsthand experience, the result of intimate, long-term acquaintance in natural settings—all essential qualities.

A basically descriptive endeavor, nonevaluative in design and guided by a principle of objectivity calling for deferred judgment (indeed, if any judgment need be made at all)—those qualities certainly seem to be what ethnography has been about. "Thick" description calls for rich detail. As Arthur Kleinman notes, ethnography requires space, "short ethnographic papers being something of an oxymoron" (Kleinman 1995:194).

Specific or particular, no doubt about that, for an ethnography is always about a particular *group* or particular *aspects* of a group. One finds courses in world ethnography, but there is no such thing as ethnography of the world. To be suited for the study of all kinds of groups, ethnography must be flexible and adaptive as an approach, and, as a consequence, idiosyncratic and individualistic as conducted and reported in each instance.

And finally, it is corroborative, all the previous named features helping the ethnographer to get the story straight, to be sure of the facts, to put things in context. "Triangulation," we call it, and I have heard overly enthusiastic doctoral students so excited by the term that they describe triangulation as *the method* that they intend to employ in conducting their research.

I emphasize that writing (and rewriting and rewriting) this book offered *me* a vehicle for pursuing a personal objective: to search out and reveal the essence of ethnography. I had assumed from the outset that identifying and elaborating on these attributes, this "essence," was where and how I would end up, in a sort of grand finale. But there was much to discuss along the way. I devoted chapters to the importance of place and serendipity in the selection of topics and to the various forms ethnography can take, from developing standard etic categories (e.g., social organization, economic organization, worldview) to letting it all bubble up from inside, to some forms that would hardly be recognizable to our forbears, such as autoethnography, ethnographic futures, critical ethnography, and ethnographic evaluation. I thought of and presented these variations and adaptations as something like ripples on a pond, with traditional Malinowski-type ethnography at the center (and not a few ethnographers writing at a very dead center) and more recent variations and adaptations emanating outward until the influence of traditional ethnography is barely discernible, if at all.

I had no trouble filling my pages, tracing ethnography to the present and looking at some current dilemmas, such as how to speed up, and thus make competitive, an approach that depends on long-term fieldwork. But my effort at teasing out the *absolutely critical* attributes did not seem to be faring too well. If collectively the items seemed adequate to convey a general sense of what ethnography is, no particular one seemed all that powerful, able to point right at the heart of what the ethnographer does that guarantees ethnography as an outcome. What is more, as I was expanding the list at one end, a shadow of doubt seemed to be forming over it at the other. None of the qualities I identified as being "of the essence" appeared, on reflection, to be absolutely essential. Desirable, yes. Customary, yes. Invaluable, yes. Inviolable, no!

Ethnographies focused narrowly on classrooms or schools, for example, seem notoriously unholistic; schools just appear out of nowhere, context free. Yet it is hard to know just where holism stops in *any* descriptive account sensitive to context. If anything, holism has always received short shrift, even in the good old days. Ethnographers early on developed a habit of relating their accounts as precontact ones, so that *even the ethnographer* disappeared from the scene in the final telling, except perhaps in a telling acknowledgment in which it seems he or she may have been there after all. Context is a splendid facet of ethnography, but one cannot pursue it indefinitely. Most of us remain oblivious of the narrow contexts in which we select our research topics or report them; we "just know" which topics are proper, which are too sensitive to study, how in-depth is deep enough.

If all research is comparative, it is difficult to discern an explicit cross-cultural dimension in some of the ethnography reported today, when nurses and other health givers, or teachers, or members of ethnic minorities, or even the great white middle class study themselves under such rubrics as "native" ethnography or the ambiguous and newly popular label of "autoethnography." Since when did we have to make the familiar strange so that we could continue to call our work ethnographic?

Firsthand experience and intimate, long-term acquaintance correspond to our image of the ethnographer at work, so commuting to a field site by subway (Passaro 1997), or Internet (Markham 1998), or doing "virtual ethnography" in distributed electronic environments (Ruhleder 2000) stretches the imagination to the limit. Just think how surprised I was to discover as long ago as the 1960s that James Spradley was literally "commuting" from Seattle to Alert Bay, British Columbia, for interviews with his informant James Sewid of *Guests Never Leave Hungry* (Spradley 1969), while there was no question in my mind (or, I think, in Spindler's) that to become a "real" anthropologist I had to live in one of the remote villages in the Alert Bay region for a year to legitimate myself. And just how intimate is intimate, as, at one extreme, those familiar with my Brad Trilogy have questioned (Wolcott 1994), or anthropologists seemingly lacking in social skills have pondered at the other?

How can a neophyte fieldworker ever hope to establish the prerequisite long-term acquaintance within the limited time and resources of doctoral research? Why are we so uncomfortable when our students turn the question on its head to ask "What's the *minimum* time for fieldwork? How *short* can a long-term acquaintance be?" How *quick* or *rapid* can ethnography be and still stake a legitimate claim to being ethnographic?

Natural settings seem a shoe-in for the ethnographer, but we turn a blind eye to the question of what is natural about the settings we study today. Hospitals, prisons, schools, soup kitchens, nursing homes—what is "natural" about any of them? Seems like they might be "natural" for sociologists—but what are ethnographers doing in them, and, once inside, do they really achieve more intimacy than their fellow researchers.

No trouble with ethnography being "basically descriptive," for, as noted, word roots remind us that it is a "picture" of people. But it is surprising how little instruction such a notion provides for beginning researchers who go forth determined to describe "everything" until they realize that such a maxim provides no help in determining which "everythings" deserve priority. And once they realize that they must attend to *something*—that they cannot possibly attend to everything at once—they also recognize that wherever they direct their attention, everything else is left unattended.

The notion of "spot" checks, whether fixed or random-interval sampling, seems to have some appeal as a way out of the dilemma, but such sampling procedures hint at someone in the field who isn't really comfortable with ethnography's own strengths and weaknesses. Ethnography should be the antithesis of randomness, not slave to it. That certainly is not to say that one cannot borrow techniques or employ systematic data-gathering procedures, but ethnography is a rather inefficient way to do surveys. Matter of fact, that is but one of several ways that ethnographers corroborate their data. In the field, it becomes far preferable to gather data through multiple *techniques*— using triangulation in that sense of the word only—rather than to go around checking up on what your informants have told you by asking whether what they are telling you is generally accepted as true. An idea that sounds so right in a text or seminar suddenly takes on unexpected implications when you attempt to put it into practice.

Nevertheless, basic description is what all this is about, and ethnographers of the past have prided themselves on their "objective" reporting. Even when judgment was inevitable—the human inclination to approve or disap-prove—it was deferred. I recall a sense of relief on hearing the explanation that a good fieldworker could be objective without having to be neutral. Then, after long having insisted that objectivity was a tenet of ethnography, it suddenly became all right, even necessary, to be *subjective* and reflexive. Quite a switch, but a necessary one when ethnographers began claiming that they were also well suited to conduct assessment studies and evaluative stud-ies. They had become as flexible and adaptive as their approach, while objec-tivity gave way to what Margaret Mead called "disciplined subjectivity" and applied work loomed as the activity in which most effort, and most employ-ment opportunities, were occurring.

No problem with ethnography being specific or particular in its focus, and no problem that, as practiced, it is idiosyncratic and individualistic. We like to think of ourselves that way and that we thrive on the latitude ethnography offers. But it raises havoc with claims about generalizability. We are caught trying to have it both ways, unique, one-of-a-kind studies rife with implica-tions for all humankind. It is more than a little discomforting to realize, or to have to admit, that when, in turn, we turn our students loose to "do eth-nography" *we really don't have a clue what they will come up with.*

## From Essence to Analogy

Teasing out critical attributes was proving to be a frustrating, and perhaps pointless, activity. It didn't seem to lead anywhere. The essence for which I was searching had become *more* elusive. No single criterion held fast; some criteria that initially seemed reasonable did not hold up at all, and for each of those I listed I could think of exceptions. The exceptions certainly did not "prove the rule"—instead, they raised doubts whether I could ever pin down the essence with anything like the certainty I had been seeking. How could an activity that consisted simply of gathering rather everyday data in rather everyday ways *sometimes* result in ethnography, and why did roughly comparable data, gathered in roughly comparable ways, end up being something else in the hands of researchers hearing other drummers—like symbolic interactionists, or ethnologists, or phenomenologists, or, going further afield, historians or biographers or investigative journalists?

I am given to analogies, another form of comparison that serves a function similar to cross-cultural study in ethnography, inviting one to examine unlike things to gain a different perspective. I began to wonder if an analogy to something different from "ethnography-making" could give me a new slant. I seemed to be dealing with a product composed of rather everyday ingredients combined in a variety of customary ways, yet no one particular ingredient appeared to be absolutely essential. Further, whatever was to result seemed to be almost entirely in the hands of the individual researcher.

The analogy that I came up with was to the making of bread: that *the making of an ethnography is rather like making a loaf of bread*. Both demand a skillful combining of customary, everyday ingredients, none of which is absolutely critical (no, not even flour ground from grass seed). The end product takes form and shape at the hands of an ethnographer—or baker—familiar with local expectations as to how it should look and who therefore selects, combines, and shapes the ingredients accordingly.

Analogies can be playful things. As I inquired into bread-making processes, I couldn't help but be amused at

- The need for "improvers"
- The preferences among bakers for either coarse *or* finely ground flours (like ethnographers who choose between raw and refined data)
- Traditions calling for the addition of a rising agent to add "life"
- The need for the dough (or a manuscript) to rest, to be reshaped, and even to be punched down a few times so it does not end up with big holes in it (caused by hot air!)

What is more, to my surprise and delight, it was the analogy that led me to what I take to be the essence of ethnography and that released me from so mechanical a way of conceptualizing the ethnographic task. I came to see that, as with the baker, it was at the hands of the ethnographer that the selection and proportion of ingredients was decided. And it was what the ethnographer—or some other researcher, with a slightly different audience and end product in mind—uses to combine the ingredients that allows them to come together in a workable mass, shaped for some particular market.

For the American ethnographer, what is added to render the raw ingredients malleable is the concept of *culture*. For a qualitative researcher of different bent, other concepts perform the comparable function but produce slightly different results. All social researchers have at hand basically the same array of ingredients, beginning with an infinite supply of potential data that can be gleaned from everyday behavior, and an assortment of readily available improvers. We admire ethnographers able to season their accounts with just enough humor, compassion, pathos, irony, wonderment, mystery, and so forth.

Researchers choose among a number of unifying concepts for the preferred one(s) they use to combine ingredients into a cohesive mass (like the baker, who selects among a wide assortment of liquids, and may use several, but wouldn't think of using them all). Until we add the concepts that enable us to form a workable and cohesive mass, the raw data are inert. At the hands of some researchers, they remain pretty much that way: dry, neither well formed nor well integrated, nor too sour, nor too sweet, nor too lacking in this or that, though we are not always able to discern just what is missing or what has been added to excess. (For me, the most obscure step in any recipe is: Correct the seasoning.)

For the ethnographer, what must be added is *culture*. Researchers of other persuasions rely on other concepts to make their accounts cohere, although many of them add a bit of culture for extra good measure. But *when ethnography is the intended end product,* culture (or some equivalent or particular subset of it—social structure, worldview, political economy) is the principal blending agent. Anthropologically, Ward Goodenough describes this process of bringing everything together to form a cohesive mass as "attributing" culture to a group (Goodenough 1976:5). Critical point: Culture is not "there," it is something added *when and if* ethnography is the intended outcome.

I note other parallels that can be drawn from the analogy. Like ethnographies, loaves of bread simply "accumulate"; they cannot be aggregated to create something new. Most have a limited shelf life and some quickly go stale. A certain uniformity is expected, but no two are exactly alike, and we recognize and applaud the superior and distinctive product. Today machines can do some of the sticky work, and those of us reared in a day when both bread making and ethnography were considered to be character-forming are sometimes aghast at what younger colleagues allow and expect mechanical gadgets to do for them. For many, a moral tone bordering on self-righteousness continues to underwrite the effort, and real ethnographers, like real bakers, cling somewhat tenaciously to the old ways for the personal significance of the work to their own lives. Old-timers also tend to pontificate and to describe the processes involved in ways more rigid than they themselves practice, hoping to set younger generations on a true course while exercising certain liberties for themselves. The way they teach it or preach it is not necessarily the way they practiced it.

## But Is It Ethnography?

Well, there you have the story of the book. What I have relayed in a few pages took place over a period of almost five years, the final draft turning out in a different way from what the author anticipated. A new appreciation for what goes into the making of ethnography, a new analogy for thinking about it.

Readers may express impatience with a penultimate chapter devoted to bread making in a book titled *Ethnography*. Developmental reviewers were not uniformly enthusiastic about what appeared as a wide, even unnecessary detour, a characteristic Wolcott meander. For myself, I'm pleased and satisfied with the book, with the analogy, and with a perspective for understanding how what goes into the making of ethnography—those common, everyday bits of observable data—differs from what comes out, depending on the concepts used to combine them and on professional expectations as to the form and shape in which the results are presented.

Perhaps it is just as well that I didn't "resolve" the criteria problem, an issue of longstanding interest to me (see Wolcott 1975) and one that continues to prompt an engaging dialogue.[3] Thinking of ethnography as being like "ripples on a pond" seemed promising to convey the idea of greater and lesser ethnographicness, but in Mitch Allen's judgment, the pond that I described seemed to be located at the edge of the world, a place where the ripples stopped abruptly.

Frankly, I do think there is some point at which studies can be judged "just not ethnographic enough," a place where the ripples are no longer discernibly traceable to ethnographic origins. Committed as I am to the concept of culture—whether stated explicitly or present in some comparable form such as Jean Lave's "community of practice"—I am inclined to see the presence or absence of a notion of culture as the ultimate criterion for judging ethnographicness. I take very seriously the notion that, as Michael Agar states it, ethnography is "much more complicated than collecting data" (Agar 1996:91). Putting it even more succinctly, *ethnography is more than method* (Wolcott 1999:67–68).

To be sure, method is part of it. That is what Mitch wanted me to acknowledge with a more welcoming message to would-be or wanna-be ethnographers outside the discipline of anthropology. But methods alone are not enough. I have long suggested and urged researchers to recognize a distinction between *borrowing ethnographic techniques in their data gathering* and *doing* ethnography. Ethnography doesn't simply happen; there is no ethnography without intent to do ethnography. As Paul Bohannan observes in *How Culture Works*, "Without an ethnographer, there is no ethnography" (1996:157).

One can say the same about baking bread: Without a baker, there is no baking. It is not that a formal role need be occupied, but that there must be intent. Not even good intentions are enough. There must be know-how, a sense of what one is trying to achieve and of how to go about it. A researcher without a good idea of what an ethnography looks like is unlikely to produce one. Even *with* a good sense of what I expect in a loaf of bread, I would need a lot of help to make one. Neither process is self-evident.

So I did not accomplish an important personal goal with the book. I have not been able precisely to say when a study is ethnographic, or "ethnographic enough." I was able to identify many of ethnography's *customary* ingredients, but its true "essence" resists rigid specification. Like the human social behavior that it purports to study, ethnography itself is *overdetermined*, a congeries of ingredients formed into something recognizable at the hands of researchers who share a general notion of what they are about. Although I was unable to pin it down more precisely, I'm convinced that a bit of consciousness-raising about "customary ingredients" and the complexity of the ethnographic process is always in order, especially among educational researchers. There have been whisperings in the corridors over the years that ethnography was never the same once educators got hold of it.

Perhaps I am particularly sensitive to the issue because my own work may have been as much a part of the problem as part of the answer. Take *The Man in the Principal's Office* (1973) as case in point. Spindler's probably long-forgotten reaction to reading it in early draft was that it looked more like sociology than anthropology. I think he had been underwhelmed by my use of concepts like socialization, socioeconomic status, role perception, role conflict, career ladder, organizational analysis, and sponsored and contest mobility, and my reliance on works by sociologists dating back to Willard Waller's *Sociology of Teaching* (1932). He may have been less attentive to my attention to the principal's out-of-school life or my use of concepts like annual cycle, real versus ideal world, or an "ethnography of encounters" not ordinarily found in studies in education. My remedy was to change only one thing: I added a subtitle to my study. I called it *An Ethnography*! That's what I intended the study to be, and I was ready to defend it, in spite of whisperings even I could hear, "Well, I didn't know you could do an *ethnography* of someone in an occupational role."

By classical standards such as Malinowski's *Argonauts of the Western Pacific* (1922), and even my own earlier *A Kwakiutl Village and School* (1967b), the principal study seemed pretty far out (or too close in?) as ethnography in its day. By current standards, it is beginning to look like the educational equivalent of *Argonauts*. Perhaps I should be more tolerant of what goes on today under the banner of educational ethnography, just as others were tolerant of me. But I underscore that although I may be among those responsible for stretching the limits, I did not simply drop in on a principal for a quick interview and a tour of the building The fieldwork was conducted over a period of two years. I also knew what ethnographies looked like, and through the experience of prior fieldwork, I brought a cross-cultural perspective to the study. It was, and is, intended as ethnography.

I did not anticipate how that study would serve as a model for work that followed, but it has proved an adequate one (see Wolcott 1982b). Looking back, I wish I had spent more time emphasizing how the study was of a man who happened to be a principal rather than of a principal who happened to be a man. Keep in mind, however, that the study was funded by an R&D center devoted to the study of educational administration. The research was completed well before Spradley and McCurdy proposed that one could study "cultural scenes" literally in one's own backyard (Spradley and McCurdy 1972).

I had pushed the limits, but I was ready to defend the study as ethnographic. I would have done battle with anyone making the suggestion that I had engaged in mere educational travel writing. I recall one educational reviewer who insisted that I might just as well have sat in a quiet corner of the library and made up the whole account, since it consisted of what everyone already knew. (He did not accuse me of doing that, he just insisted that I would have come out at the same place.) I accepted that criticism as inevitable in doing ethnography close to home. I do not mind being accused of making the obvious obvious. I was confident there was plenty in the study to think about. Witness that the monograph remained in print for about twenty years.

## Ethnography? Or Educational Travel Writing?

In my reading while preparing the new book, I was reminded that ethnography grew out of a tradition of travel writing based on the accounts of travelers, explorers, and missionaries (see, for example, MacClancy 1996:239). We might keep the phrase "educational travel writing" in mind as a handy epithet as we look at some of the work offered up as ethnography today. Perhaps the phrase itself need not be uttered so much as simply held in abeyance, a caution to students (and colleagues) too eager to appropriate the label but otherwise oblivious to all the elements customarily associated with the making of ethnography. To be accused of travel writing—"research tourism," as it is known in some circles—might be something educational researchers wish to avoid, easy enough to do simply by not borrowing the label unless the claim is warranted.

An epithet is a disparaging phrase. I underscore that the label *educational travel writing* be reserved for those studies of "questionable quality" to which our attention has been invited. Perhaps the phrase need only be whispered, not said aloud, a caution for educational researchers tempted to make unwarranted claims as to the intent or depth—or impartiality?—of their studies.

I do not mean to disparage the art of travel writing itself. I admire writers who do it well and note that some of them even make money at it. Our local newspaper devotes an entire section each Sunday to travel writing, but nary a word to ethnography. And in James Spradley's suggestion for beginning an ethnographic interview with a Grand Tour Question, Do you recognize the idea of the Grand Tour itself as a travel notion?

I have come to realize that travel writers share many concerns familiar to ethnographers. Here is a sampling of topics discussed and advice given in one current source on travel writing (Edwards 1999; see also Zinsser 1991):

- Finding a great story is often a matter of being receptive to opportunities and recognizing a first-rate possibility when it comes your way. (p. 117) [We call that serendipity.]

- Double check all your facts. The information you furnish must be accurate. (p. 134)
- Wherever your travels take you, keep your eyes open, your notebook handy, and your camera loaded. (p. 117)
- Long descriptions are boring. (p. 23)
- When you can use a quote . . . it has a tremendous effect on whatever you're writing. (p. 144)
- The hardest thing . . . to overcome when conducting an interview is chiming in with [one's] own stories. (p. 175)
- Writing is 10% writing and 90% rewriting. (p. 166)
- You have to read every possible publication you can in an area—you just cannot sop up too much information. (p. 145)
- Putting it down while it's still fresh makes all the difference. (p. 178)
- Make it comfortable for your interviewees. Always get their permission to record the conversation. (p. 176)
- Start as soon as possible to transcribe interviews and notes from your journal. (p. 192)
- And the subheading in one chapter include these familiar problems:

> How "Narrow" a Focus Is Too Narrow?
> The Thin Line between a Great Idea and a Futile Endeavor
> Switching Your Focus to New Possibilities
> Spreading Your Focus Too Thinly
> Hang On to Your Sense of Humor

Or consider the following quote from an essay on travel writing, closely paralleling a dialogue heard among anthropologists in the last thirty years. Just substitute "ethnographers" for "travelers" in the opening sentence:

> Western travelers [read "ethnographers"] have tended to adopt a colonialist style of writing which assumes the superiority of the traveler's cultural and moral values and which leads to this figure taking possession of what he sees in a voyeuristic gaze. Even when sympathetic towards the people being visited, this colonial rhetoric positions the indigenous people as childlike or lacking in reason. [Sharp 1999: 200.]

We might keep "educational travel writing" in mind for cautioning colleagues to be circumspect, to refrain from slapping the label "ethnography" on every descriptive study seeking an academic upgrade. Like loaves of bread, ethnographies cannot be judged until we see the final product. It is not as simple as holding up a checklist of ingredients or asking a researcher what he or she hoped would be the final outcome. But neither borrowing a fieldwork technique or two, nor providing a descriptive vignette or two, nor simply having "been there" makes a study ethnographic. We can only note that the fewer the customary criteria met, or the less steeped in the ethnographic tradition the researcher, the less likely the outcome will be satisfying or convincing as ethnography.

I am not pleading on behalf of an ethnography-of-yesterday that may have become outmoded. I certainly do not insist that some standard list of ingredients must always be included; if anything, I have tried to show by analogy that exactly what those ingredients are, which of them are to be included and in what proportion, is always subject to wide variation. But educational ethnography is not well served if anyone can slap the label on a study simply because they took an afternoon off to visit a classroom, interview a few students or teachers, or once attended school themselves.

There aren't all that many situations today in educational research that demand or even allow the kind of contextualized firsthand knowledge-in-depth we expect from an ethnographer. Borrow and adapt the fieldwork techniques freely, but save the label *ethnography* for studies that warrant it. If a series of vignettes or case histories are sufficient to set a problem, provide an illustration, or unleash yet another diatribe about what is wrong with schools, don't appropriate a label that implicates a more thorough, time-consuming, culturally based examination of what goes on in them and how they got that way. Otherwise you may be the researcher about whose work some future reviewer begins an essay with these words, "Educational travel writing, perhaps. Whatever it is, it's not ethnography!"

## Notes

1. Richard King's monograph *The School at Mopass* was published later that same year (1967) but was not one of the four monographs that introduced the series.

2. Full citations for these references can be found in the original article. See Wolcott 1967.

3. On page 9 in volume 1 of their seven-volume *Ethnographer's Toolkit*, published in 1999, editors Margaret LeCompte and Jean Schensul set forth "the seven characteristics that mark a study as ethnographic." Paraphrased, they are that ethnography:

- Is carried out in a natural setting, not in a laboratory.
- Involves intimate, face-to-face interaction with participants.

- Presents an accurate reflection of participant's perspectives and behaviors.
- Uses inductive, interactive, and recursive data collection and analytic strategies to build local cultural theories.
- Frames all human behavior and belief within a sociopolitical and historical context.
- Uses multiple data sources, including both quantitative and qualitative data.
- Uses the concept of culture as a lens through which to interpret results.

# References

Agar, M. H. *The Professional Stranger*. 2nd ed. San Diego, Calif.: Academic Press, 1996.

Bohannan, P. *How Culture Works*. New York: Free Press, 1996.

Edwards, J. *Travel Writing in Fiction & Fact*. Portland, Ore.: Blue Heron Publishing Co., 1999.

Gay, J., and M. Cole. *The New Mathematics and an Old Culture: A Study of Learning among the Kpelle of Liberia*. New York: Holt, Rinehart and Winston, 1967.

Goodenough, W. H. "Multiculturalism as the Normal Human Experience." *Anthropology and Education Quarterly*, 7, 1 (1976):4–7.

King, A. R. *The School at Mopass: A Problem of Identity*. New York: Holt, Rinehart and Winston, 1967.

Kleinman, A. *Writing at the Margin: Discourse between Anthropology and Medicine*. Berkeley: University of California Press, 1995.

LeCompte, M. D., and J. J. Schensul. *Designing and Conducting Ethnographic Research: Volume 1 of The Ethnographer's Toolkit*. J. J. Schensul and M. D. LeCompte, series ed. Walnut Creek, Calif.: AltaMira Press, 1999.

MacClancy, J. "Fieldwork Styles." Pp. 225–44 in J. MacClancy and C. McDonaugh, ed., *Popularizing Anthropology*. New York: Routledge, 1996.

Malinowski, B. *Argonauts of the Western Pacific*. London: George Routledge & Sons,1922.

Markham, A. N. *Life Online: Researching Real Experience in Virtual Space*. Walnut Creek, Calif.: AltaMira Press, 1998.

Passaro, J. "You Can't Take the Subway to the Field!: 'Village' Epistemologies in the Global Village." Pp. 147–62 in A. Gupta and J. Ferguson, ed., *In Anthropological Locations*. Berkeley: University of California Press, 1997.

Ruhleder, K. "The Virtual Ethnographer: Fieldwork in Distributed Electronic Environments." *Field Methods*, 12, 1 (2000):3–17.

Singleton, John. *Nichu: A Japanese School*. New York: Holt, Rinehart and Winston,1967.

Sharp, J. P. "Writing over the Map of Provence: The Touristic Therapy of 'A Year in Provence.'" Pp. 200–18 in J. Duncan and D. Gregory, ed., *Writes of Passage: Reading Travel Writing*. London: Routledge, 1999.

Spindler, G. D., ed. *Education and Anthropology*. Stanford, Calif.: Stanford University Press, 1955.

Spindler, G. D. *Education and Culture: Anthropological Approaches*. New York: Holt, Rinehart and Winston, 1963.

Spradley, J. P., ed. *Guests Never Leave Hungry: The Autobiography of James Sewid, A Kwaki-utl Indian*. New Haven, Conn.: Yale University Press, 1969.

Spradley, J. P., and D. W. McCurdy. *The Cultural Experience: Ethnography in Complex Society*. Chicago: Science Research Associates, 1972.

Waller, W. *The Sociology of Teaching*. New York: John Wiley & Sons, 1932.

Warren, R. L. *Education in Rebhausen: A German Village*. New York: Holt, Rinehart and Winston, 1967.

Wolcott, H. F. "Anthropology and Education." *Review of Educational Research*, 37 (1967a):82–95.

Wolcott, H. F. *A Kwakiutl Village and School*. New York: Holt, Rinehart and Winston, 1967b.

Wolcott, H. F. "Handle with Care: Necessary Precautions in the Anthropology of Schools." Pp. 98–117 in M. L. Wax, S. Diamond, and F. O. Gearing, ed., *Anthropological Perspectives on Education*. New York: Basic Books, 1971.

Wolcott, H. F. *The Man in the Principal's Office: An Ethnography*. New York: Holt, Rinehart and Winston, 1973.

Wolcott, H. F. "Criteria for an Ethnographic Approach to Research in Schools." *Human Organization*, 34, 2 (1975):111–27.

Wolcott, H. F. "How to Look Like an Anthropologist Without Really Being One." *Practicing Anthropology*, 3, 1 (1980):6–7, 56–59. (Reprinted pp. 43–50 in P. Higgins and A. Paredes, ed., *Classics of Practicing Anthropology: 1978–1998*. Oklahoma City, Okla.: Society for Applied Anthropology, 2000.)

Wolcott, H. F. "Differing Styles of On-Site Research, Or, 'If It Isn't Ethnography, What Is It?'" *Review Journal of Philosophy and Social Science*, 7, 1, 2 (1982a):154–69. (Special issue on Naturalistic Research Paradigms.)

Wolcott, H. F. "Mirrors, Models, and Monitors: Educator Adaptations of the Ethnographic Innovation." Pp. 68–95 in G. Spindler, ed., *Doing the Ethnography of Schooling*. New York: Holt, Rinehart and Winston,1982b.

Wolcott, H. F. "Ethnographers sans Ethnography: The Evaluation Compromise." Pp. 177–210 in David M. Fetterman, ed., *Ethnography in Educational Evaluation*. Beverly Hills, Calif.: Sage, 1984.

Wolcott, H. F. "On Ethnographic Intent." Pp. 37–57 in G. Spindler and L. Spindler, ed., *Interpretive Ethnography of Education: At Home and Abroad*. Hillsdale, N.J.: Lawrence Erlbaum Associates, 1988.

Wolcott, H. F. "Making a Study 'More Ethnographic.'" *Journal of Contemporary Ethnography*, 19, 1 (1990a):44–72.

Wolcott, H. F. *Writing Up Qualitative Research*. Sage University Press Series on Qualitative Research, Volume 20. Newbury Park, Calif.: Sage,1990b.

Wolcott, H. F. "Posturing in Qualitative Inquiry." Pp. 3–52 in M. D. LeCompte, W. L. Millroy, and J. Preissle, ed., *Handbook of Qualitative Research in Education.*. San Diego, Calif.: Academic Press, 1992.

Wolcott, H. F. *Transforming Qualitative Data: Description, Analysis, and Interpretation.* Thousand Oaks, Calif.: Sage, 1994.

Wolcott, H. F. *The Art of Fieldwork.* Walnut Creek, Calif.: AltaMira Press, 1995.

Wolcott, H. F. *Ethnography: A Way of Seeing.* Walnut Creek, Calif.: AltaMira Press, 1999.

Zinsser, W., ed. *They Went: The Art and Craft of Travel Writing.* Boston, Mass.: Houghton Mifflin, 1991.

CHAPTER THREE

~

# The Destructive Desire for a Depoliticized Ethnographic Methodology: Response to Harry F. Wolcott

*James J. Scheurich*

In many ways, critiquing Harry Wolcott is not easy. He comes across in his books as this friendly, helpful person. I sometimes use his books in the courses that I teach, and I am using one of them now, *Transforming Qualitative Data*, so I am rereading it. Once again, I have an experience of this warm, open person who simply wants to share his knowledge and expertise in a helpful way. I have also heard him speak one other time, besides today, and I got the same impression from that experience. Here is a person who is not as egotistical as many well-known academics become.

Another part of this friendly persona is that while he certainly indicates an awareness of paradigm and political debates throughout his written work, he always seems to *not* take them very seriously. He will make minor comments, almost like asides, about such debates, and then will proceed to do his ethnography or discussions of ethnography.

I am afraid, however, that this is part of what makes an approach like that of Harry Wolcott's dangerous. Having read several of his books and articles, but certainly less than half of them, I have come to realize that his comments, or asides, on various debates, especially political debates, are highly problematic. It is not, as I used to assume, that Harry Wolcott is not political;

he is in fact *very* political. His brand of politics, like many Americans', particularly white Americans, is that all of those words and actions about inequity and oppression by other, more politicized researchers have only a little to do with "reality," and certainly nothing to do with research methodologies, like ethnography. Otherwise, how could he go on this meandering travel, writing about, musing about the nature of ethnography without ever addressing the politics of epistemology and methodology, of research and the university.

You cannot just discuss what ethnography is when our society sends an extraordinarily disproportionate percentage of men of color, particularly Hispanic and African American men, to prison. That over the past ten or more years we have embarked on this incredible expansion of our prison system, easily the largest among the so-called advanced nations, and stocked these prisons with men of color is hideous. In fact, 25–50 percent of young men of color in many urban areas are somehow involved with the law enforcement and the penal systems. What does this say about our society, about us? How is this one situation so ignored? Surely, this has nothing to do with ethnography in general, nothing to do with methodology and epistemology, nothing to do with the social functions of social science research and the university.

You cannot just discuss what ethnography is when in our schools, kindergarten to graduate, students of color are mistreated so badly that their self-esteem is often destroyed as is their belief that they too can be smart and knowledgeable. Children of color in our schools get disproportionately the most discipline, the most assignment to special education, the most tracking in the lowest educational tracks, the least positive and the most negative attention of the teachers, the least assignment to programs for the gifted, the least attention in the curriculum, and the least understanding of their culture. Surely, though, this has nothing to do with ethnography in general, nothing to do with methodology and epistemology, nothing to do with the social functions of social science research and the university.

Adults of color disproportionately hold the lowest paying jobs. The hierarchy of most corporations in Houston is a color chart. As you start at the bottom with those earning the least, the color is brown and black. As you work your way up the hierarchy, the color slowly turns lighter, until by the time you get to the top, it is almost all white. People of color are largely segregated inside the worst housing in any city. As a person of color you will have much more difficulty getting loans, buying houses, obtaining rentals, and being treated decently by clerks at retail counters. A good example of this comes from a recent report that indicates that for every one dollar of family wealth the median white family had in 1999, the median African American family held barely 9 cents. While most of the white faculty in American universities, including myself, are likely to be above the median for whites, just think, at a maximum, for every $100 dollars you have, an African American family has $9 dollars, and I doubt that the wealth of Hispanic families is much different than the latter.

Our society is, in fact, this massive hierarchy of inequality by race that at a minimum substantially limits the potential of people of color to succeed in school, to earn a decent salary, to live in decent housing, to be treated as an equal human being, and to enjoy a decent life. At a maximum this hierarchy literally destroys people of color, particularly children of color, in a thousand different ways, and then usually blames them as the cause of their own destruction. We simply do not live in a free and clear world; we do not live in an apolitical world. Our society is massively political, outrageously inequitable. Surely, though, this has nothing to do with ethnography in general, nothing to do with methodology and epistemology, nothing to do with the social functions of social science research and the university.

Our world, our society, is a social construction. I don't mean that the streets or trees are social constructions. I mean the meaning we make of the world is a large social construction. And the dominant social construction in our society, whether it is in the popular media or in the university, is a white racist one. Ethnography did not just pop out of a historical hat like a rabbit, though if it is a rabbit, it is certainly a white one. Social science research in general has a social function, a conservative social function with an apolitical white face, to help create and legitimate a certain kind of inequitable social construction of what we then come to think of as "reality."

Consequently, inequity and white racism are ontological. That is, our socially constructed world, which is historically and daily constructed through semiotic categories of all kinds (including but not limited to language), in its most fundamental being is a white racist construction. It is not that white racism is just an action at the surface of human thoughts and actions, so that as long as you are not an explicitly racist individual, you are free and clear to think and write about just ethnography. The very nature of reality as we know and live it in our society is a white racist one. Thus, the inequity cannot be critiqued and fought as if reality, or ethnography, just exists apolitically. Social reality, at the level of its deepest assumptions, is a white racist reality. Research epistemology and methodology, at the level of their deepest assumptions, are racist.

The ontological and epistemological struggle to critique and remove this racism obviously has many implications for ethnography and for critical ethnography, many more than I can address in this chapter. What I want to do, then, is to turn to one issue this struggle raises, an issue I think Anglo critical ethnographers have in general not sufficiently addressed. And in these remarks to follow I only address other Anglo critical researchers like myself. In my view of white racism, it is none of my activist or philosophical business to be critiquing the subjectivities of researchers of color. I want to repeat this point: The remarks that follow are for me part of my efforts as a white scholar to address other white scholars on the issue of white racism.

Our selves, our subjectivities, do not stand outside of ontology, outside of the social construction of reality. This view that the self walks through history rather than is deeply constructed by history is one aspect of white racism. The idea that an individual self is separate from history, that an individual self can autonomously choose her or his life, this is the self of the elite Anglo male. Only those in this category possess the power and resources to come anywhere near to accomplishing this positionality. This so-called individual self, which we all live under the sign of, is the creation of modernism, the individual that Lacan called the transcendental signifier of history. In other words, the individual, autonomous self we are taught to have as our "birthright" as a person is an elitist, masculinist, heterosexist, and white racist trope.

And this trope haunts all of us as we daily try to live it. It is inside all of us, including me. In other words, emancipation, revolution, struggle, transformation are not just issues of the critique of the socially constructed, inequitable world; they are issues that come home to our own subjectivities. In general, I find that we white critical theorists want the critique and political struggle to be out there in the world. In general, I find that we are very good at criticizing the inequitable world. But this overload, this imbalance in one direction toward the critique of the world out there is itself a failure of critical theory, an instance of reproduction within ourselves of the white racist ontology. In other words, by not attending to the nature of our own subjectivity, and the roles it plays in the reproduction of an inequitable status quo, we too are guilty of participating in the creation of that status quo. We can criticize the world out there day after day, but if we don't also criticize our own subjectivity, we leave one of the main tropes of white racist modernism not only untouched but also active in reproduction.

In fact, we white critical researchers can live a good life, get lots of attention, live in nice houses and drive nice cars, travel around to conferences staying in nice hotels. We can become well paid and well known criticizing the world. Consequently, in my view, Anglo critical theorists, including myself, have a serious problem. Because we have not been sufficiently onto-logical in our critique, we often leave the socially constructed, white racist nature of reality itself off our table. Then, when we do address this, we still leave our own subjectivities off the table. And I don't mean just subjectivity as another general category. I mean we leave who each of us criticalists is in our selves off the table. How is the self that I live, not the self of someone else, but the self that I live, how am I reproductive of the inequitable status quo? Am I living the egotism of the white racist, transcendental signifier? Yes, I am. It is in and of me. The way that I talk to myself, the way that I talk to others, the way that I see myself, the effects of my white skin privilege are inside me, deeply a part of me.

Thus, we cannot just operate freely in the world as critical researchers. We cannot just critique the world out there. We have to place our selves, our subjectivities, our personal selves inside the circle of critique and struggle. Our critique of the world out there is very fine; it is complex, it is deep, it is thorough. Our critique of ourselves as selves, our struggle with our selves in collaboration with each other is virtually nonexistent. We offer the world a fine critique of inequity, but we leave out subjectivity, we leave out the per-sonal space in which we live. When we do this, we end up as just another elite white group.

The question for me then is how can we participate in the world in a way that acts to create a world of sister and brotherhood both that is open, supportive, and loving and critically struggles with each other about our own subjectivities? How do we participate in the world as researchers in a way that brings our subjectivities inside the circle of our critique and struggle? Transforming the world is not just about critiquing it while living safe and easy lives in our elite white subjectivities. Transforming the world requires, through a loving struggle with others, our very selves becoming part of the ongoing social struggle for transforming society.

Returning to where I started this brief, almost completed, journey, I want to say that I do respect Harry Wolcott for placing his subjectivity inside the circle of his work. With his Brad trilogy, which I am sure most of you are familiar with, and generally throughout his writings, Wolcott has, to some extent, placed himself inside, and he advocates others doing this, also. I think his Brad trilogy does provide us with a useful example. However, what is dangerously missing from this example, as with Wolcott's work in general, is a critical perspective, about himself, about his work, and about the white racism that is deeply "indigenous" to reality itself, to research epistemology and methodology, and to social science research and the university. However, what I hope can receive some attention, and what I am most concerned about among those of us Anglos who consider ourselves to be critical theorists, is our strong tendency to only critique the world out there while leaving our selves, our lives, and our lifestyles, outside of the struggle. In my view, university-based critical research will continue to have little effect on the society at large until through our own loving struggles with others from both inside and outside the university we have learned to critique and change our own subjectivities in parallel with our critiques of the appallingly inequitable world.

CHAPTER FOUR

~

# The Hidden History of Praxis Theory within Critical Ethnography and the Criticalism/ Postmodernism Problematic

*Phil Francis Carspecken*

## I. The Dialectic of Sameness and Difference

**Paradigm Proliferation in Qualitative Social Research**
In the autumn of 1999 I attended a conference at the Bergamot retreat center in Ohio. There I observed an extremely interesting presentation on "paradigm proliferation" in qualitative social research. The presenters were Bob Donmoyer and Patti Lather, who began by explaining what they meant by "paradigm proliferation." The expression refers to a sort of discourse on paradigms that has been prevalent within certain communities of qualitative social researchers for about fifteen years. Yvonna Lincoln and Egon Guba initiated the discourse in 1985, when they published a now famous book: *Naturalistic Inquiry*. In this book the authors argue that qualitative research should be called "naturalistic research" and that it is paradigmatically incommensurable with quantitative social research. A few years later the same authors published books and papers that divided social research, and qualitative research itself, into distinctive, incommensurable paradigms: positivist, postpositivist, critical, and constructivist (Guba 1990a). Other writers have followed suit, sometimes inventing their own categories to distinguish

between various ways of pursuing qualitative research. Today we are used to reading about "ludic postmodernism," "critical postmodernism," "colored epistemology," and "feminist epistemology." All in all both the discourse on paradigms in qualitative research and the number of paradigms claimed to exist have indeed been proliferating. I was very interested in finding out what Bob Donmoyer and Patti Lather would have to say. I have been irritated by the paradigm typologies, particularly by the manner in which those who employ them usually characterize critical ethnography. I have published arguments against paradigm typologies for qualitative social research though I have done so as part of a more general argument that critical ethnography has demonstrated something like a real paradigm shift for *all* social research, potentially including quantitative, even though this has not yet been fully explicated or understood even by those who call their research "critical" (Carspecken 1996, 1999b: ch. 1). Patti Lather, in contrast, has published her own typological scheme for qualitative research, distinguishing between realist, interpretive, critical, and postmodern orientations (Lather 1991). And I quickly learned during this presentation that Bob Donmoyer has long held the view that the paradigm discourse has been a fiction from the start.

## To Agree or Not Agree
The presentation was framed in an interesting and surprising manner. The audience was asked to listen to each presentation and then decide whether or not Bob Donmoyer and Patti Lather really agreed with each other even though Patti Lather thought they held different positions (Bob Donmoyer believed they were in basic agreement).

As the presentation proceeded I found that I completely agreed with what Bob Donmoyer had to say. The concept of a "research paradigm" is inappropriate for describing and comparing the various communities of qualitative researchers practicing and publishing today because the different orientations that may be identified do not amount to totalizing views that are incommensurable with each other. Bob Donmoyer regards the paradigm talk initiated by Lincoln and Guba to be a fiction that had strategic importance for legitimating qualitative research during the 1980s but that is no longer useful. The only thing I would have added to his arguments is something I am sure he would not immediately agree with: critical ethnography does indeed implicate a distinctive paradigm.

I agreed with what Bob Donmoyer had to say but then also found myself in complete sympathy with Patti Lather's presentation. I applauded Patti Lather's work while agreeing with Bob Donmoyer's arguments, but not because I thought she and Bob were in basic agreement while she was unaware of this. To agree or not agree was cast as a political question by Patti Lather.

Patti Lather's paper sounded complex. It was read rapidly. I am sure I didn't catch everything she had to say. But I do think I captured the root metaphors in play and the core dynamic of the arguments. Patti Lather was in tune with the dialectic of sameness and difference. In fact she explicitly referred to Hegelian dialectic and the sort of power play that occurs whenever Hegel's *aufheben* steps in to make a sameness out of two differences.

To put it more crudely and formulaically than Hegel himself did, Hegelian dialectic generates a "synthesis" out of a "thesis" and its "antithesis." It does this by sublating the difference involved between thesis and antithesis to make it the principle of a new unity. The movement from difference to a new level of sameness is called *aufheben*: The difference is *aufgehoben* when the movement to unity is completed. *Aufgehoben* means preserved but understood from a broader perspective. For example, the concept of "being" first appears to be most fundamental in understanding the so-called absolute. The absolute is "pure being" or "substance" as Spinoza conceived of it. But then we are invited to become aware of the fact that the concept of being depends upon a backgrounded concept that is opposite to it in order to be intelligible. Being implicates its antithesis, "nothing." The dialectic next proceeds to unify being and nothing, and the difference between them, in the synthesis: "becoming." The difference between being and nothing is made *aufgehoben* in becoming. Hegelian dialectic makes sameness out of difference.

Patti Lather stated that there never really is sameness, there is only a power claim that will make two differences appear to be united within a broader view when this broader view in fact favors one of the opposed moments. This is a well-known postmodern argument and not unique to Patti Lather. Hegelian dialectic pretends to be a "friend of the flux" while actually theorizing the flux away (e.g., see Caputo 1987). "Reality," if we want to risk using this word, is a proliferation of incommensurable differences. Postmodern qualitative researchers apply this principle to social reality. The people and cultures that social researchers study are irreducibly heterogeneous. Research always risks subsuming the voices of people within regimes of power when they explain these voices and subject them to their a priori concepts of truth, validity, and knowledge. Research often does emphasize the differences between cultures but it does so in a quasi-Hegelian manner by representing difference within one dominant voice so as to, in effect, theorize difference away.

So the same view might be held of research communities, the view that they are incommensurably heterogeneous. Patti Lather basically argued from a postmodern position on "reality" to a similar position on specifically social reality, and from there to an argument in favor of keeping research communities distinct. She described research communities as "discourse-formations" rather than in terms of epistemologies, which does seem closer to the mark and in fact would skirt the paradigm discourse if used with this purpose in mind. But the incommensurability thesis remained central to her discussion. The political usefulness of keeping such communities distinct so as to prevent the formation of a hegemonic knowledge-power formation among researchers seemed to be the principal point of her paper. The epistemology and/or metatheory of any research design is a claim to power that will necessarily be opposed (in terms of interests and identity repertoires) to many of the people "studied," so it is therefore wise to keep multiple paradigms or discourse communities going. All too often people of color have been studied by whites, women have been studied by men, gay and lesbian people have been studied by heterosexuals, and non-Western cultures have been studied by Europeans and Americans. Such "studies" have served the purposes of subjugation.

As I listened I definitely sympathized with Patti Lather's strategy. In terms of theorizing and representing "truth" I think there are two basic positions one can occupy. One can be a "sameness theorist" or one can be a "difference theorist." Bob Donmoyer spoke as a sameness theorist, seeking ways to integrate the various practices of qualitative research communities under one epistemological umbrella. Patti Lather spoke as a difference theorist, though difference theorists cannot at the end of the day be "theorists": they must rather be *strategists*. Though she emphasized differences, Patti Lather's own use of a paradigm typology as *theory* is at face value "sameness": it uses one framework and one set of parameters by which to contrast the orientations of different research communities. Because it does this, difference is in fact made *aufgehoben* within her typology. In addition, Patti Lather's presentation suggested stable concepts such as "heterogeneity," "knowledge-power," and "discourse formations," and to do this is also to embrace a version of sameness. She presented, *on the face* of her presentation, a singular and internally coherent view of society and the process of knowing. But Patti Lather performed her presentation in a postmodern way so as to differentiate the theoretical appearance of her typology, concepts, and metaphors—their "face value"—from their role as tools for deconstruction. She was quick to make a point, then explicate the metaphor underlying the point she just made, and then indicate a willingness to scrap that metaphor for alternatives. She kept things open with her talk. She was a strategist: a person committed to disrupt the formation of hegemonic beliefs about truth that appear to be "neutral" but in fact aim to establish regimes of power. Her performance delivered herself as a ludic theorist, or strategist, rather than as a theorist per se.

To agree or not agree thus appeared as a political question in the talk of Patti Lather. To say that Bob Donmoyer and Patti Lather really "agree" is to embrace sameness theory. To say that they in fact disagree is to embrace difference strategy. But it is right here that a critical epistemology may find entrance to the issues raised by Lather and Donmoyer. Critical epistemology, as I outline it in sections to follow, makes the dialectic of sameness and difference an internal structure of all knowledge claims—not as something *aufgehoben* within the fixed theory of one community of authors but rather as a pragmatic structure conjoined with the invitation to agree made necessarily in the full meaning horizon of every speech act. All acts of agreement, whether they are contextualized in everyday life situations or in dialogs between social theorists, are acts that embrace sameness on some level. All acts of disagreement entail new sameness claims that members of some discoverable audience are invited to endorse. Critical epistemology is based on this very structure common to all communicative acts.

## Two Problematics: Structure vs. Agency and Criticalism vs. Postmodernism

For many critical ethnographers the distinction between sameness theory and difference strategy entails a problematic that I will here call "criticalism versus postmodernism." But critical ethnography originated within a different problematic: "structure versus agency." Critical ethnography was initiated in the 1970s with the publication of *Learning to Labor* by Paul Willis (1977). I have argued elsewhere that this is the inaugural work for what we call critical ethnography today, even though the work of Paulo Freire and Pierre Bourdieu played an important role early on, and even though newer movements in feminist theory, queer theory, and postcolonial theory are now infused within the loosely bounded genre of critical ethnography (Carspecken 1999b). *Learning to Labour* quickly made a huge impact on those working in cultural studies and social theory as well as those ethnographers who had a neo-Marxist and/or feminist orientation. It was successful partly because it embodied a reformulated theory of praxis that resolved the structure versus agency debates.

In the following sections I review the origins of critical ethnography and its original significance in terms of the structure versus agency debates of the 1970s and early 1980s. Then I clarify certain features of the criticalism versus postmodernism problematic to establish a context for the central thrust and final arguments of this chapter: Willis's reformulation of praxis theory has epistemological implications that suggest a way through the criticalism versus postmodernism divide.

Willis's reformulation of praxis theory has remained implicit and hidden within the tradition of critical ethnography he initiated through the take-up of his concept of "cultural production." Praxis as cultural production explicitly solved metatheoretical and social-ontological problems generated by previous conceptualizations of structure and agency. But the manner in which Willis reformulated praxis theory has implications that go beyond the concept of cultural production. The full theory of praxis embodied within the tradition of critical ethnography remains implicit and yet suggests praxis as a will to knowledge and a will to power. Praxis as a will to knowledge, when located within a critical pragmatist theory of truth, resolves epistemological problems of the criticalism versus postmodernism debates. It makes the dialectic of sameness and difference a structure of knowledge claims and it casts the question of agreement in disagreement in new light.

## II. Early Critical Ethnography and Willis's Reformulation of Praxis Theory

### The Structure vs. Agency Problematic and the Concept of Cultural Production

During the 1970s major debates were taking place between Marxist-structuralists like Althusser (1969) and Marxist-culturalists like E. P. Thompson (1963, 1978). Both theoretical camps found problems with what might be called "old left" Marxism and the functionalism of its base-superstructure model of society (Kaye 1984, Johnson 1979). Marxist-culturalists emphasized human agency in their arguments and Marxist-structuralists argued that agency is determined by structure.

With *Learning to Labour* Willis introduced a formulation that skirted the structure versus agency problematic. With the concept of "cultural production" Willis provided a nonreified way to think about social structure, preserving an emphasis on human agency and the cultural conditions within which agency always takes place. Action is not determined by structure, it is rather conditioned by cultural milieu and is always productive of new cultural forms. Yet cultural milieu is itself explicable in terms of the life conditions within which it is produced, such as conditions of work, and also in terms of the inertia of cultural milieu: its formation into traditions. Actors continuously produce cultural innovations but must draw upon preexisting milieu in order to do so. Cultural inertia, life environments, institutional and organizational structures, and the social relations of economic production and consumption shape modes of social reproduction *through* cultural production and reproduction. Culture constantly emerges in new forms through human activity but does so in a way that will preserve certain deep structures or support certain trends in system change by taking on system functions. The system functions occur often without the discursive awareness of those whose actions bring them about.

The structure versus agency problematic pertained to "metatheory," or the social ontology assumed by theorists and researchers prior to their theoretical and empirical endeavors. "Metatheory," or social ontology, pertains to such concepts as social action, social system, culture, and identity that guide the very formulation of a research design. The concept of cultural production deconstructed the opposition between structure and agency at the level of metatheory. Willis basically relocated the concept of "structure," as used by Marxist-structuralists, within the concept of culture rather than within the concept of a "social order." Culture is structured in the sense that every human act draws upon complex cultural milieu and reproduces it in new forms: forms that often retain basic themes that mutually implicate each other in patterns ("structures") of binary opposition, hierarchical subordination, homology, and metaphor. Each meaningful act carries huge realms of implicate cultural structure constituting its explicit sense (see Carspecken 1991, 1992, 1996, 1999a for examples and further discussion).

The culture generated by Willis's "lads" is clearly structured. For example, one can easily reconstruct binary oppositions within homologous strings from Willis's data on the lads' culture: Masculinity is to femininity as nonconformity is to conformity as street knowledge is to school knowledge as being ordinary is to being posh, and so on. Anthony Giddens codified this view of culture with his theory of "structuration": structure is the medium and outcome of action. Structure pertains to the implicate orders of lived culture. Giddens has explicitly cited *Learning to Labour* by Paul Willis as an exemplar of structuration theory (Giddens 1984). The structure of binary oppositions in homologous strings, as well as other cultural structures distinctive of the "lads," was both drawn upon and reproduced (with the possibility of alterations and innovations) through the typical and routine activities of these boys. It was the medium and outcome of their action.

This relocation of structure within the concept of culture is, of course, consistent with the original anthropological structuralism of Levi-Strauss, though Willis's analysis importantly placed structure within the concept of "action conditions" rather than action determinants. Society is not reduced to culture in this view. Willis preserved the important Marxist distinction between culture and other features of society whose organization and dynamics cannot be explained by culture alone (e.g., the social relations of production, the government, markets, complex organizations). The objective features of "social order" are preserved in Willis's work through attention to the functions that culturally conditioned actions serve; that is, to the functional interconnection of action *consequences* in the formation of self-maintaining systems. Thus "social structure" in the sense of the Marxist debates of the 1970s would be more appropriately called "social system" from the orientation developed by Willis.

The importance of *Learning to Labour* for the tradition of critical ethnography that followed cannot be overstated. This legacy has built upon Willis's metatheory or social ontology, which has cultural production at its heart. Ethnographers working within this tradition basically have made innovations *within* the model established by Willis: First, reconstruct the culture of a group one is interested in, allowing members plenty of input into the analysis itself. Look for deep structures in this culture: core views, values, beliefs, and the structural relations between them that are implicated by routine activities and interactions. Show how these deep structures are employed in the continuous construction of identities. Second, examine the resulting cultural reconstructions for their relationship to institutional orders and self-maintaining, self-adapting systems. This basic methodology has been employed by many critical ethnographies influenced by *Learning to Labour* (e.g., Everhart 1983; McRobbie 1978; McLaren 1993; Carspecken 1991). The results have always been *critical*: displaying how cultural formations both challenge and play into systems of unequal social relations and how research may contribute to the challenges.

**Praxis Theory**
Willis's analysis suggests that human beings are strongly motivated to continuously produce themselves and that this motivational structure is what drives cultural production. This is what makes his theory of social action a theory of praxis. Praxis theory is introduced in some of Marx's early writings,

particularly *The Philosophical Manuscripts of 1848* and the *Theses on Feuerbach* (Marx and Engels 1976:Vol. 5). At that time, Marx was still working under Hegelian influences and praxis was discussed within core Hegelian categories: alienation, objectification, and self-production. In Hegel's philosophy, *Geist* is the agent of praxis. *Geist* is the impetus, process, and product of its own self-production. Any "moment" of *Geist* will display a process of something implicit expressed to make an objective form, an objective manifestation of *Geist*. But *Geist* is never captured by any objective expression and therefore all such expressions reveal a contradiction that drives expression onward in a dialectical manner. This dialectical movement is, of course, the dialectic of difference and sameness at bottom.

The early writings of Marx rejected the concept of *Geist* but retained the notion of self-production for the human subject. Self-expression through self-objectification is a core feature of being human, not the core nature of an abstract entity, *Geist*. In line with his materialist orientation, Marx located human self-production within the work humans do. Human work to produce useful objects is simultaneously human work to produce themselves. Marx truncated an important insight, the insight of self-production, by emphasizing the production of material products in a deliberate effort to escape Hegelian idealism and to locate self-production, praxis, within objective social conditions and historical development.

The work of the artisan was the paradigm case for Marx. The artisan creates material products much as an artist creates a work of art: the product is conceived by the artisan who then skillfully, artfully, produces it. When it is finished the artisan has in some senses created him or herself, or contributed to ongoing self-creation (see Habermas 1987a: ch. 3 for a critique of the artisan paradigm for conceptualizing work). One develops pride, dignity, and self-understanding through one's work in this way.

Marx really presented a theory of human motivation in his theory of praxis. People have "praxis needs." For praxis needs to be met certain social conditions must be in place. Work as praxis requires control of the conceptualization of production, control of the tools and resources used for work, and control of the product. Conception and execution must be united. Expressive needs, praxis needs, are only satisfied if these objective social conditions are established.

Praxis needs are basically the need to become a self, maintain a self, and develop a self through expressive activity. Because the social conditions required for the satisfaction of these needs are contradicted by the relations of capitalist production, capitalist workers are alienated. Workers merely execute the conceptualizations of others; their employers, foremen, and managers. The expressive process is fragmented within capitalist work organization, each worker contributing one small menial act to a product as it moves down the assembly line. Thus, work is no longer expressive, no longer self-developing, for capitalist workers. Furthermore, the products of work are not owned by the workers who make them, workers must rather buy such products with their wages. Taken together, capitalist relations of production alienate workers from their need for praxis and from the products of their work. Alienation is the denial of those conditions workers would need for praxis to take place.

Marx's conceptualization of praxis was consistent with a tradition of "expressivist philosophy" that Charles Taylor traces back to Herder (Taylor 1979). Hegel also incorporated Herderian ideas within his work. The same insight seems to be formulated in different directions by Herder, Hegel, and Marx and it is an insight taken up within various philosophical movements of the twentieth century as well (e.g., in existentialism, Sartre, Bernstein). Marx improved upon the basic ideas presented in Herder's philosophy by analyzing the conditions for praxis in terms of economic organization and thus making a distinction between culture and other features of society. But Marx also truncated the idea by limiting it to the relationship between human beings and a material world. The production of useful and beautiful items is not the only sphere for self-production. Praxis needs can be met without producing a material product. In fact, human-to-human relations are most immediately involved in praxis; the need to produce a self through social relations and the desire for recognition that is attendant to this need. Work and the production of material products meet praxis needs primarily through the social character of work: the potentiality that others will recognize the expressed self *through* one's products. A better theory of praxis would tie it to the social-communicative preconditions for the emergence of a self and the motivational structures that come forth as emergent properties as soon as these preconditions are in place.

Willis's development of praxis theory does not limit praxis to the production of material objects though it preserves the distinction between culture and society. His theory of praxis is less explicit in *Learning to Labour* than it is in his two earlier publications based on the same field study (Willis 1975, 1976), but it implicitly permeates *Learning to Labour* just the same. In this chapter I argue that praxis theory has remained hidden within the critical ethnography tradition initiated by Willis, through the take-up of his meta-theory, and has born unexplored implications for a critical epistemology.

One of Willis's earlier publications, "The Main Reality" (1976), argued that "the main reality" for the "lads" Willis studied was their socially constructed identities. The need of the lads to construct and maintain identities of which they could feel proud was the driving force behind their culture. The careers master at the lads' school, and the teachers, tried to convince these adolescent boys to take school seriously and to plan for their futures. But Willis showed that actions oriented toward the construction and maintenance of positive identities were much more important to the "lads" than were actions oriented instrumentally toward goals. Dramaturgical action dominated over instrumental action. The lads were producers of culture first and foremost, goal-seeking agents only on occasion. The "main reality" was the process of constructing and maintaining identity. This was the driving force underlying cultural production.

Marx's concept of praxis is retained in Willis's work but relocated within a more encompassing theory of social action. In brief, Willis's theory of praxis could be articulated as follows: Human beings are expressive organisms essentially concerned with their identities. Identities are constructed and maintained, not primarily through work oriented toward the physical world, but interactively and thus culturally. The expressive importance of work is not denied in Willis's theory of praxis, it is rather *explained* as the result of communicative structure. Work that produces material products may be expressive because other people use and appreciate the products. Material products can, but need not, symbolize the selves of those who make them. Willis's standard for determining whether alienation exists or not, and to what degree, involves the extent to which actors have control over their self-expression within any environment (and thus not just work environments). Most action is praxis or praxis-relevant in that most action will include a motivating "identity claim" (see Carspecken 1996, 1999b). Whether pursuing goals, undertaking prescribed tasks, or interacting with others for intrinsic and not task-related reasons, an actor's identity will be one of the things at stake. Action thus appears to have at least three dimensions: the goal-rational dimension oriented toward an objective world, a self-expressive dimension oriented from one self to an audience of others, and a cultural dimension concerned with the development of values, norms, and identity repertoires *through which* self-expression is achieved. Most acts will involve all three dimensions simultaneously though the degree of investment within specific dimensions will vary from act to act.

The theory of action here is at least three dimensional and the three dimensions I have just explicated (goal-oriented, self-expressive, and culturally productive) are obviously congruent with Habermas's three "formal worlds" of objectivity, subjectivity, and the social (Habermas 1981). Willis implicitly provides a richer view of action than Habermas, however, by regarding action fundamentally as praxis. Habermas's category of the subjective claim can be distinguished from the motivational features of the identity claim. The identity claim is core to action-as-praxis and should be regarded as distinctive, as a sort of "fourth dimension" to each act that, however, fuses subjective, normative, and objective validity claims while not accounting for all such claims within the pragmatic horizon of a meaningful act. I have made these distinctions and elaborated their sense and use in other publications (Carspecken 1996, 1999a, 1999b). To reconceive communicative action as a form of praxis is to deepen Habermas's theory by more carefully theorizing act constitution and motivational complexes.

With this expanded model of action in praxis theory, alienation may next be theorized as a state of affairs occurring when one or more dimension of action is under the control of other people and/or social institutions. Because action is multidimensional and praxis a need, human responses to alienation include the development of cultures that emphasize those dimensions still under the actor's control. This is how we may understand the significance of a "resistance culture," which is another concept we can trace back to the early Willis. A resistance culture is developed under social conditions that place the goal-directed dimension of action under the control of others so that praxis needs may only be met through social interactions and cultural production alone. Resistance cultures produce identity repertoires that counter the ideologies legitimating external controls over the goal and task dimensions of action.

In other words, praxis needs will always be pursued in some relation to the goal-oriented tasks of one's institutional life. An ideal human situation is one in which all three dimensions of action are under one's control and self-expression may be pursued in synthesis with the goal-oriented features of one's acts. But when goal-oriented tasks are controlled by others, are menial, fragmented, and do not facilitate self-expression, then people will develop cultures that try to maximize what few opportunities for self-expression do exist in the tasks themselves (e.g., the pride taken by Willis's lads and their fathers in hard physical labor) and simultaneously meet praxis needs by resisting cultural forms associated with the authority figures of the setting: teachers, foremen, employers.

Action becomes a concept divisible into diverse dimensions, and *praxis becomes a concept of human expressive need that will seek to unify all such dimensions of action under the control of a self-actualizing, autonomous subject.* Praxis theory thus poses an internal relationship between power, action, and human motivation. A key feature of the resistance culture reconstructed in *Learning to Labor* was its recapture of power over as much of the lads' environment as possible. The recapture of power was central to the identity claims of the lads and their fathers working in factories. Power is a central structure of autonomy and praxis needs include a need for autonomy.

### Power

Therefore, by expanding the concept of praxis toward a more complex model of human action, Willis located power within the human subject. Conditions of action, such as the constraints in play and the resources available with which to manifest intentions and satisfy needs, establish social relations of power, not by being "powerful in themselves" but rather through their relation to human agency. Power is at bottom logically tied to agency when agency is understood as inclusive of a need for self-production. This way of understanding power makes it possible to consistently analyze political, economic, and institutional modes of power in terms of action *conditions* and to analyze the extent to which individuals are *empowered* in terms of the extent to which they can meet needs, actualize intentions, and develop a self through expressive activity. The unconstrained pursuit of praxis needs results in empowerment. The constraints of class location and ethnic, racial, and gender status manifest system-level modes of power because they constrain agency. Praxis needs are needs for power; but not for power at the expense of other people. The internal relation between power and praxis is one of the ways in which Willis's reformulation of praxis theory may address the criticalism versus postmodernism problematic because it has epistemological implications, as the following sections argue.

## III. Praxis vs. Ocular-Centrism

In commentaries on two of my previous publications (Carspecken 1996, 1999a) Peter McLaren coined the expression "ocular-centrism" (McLaren 1999). I appreciate the expression and will use it as he did, to represent the paradigmatically dominant use of visual perception in many Western epistemologies and philosophies. Willis's reformulation of praxis theory has epistemological significance partly because it informs a nonocular-centric theory of knowledge that yet retains certain important postmodern and poststructural themes.

Visual perception has been a root metaphor employed in the concept of knowledge within much of Western philosophy. It has been a root metaphor employed by those who have divided qualitative research into distinctive paradigms. Knowing is construed to be a form of seeing clearly. In another publication, for example, I have examined Lincoln and Guba's four "paradigms" within qualitative research and shown how each so-called paradigm is really a different manifestation of ocular-centrism (see especially Guba 1990a). Knowing is seeing in each case but in the positivist camp seeing supposedly takes place directly and unproblematically, in the post-positivist camp seeing is always through a symbolic window of some kind, in the critical camp seeing is always through a value window of some kind and in the constructivist camp seeing and what is seen turn out to be indistinguishable (though this is argued by beginning with the distinction between the one who sees and the object seen and then collapsing the objective side of the framework). In each case a single paradigm is in play and this paradigm has placed visual perception at the heart of what is to be understood by "knowledge."

To establish a framework for presenting the major ways in which praxis theory may inform a critical epistemology let me begin with a discussion of ocular-centrism in relation to postmodern and poststructural orientations. Postmodern and poststructural insights seem to have had specific influences on the methodological theories of qualitative researchers through two ocular-centric image clusters. These image clusters are often brought together in postmodern writings on methodological theory but they are distinctive in their origins and in their origins served purposes at odds with each other. One cluster can be traced back to Michel Foucault and the other can be traced back to Jacques Derrida.

### "Gaze Theory": Power as Being Seen and Knowledge as Seeing

The discourse that can be traced back to Michel Foucault presents knowledge as seeing but equates knowledge with power through the metaphor of the gaze. The famous example of the panoptical (Foucault 1979) has had a major influence on postmodern and/or poststructural qualitative researchers. A centrally located gaze commands both knowledge of and power over the prisoners of Bentham's ideal and "enlightened" prison. Knowledge is the gaze and the gaze is power. Foucault analyzed the various social disciplines of Western knowledge (psychology, sociology, criminal science, and so on) as discourse-practices that both construct the subjects to be known through their specialized jargon and subjugate the resulting subjects to practices of control (Foucault 1973, 1979). Though the characterization of knowledge as discourse-practices suggests a sort of action orientation on Foucault's part, the metaphor of the subjugating gaze underlies the way Foucault's work has been taken up by many subsequent writers. Foucault's explicit equation of knowledge and power and his famous codification of this equation in the slogan "knowledge is a regime" have been widely employed by postcolonial, race, and feminist theorists. Such theorists correctly draw attention to ideology as the control of identity formation through a hegemonic gaze but then relativize knowledge as always being only one of many possible gazes, always basically being a form of ideology. Moreover, the classic Foucaultian position is to regard gazes as the product of "strategies" pursued by "anonymous power" rather than through the work of people who, knowingly or unknowingly construct views to favor their own social positions and interests. People, whether they occupy the position of gazers or gazees, whether they are the subject or the object of the gaze, are themselves constructed by the same strategy of power which is why Foucault proclaimed the "death of the subject," the death of humanistic theories and philosophies, in his version of poststructuralism.

This full employment of Foucaultian formulations places power outside the subject and inside or equal to knowledge. Habermas has critiqued the reduction and/or equalization of knowledge and power in Foucault (Habermas 1987a) and I review the gist of this critique a little later on. Willis has implicitly critiqued Foucault's displacement of power from the subject and this will also be explained below. For now, however, consider how a study of mental hospitals, prisons, and the like would proceed from a Willis, critical ethnographic, orientation. The culture of prisoners and patients would have to be examined from this orientation to look for the extent to which the dominant gaze has been internalized and the extent to which it has been resisted. Prisoners and patients would not be assumed to be "products" of a power-gaze but rather praxis-seeking agents who will respond to their conditions in ways that only an empirical investigation could reveal.

Now let us examine the gaze metaphor more carefully. The metaphor, as it manifests within poststructural writings, constitutes a theory of knowledge in two ways. These two distinctive manifestations are presented as one in many take-ups of Foucault, and in these same take-ups the gaze metaphor appears in a third manifestation that is usually left unacknowledged. A second and third person articulation of the gaze metaphor are generally put together, and a first person articulation is left implicit.

From the second person position, the gaze is the reference through which people construct their identities. The position from which actors, thinkers, and theorists understand and judge their actions, thoughts, theories, and selves is "captured" by one or more hegemonic gazes. The gaze is generally constructed as that of whites, men, heterosexuals, and Europeans. Its power is noted from the second person position as its dominance in the position-taking one must undergo to think any thought, act any act, write any theory, and attain any objectification of the self. We thinkers, actors, and theorists construct both our actions and our selves *for* the gaze and therefore within its terms. Conceptualized from the second person position, the gaze is the hegemonic, internalized audience.

Conceptualized from the third person position the gaze becomes a center within a periphery it has generated. The periphery is also the "margin." This is a view of society as a whole, a metatheory. Knowledge production appears from this third person position as a competition for centers with the gaze of several intersecting groups (whites, males, Europeans, heterosexuals) taking on dominance and marginalizing the perspectives of other groups. From this third person perspective a model of society is constructed and a way to deconstruct hegemonic ideologies is suggested. Many diverse discourse-practices form and compete within a collection of discourses and practices, and society is a pattern of subjugating social relations constructed of knowledge formations, only some of which attain dominance over wide regions of the whole. Viewed in this way, knowledge formations can be deconstructed by articulating what they have silenced and showing up the real power relations they support but simultaneously mask with their claims to universality and neutrality.

The third person position articulates the gaze metaphor into a "view of gazes," discourse-practices, conceptualized by the theorist as if she herself gazed upon the gazes of others to reveal the true state of affairs. Thus, use of this imagery provides a first person position for the author and the audience of the poststructural text. It is a first person position from which gazing does take place but from which a unique and singular freedom from power is tacitly claimed since it is only a "correct view" of the social order, *the* correct view, that is implicitly claimed into being. When a dominant knowledge-formation is deconstructed by showing the silences it has created and the power relations it has produced then *real* silenced people and *real* power relations are claimed to exist rather than to be constructed by this privileged and powerless gaze. The first person articulation of the gaze metaphor is in contradiction with the third person perspective that renders all knowledge a form of power and seeing simultaneously, unless the theorist herself makes a next move by problematizing the metaphor *in total* after its work of deconstructing the knowledges of others is completed. This would mean that the theorist is really a postmodern strategist. This is the issue Patti Lather addressed through her performance at Bergamot. She problematized her own concepts and metaphors just after employing them. She further explained that she believed knowledge always works by producing "containers" and it is necessary to use what the containers attempt to contain against the containers themselves. The consistent poststructural theorist must perform to deconstruct her own formulations just after producing them. The third person articulation of the gaze metaphor gives a picture of society (collection of discourse-practices formed through strategies of power) that is itself a container, but then it is necessary to deconstruct this picture in the next move.

I soon argue that with praxis theory we may retain the metaphor of the gaze as it works through the second person position but deconstruct the other two articulations of "gaze theory" for their ocular-centrism. The metaphor of the gaze will then take its sense within more fundamental metaphors that are not ocular-centric and that resolve the tension between the content and the performance of an academic paper or research report.

### Deconstructing Presence

The other ocular-centric image cluster influencing postmodern qualitative researchers can be traced back to Jacques Derrida and his deconstruction of presence. This cluster is actually at odds with the metaphor of the gaze because the full deconstruction of presence is a deconstruction of the epistemological paradigm of seeing. One of Derrida's many accomplishments has been to show that knowledge is not seeing though Derrida certainly has not wished to try to represent what knowledge "is" at all.

Derrida's deconstruction of presence, begun with his work on Husserl's philosophy of phenomenology (Derrida 1973), implodes ocular-centric logic. Visual perception enters paradigmatically into epistemological theories of many various types when the theorist begins by considering the sense of certainty one feels in visual perception, as in: "What I am seeing before me now certainly exists." An effort is then made to explain this certainty, explain cases in which such certainty does indeed indicate knowledge and cases in which it does not, and build an entire theory of knowledge from these foundations. Derrida struck at the heart of this approach in epistemological theories (as well as in ontologies and philosophies generally) not by deconstructing the seeing metaphor per se but rather by deconstructing the more general category of "presence." I feel certain that this object is *present* before me because I see (feel, hear, smell, taste, or think) it now.

Ocular-centrism seems paradigmatic to me in all cases of presence because the distinction between the knowing subject and the object known, or the distinction between consciousness and phenomena as Husserl examined it, seems everywhere framed in terms of visual experience. How is a thought or concept present to consciousness? The difference between a mental *image* and that which *perceives* it comes to mind. How is a sound present to consciousness? It is difficult to note the sound in order to try to answer this question without making a visual representation. The paradigm of seeing is difficult to escape when considering the concept of presence.

Be that as it may, the converse relationship between presence and seeing is certainly obvious. When considering visual perception itself the concept of presence seems to be immediately implied. To deconstruct presence is certainly to deconstruct ocular-centrism. Ocular-centrism operates within epistemological theories to prioritize *observations* and a passive-receptive notion of consciousness when developing such notions as "truth" and "validity." The alternative offered by critical pragmatism is to make consensus between communicating subjects paradigmatic. Derrida's deconstruction of presence provides good reasons for seeking an alternative paradigm or "originary scene" (Carspecken 1999a) because it strikes at the heart of ocular-centrism.

For various reasons it is worth our while to here review certain features of Derrida's famous deconstruction of Husserl's phenomenological philosophy. The concept of presence is only intelligible against the horizon of a notion of time. What is phenomenologically present to us must always be present *now*. Derrida shows that the most primordial consideration of presence, and thus in Husserl's work the most phenomenological and prior-to-reflection consideration, actually assumes a structure of absence at its heart because of the time problematic. A "now" always simultaneously implies a "just has been" (Husserl called this a "retention") and a "soon to be" (Husserl called this a protention). But a "just has been" is also a "is no longer, is not *now*." Absence inhabits presence. Presence (which also informs our concept of sameness or object-identity) is structured by difference and this partly because of the time problematic. Sameness is never immediate but is constituted by difference, has difference internal to it.

To make this formulation less abstract let's consider the situation from the standpoint of ocular-centric knowing. "Certain knowledge" is a belief that is usually constructed from the paradigm case of seeing something before us in a single moment and feeling certain that it is there, that it is "known" to be there, now. But the moment in which we can *note* something to be present to us is not the same moment in which we believe it must just have been immediately present to us. To experience presence and to know that we experience presence are two distinctive moments in time. This is merely one way of articulating the deconstruction that Derrida performed on many simultaneous levels. But it is an easily understood way of illuminating the deconstruction. Presence is not knowledge-imparting, a second act must take place to make an experience something known.

This means that ocular-centric knowledge claims *defer* to a presence that is never self-evident, never knowledge-imparting. As soon as we feel something is known because of an experience this something known is no longer present. So knowledge claims of the sort: "I know this is here before me now," claims that seem so certain as to constitute the paradigm of certainty for us, actually defer to a moment of real presence already gone by. They defer to it as their authority or ground. In fact they construct this previous moment. One could argue that the brain has retained an impression of just prior experience, but this kind of argument would step out of phenomenology into an objective theory of brains and brain processes that phenomenology has not yet grounded. One cannot do this as a phenomenological argument. Perhaps, then, one could follow Husserl and argue that it is possible to phenomenologically detect a "trace" (retention) of previous experience. But this is self-contradictory because such a "trace" is conceptualized in terms of its being present to consciousness and therefore is not really a trace but a trace of a trace, which gives us a regress. A trace is a concept contradictory to phenomenological theory since it combines a here-and-now with a no-longer-here-and-now into one experience within a present moment. Thus presence itself is a concept contradictory to phenomenological theory. This is why ocular-centric knowledge claims defer to an experience of presence that can never be reached.

Let's explore things a little further to iterate Derrida's neo-logism "difference." Deferring works in two ways with ocular-centric claims: deferring to the authority of self-evident presence and deferring this experience of self-evident presence in time. When we say "this is here now" we defer to a moment of presence already gone by as the authority or ground for this claim. But we also usually defer to future moments in which the experience will come back. We then say, "this is here now" with the expectation that it will continue to be here in immediately future nows. We defer to presence once again but this time to its quality of always coming again or repeating. And if our claim is structured as an objective one then we say "this is here now, look for yourself" and make the repetition of presence something shared with other people or in other words an intersubjective structure. We defer to the authority of an unreachable presence in every case.

Knowledge claims based on presence defer to presence in two ways and yet *differ* from presence as a moment always already gone by and usually always about to come. The case of claims that require the "always about to come" factor are the most usual, though it is possible to claim something that only has the presence-gone structure, something like: "I know I experienced a red light that I am sure will never return and was never experienced by any other." In the more usual cases presence is temporally deferred in the sense of delayed: "Look for yourself" or "look again." In the case of knowledge claims structured by a belief in temporal duration the final "proof" is always deferred in time because presence cannot be reached. So Derrida famously, and brilliantly, put three terms together with his neo-logism "difference." Presence deconstructs through difference, which implicates the three terms of deference to authority, deferring as delaying, and difference as a structure internal to the concept of presence. From this term "difference" many secondary sorts of deconstructive terms were produced by Derrida in different projects. Difference means that knowledge production often takes the form of "detours" as the promise to bring about genuine presence continuously undergoes delay. Knowledge claims are always in need of "supplements" because their claim to a ground in presence is never self-sufficient. Knowledge claims never have a certain ground and therefore "disseminate" rather than inseminate and thus another metaphor for certainty and goal-completion, a psychoanalytic one in this case, is deconstructed. And so on. Derrida's brilliantly playful, self-referencing, and discipline-transversing deconstructions are well known.

The phrase "metaphysics of presence" coined by Derrida has produced a postmodern discourse that has iterated and disseminated in ways true to Derridian themes themselves. This discourse shows up in much of the postmodern methodological writings, however, not so much in terms of the enormous doubt Derrida has placed in ocular-centric epistemologies but rather in terms of insights one can skim from the wakes of Derrida's many travels. The notions of sameness, homogeneity, univocality, and representation are all deconstructable where they implicate a belief in presence. Postmodern methodologists will consequently claim that representations must always be multiple, multivocal, and reality a flux of heterogeneity.

Thus it is easy to combine Derridian formulations with a notion of power. Knowledge claims assert certainty over an abyss of uncertainty. They try to claim sameness into being when the concept of sameness is presence-dependent. Hence knowledge claims can easily be regarded as the products of a will-to-power. When this is social theorizing we are talking about then the production of knowledge will always be an effort to subsume what can only be radically heterogeneous peoples and cultures and lifestyles within an arbitrary homogeneity that seeks to disguise its arbitrariness. Clearly, metaphors and themes can be gathered from the wakes of Derrida's various intellectual journeys and then iterated within quite different contexts. They can be placed alongside themes from Foucault: knowledge is a gaze that is also power, knowledge is arbitrary because gazes are deconstructable, knowledge is a will to power, knowledge is a regime.

Themes from the wakes of Derrida's travels include the suggestion that the self is a sort of infinite longing for recognition and for a certain world and thus constituted by an infinite and unreachable longing for presence. The longing for presence and the related longing for recognition so that the self may be known and validated, put a different twist on the power and knowledge connection. Gayatri Spivak articulates this in her introduction to Derrida's *of Grammatology* as follows: "to recognize that one is shaped by difference, to recognize, that the 'self' is constituted by its never-fully-to-be-recognized-ness" (1974:xliv). The will to power is a will to exist that can never be consummated but only continuously asserted. And here we have the expressivist theme, once again, that informed Hegel's philosophy, Marx's theory of praxis, Sartrian existentialism, and other philosophical theories and movements. Gayatri Spivak's articulation of the theme in the above quotation is close to Willis's theory of praxis minus Willis's location of praxis within social and historical conditions. The need to construct and maintain a self is a "main reality" for human beings. Yet with Spivak and Derrida an actual theory of self production is not proposed, it is rather suggested during the course of deconstruction.

## IV. Critical Epistemology

### Praxis and Metatheory

On the level of metatheory, or social ontology, praxis theory allows us to retain some of the components within the poststructuralist view of society (strategies of power, hegemonic gazes) while not proclaiming the death of the subject. Earlier in this chapter the basic features of Willis's theory of praxis were outlined. Human beings are expressive beings with expressive needs. Human beings act socially in part to construct and maintain positive identities and to explore their further potentialities as self-producers. This is a driving force for the production of *culture* because self-production is dependent on the recognition of others and culture is the medium through which such recognition must take place. Human acts are complex and simultaneously work in three dimensions to claim and evaluate the nature of the actor, the social world shared by the actor with others, and the world of objects, events, resources, and constraints within which the actor and her communities must live. When social conditions inhibit, constrain, and/or control any one of these dimensions of action then self-production will be affected. Often self-production will include the internalization of hurts and limitations but with at least a tacitly understood opposition to these things. Often self-production under conditions of alienation will act out some of the oppositional forces felt inside and a resistance culture will take shape.

Why do cultures of alienation hurt, become as Peter McLaren called them "cultures of pain?" Willis's theory of praxis answers that human beings are not fully a product of culture, they *produce* culture continuously. But the production of culture is always positioned within institutional, political, and economic environments and it always must draw upon preexisting cultural milieu. If the resources available in such milieu make it difficult to produce a culture in which one can recognize one's self as worthy, autonomous, and with expressive potentiality then cultural production will result in pain. One way in which this takes place occurs when cultural milieu has been captured by dominant ideologies that in this case function as a hegemonic gaze. Actors in these conditions find themselves gaining knowledge of themselves only through an internalized gaze that maintains and downgrades their "place" in society. Willis reformulated praxis theory to show up the communicative structures essential to self-construction. The same theory makes it easy to understand how such communicative structures, which always take particular forms shaped by cultural milieu, can be captured by hegemonic ideologies produced by class, gender, and racial others.

And how is it that resistance cultures can be formed, cultures that rebel against hegemonic gazes to produce counter repertoires with which to produce the self? Only praxis theory or something like it can explain this. Human beings are expressive beings with praxis needs. They are not constructed by culture or discourses; only available repertoires of identities that must be used to construct a self are discourse-determined. Yet these repertoires are just the medium of action and do not determine the outcome of acts. The outcome of acts will always make alterations and this is how resistance cultures can be and are indeed produced. Existing cultural milieu constrains the actions and selves of actors but it determines neither. Within the theory of praxis is a theory of human motivation that suggests people will always resist and attempt to self-actualize even though resistance will always be both resourced and constrained by social and cultural conditions.

This is the metatheory one can reconstruct from Willis's early critical ethnographies. It has a place for certain poststructural and postmodern metaphors: those of the gaze, the discourse-practice, and the longing for recognition. It goes beyond these metaphors by modeling society as something more than just discourse practices. Society is this plus the conditions within which discourse practices are acted out and iterated. Such conditions include the way in which action consequences in selective and aggregate form take on functional significance for self-maintaining systems. Moreover, discourse-practices are the medium and outcome of action produced by agents: they condition agency but are also altered by agency and they do not determine agents.

### Critical Pragmatism

The criticalism versus postmodernism problematic, however, is primarily epistemological rather than metatheoretical. Praxis theory provides solutions for epistemological issues as well. What I have in mind is something that could be called "praxis epistemology" which can be articulated by informing critical pragmatism with praxis theory. First I review the basic features of critical pragmatics, then its relation to praxis theory.

By "critical pragmatism" I refer to the Habermasian school of critical theory. Within this school "truth" and "validity" are not concepts dependent on a belief in presence. "Truth" is rather a concept emergent from pragmatic structures of communicative action. Truth *only* becomes important as an explicit concept when people attempt to reach understandings with each other. Of course truth is also important when representations of the world are to guide goal-oriented acts, but the representations themselves are structured in line with communicative imperatives.

When people communicate they do so through pragmatic coordinates with which to establish working commonalties. Habermas's three formal worlds are the system of coordinates (Habermas 1981): meaningful acts make simultaneous claims about a reality shared through the senses (objectivity), a reality shared by virtue of belonging to a shared community (the social), and a world to which only one actor has access (subjectivity). Truth claims, or more generally, *validity* claims (Carspecken 1996) are continuously made when people interact or act in ways they could explain to others.

The validity claims constitutive of communicative acts are "sameness claims" but only *claims*. They are a special form of sameness claim, structured by a formulation I used as a subheading above: *to agree or not agree*. It is intersubjective sameness that is the heart of the matter rather than perceptual sameness. Sameness is most primordially a *presupposition* that regulates agreements, not an experience. The certainty of sameness is always deferred because of the impossibility of ever knowing without doubt exactly what another person thinks and experiences, not because of time per se. Sameness structures working *agreements* that are always fallible.

Indeed the deconstruction of presence could be understood as the ultimate push on what Habermas calls the limit cases of pragmatic-communicative infrastructure. Ultimate, certain consensus on objective truth claims is impossible and the deconstruction of presence is one way of showing up this impossibility, because objective validity claims are structured by multiple access to sense experiences. Certain consensus on subjective validity claims is impossible simply and directly because these claims are structured by privileged access. But in addition, presence within subjectivity is always deferred because the act of noting a subjective state involves position-taking with internalized audiences. The moment of presence in both cases is always different than the moment of noting presence because "noting" requires a shift from the first to the third person position. Consensus on normative-evaluative validity claims similarly requires position-taking but without any presuppositions of presence as I will argue later on. Taken together, all validity claims are made with a *working* consensus in mind. There are many specifically methodological principles and data-analytic techniques that can be derived from the theory of three pragmatic "coordinates" and their associated validity claims but I have explored those principles and techniques in other publications (especially Carspecken 1996).

In critical pragmatism truth claims, validity claims, are always fallible. What arguments, then, could be presented to accept the critical pragmatist position itself, given that all arguments are acknowledged to be fallible and uncertain? As partially discussed above, postmodern themes in methodological theory are deployed with self-contradiction if an actual theory or epistemology is constructed from them because self-reference results in self-deconstruction. Is the case similar with critical pragmatics?

Critical pragmatism best defends itself through the principle of fallibility and the "performative contradiction." It regards itself, as an epistemological theory, to be essentially a set of logically connected claims that others are invited to discuss, challenge, and debate. It is meant to be fallible itself, dependent on the responses of others and open to continuous reformulations and improvements. Critical pragmatism is recursive, it has self-reference built consistently within.

It seems, moreover, that critiques of the very foundations of critical pragmatism always display "the performative contradiction": they assume the very principles formulated within critical pragmatics as soon as they are expressed. The performative contradiction has so far been the ultimate defense of critical pragmatist theory. Critical pragmatism is consequently not ocular-centric. It does not defer to presence, it defers within the category of expectation: expectation that consensus to itself will be maintained over time.

Yet certain issues are not satisfactorily understood from the perspective of critical pragmatism alone. Critical pragmatism may not be self-contradictory and it may be consistently supported by the performative contradiction, but what can we say about *agreements* to the theory? What would motivate people to agree to the epistemology of critical pragmatism, as a working agreement? Various plausible answers come to mind when this question is asked that have to do with its explanatory power and usefulness. But the question itself is deeper than a specification of advantages to working with this theory and the fact that it is hard, perhaps impossible, to contradict it.

The question of why one ought to agree with critical pragmatism is most fully answered through an appeal to the concept of *recognition*. Critical pragmatism consists of formulations that others ought to recognize as true of their own communicative practice. The formulation of the theory should produce the experience of recognizing something one already knew, but in tacit ways. Thus a core epistemological issue at stake has to do with the concept of recognition. A push on the concept of recognition, from within the critical pragmatist framework, will suggest the epistemological importance of praxis theory.

### Power, Recognition, and Praxis Theory

Critical pragmatism in its Habermasian formulation well explains how knowledge may serve the purposes of power through the establishment of a hegemonic gaze. But knowledge in such cases is clearly deformed in relation to the ideal speech situation (see below). On the other hand, the theory does not seem immediately congruent with the idea of a "will to knowledge" and/ or a "will to power." Nor does it really capture the insight expressed as the "longing for presence."

In Habermas's theory of communicative action knowledge rather seems to come from a need to cooperate which depends on the ability to reach understandings. The need to reach agreements, so as to coordinate the activities of an entire group of people, produces a distinctive *type* of action: action oriented toward understanding. This type of action is distinguished from action oriented toward success in Habermas's theory, and action oriented toward success is evolutionarily antecedent to action oriented toward understanding (Habermas 1987b: ch.5).

Thus in a lot of Habermas's writings one gets the impression that action oriented toward understanding is employed in its purest forms only when action coordination breaks down, assumedly shared understandings (sameness) turn out to be misunderstandings, and actors must strive to reach agreements explicitly so that they may then resume their coordinated projects of pursuing goal-rational acts.

Habermas uses the firm distinction between action oriented toward understanding and action oriented toward success in his critique of Foucault (Habermas 1987a). Symbolic knowledge is the product of action oriented toward understanding. Knowledge cannot be equated with power because action oriented toward understanding *must* presuppose the limit case of an ideal speech situation. The ideal speech situation is presupposed as a limit case, which means that it may never be actualized in real-life contexts but it serves as a set of regulating principles for activities in which reaching understanding is the main goal. If someone feels that a debate or discussion went wrong or was somehow flawed, then the reasons why it went wrong will generally be articulated as violations of one or more ideal speech conditions.

The ideal speech situation is a situation in which all people affected by the knowledge to be generated may contribute with equal voices and without any distortions of power. All such people must participate with only the motivation to reach an understanding and thus must be open to criticism. Consent must be won through the "force of the better argument" and nothing else (Habermas 1981). Therefore, knowledge may be "powerful" only in the sense that it may guide action oriented toward success in productive ways, *after* it has been produced. In the effort to produce knowledge power must be put out of play. These arguments make excellent sense but suggest a concept of power in terms of action *conditions* only (though Habermas himself does not necessarily view the situation in this way).

Willis reformulated praxis theory in such a way as to suggest the opposite notion of power: that it is logically tied to the concept of agency and that all acts exhibit power. Power is found within macro-sociological relations via the manner in which conditions of action either resource or constrain agency. Without agency it would make no sense to speak of power. Power is not just the distortion of the ideal speech situation, rather the distortion of the ideal speech situation manifests power by constraining agency.

All this means that actions oriented toward understanding are also acts of power even when the ideal speech situation is well approximated. When the ideal speech situation is well approximated power is not put out of play but rather *equalized*. I believe that this insight is consistent with Habermas's general arguments and yet deepens critical pragmatism in a way that preserves but relocates some of the postmodern themes discussed earlier on. This insight pushes critical pragmatism toward something like a praxis epistemology.

Here is how a reformulated praxis theory may generate a praxis epistemology, in very short form (see Carspecken 1999a: ch.3 for extended arguments). What motivates agreement to "the force of the better argument" that Habermas refers to when he presents his theory of the ideal speech situation? It is different, in its specifics, for each type of validity claim. In the case of objective validity claims an extra-linguistic ground is presupposed in the form of a world of objects and events to which there is multiple access. The force of the better argument here would include whether or not predictions are born out and whether or not actions oriented toward success may employ accurate means deduced from the knowledge claims.

In the case of subjective validity claims an extra-linguistic ground is presupposed such that those engaged in discussion find reasons to believe that a subjective state has been authentically and sincerely represented. Notice that the concept of presence crops up as a secondary structure to the presupposition of an extra-linguistic ground in the case of both objectivity and subjectivity.

In the case of purely normative claims we have a special situation whereby the force of the better argument may not include appeals to an extra-linguistic reference. Habermas has discussed this peculiarity of the normative claim in several places within chapter five of *The Theory of Communicative Action* (1987b:61). He also argues in that same chapter that the form of both objective and subjective validity claims may have evolved via metaphoric extension from the normative claim which seems to be evolutionarily prior to the other two. What grounds normative claims when actors discuss them with the intention of reaching understanding alone?

Ultimately it would seem that *complete* intersubjective recognition is the ground but as an unreachable limit case. Intersubjectivity presupposes norms that depend upon significant symbols (minimally, gestures) and thus it is the sameness of the symbol that is the limit case ground for normative validity claims. Derrida has shown that the sameness of symbols deconstructs when symbolic theory is based on presence. But in critical pragmatism the sameness of the symbol is based on the presupposition that it means the same thing to two or more people and in normal situations sameness of meaning is only what *counts* as sameness in the coordination of action. Sameness of the symbol is not based on presence or perception in critical pragmatism and, in fact, sameness is a secondary structure generated when the other in communication does not say "no" to a claim or to the use of a symbol. Sameness is the negation of a negation.

Theories of human development and of the phylogenesis of symbolic systems are implied in Habermas's theory. At first the sameness of the symbol for two or more persons is a backgrounded and implicit presupposition for acts oriented toward understanding but conducted *in order to coordinate acts oriented toward success.* With evolutionary development more and more often communicative acts become intrinsically motivated as people construct selves and desire the understanding and recognition of others. This is what praxis theory is all about, the expressive and self-productive motivation complexes in people. People continuously try to "find themselves" through expression toward audiences and this continuous effort is part of what it means to be a person.

The limit case of self-production would be the recognition of one's self through taking the position of others on one's own expressions. This is impossible because of the distinction between a self-expression and the intentions and full subjectivity of the actor. The desire for recognition is a desire to find an "I" objectified through the production of a "me." The "I" is not self conscious but the "me" is the object of self-consciousness. Yet a "me" can never fully manifest the "I." In everyday life situations a sense of self is maintained short of the impossible limit case of full intersubjective recognition when identity claims do not produce the response of "no." The social self, which never satisfies the desire for self, is a negation of a negation.

The desire to recognize the "I" is a motivational structure core to praxis theory. This same motivation is found when one pushes continuously upon the reasons why anyone would agree to normative validity claims for intrinsic reasons only. Such a push will first reveal the need for cooperation but peel back toward the desire to know and create the self via position-taking with others. This explains the intrinsic reasons for engaging in acts purely oriented toward understanding. The quest for certainty peels back toward a quest for the self that is structured by an unreachable limit case in which difference and sameness would be united within the *self-recognition* of all subjects. In a certain sense, an argument could be developed that praxis theory articulates the ultimate limit case and ground of all types of validity claims given the special status of the normative claim in relation to the other two.

Therefore, if we inform critical pragmatism with Willis's version of praxis theory we find several postmodern themes illuminated in new ways. Knowledge is indeed the product of a will-to-power and is indeed infused with desire and longing. But from the perspective of a praxis epistemology this does not mean that knowledge is always a regime nor that it is arbitrary. Where knowledge functions as a regime it is flawed internally and where knowledge appears arbitrary it has failed to meet regulating principles intrinsic to communicative structure. Presence is only a belief. But in praxis epistemology this is revealed through the necessity of presupposing extra-linguistic grounds for subjective and objective validity claims. Since presence is not a ground for the claim that praxis epistemology itself is a valid theory the metaphysics of presence does not undermine criticalism. One can communicate the deconstructability of presence but when one does so one employs pragmatic-communicative structures.

The dialectic of sameness and difference is unavoidable whenever communication is taking place. Sameness claims of many types and varieties are made with every communicative act. Sameness is always deconstructable but to deconstruct it communicatively and as a fundamental category in itself is to find oneself within the performative contradiction (i.e., making new sameness claims). The dialectic of sameness and difference can indeed result in regimes of power when a unity is claimed out of difference at the expense of peoples and cultures. But this does not mean that one can have no epistemological theory. This rather means that an epistemological theory must take this dialectic self-reflectively, recursively, into account such that knowledge-power formations are internally flawed as claims to knowledge. More than anything else, the "praxis epistemology" I have barely sketched in this chapter takes sameness and difference into account by always being open to new differences (fallibility) and by requiring the voices of all people to be affected by a theory to take part in the production of the theory for it to be valid.

## V. Conclusion

One may read this chapter and wonder what all the fuss is about: Why worry about "presence" or deconstruct ocular-centrism? What does this have to do with real research situations and methodological problems? Yet few critical ethnographers today can be unaware of the criticalism versus postmodernism problematic. Many postmodern insights are attractive to those in the critical camp. Postmodern writings are very insightful when it comes to the subtle manifestations of power in societies today. Postmodern writings seem to have captured some of the deepest penetrations of ideologies, particularly when they work through social science itself. But too often postmodern slogans and formulas are employed without taking the next necessary step: to deconstruct one's own work along postmodern and poststructural lines. And when the next step is indeed taken one is left wondering whether one's work can have any force other than to win the approval of a small number of other academics working within postmodern discourses. Finally, postmodern insights, when used inappropriately and without sufficient self-reflection, make it possible to produce basically sloppy and biased social research. If others object to such work then all the author need do is claim that all knowledge is nothing but interpretation, all truth claims rhetoric meant to persuade only.

Critical ethnographers are in the position of wishing to claim that real social inequalities exist, that research can discover and represent them without bias, and that social inequalities are morally unacceptable. Postmodern themes, taken in any totalizing way, will not help but rather hinder them in this project. This paper has accordingly sought to challenge and relocate postmodern and poststructural insights within the very rough outlines of an epistemological theory that has yet to be fully articulated. I call this critical epistemology. It makes heavy use of critical pragmatism but critical pragmatism as informed by a reformulated theory of praxis. The basic features of this reformulated theory of praxis are already implicit in the critical ethnographic tradition, hidden there within the concept of cultural production as introduced to us by Paul Willis.

# References

Althusser, L. For Marx. London: Allen Lane, 1969.

Bernstein, R. Praxis and Action. Philadelphia: University of Pennsylvania Press, 1971.

Caputo, J. Radical Hermeneutics: Repetition, Deconstruction, and the Hermeneutic Project. Bloomington: Indiana University Press, 1987.

Carspecken, P. F. Community Schooling and the Nature of Power, The Battle for Croxteth Comprehensive. London and New York: Routledge, 1991.

Carspecken, P. F. "Pragmatic Binary Oppositions and Intersubjectivity in an Illegally Occupied School." International Journal of Qualitative Research in Education, 5, 1 (January–March 1992).

Carspecken, P. F. *Critical Ethnography in Educational Research: A Theoretical and Practical Guide*. New York and London: Routledge, 1996.

Carspecken, P. F. *Four Scenes for Posing the Question of Meaning, and Other Explorations in Critical Philosophy and Critical Methodology*. New York: Peter Lang, 1999a.

Carspecken, P. F. "There Is No Such Thing as 'Critical Ethnography': A Historical Discussion and an Outline of One Methodological Theory." Pp. 29–56 in A. Massey and G. Walford, ed., *Studies in Educational Ethnography Volume 2, Explorations in Methodology*. Stamford, Conn.: Jai Press Co., 1999b.

Carspecken, P. F., and M. Apple. "Critical Qualitative Research, Theory, Method, and Practice. In M. LeCompte, W. Millroy, and J. Preissle, ed., *Handbook of Qualitative Research in Education*. Florida: Academic Press, 1992.

Carspecken, P. F., and P. Cordeiro. "Being, Doing, and Becoming: Textual Models of Social Identity and a Case Study." *Qualitative Inquiry*, 1, 1 (1995).

Carspecken, P. F., and L. MacGillivray. "Raising Consciousness about Reflection, Validity and Meaning." In G. Shacklock and J. Symth, ed., *Being Reflexive in Critical Educational and Social Research*. London: Falmer Press, 1998.

Derrida, J. *Speech and Phenomena: And Other Essays on Husserl's Theory of Signs*. Trans. David Allison. Evanston: Northwestern University Press, 1973.

Derrida, J. *Of Grammatology*. Trans. Gayatri Chakravorty Spivak. Baltimore: Johns Hopkins University Press, 1974.

Everhart, R. *Reading, Writing, and Resistance: Adolescence and Labor in a Junior High School*. London: Routledge and Kegan Paul, 1983.

Foucault, M. *Madness and Civilization: A History of Insanity in the Age of Reason*. New York: Vintage/Random House, 1973.

Foucault, M. *Discipline and Punish: The Birth of the Prison*. New York: Vintage/Random House, 1979.

Giddens, A. *Central Problems in Social Theory*. London: Macmillan, 1979.

Giddens, A. *The Constitution of Society*. Cambridge, UK: Polity Press, 1984.

Guba, E. "The Alternative Paradigm Dialog." Pp. 17–27 in E. Guba, ed., *The Paradigm Dialog*. Newbury Park, Calif.: Sage Publications, 1990a.

Guba, E., ed. *The Paradigm Dialog*. Newbury Park, Calif.: Sage Publications, 1990b.

Habermas, J. *The Theory of Communicative Action*. *Volume I: Reason and the Rationalization of Society*. Boston: Beacon Press, 1981.

Habermas, J. *The Philosophical Discourse of Modernity: Twelve Lectures*. Cambridge, Mass.: MIT Press, 1987a.

Habermas, J. *The Theory of Communicative Action*. *Volume II: Life-World and System: A Critique of Functionalist Reason*. Boston: Beacon Press, 1987b.

Johnson, R. "Three Problematics: Elements of a Theory of Working Class Culture." In J. Clarke, C. Critcher and R. Johnson, ed., *Working Class Culture: Studies in History and Theory*. London: Hutchinson and Co. 1979.

Kaye, H. *The British Marxist Historians: An Introductory Analysis*. Cambridge, UK: Polity Press, 1984.

Kuhn, T. *The Structure of Scientific Revolutions.* 2nd ed. Chicago: University of Chicago Press, 1970.

Lather, P. *Getting Smart: Feminist Research and Pedagogy with/in the Postmodern.* New York and London: Routledge, 1991.

Lincoln, Y., and E. Guba. *Naturalistic Inquiry.* Beverly Hills, Calif.: Sage Publications, 1985.

Marx, K. *Early Writings.* Harmondsworth, UK: Penguin Books, 1977.

Marx, K., and F. Engels. *Complete Works.* London: Lawrence and Wishart, 1976.

McLaren, P. *Schooling as a Ritual Performance: Towards a Political Economy of Educational Symbols and Gestures.* 2nd ed. New York and London: Routledge, 1993.

McLaren, P. Foreword. In P. F. Carspecken, ed., *Four Scenes for Posing the Question of Meaning, and Other Explorations in Critical Philosophy and Critical Methodology.* New York: Peter Lang, 1999.

McRobbie, A. "Working Class Girls and the Culture of Femininity." In Center for Contemporary Cultural Studies, ed., *Women Take Issue.* London: Hutchinson and Co., 1978.

Spivak, G. C. Translator's preface. *Of Grammatology.* By J. Derrida. Baltimore: Johns Hopkins University Press, 1974.

Taylor, C. *Hegel and Modern Society.* Cambridge, UK: Cambridge University Press, 1979.

Thompson, E. P. *The Making of the English Working Class.* London: Victor Gollancz Ltd., 1963.

Thompson, E. P. *The Poverty of Theory and Other Essays.* London: Merlin Press, 1978.

Willis, P. "How Working Class Kids Get Working Class Jobs." University of Birmingham Occasional Papers, 1975.

Willis, P. "The Main Reality." University of Birmingham Occasional Papers, 1976.

Willis, P. *Learning to Labor: How Working Class Kids Get Working Class Jobs.* London: Gower, 1977.

~

# CHAPTER FIVE

# Rethinking Critical Theory and Qualitative Research

*Joe L. Kincheloe and Peter McLaren*

## The Roots of Critical Research

Some seventy years after its development in Frankfurt, Germany, critical theory retains its ability to disrupt and challenge the status quo. In the process, it elicits highly charged emotions of all types—fierce loyalty from its proponents, vehement hostility from its detractors. Such vibrantly polar reactions indicate at the very least that critical theory still matters. We can be against critical theory or for it, but, especially at the present historical juncture, we cannot be without it. Indeed, qualitative research that frames its purpose in the context of critical theoretical concerns still produces, in our view, undeniably dangerous knowledge, the kind of information and insight that upsets institutions and threatens to overturn sovereign regimes of truth.

*Critical theory* is a term that is often evoked and frequently misunderstood. It usually refers to the theoretical tradition developed by the Frankfurt school, a group of writers connected to the Institute of Social Research at the University of Frankfurt. However, none of the Frankfurt school theorists ever claimed to have developed a unified approach to cultural criticism. In its beginnings, Max Horkheimer, Theodore Adorno, and Herbert Marcuse initiated a conversation with the German tradition of philosophical and social thought, especially Marx, Kant, Hegel, and Weber. From the vantage point of these critical theorists, whose political sensibilities were influenced by the devastation of World War I, postwar Germany with its economic depression marked by inflation and unemployment, and the failed strikes and protests in Germany and Central Europe in this same period, the world was in urgent need of reinterpretation. From this perspective, they defied Marxist orthodoxy while deepening their belief that injustice and subjugation shaped the lived world (Bottomore 1984; Gibson 1986; Held 1980; Jay 1973). Focusing their attention on the changing nature of capitalism, the early critical theorists analyzed the mutating forms of domination that accompanied this change (Giroux, 1983, 1997; McLaren 1997; Agger 1998; Kellner 1989; Kincheloe and Pinar 1991; Gall, Gall, and Borg 1999).

Only a decade after the Frankfurt school was established, the Nazis controlled Germany. The danger posed by the exclusive Jewish membership of the Frankfurt school, and its association with Marxism, convinced Horkheimer, Adorno, and Marcuse to leave Germany. Eventually locating themselves in California, these critical theorists were shocked by American culture. Offended by the taken-for-granted empirical practices of American social science researchers, Horkheimer, Adorno, and Marcuse were challenged to respond to the social science establishment's belief that their research could describe and accurately measure any dimension of human behavior. Piqued by the contradictions between progressive American rhetoric of egalitarianism and the reality of racial and class discrimination, these theorists produced their major works while residing in the United States. In 1953, Horkheimer and Adorno returned to Germany and reestablished the Institute of Social Research. Significantly, Herbert Marcuse stayed in the United States, where he would find a new audience for his work in social theory. Much to his own surprise, Marcuse skyrocketed to fame as the philosopher of the student movements of the 1960s. Critical theory, especially the emotionally and sexually liberating work of Marcuse, provided the philosophical voice of the New Left. Concerned with the politics of psychological and cultural revolution, the New Left preached a Marcusian sermon of political emancipation (Gibson 1986; Wexler 1991, 1996; Hinchey 1998; Kincheloe and Steinberg 1997; Surber 1998).

Many academicians who had come of age in the politically charged atmosphere of the 1960s focused their scholarly attention on critical theory. Frustrated by forms of domination emerging from a post–Enlightenment culture nurtured by capitalism, these scholars saw in critical theory a method of temporarily freeing academic work from these forms of power. Impressed by critical theory's dialectical concern with the social construction of experience, they came to view their disciplines as manifestations of the discourses and power relations of the social and historical contexts that produced them. The "discourse of possibility" implicit within the constructed nature of social experience suggested to these scholars that a reconstruction of the social sciences could eventually lead to a more egalitarian and democratic social order. New poststructuralist conceptualizations of human agency and their promise that men and women can at least partly determine their own existence offered new hope for emancipatory forms of social research when compared with orthodox Marxism's assertion of the iron laws of history, the irrevocable evil of capitalism, and the proletariat as the privileged subject and anticipated agent of social transformation. For example, when Henry Giroux and other critical educators criticized the argument made by Marxist scholars Samuel Bowles and Herbert Gintis—that schools were capitalist agencies of social, economic, cultural, and bureaucratic reproduction—they contrasted the deterministic perspectives of Bowles and Gintis with the idea that schools, as venues of hope, could become sites of resistance and democratic possibility through concerted efforts among teachers and students to work within a liberatory pedagogical framework. Giroux (1988), in particular, maintained that schools can become institutions where forms of knowledge, values, and social relations are taught for the purpose of educating young people for critical empowerment rather than subjugation.

## Critical Humility: Our Ideosyncratic Interpretation of Critical Theory and Critical Research

Over the last twenty years of our involvement in critical theory and critical research, we have been asked by hundreds of people to explain more precisely what critical theory is. We find that question difficult to answer because: (a) there are many critical theories not just one; (b) the critical tradition is always changing and evolving; and (c) critical theory attempts to avoid too much specificity since there is room for disagreement among critical theorists. To lay out a set of fixed characteristics of the position is contrary to the desire of such theorists to avoid the production of blueprints of sociopolitical and epistemological beliefs. Given these disclaimers, we will now attempt to provide one idiosyncratic "take" on the nature of critical theory and critical research at the beginning of the millennium. Please note that this is merely our subjective analysis, and there are many brilliant critical theorists who will find many problems with our pronouncements.

In this humble spirit, we tender a description of a reconceptualized, end-of-century critical theory that has been critiqued and overhauled by the "post-discourses" of the last quarter of the twentieth century (Bauman 1995; Kellner 1995; Carlson and Apple 1998; Giroux 1997; Collins 1995; Steinberg and Kincheloe 1998; Roman and Eyre 1997). In this context, a reconceptualized critical theory questions the assumption that societies such as the United States, Canada, Australia, New Zealand, and the nations in the European Union, for example, are unproblematically democratic and free. Over the twentieth century, especially since the early 1960s, individuals in these societies have been acculturated to feel comfortable in relations of domination and subordination rather than equality and independence. Given the social and technological changes of the last half of the century that led to new forms of information production and access, critical theorists argued that questions of self-direction and democratic egalitarianism should be reassessed. The post-discourses (e.g., postmodernism, critical feminism, post-structuralism centered) are more shaped by social and historical forces than previously believed. Given the changing social and informational conditions of the latter twentieth century media-saturated Western culture, new ways of researching and analyzing the construction of individuals were needed by critical theorists (Smith and Wexler 1995; Leistyna, Woodrum, and Sherblom 1996; Hinchey 1998; Agger 1992; Flosser and Otto 1998; Sünker 1998). The following points briefly delineate our interpretation of a critical theory for the new millennium.

## A Reconceptualized Critical Theory

In this context, it is important to note that we understand a social theory as a map or a guide to the social sphere. In a research context, it does not determine how we see the world but helps us devise questions and strategies for exploring it. A critical social theory is concerned in particular with issues of power and justice and the ways that the economy; matters of race, class, and gender; ideologies; discourses; education; religion and other social institutions; and cultural dynamics interact to construct a social system.

1) *Critical Enlightenment.* In this context, critical theory analyzes competing power interests between groups and individuals within a society—identifying who gains and who loses in specific situations. Privileged groups, criticalists argue, often have an interest in supporting the status quo to protect their advantages; the dynamics of such efforts often become a central focus of critical research. Such studies of privilege often revolve around issues of race, class, gender, and sexuality (Kincheloe and Steinberg 1997; Kin-

cheloe, Steinberg, Rodriguez, and Chennault 1998; Rodriguez and Villaverde 1999; McLaren 1997; Sleeter and McLaren 1995; Carter 1998; Howell 1998). In this context, to seek critical enlightenment is to uncover the winners and losers in particular social arrangements and the process by which such power plays operate (Cary 1996; King 1996; Fehr 1993; Pruyn 1994; Wexler 1996).

2) *Critical Emancipation.* Those who seek emancipation attempt to gain the power to control their own lives in solidarity with a justice-oriented community. Here, critical research attempts to expose the forces that prevent individuals and groups from shaping the decisions that crucially affect their lives. In this way, greater degrees of autonomy and human agency can be achieved. At the beginning of the new millennium we are cautious in our use of the term emancipation, because, as many critics have pointed out, no one is ever completely emancipated from the sociopolitical context that has produced him or her. Also, many have questioned the arrogance that may accompany feelings of personal emancipation. These are important criticisms and must be carefully taken into account by critical researchers. Thus, as critical inquirers who search for those forces that insidiously shape who we are, we respect those who reach different conclusions in their personal journeys (Kincheloe and Steinberg 1998; Cannella 1997; Butler 1998; Kellogg 1998; Weil 1998).

3) *The Rejection of Economic Determinism.* A caveat of a reconceptualized critical theory involves the insistence that the tradition does not accept the Marxist notion that "base" determines "superstructure"—meaning that economic factors dictate the nature of all other aspects of human existence. Critical theorists understand at the beginning of the twenty-first century that there are multiple forms of power including the aforementioned racial, gender, and sexual axes of domination. In issuing this caveat, however, a reconceptualized critical theory in no way attempts to argue that economic factors are unimportant in the shaping of everyday life. Economic factors can never be separated from other axes of oppression (Kincheloe and Steinberg 1999; Kincheloe 1995, 1999; Gee, Hull, and Lankshear 1996; Rifkin 1995; Gibson 1986).

4) *The Critique of Instrumental or Technical Rationality.* A reconceptualized critical theory sees instrumental/technological rationality as one of the most oppressive features of contemporary society. Such a form of "hyper-reason" involves the obsession with means in preference to ends. Critical theorists claim that instrumental/technical rationality is more interested with method and efficiency than purpose. It delimits its questions to "how to" instead of

"why should." In a research context, critical theorists claim that many ratio-nalistic scholars become so obsessed with issues of technique, procedure, and correct method that they forget the humanistic purpose of the research act. Instrumental/technical rationality often separates fact from value in its obsession with "proper" method, losing in the process an understanding of the value choices always involved in the production of so-called facts (Kin-cheloe 1993; McLaren 1998; Giroux 1997; Hinchey 1998; Alfino, Caputo, and Wynyard 1998; Stallabrass 1996; Weinstein 1998).

5) *The Impact of Desire.* A reconceptualized critical theory appreciates poststructuralist psychoanalysis as an important resource in pursuing an emancipatory research project. In this context, critical researchers are empowered to dig more deeply into the complexity of the construction of the human psyche. Such a psychoanalysis helps critical researchers discern the unconscious processes that create resistance to progressive change and induce self-destructive behavior. A poststructural psychoanalysis, in its rejec-tion of traditional psychoanalysis's tendency to view individuals as rational and autonomous beings, allows critical researchers new tools to reconfigure the interplay among the various axes of power, identity, libido, rationality, and emotion. In this configuration the psychic is no longer separated from the sociopolitical realm; indeed, desire can be socially constructed and used by power wielders for destructive and oppressive outcomes. On the other hand, critical theorists can help mobilize desire for progressive and emanci-patory projects. Taking their lead from feminist theory, critical researchers are aware of the patriarchal inscriptions within traditional psychoanalysis and work to avoid its bourgeois, ethnocentric, and misogynistic tendencies. Freed from these blinders, poststructural psychoanalysis helps researchers gain a new sensitivity to the role of fantasy and imagination and the struc-tures of sociocultural and psychological meaning they reference (Kincheloe, Steinberg, and Villaverde 1999; Alford 1993; Samuels 1993; Elliot 1994; Barrows 1995; Block 1995; Slattery 1995; Pinar 1998; Atwell-Vasey 1998; Pinar, Reynolds, Slattery, and Taubman 1995; Britzman and Pitt 1996).

6) *A Reconceptualized Critical Theory of Power: Hegemony.* Our concep-tion of a reconceptualized critical theory is intensely concerned with the need to understand the various and complex ways that power operates to dominate and shape consciousness. Power, critical theorists have learned, is an extremely ambiguous topic that demands detailed study and analysis. A consensus seems to be emerging among criticalists that power is a basic con-stituent of human existence that works to shape the oppressive and produc-tive nature of the human tradition. Indeed, we are all empowered and we are

all unempowered, in that we all possess abilities and we are all limited in the attempt to use our abilities. Because of limited space, we will focus here on critical theory's traditional concern with the oppressive aspects of power, although we understand that an important aspect of critical research focuses on the productive aspects of power—its ability to empower, to establish a critical democracy, to engage marginalized people in the rethinking of their sociopolitical role (Fiske 1993; Macedo 1994; Apple 1996; Giroux 1997; Nicholson and Seidman 1995).

In the context of oppressive power and its ability to produce inequalities and human suffering, Antonio Gramsci's notion of hegemony is central to critical research. Gramsci understood that dominant power in the twentieth century is not always exercised simply by physical force but via social-psychological attempts to win people's consent to domination through cultural institutions such as the media, the schools, the family, and the church. Gramscian hegemony recognizes that the winning of popular consent is a very complex process and must be researched carefully in a case-by-case basis. Students and researchers of power, educators, sociologists, all of us are hegemonized as our field of knowledge and understanding is structured by limited exposure to competing definitions of the sociopolitical world. The hegemonic field, with its bounded sociopsychological horizon, garners consent to an inequitable power matrix—a set of social relations that are legitimated by their depiction as natural and inevitable. In this context critical researchers note that hegemonic consent is never completely established, for it is always contested by various groups with different agendas (McLaren 1995a; McLaren, Hammer, Reilly, and Sholle 1995; West 1993; Grossberg 1997; Lull 1995).

7) *A Reconceptualized Critical Theory of Power: Ideology.* Critical theorists understand that hegemony cannot be separated from ideology. If hegemony is the larger effort of the powerful to win the consent of their "subordinates," then dominant or hegemonic ideology involves the cultural forms, the meanings, the rituals, and the representations that produce consent to the status quo and individuals' particular places within it. Ideology vis-à-vis hegemony moves critical inquirers beyond simplistic explanations of domination that have used terms such as propaganda to describe the way media, political, educational, and other sociocultural productions coercively manipulate citizens to adopt oppressive meanings. A reconceptualized critical research understands a much more subtle, ambiguous, and situationally specific form of domination that refuses the propaganda model's assumption that people are passive, easily manipulated victims. Researchers operating with an awareness

of this hegemonic ideology understand that dominant ideological practices and discourses socially construct our vision of reality (Lemke 1995, 1998). Thus, our notion of hegemonic ideology is a critical form of epistemological constructivism buoyed by a nuanced understanding of power's complicity in the constructions people make of the world and their role in it (Kincheloe 1998). Such an awareness corrects earlier delineations of ideology as a mono-lithic, unidirectional entity that was imposed on individuals by a secret cohort of ruling-class tsars. Understanding domination in the context of concurrent struggles among different classes, racial and gender groups, and sectors of capital, critical researchers of ideology explore the ways such com-petition engages different visions, interests, and agendas in a variety of social locales—venues previously thought to be outside the domain of ideological struggle (Brosio 1994; Tanaka 1996).

8) *A Reconceptualized Critical Theory of Power: Linguistic/Discursive Power.* Critical researchers have come to understand that language is not a mirror of society. It is an unstable entity that finds its meaning shifting depending on the context in which it is used. Contrary to previous understandings, critical researchers appreciate the fact that language is not a neutral and objective conduit of description of the "real world." Rather from a critical perspective, linguistic descriptions are not simply about the world but serve to construct it. With these linguistic notions in mind, criticalists begin to study the way language in the form of discourses serves as a form of regulation and domina-tion. Discursive practices are defined as a set of tacit rules that regulate what can and cannot be said; who can speak with the blessings of authority and who must listen; and whose social constructions are valid and whose are erro-neous and unimportant. In an educational context, for example, legitimized discourses of power insidiously tell educators what books may be read by stu-dents, what instructional methods may be utilized, and what belief systems and views of success may be taught. In all forms of research, discursive power validates particular research strategies, narrative formats, and modes of repre-sentation. In this context, power discourses undermine the multiple mean-ings of language, establishing one correct reading that implants a particular hegemonic/ideological message into the consciousness of the reader. This is a process often referred to as the attempt to impose discursive closure. Critical researchers interested in the construction of consciousness are very attentive to these power dynamics (Blades 1997; Gee 1996; Lemke 1993; Morgan 1996; McWilliam and Taylor 1996).

9) *Focusing on the Relationship among Culture, Power, and Domination.* In the last decades of the twentieth century, culture has taken on a new impor-

tance in the effort to understand power and domination. Critical researchers (Kincheloe and Steinberg 1997; Steinberg and Kincheloe 1997; McLaren 1997; Giroux 1997) have argued that culture has to be viewed as a domain of struggle where the production and transmission of knowledge is always a contested process. Dominant and subordinate cultures deploy differing systems of meaning based on the forms of knowledge produced in their cultural domain. The realm of culture known as popular culture with its TV, movies, video games, computers, music, dance, and other productions, plays an increasingly important role in critical research on power and domination. Cultural studies, of course, occupies an ever-expanding role in this context, as it studies not only popular culture but the tacit rules that guide cultural production. Arguing that the development of mass media has changed the way the culture operates, cultural studies researchers maintain that cultural epistemologies at the beginning of the new millennium are different than they were only a few decades ago. In this new epistemological era new forms of culture and cultural domination are produced as the distinction between the real and simulated is blurred. This blurring effect of hyperreality constructs a social vertigo characterized by a loss of touch with traditional notions of time, community, self, and history. New structures of cultural space and time generated by bombarding electronic images from local, national, and international spaces shake our personal sense of place. This proliferation of signs and images functions as a mechanism of control in contemporary Western societies. The key to successful counterhegemonic cultural research involves: 1) the ability to link the production of representations, images, and signs of hyperreality to power in the political economy, and 2) the capacity, once this linkage is exposed and described, to delineate the highly complex effects of the reception of these images and signs on individuals located at various race, class, gender, and sexual coordinates in the web of reality (Grossberg 1995; Thomas 1997; Garnham 1997; Ferguson and Golding 1997; Joyrich 1996).

10) *The Role of Cultural Pedagogy in Critical Theory.* Cultural production can often be thought of as a form of education, as it generates knowledge, shapes values, and constructs identity. From our perspective such a framing can help critical researchers make sense of the world of domination and oppression, as they work to bring about a more just, democratic, and egalitarian society. In recent years this educational dynamic has been referred to as cultural pedagogy (McLaren 1997; Kincheloe 1995; Giroux 1997; Pailliotet 1998; Semali 1998; Soto 1998; Berry 1998). Pedagogy is a useful term that was traditionally used to refer only to teaching and schooling. By using the

term cultural pedagogy, we are specifically referring to the ways particular cultural agents produce particular hegemonic ways of seeing. In our critical interpretive context our notion of cultural pedagogy asserts that the new "educators" in the electronically wired contemporary era are those who possess the financial resources to use mass media. This corporate dominated pedagogical process has worked so well that few complain about it at the beginning of the new millennium—such informational politics doesn't even make the evening news. Can we imagine another institution in contemporary society gaining the pedagogical power corporations now assert over information and signification systems? What if the Church of Christ was sufficiently powerful to run pedagogical "commercials" every few minutes on TV and radio touting the necessity for everyone to accept their denomination's faith? Replayed scenes of Jews, Muslims, Hindus, Catholics, and Methodists being condemned to hell if they rejected the official pedagogy (the true doctrine) would greet North Americans and their children seven days a week. There is little doubt that many people would be outraged and would organize for political action. Western societies have to some degree capitulated to this corporate pedagogical threat to democracy, passively watching an elite gain greater control over the political system and political consciousness via a sophisticated cultural pedagogy. Critical researchers are intent on exposing the specifics of this process (Deetz 1993; Boyles 1998; Steinberg and Kincheloe 1997; Molnar 1996; Drummond 1996; Pfeil 1995).

## Critical Research and the Centrality Of Interpretation: Critical Hermeneuticics

One of the most important aspects of a critical theory–informed qualitative research involves the often-neglected domain of the interpretation of information. As we have taught and written about critical research in the 1990s, this interpretive or hermeneuticical aspect becomes increasingly important. Many students of qualitative research approach us in classes and presentations with little theoretical background involving the complex and multidimensional nature of data interpretation in their work. While there are many moments within the process of researching where the *critical* dynamic of critical theory–informed research, there is none more important than the moment(s) of interpretation. In this context we will begin our discussion of critical qualitative research, linking it as we go to questions of the relationship between critical hermeneutics and knowledge production (Slattery 1995).

The critical hermeneuticical tradition (Gross and Keith 1997; Rosen 1987; Grondin 1994; Vattimo 1994) that in qualitative research there is only interpretation, no matter how vociferously many researchers may argue that the facts speak for themselves. The hermeneuticic act of interpretation involves in its most elemental articulation making sense of what has been observed in a way that communicates understanding. Not only is all research merely an act of interpretation but hermeneuticics contends that perception itself is an act of interpretation. Thus, the quest for understanding is a fundamental feature of human existence, as encounter with the unfamiliar always demands the attempt to make meaning, to make sense. The same, however, is also the case with the familiar. Indeed, as in the study of commonly known texts, we come to find that sometimes the familiar may be seen as the most strange. Thus, it should not be surprising that even the so-called objective writings of qualitative research are interpretations, not value-free descriptions (Denzin 1994; Gallagher 1992; Jardine 1998).

Learning from the hermeneuticic tradition and the postmodern critique, critical researchers have begun to reexamine textual claims to authority. No pristine interpretation exists—indeed, no methodology, social or educational theory, and discursive form can claim a privileged position that enables the production of authoritative knowledge. Researchers must always speak/write about the world in terms of something else in the world, in relation to. . . . As creatures of the world, we are oriented to it in a way that prevents us from grounding our theories and perspectives outside of it. Thus, whether we like it or not we are all destined as interpreters to analyze from within its boundaries and blinders. Within these limitations, however, the interpretations emerging from the hermeneuticic process can still move us to new levels of understanding, appreciations that allow us to "live our way" into an experience described to us. Despite the impediments of context, hermeneuticical researchers can transcend the inadequacies of thin descriptions of decontextualized facts and produce thick descriptions of social texts characterized by the context of their production, the intentions of its producers, and the meanings mobilized in the process of its construction. The production of such thick descriptions/interpretations follows no step-by-step blueprint or mechanical formula. As with any art form, hermeneuticical analysis can be learned only in the Deweyan sense—by doing it. Researchers in the context practice the art by grappling with the text to be understood, telling its story in relation to its contextual dynamics and other texts first to themselves and then to a public audience (Slattery 1995; Denzin 1994; Gallagher 1992; Slattery and Kincheloe forthcoming; Jardine 1998; Carson and Sumora 1997).

1) *Critical Hermeneuticical Methods of Interpretation*
These concerns with the nature of hermeneuticical interpretation come
under the category of philosophical hermeneuticics. Working in this domain,
hermeneuticical scholars attempt to think through and clarify the conditions
under which interpretation and understanding take place. The critical hermeneuticics that grounds critical qualitative research moves more in the
direction of normative hermeneuticics in that it raises questions about the
purposes and procedures of interpretation. In its critical theory–driven context, the purpose of hermeneuticical analysis is to develop a form of cultural
criticism revealing power dynamics within social and cultural texts. Qualitative researchers familiar with critical hermeneutics build bridges between
reader and text; text and its producer; historical context and present; and
one particular social circumstance and another. Accomplishing such interpretive tasks is a difficult endeavor, and researchers situated in normative hermeneutics push ethnographers, historians, semioticians, literary critics, and
content analysts to trace the bridge-building processes employed by successful interpretations of knowledge production and culture (Gallagher 1992;
Kellner 1995; Kogler 1996; Rapko 1998).

Grounded by the hermeneuticical bridge-building, critical researchers in
a hermeneuticical circle (a process of analysis where interpreters seek the
historical and social dynamics that shape textual interpretation) engage in
the back and forth of studying parts in relation to the whole and the whole
in relation to parts. No final interpretation is sought in this context, as the
activity of the circle proceeds with no need for closure (Pinar, Reynolds,
Slattery, and Taubman 1995; Gallagher 1992; Peters and Lankshear 1994).
This movement of whole to parts is combined with an analytical flow
between abstract and concrete. Such dynamics often tie interpretation to the
interplay of larger social forces (the general) to the everyday lives of individuals (the particular). A critical hermeneuticics brings the concrete, the parts,
and the particular into focus, but in a manner that grounds them contextually in a larger understanding of the social forces, the whole, and the abstract
(the general). Focus on the parts is the dynamic that brings the particular
into focus, sharpening our understanding of the individual in light of the
social and psychological forces that shape him or her. The parts and the
unique places they occupy ground hermeneuticical ways of seeing by providing the contextualization of the particular—a perspective often erased in traditional inquiry's search for abstract generalizations (Kellner 1995; Gallagher
1992; Peters and Lankshear 1994; Miller and Hodge 1998).

The give and take of the hermeneuticical circle induces analysts to review

existing conceptual matrixes in light of new understandings. Here, precon-
ceptions are reconsidered and reconceptualized so as to provide a new way of
exploring a particular text. Making use of an author's insights hermeneutici-
cally does not mean replicating his or her response to his or her original question. In the hermeneuticical process, the author's answer is valuable only if
it catalyzes the production of a new question for our consideration in the
effort to make sense of a particular textual phenomenon (Gallagher 1992).
In this context, participants in the hermeneuticical circle must be wary of
techniques of textual defamiliarization that have become cliched. For example, feminist criticisms of Barbie's figure and its construction of the image of
ideal woman became such conventions in popular cultural analysis that other
readings of Barbie were suppressed. Critical hermeneuticical analysts in this
and many other cases have to introduce new forms of analysis to the hermeneuticical circle—to defamiliarize conventional defamiliarizations—in order
to achieve deeper levels of understanding (Berger 1995).

Within the hermeneuticical circle, we may develop new metaphors to
shape our analysis in ways that break us out of familiar modes. For example,
thinking of movies as mass-mediated dreams may help critical researchers of
popular culture reconceptualize the interpretive act as a psychoanalytic form
of dream study. In this way, critical researchers could examine psychoanalyti-
cal work in the analysis of dream symbolization for insights into their cultural
studies of the popular culture and the meanings it helps individuals make via
its visual images and narratives. As researchers apply these new metaphors
in the hermeneuticic circle, they must be aware of the implicit metaphors
researchers continuously bring to the interpretive process (Berger 1995;
Clough 1998). Such metaphors are shaped by the sociohistorical era, the culture, and the linguistic context in which the interpreter operates. Such
awarenesses are important features that must be introduced into the give and
take of the critical hermeneuticical circle. As John Dewey (1916) wrote decades ago, individuals adopt the values and perspectives of their social groups
in a manner that such factors come to shape their views of the world. Indeed,
the values and perspectives of the group help determine what is deemed
important and what is not (i.e., what is granted attention and what is
ignored). Hermeneuticical analysts are aware of such interpretational
dynamics and make sure they are included in the search for understanding
(Slattery and Kincheloe, forthcoming).

Critical researchers with a hermeneuticical insight take Dewey's insight
to heart as they pursue their inquiry. They are aware that the consciousness
and the interpretative frames they bring to their research are historically-

situated, ever changing, and ever evolving in relationship to the cultural and ideological climate (Hinchey 1998; Kincheloe, Steinberg, and Hinchey 1999). Thus, there is nothing simple about the social construction of interpretative lenses—consciousness construction is contradictory and the result of the collision of a variety of ideologically oppositional forces. Critical qualitative researchers understanding the relationship between identity formation and interpretive lenses are better equipped to understand the etymology of their own assertions—especially the way power operates to shape them. Linguistic, discursive, and many other factors typically hidden from awareness insidiously shape the meanings researchers garner from their work (Goodson 1997). It was this dynamic Antonio Gramsci had in mind when he argued that a critical philosophy should be viewed as a form of self-criticism. The starting point, he concluded, for any higher understanding of self involves consciousness of oneself as a product of power-driven sociohistorical forces. A critical perspective, he once wrote, involves the ability of its adherents to criticize the ideological frames that they use to make sense of the world (Coben 1998).

Analyzing Dewey's and Gramsci's notions of self-production in light of the aims of critical hermeneuticics vis-à-vis critical qualitative research, we begin to gain insight into how the ambiguous and closeted interpretive process operates. This moves us in a critical direction, as we understand that the "facts" do not simply demand particular interpretations.

2) *Hermentucial Horizons: Situating Critical Research*
Researchers who fail to take these points into account operate at the mercy of unexamined assumptions. Since all interpretation is historically and culturally situationed, it befalls the lot of critical researchers to study the ways both interpreters (often the analysts themselves) and the object of interpretation are constructed by their time and place. In this context, the importance of social theory emerges. Operating in this manner, researchers inject critical social theory into the hermeneuticic circle to facilitate an understanding of the hidden structures and tacit cultural dynamics that insidiously inscribe social meanings and values (Gallagher 1992; Kellner 1995; Cary 1996). This social and historical situating of interpreter and text is an extremely complex enterprise that demands a nuanced analysis of the impact of hegemonic and ideological forces that connect the micro-dynamics of everyday life with the macro-dynamics of structures such as white supremacy, patriarchy, and class elitism. The central hermeneuticic of many critical

qualitative works involve the interaction among research, subject(s), and these situating sociohistorical structures.

When these aspects of the interpretation process are taken into account, analysts begin to understand Hans-Georg Gadamer's (1989) contention that social frames of reference influence researchers' questions, which, in turn, shape the nature of interpretation itself. In light of this situating process, the modernist notion that a social text has one valid interpretation evaporates into thin air. Researchers, whether they admit it or not, always have a point of view, a disciplinary orientation, a social or political group with which they identify (Kincheloe 1991; Lugg 1996). Thus, the point, critical hermeneutics argue, is not for researches to shed all worldly affiliations but to identify them and understand their impact on the ways they approach a social and educational phenomenon. Gadamer labels these world affiliations of researchers their "horizons" and deems the hermeneuticic act of interpretation the "fusion of horizons." When critical researchers engage in the fusion of horizons they enter the tradition of the text. Here they study the conditions of its production and the circle of previous interpretations. In this manner, they begin to uncover the ways the text has attempted to represent truth (Berger 1995; Slattery 1995; Miller and Hodge 1998; Jardine 1998; Ellis 1998).

In the critical hermeneuticical tradition, these analyses of the ways interpretation is situated are considered central to the critical project. Researchers, like all human beings, critical analysts argue, make history and live their lives within structures of meaning they have not necessarily chosen for themselves. Understanding this, critical hermeneutics realize that a central aspect of their sociocultural analysis involves dissecting the ways people connect their everyday experiences to the cultural representations of such experiences. Such work involves the unraveling of the ideological codings embedded in these cultural representations. This unraveling is complicated by the taken-for-grantedness of the meanings promoted in these representations and the typically undetected ways these meanings are circulated into everyday life (Denzin 1992; Kogler 1996). The better the analyst, the better he or she can expose these meanings in the domain of the "what-goes-without-saying"— that activity previously deemed unworthy of comment.

At this historical juncture—the postmodern condition or hyperreality, as it has been labeled—electronic modes of communication become extremely important to the production of meanings and representations that culturally situate human beings in general and textual interpretations in particular (Goldman and Papson 1994; Hall 1997; Boyles 1998). In many ways, it can be argued that the postmodern condition produces a secondhand culture, filtered and preformed in the marketplace and constantly communicated via popular cultural and mass media. Critical analysts understand that the pedagogical effects of such a mediated culture can range from the political/ideological to the cognitive/epistemological. For example, the situating effects of print media tend to promote a form of linearity that encourages rationality, continuity, and uniformity. On the other hand, electronic media promotes a nonlinear immediacy that may encourage more emotional responses that lead individuals in very different directions (du Gay, et al. 1997; Shelton and Kincheloe 1999). Thus, the situating influence and pedagogical impact of electronic media of the postmodern condition must be assessed by those who study cultural and political processes and, most importantly at the turn of the millennium, the research processes itself (Kellner 1995; Berger 1995; Slattery 1995; Denzin 1992; Bell and Valentine 1997; Bertman 1998).

### 3) Critical Hermeneuticics: Laying the Groundwork of Critical Research

Understanding the forces that situate interpretation, critical hermeneuticics is suspicious of any model of interpretation that claims to reveal the final truth, the essence of a text, or any form of experience (Goodson and Mangan 1996). Critical hermeneuticics is more comfortable with interpretive approaches that assume that the meaning of human experience can never be fully disclosed—neither to the researcher nor to the human that experienced it. Since language is always slippery with its meanings ever "in process," critical hermeneuticics understand that interpretations will never be linguistically unproblematic, will never be direct representations. Critical hermeneuticics seeks to understand how textual practices such as scientific research and classical theory work to maintain existing power relations and to support extant power structures (Denzin 1992). As critical researchers, we draw, of course, on the latter model of interpretation with its treatment of the personal as political. Critical hermeneuticics grounds a critical research that attempts to connect the everyday troubles individuals face to public issues of power, justice, and democracy. Typically, within the realm of the cultural studies and cultural analysis in general, critical hermeneuticics has deconstructed sociocultural texts that promote demeaning stereotypes of the disempowered (Denzin 1992; Rapko 1998; Gross and Keith 1997). In this context, critical hermeneuticics is also being deployed in relation to cultural texts that reinforce an ideology of privilege and entitlement for empowered members of the society (Kincheloe, Steinberg, Rodriquez, and Chennault

1998; Rodriguez and Villaverde 1999; Frankenberg 1993; Fine, Weis, Powell, and Wong 1997; Rains 1998; Allison 1998).

In its ability to render the personal political, critical hermeneuticics provides a methodology for arousing a critical consciousness through the analysis of the generative themes of the present era. Such generative themes can often be used to examine the meaning-making power of the contemporary cultural realm (Peters and Lankshear 1994). Within the qualitative research community there is still resistance to the idea that movies, TV, and popular music are intricately involved in the most important political, economic, and cultural battles of the contemporary epoch. Critical hermeneuticics recognizes this centrality of popular culture in the postmodern condition and seeks to uncover the ways it impedes and advances the struggle for a democratic society (Kellner 1995). Appreciating the material effects of media culture, critical hermeneuticics traces the ways the cultural dynamics position audiences politically in ways that not only shape their political beliefs but formulate their identities (Steinberg and Kincheloe 1997). In this context, Paulo Freire's (1985) contribution to the development of a critical hermeneuticics is especially valuable. Understanding that the generative themes of a culture are central features in a critical social analysis, Freire assumes that the interpretive process is both an ontological (pertaining to being) and an epistemological (pertaining to knowledge) act. It is ontological on the level that our vocation as humans, the foundation of our being, is grounded on the hermeneuticical task of interpreting the world so we can become more fully human. It is epistemological in the sense that critical hermeneuticics offers us a method for investigating the conditions of our existence and the generative themes that shape it. In this context, we gain the prowess to both live with a purpose and operate with the ability to perform evaluative acts in naming the culture around us. This ability takes on an even greater importance in the contemporary electronic society when the sociopolitical effects of the cultural domain have often been left unnamed, allowing our exploration of the shaping of our own humanness to go unexplored in this strange new social context. Critical hermeneuticics address this vacuum (Peters and Lankshear 1994; Kincheloe and Steinberg 1997; McLaren 1997).

Critical hermeneuticics names the world as a part of a larger effort to evaluate it and make it better. Knowing this, it is easy to understand why critical hermeneuticics focuses on domination and its negation, emancipation. Domination limits self-direction and democratic community-building while emancipation enables it. Domination, legitimated as it is by ideology, is decoded by critical hermeneutics who help critical researchers discover the ways they and their subjects have been entangled in the ideological process. The exposé and critique of ideology is one of critical hermeneuticics' main objectives in its effort to make the world better. As long as our vision is obstructed by the various purveyors of ideology, our effort to live in democratic communities will be thwarted (Gallagher 1992). Power wielders with race, class, and gender privilege (Kincheloe and Steinberg 1997) have access to the resources that allow them to promote ideologies and representations in a way individuals without such privilege cannot (Denzin 1992; Peters and Lankshear 1994; Hinchey 1998; Leistyna, Woodrum, and Sherblom 1996; Pinar 1998; Jipson and Paley 1997; Carlson and Apple 1998; Bartolome 1998).

## Partisan Research in a "Neutral" Academic Culture

In the space available here, it is impossible to do justice to all of the critical traditions that have drawn inspiration from Marx, Kant, Hegel, Weber, the Frankfurt school theorists, continental social theorists (such as Foucault, Habermas, and Derrida), Latin American thinkers (such as Paulo Freire), French feminists (such as Irigaray, Kristeva, or Cixous), or Russian sociolinguists (such as Bakhtin and Vygotsky)—most of whom regularly find their way into the reference lists of contemporary critical researchers. Today there are criticalist schools in many fields, and even a superficial discussion of the most prominent of these schools would demand much more space than we have available.

The fact that numerous books have been written about the often-virulent disagreements among members of the Frankfurt school only heightens our concern with "packaging" the different criticalist schools. Critical theory should not be treated as a universal grammar of revolutionary thought objectified and reduced to discrete formulaic pronouncements or strategies. Obviously, in presenting our idiosyncratic version of a reconceptualized critical theory, we have defined the critical tradition very broadly for the purpose of generating understanding; as we asserted earlier, this will trouble many critical researchers. In this move, we decided to focus on the underlying commonality among critical schools of thought, at the risk of focusing on differences. This, of course, is always risky business in terms of suggesting a false unity or consensus where none exists, but such concerns are unavoidable in a survey chapter such as this. We are defining a criticalist as a researcher or theorist who attempts to use her or his work as a form of social or cultural criticism and who accepts certain basic assumptions: that all thought is fundamentally mediated by power relations that are social and historically constituted; that facts can never be isolated from the domain of values or removed from some form of ideological inscription; that the relationship between concept and object and between signifier and signified is never stable or fixed and is often mediated by the social relations of capitalist production and consumption; that language is central to the formation of subjectivity (conscious and unconscious awareness); that certain groups in any society are privileged over others and, although the reasons for this privileging may vary widely, the oppression that characterizes contemporary societies is most forcefully reproduced when subordinates accept their social status as natural, necessary, or inevitable; that oppression has many faces and that focusing on only one at the expense of others (e.g., class oppression versus racism) often elides the interconnections among them; and, finally, that mainstream research practices are generally, although most often unwittingly, implicated in the reproduction of systems of class, race, and gender oppression (Kincheloe and Steinberg 1997).

In today's climate of blurred disciplinary genres, it is not uncommon to find literary theorists doing anthropology and anthropologists writing about literary theory, or political scientists trying their hand at ethnomethodological analysis, or philosophers doing Lacanian film criticism. We offer this observation not as an excuse to be wantonly eclectic in our treatment of the critical tradition but to make the point that any attempts to delineate critical theory as discrete schools of analysis will fail to capture the hybridity endemic to contemporary critical analysis.

Readers familiar with the criticalist traditions will recognize essentially four different "emergent" schools of social inquiry in this chapter: the neo-Marxist tradition of critical theory associated most closely with the work of Horkheimer, Adorno, and Marcuse; the genealogical writings of Michael Foucault; the practices of poststructuralist deconstruction associated with Derrida; and postmodernist currents associated with Derrida, Foucault, Lyotard, Ebert, and others. In our view, critical ethnography has been influenced by all of these perspectives in different ways and to different degrees. From critical theory, researchers inherit a forceful criticism of the positivist conception of science and instrumental rationality, especially in Adorno's idea of negative dialectics, which posits an unstable relationship of contradiction between concepts and objects; from Derrida, researchers are given a means for deconstructing objective truth or what is referred to as "the metaphysics of presence." For Derrida, the meaning of a word is constantly deferred because it can have meaning only in relation to its difference from other words within a given system of language; Foucault invites researchers to explore the ways in which discourses are implicated in relations of power and how power and knowledge serve as dialectically reinitiating practices that regulate what is considered reasonable and true. We have characterized much of the work influenced by these writers as the "ludic" and "resistance" post-modernist theoretical perspectives.

Critical research can be best understood in the context of the empowerment of individuals. Inquiry that aspires to the name "critical" must be connected to an attempt to confront the injustice of a particular society or sphere within the society. Research thus becomes a transformative endeavor unembarrassed by the label "political" and unafraid to consummate a relationship with an emancipatory consciousness. Whereas traditional researchers cling to the guard rail of neutrality, critical researchers frequently announce their partisanship in the struggle for a better world. Traditional researchers see their task as the description, interpretation, or reanimation of a slice of reality, whereas critical researchers often regard their work as a first step toward forms of political action that can redress the injustices found in the field site or constructed in the very act of research itself. Horkheimer (1972) put it succinctly when he argued that critical theory and research are never satisfied with merely increasing knowledge (see also Giroux 1983, 1988, 1997; Agger 1998; Shor 1996; Anderson 1989; Britzman 1991; Kincheloe 1991; Kincheloe and Steinberg 1993; Quantz 1992; Villaverde and Kincheloe 1998).

Research in the critical tradition takes the form of self-conscious criticism—self-conscious in the sense that researchers try to become aware of the ideological imperatives and epistemological presuppositions that inform their research as well as their own subjective, intersubjective, and normative reference claims. Thus critical researchers enter into an investigation with their assumptions on the table, so no one is confused concerning the epistemological and political baggage they bring with them to the research site. Upon detailed analysis, these assumptions may change. Stimulus for change may come from the critical researchers' recognition that such assumptions are not leading to emancipatory actions. The source of this emancipatory action involves the researchers' ability to expose the contradictions of world of appearances accepted by the dominant culture as natural and inviolable (Giroux 1983, 1988, 1997; McLaren 1992a, 1997; San Juan 1992; Zizek 1990). Such appearances may, critical researchers contend, conceal social relationships of inequality and injustice. For instance, if we view the violence we find in classrooms not as random or isolated incidents created by aberrant individuals willfully stepping out of line in accordance with a particular form of social pathology, but as narratives of transgression and resistance, then this could indicate that the "political unconscious" lurking beneath the surface of everyday classroom life is not unrelated to issues of race, class, and gender oppression.

## Babes in Toyland: Critical
## Theory in Hyperreality

### Postmodern Culture

Over the last quarter of the twentieth century, traditional notions of critical theory have had to come to terms with the rise of postmodernism. Our reconceptualized notion of critical theory is our way of denoting the conversation between traditional criticalism and postmodernism (Kincheloe, Steinbreg, and Tippins 1999). We will first analyze postmodernism and then address the relationship between it and our notion of critical theory.

In a contemporary era marked by the delegitimation of the grand narratives of Western civilization, a loss of faith in the power of reason, and a shattering of traditional religious orthodoxies, scholars continue to debate what the term *postmodernism* means, generally positing it as a periodizing concept following modernism. Indeed, scholars have not agreed if this epochal break with the "modern" era even constitutes a discrete period. In the midst of such confusion it seems somehow appropriate that scholars are fighting over the application of the term postmodernism to the contemporary condition. Accepting postmodernism as an apt moniker for the end of the twentieth century, a major feature of critical academic work has involved the exploration of what happens when critical theory encounters the postmodern condition, or hyperreality. Hyperreality is a term used to describe an information society socially saturated with ever-increasing forms of representation: filmic, photographic, electronic, and so on. These have had a profound effect on constructing the cultural narratives that shape our identities. The drama of living has been portrayed so often on television that individuals, for the most part, are increasingly able to predict the outcomes and consider such outcomes to be the "natural" and "normal" course of social life (Gergen 1991; Kellner 1995; Morley and Chen 1996; Nicholson and Seidman 1995; Fraser 1995; Heshusius and Ballard 1996).

As many postmodern analysts have put it, we become pastiches, imitative conglomerations of one another. In such a condition, we approach life with low affect, with a sense of postmodern ennui and irremissible anxiety. Our emotional bonds are diffused as television, computers, VCRs, and stereo headphones assault us with representations that have shaped our cognitive and affective facilities in ways that still remain insufficiently understood. In the political arena, traditionalists circle their cultural wagons and fight off imagined bogeymen such as secular humanists, "extreme liberals," and utopianists, not realizing the impact that postmodern hyperreality exerts on their hallowed institutions. The nuclear family, for example, has declined in importance not because of the assault of "radical feminists," but because the home has been redefined through the familiar presence of electronic communication systems. Particular modes of information put individual family members in constant contact with specific subcultures. While they are physically in the home, they exist emotionally outside of it through the mediating effects of various forms of communication (Gergen 1991; McLaren 1997; Poster 1989; Steinberg and Kincheloe 1997; McGuigan 1996). We increasingly make sense of the social world and judge other cultures through conventional and culture-bound television genres. Hyperreality has presented us with new forms of literacy that do not simply refer to discrete skills but rather constitute social skills and relations of symbolic power. These new technologies cannot be seen apart from the social and institutional contexts in which they are used and the roles they play in the family, the community, and the workplace. They also need to be seen in terms of how "viewing competencies" are socially distributed and the diverse social and discursive practices in which these new media literacies are produced (Buckingham 1989; Taylor and Saarinen 1994; Hall 1997).

Electronic transmissions generate new formations of cultural space and restructure experiences of time. We often are motivated to trade community membership for a sense of psuedo belonging to the mediascape. Residents of hyperreality are temporarily comforted by proclamations of community offered by "media personalities" on the 6 o'clock Eyewitness News. "Bringing news of your neighbors in the Tri-State community home to you," media marketers attempt to soften the edges of hyperreality, to soften the emotional effects of the social vertigo. The world is not brought into our homes by television as much as television brings its viewers to a quasi-fictional place—hyperreality (Luke 1991).

## Postmodern Social Theory

We believe that it is misleading to identify postmodernism with poststructuralism. Although there are certainly similarities involved, they cannot be considered discrete homologies. We also believe that it is a mistake to equate postmodernism with postmodernity or that these terms can be contrasted in some simple equivalent way with modernism and modernity. As Michael Peters (1993) notes, "To do so is to frame up the debate in strictly (and naively) modernist terminology which employs exhaustive binary oppositions privileging one set of terms against the other" (p. 14). We are using the term postmodernity to refer to the postmodern condition that we have described as *hyperreality* and the term postmodern theory as an umbrella term that includes antifoundationalist writing in philosophy and the social sciences. Again, we are using the term in a very general sense that includes poststructuralist currents.

Postmodern theoretical trajectories take as their entry point a rejection of the deeply ingrained assumptions of Enlightenment rationality, traditional Western epistemology, or any supposedly "secure" representation of reality that exists outside of discourse itself. Doubt is cast on the myth of the autonomous, transcendental subject, and the concept of praxis is marginalized in favor of rhetorical undecidability and textual analysis of social practices. As a species of criticism, intended, in part, as a central requestioning of the humanism and anthropologism of the early 1970s, postmodernist social theory rejects Hegel's ahistorical state of absolute knowledge and resigns itself to the impossibility of an ahistorical, transcendental, or self-authenticating version of truth. The reigning conviction that knowledge is knowledge only if it reflects the world as it "really" exists has been annihilated in favor of a view in which reality is socially constructed or semiotically posited. Furthermore, normative agreement on what should constitute and guide scientific practice and argumentative consistency has become an intellectual target for epistemological uncertainty (Shelton 1996; Pinar, Reynolds, Slattery, and Taubman 1995).

Postmodern criticism takes as its starting point the notion that meaning is constituted by the continual playfulness of the signifier, and the thrust of its critique is aimed at deconstructing Western metanarratives of truth and the ethnocentrism implicit in the European view of history as the unilinear progress of universal reason. Postmodern theory is a site of both hope and fear, where there exists a strange convergence between critical theorists and political conservatives, between a cynical complicity with status quo of social and institutional relations and a fierce criticism of ideological manipulation.

## Ludic and Resistance Postmodernism

Postmodernist criticism is not monolithic, and for the purposes of this essay we would like to distinguish between two theoretical strands. The first has been astutely described by Teresa Ebert (1991) as "ludic postmodernism" (p. 115)—an approach to social theory that is decidedly limited in its ability to transform oppressive social and political regimes of power. Ludic postmodernism generally occupies itself with a reality that is constituted by the continual playfulness of the signifier and the heterogeneity of differences. As such, ludic postmodernism (see, e.g., Lyotard, Derrida, Baudrillard) constitutes a moment of self-reflexivity in deconstructing Western metanarratives, asserting that "meaning itself is self-divided and undecidable."

We want to argue that critical researchers should assume a cautionary stance toward ludic postmodernism critique because, as Ebert (1991) notes, it tends to reinscribe the status quo and reduce history to the supplementarity of signification or the free-floating trace of textuality. As a mode of critique, it rests its case on interrogating specific and local enunciations of oppression, but often fails to analyze such enunciations in relation to larger dominating structures of oppression (Aronowitz and Giroux 1991; McLaren 1995; Sünker 1998).

The kind of postmodern social theory we want to pose as a counterweight to skeptical and spectral postmodernism has been referred to as oppositional postmodernism, radical critique-al theory, "postmodern education" (Aronowitz and Giroux 1991), "resistance postmodernism" (Ebert 1991), "affirmative postmodernism" (Slattery 1995), and "critical postmodernism" (Giroux 1997; McLaren and Hammer 1989), and "postformalism" (Kincheloe 1993, 1995; Kincheloe and Steinberg 1993; Kincheloe, Steinberg, and Hinchey 1999; Kincheloe, Steinberg, and Villaverde 1999). These forms of critique are not alternatives to ludic postmodernism but appropriations and extensions of this critique. Resistance postmodernism brings to ludic critique a form of materialist intervention, because it is not solely based on a textual theory of difference but rather on one that is also social and historical. In this way, postmodern critique can serve as an interventionist and transformative critique of Western culture. Following Ebert (1991), resistance postmodernism attempts to show that "textualities (significations) are material practices, forms of conflicting social relations" (p. 115). The sign is always an arena of material conflict and competing social relations as well as ideas. From this perspective, we can rethink a signifier as an ideological dynamic ever related to a contextually possible set of signifieds. In other words, difference is politicized by being situated in real social and historical conflicts.

The synergism of the conversation between resistance postmodernism and critical theory involves an interplay between the praxis of the critical and the radical uncertainty of the postmodern. As it invokes its strategies for the emancipation of meaning, critical theory provides the postmodern critique with a normative foundation (i.e., a basis for distinguishing between oppressive and liberatory social relations). Without such a foundation, the postmodern critique is ever vulnerable to nihilism and inaction. Indeed, the normatively ungrounded postmodern critique is incapable of providing an ethically challenging and politically transformative program of action. Aronowitz, Giroux, Kincheloe, and McLaren argue that if the postmodern critique is to make a valuable contribution to the notion of schooling as an emancipatory form of cultural politics, it must make connections to those egalitarian impulses of modernism that contribute to an emancipatory democracy. In doing this, the project of an emancipatory democracy and the schooling that supports it can be extended by new understandings of how power operates and by incorporating groups who had been excluded by their race, gender, or class (Aronowitz and Giroux 1991; Codd 1984; Godzich 1992; Lash 1990; McLaren 1995b, 1997; Morrow 1991; Rosenau 1992; Welch 1991; Yates 1990; Kincheloe 1995, 1999; Steinberg and Kincheloe 1998; Surber 1998; Wexler 1996a, 1996b, 1997; Pinar 1994, 1998).

## Critical Research and Cultural Studies

Cultural studies is an interdisciplinary, transdisciplinary, and sometimes counter-disciplinary field that functions within the dynamics of competing definitions of culture. Unlike traditional humanistic studies, cultural studies questions the equation of culture with high culture; instead, cultural studies asserts that myriad expressions of cultural production should be analyzed in relation to other cultural dynamics and social and historical structures. Such a position commits cultural studies to a potpourri of artistic, religious, political, economic, and communicative activities. In this context, it is important to note that while cultural studies is associated with the study of popular culture, it is not primarily about popular culture. Cultural studies interests are much broader and tend to generally involve the production and nature of the rules of inclusivity and exclusivity that guide academic evaluation—in particular, the way these rules shape and are shaped by relations of power. The rules that guide academic evaluation are inseparable from the rules of knowledge production and research. Thus, cultural studies provides a disciplinary critique that holds many implications (Grossberg 1995; McLaren 1995b; Abercrombie 1994; Woodward 1997; Ferguson and Golding 1997; Hall and du Gay 1996).

One of the most important sites of theoretical production in the history of critical research has been the Centre for Contemporary Cultural Studies (CCCS) at the University of Birmingham. Attempting to connect critical theory with the particularity of everyday experience, the CCCS researchers have argued that all experience is vulnerable to ideological inscription. At the same time, they have maintained that theorizing outside of everyday experience results in formal and deterministic theory. An excellent representative of the CCCS's perspectives is Paul Willis, who published *Learning to Labour: How Working Class Kids Get Working Class Jobs* in 1977, seven years after Colin Lacey's *Hightown Grammar* (1970). Redefining the nature of ethnographic research in a critical manner, *Learning to Labour* inspired a spate of critical studies: David Robins and Philip Cohen's *Knuckle Sandwich: Growing Up in the Working-Class City* in 1978, Paul Corrigan's *Schooling the Smash Street Kids* in 1979, and Dick Hebdige's *Subculture: The Meaning of Style* in 1979.

Also following Willis's work were critical feminist studies, including an anthology titled *Women Take Issue* (Centre for Contemporary Culture Studies 1978). In 1985 Christine Griffin published *Typical Girls?*, the first extended feminist study produced by the CCCS. Conceived as a response to Willis's *Learning to Labour, Typical Girls?* analyzes adolescent female consciousness as it is constructed in a world of patriarchy. Through their recognition of patriarchy as a major disciplinary technology in the production of subjectivity, Griffin and the members of the CCCS gender study group move critical research in a multicultural direction. In addition to the examination of class, gender and racial analyses are beginning to gain in importance (Quantz 1992). Poststructuralism frames power not simply as one aspect of a society, but as the basis of society. Thus patriarchy is not simply one isolated force among many with which women must contend; patriarchy informs all aspects of the social and effectively shapes women's lives (see also Frankenberg 1993; Franz and Stewart 1994; Douglas 1994; Fine, Weis, Powell, and Wong 1997; Shohat and Stam 1994; Finders 1997).

Cornel West (1993) pushes critical research even further into the multicultural domain as he focuses critical attention on women, the Third World, and race. Adopting theoretical advances in neo-Marxist postcolonialism criticism and cultural studies, he is able to shed greater light on the workings of power in everyday life. In this context Ladislaus Semali and Joe Kincheloe (1999) in *What Is Indigenous Knowledge? Voices from the Academy* explore the power of indigenous knowledge as a resource for critical attempts to bring about social change. Critical researchers, they argue, should analyze such knowledges in order to understand emotions, sensitivities, and epistemologies that move in ways unimagined by many Western knowledge producers. In this post-colonially informed context Semali and Kincheloe employ concerns raised by indigenous knowledge to challenge the academy, its "normal science," and its accepted notions of certified information. Moving the conversation about critical research in new directions, the authors understand the conceptual inseparability of valuing indigenous knowledge, developing postcolonial forms of resistance, academic reform, the reconceptualization of research and interpretation, and the struggle for social justice.

In *Schooling as a Ritual Performance*, Peter McLaren (1995b) integrates poststructuralist and postcolonial theory with the project of cultural studies, critical pedagogy, and critical ethnography. He grounds his theoretical analysis in the poststructuralist claim that the connection of signifier and signified is arbitrary yet shaped by historical, cultural, and economic forces. The primary cultural narrative that defines school life is the resistance by students to the school's attempts to marginalize their street culture and street knowledge. McLaren analyzes the school as a cultural site where symbolic capital is struggled over in the form of ritual dramas. *Schooling as a Ritual Performance* adopts the position that researchers are unable to grasp themselves or others introspectively without social mediation through their positionalities with respect to race, class, gender, and other configurations. The visceral, bodily forms of knowledge, and the rhythms and gestures of the street culture of the students, are distinguished from the formal abstract knowledge of classroom instruction. Knowledge as it is constructed informally outside of the culture of school instruction is regarded by the teachers as threatening to the universalist and decidedly Eurocentric ideal of high culture that forms the basis of the school curriculum.

As critical researchers pursue the reconceptualization of critical theory pushed by its synergistic relationship with cultural studies, postmodernism, and poststructuralism, they are confronted with the post-discourses' redefinition of critical notions of democracy in terms of multiplicity and difference. Traditional notions of community often privilege unity over diversity in the name of Enlightenment values. Poststructuralists in general and post-structuralist feminists in particular see this communitarian dream as politically disabling because of the suppression of race, class, and gender differences and the exclusion of subaltern voices and marginalized groups whom community members are loath to engage. What begins to emerge in this instance is the movement of feminist theoretical concerns to the center of critical theory. Indeed, after the feminist critique critical theory can never return to a paradigm of inquiry in which the concept of social class is antiseptically privileged and exalted as the master concept in the Holy Trinity of Race, Class, and Gender. A critical theory reconceptualized by poststructuralism and feminism promotes a politics of difference that refuses to pathologize or exoticize the Other. In this context, communities are more prone to revitalization and revivification (Wexler 1996b, 1997); peripheralized groups in the thrall of a condescending Eurocentric gaze are able to edge closer to the borders of respect, and "classified" objects of research potentially acquire the characteristics of subjecthood. Kathleen Weiler's *Women Teaching for Change: Gender, Class, and Power* (1988) serves as a good example of critical research framed by feminist theory. Weiler shows not only how feminist theory can extend critical research, but how the concept of emancipation can be reconceptualized in light of a feminist epistemology (Aronowitz and Giroux 1991; Lugones 1987; Morrow 1991; Young 1990; Rand 1995; King and Mitchell 1995; Steinberg 1997; Maher and Tetreault 1994; Christian-Smith 1999; Hammer 1999; Bersani 1995; Clatterbaugh 1997; Cooper 1994; Hedley 1994; Johnson 1996; Kelly 1996; Sedgwick 1995; Britzman 1995; Clough 1995; Behar and Gordon 1995; Brents and Monson 1998; Scott 1992).

## Focusing on Critical Ethnography

As critical researchers attempt to get behind the curtain, to move beyond assimilated experience, to expose the way ideology constrains the desire for self-direction, and to confront the way power reproduces itself in the construction of human consciousness, they employ a plethora of research methodologies. In this context Patti Lather (1991, 1993) extends our position with her notion of catalytic validity. Catalytic validity points to the degree to which research moves those it studies to understand the world and the way it is shaped in order for them to transform it. Noncritical researchers who operate within an empiricist framework will perhaps find catalytic validity to be a strange concept. Research that possesses catalytic validity will not only display the reality-altering impact of the inquiry process, it will also direct this impact so that those under study will gain self-understanding and self-direction.

Theory that falls under the rubric of "post-colonialism" (see Semali and Kincheloe 1999; McLaren 1999) involves important debates over the knowing subject and object of analysis. Such works have initiated important new modes of analysis, especially in relation to questions of imperialism, colonialism, and neo-colonialism. Recent attempts by critical researchers to move beyond the objectifying and imperialist gaze associated with the Western anthropological tradition (which fixes the image of the so-called informant from the colonizing perspective of the knowing subject), although laudatory and well-intentioned, are not without their shortcomings (Bourdieu and Wacquaat 1992). As Fuchs (1993) has so presciently observed, serious limitations plague recent efforts to develop a more reflective approach to ethnographic writing. The challenge here can be summarized in the following questions: How does the knowing subject come to know the Other? How can researchers respect the perspective of the Other and invite the Other to speak (Semali and Kincheloe 1999; Prakash and Esteva 1998; Myrsiades and Myrsiades 1998; Macedo 1994; Abdullah and Stringer 1999; Ashcroft, Griffiths, and Tiffin 1995; Brock-Utne 1996; Pieterse and Parekh 1995; Schurich and Young 1997; Goldie 1995; Viergever 1999; Swartz 1998; Rains 1998)?

Although recent confessional modes of ethnographic writing attempt to treat so-called informants as "participants" in an attempt to avoid the objectification of the Other (usually referring to the relationship between Western anthropologists and non-Western culture), there is a risk that uncovering colonial and postcolonial structures of domination may, in fact, unintentionally validate and consolidate such structures as well as reassert liberal values through a type of covert ethnocentrism. Fuchs (1993) warns that the attempt to subject researchers to the same approach to which other societies are subjected could lead to an "'othering' of one's own world" (p. 108). Such an attempt often fails to question existing ethnographic methodologies and therefore unwittingly extends their validity and applicability while further objectifying the world of the researcher.

Michel Foucault's approach to this dilemma is to "detach" social theory from the epistemology of his own culture by criticizing the traditional philosophy of reflection. However, Foucault falls into the trap of ontologizing his own methodological argumentation and erasing the notion of prior understanding that is linked to the idea of an "inside" view (Fuchs, 1993). Louis Dumont fares somewhat better by arguing that cultural texts need to be viewed simultaneously from the inside and from the outside. However, in trying to affirm a "reciprocal interpretation of various societies among themselves" (Fuchs 1993: 113) through identifying both transindividual structures of consciousness and transsubjective social structures, Dumont aspires to a universal framework for the comparative analysis of societies. Whereas Foucault and Dumont attempt to "transcend the categorical foundations of their own world" (Fuchs 1993: 118) by refusing to include themselves in the process of objectification, Pierre Bourdieu integrates himself as a social actor into the social field under analysis. Bourdieu achieves such integration by "epistemologizing the ethnological content of his own presuppositions" (p.121). But the self-objectification of the observer (anthropologist) is not unproblematic. Fuchs (1993) notes, after Bourdieu, that the chief difficulty is "forgetting the difference between the theoretical and the practical relationship with the world and of imposing on the object the theoretical relationship one maintains with it" (p. 120). Bourdieu's approach to research does not fully escape becoming, to a certain extent, a "confirmation of objectivism," but at least there is an earnest attempt by the researcher to reflect on the preconditions of his own self-understanding—an attempt to engage in an "ethnography of ethnographers" (p. 122).

Postmodern ethnography often intersects—to varying degrees—with the concerns of postcolonialist researchers, but the degree to which it fully addresses issues of exploitation and the social relations of capitalist exploitation remains questionable. Postmodern ethnography—and we are thinking here of works such as Paul Rabinow's *Reflections on Fieldwork in Morocco* (1977), James Boon's *Other Tribes, Other Scribes* (1982), and Michael Taussig's *Shamanism, Colonialism, and the Wild Man* (1987)—shares the conviction articulated by Marc Manganaro (1990) that "no anthropology is apolitical, removed from ideology and hence from the capacity to be affected by or, as crucially, to effect social formations. The question ought not to be if an anthropological text is political, but rather, what kind of sociopolitical affiliations are tied to particular anthropological texts" (p. 35).

Judith Newton and Judith Stacey (1992–1993) note that the current postmodern textual experimentation of ethnography credits the "postcolonial predicament of culture as the opportunity for anthropology to reinvent itself" (p. 56). Modernist ethnography, according to these authors, "constructed authoritative cultural accounts that served, however inadvertently, not only to establish the authority of the Western ethnographer over native others but also to sustain Western authority over colonial cultures." They argue (following James Clifford) that ethnographers can and should try to escape the recurrent allegorical genre of colonial ethnography—the pastoral, a nostalgic, redemptive text that preserves a primitive culture on the brink of extinction for the historical record of its Western conquerors. The narrative structure of this "salvage text" portrays the native culture as a coherent, authentic, and lamentably "evading past," while its complex, inauthentic, Western successors represent the future (p. 56).

Postmodern ethnographic writing faces the challenge of moving beyond simply the reanimation of local experience, an uncritical celebration of cultural difference (including figural differentiations within the ethnographer's own culture), and the employment of a framework that espouses universal values and a global role for interpretivist anthropology (Silverman 1990). What we have described as resistance postmodernism can help qualitative researchers challenge dominant Western research practices that are underwritten by a foundational epistemology and a claim to universally valid knowledge at the expense of local, subjugated knowledges (Peters 1993). The choice is not one between modernism and postmodernism, but one of whether or not to challenge the presuppositions that inform the normalizing judgments one makes as a researcher. Vincent Crapanzano (1990) warns that "the anthropologist can assume neither the Orphic lyre nor the crown of thorns, although I confess to hear salvationist echoes in his desire to protect his people" (p. 301).

The work of James Clifford, which shares an affinity with ethnographic work associated with Georges Bataille, Michel Lerris, and the College de Sociologie, is described by Connor (1992) as not simply the "writing of culture" but rather "the interior disruption of categories of art and culture correspond[ing] to a radically dialogic form of ethnographic writing, which takes place across and between cultures" (p. 251). Clifford (1992) describes his own work as an attempt "to multiply the hands and discourses involved in 'writing culture' . . . not to assert a naive democracy of plural authorship, but to loosen at least somewhat the monological control of the executive writer/ anthropologist and to open for discussion ethnography's hierarchy and negotiation of discourses in power-charged, unequal situations" (p. 100). Citing the work of Marcus and Fischer (1986), Clifford warns against modernist ethnographic practices of "representational essentializing" and "metonymic freezing" in which one aspect of a group's life is taken to represent them as a whole; instead, Clifford urges forms of multilocale ethnography to reflect the "transnational political, economic and cultural forces that traverse and constitute local or regional worlds" (p. 102). Rather than fixing culture into reified textual portraits, culture needs to be better understood as displacement, transplantation, disruption, positionality, and difference.

Although critical ethnography allows, in a way conventional ethnography does not, for the relationship of liberation and history, and although its hermeneuticical task is to call into question the social and cultural conditioning of human activity and the prevailing sociopolitical structures, we do not claim that this is enough to restructure the social system. But it is certainly, in our view, a necessary beginning. We follow Patricia Ticineto Clough (1998) in arguing that "realist narrativity has allowed empirical social science to be the platform and horizon of social criticism" (p. 135). Ethnography needs to be analyzed critically not only in terms of its field methods but also as reading and writing practices. Data collection must give way to "rereadings of representations in every form" (p. 137). In the narrative construction of its authority as empirical science, ethnography needs to face the unconscious processes upon which it justifies its canonical formulations, processes that often involve the disavowal of oedipal or authorial desire and the reduction of differences to binary oppositions. Within these processes of binary reduction, the male ethnographer is most often privileged as the guardian of "the factual representation of empirical positivities" (p. 9).

## New Questions Concerning
## Validity in Critical Ethnography

Critical research traditions have arrived at the point where they recognize that claims to truth are always discursively situated and implicated in relations of power. Yet, unlike some claims made within "ludic" strands of postmodernist research, we do not suggest that because we cannot know truth absolutely, that truth can simply be equated with an effect of power. We say this because truth involves regulative rules that must be met for some statements to be more meaningful than others. Otherwise, truth becomes meaningless and, if this is the case, liberatory praxis has no purpose other than to win for the sake of winning (Carspecken 1993). As Phil Carspecken remarks, every time we act, in every instance of our behavior, we presuppose some normative or universal relation to truth. Truth is internally related to meaning in a pragmatic way through normative referenced claims, intersubjective referenced claims, subjective referenced claims, and the way we deictically ground or anchor meaning in our daily lives.

Carspecken explains that researchers are able to articulate the normative evaluative claims of others when they begin to see them in the same way as their participants by living inside the cultural and discursive positionalities that inform such claims. Claims to universality must be recognized in each particular normative claim and questions must be raised about whether such norms represent the entire group. When the limited claim of universality is seen to be contradictory to the practices under observation, power relations become visible. What is crucial here, according to Carspecken, is that researchers recognize where they are ideologically located in the normative and identity claims of others and, at the same time, be honest about their own subjective referenced claims and not let normative evaluative claims interfere with what is observed. Critical research continues to problematize normative and universal claims in a way that does not permit them to be analyzed outside of a politics of representation, divorced from the material conditions in which they are produced, or outside of a concern with the constitution of the subject in the very acts of reading and writing.

In his latest book, *Critical Ethnography in Educational Research*, Carspecken (1996) addresses the issue of critical epistemology, an understanding of the relationship between power and thought, and power and truth claims. In a short exposition of what is "critical" to critical epistemology, he debunks facile forms of social constructivism and offers a deft criticism of mainstream epistemologies by way of continental phenomenology, poststructuralism, and postmodernist social theory, mainly the work of Edmund Husserl and Jacques Derrida. Carspecken makes short work of facile forms of constructivist thought which purports that what we see is strongly influenced by what we already value and that criticalist research simply indulges itself in the 'correct ' political values. For instance, some constructivists argue that all that criticalists need to do is to 'bias' their work in the direction of social justice. This form of constructivist thought is not viable according to Carspecken because it is plainly ocularcentric, that is, it depends upon visual perception to form the basis of its theory. Rather than rely on perceptual metaphors found in mainstream ethnographic accounts, critical ethnography, in contrast, should emphasize communicative experiences and structures as well as cultural typifications.

Carspecken argues that critical ethnography needs to differentiate among ontological categories (i.e., subjective, objective, normative-evaluative) rather than adopt the position of "multiple realities" defended by many constructivists. Carspecken adopts a principled position that research value orientations should not determine research findings, as much as this is possible. Rather, critical ethnographers should employ a critical epistemology; that is, they should uphold epistemological principles that apply to all researchers. In fecundating this claim, Carspecken rehabilitates critical ethnography from many of the misperceptions of its critics who believe that it ignores questions of validity.

To construct a socially critical epistemology, critical ethnographers need to understand holistic modes of human experience and their relationship to communicative structures. Preliminary stages of this process articulated by Carspecken include examining researcher bias and discovering researcher value orientations. Following stages include: compiling the primary record through the collection of monological data; preliminary reconstructive analysis; dialogical data generation; discovering social systems relations; and using systems relations to explain findings. Anthony Giddens's work forms the basis of Carspecken's approach to systems analysis. Accompanying discussions of each of the complex stages developed by Carspecken are brilliantly articulated approaches to horizontal and vertical validity reconstructions and pragmatic horizons of analysis. In order to help link theory to practice, Carspecken uses data from his study of an inner-city Houston elementary school program that is charged with helping students learn conflict management skills.

Another impressive feature is Carspecken's exposition and analysis of communicative acts, especially his discussion of meaning as embodiment and of understanding as intersubjective, not objective or subjective. Carspecken works from a view of intersubjectivity that combines Hegel, Mead, Habermas, and Taylor. He recommends that critical ethnographers record body language carefully because the meaning of an action is not in the language, it is rather in the action and bodily states. In Carspecken's view, subjectivity is derivative from intersubjectivity (as is objectivity). And intersubjectivity involves the dialogical constitution of the "feeling body." Finally, Carspecken stresses the importance of macrolevel social theories, environmental conditions, socially structured ways of meeting needs and desires, effects of cultural commodities on students, economic exploitation, and political and cultural conditions of action.

Much of Carspecken's inspiration for his approach to validity claims is taken from Habermas's theory of communicative action. Carspecken reads Habermas as grasping the prelinguistic foundations of language and intersubjectivity, making language secondary to the concept of intersubjectivity. Yet Carspecken departs from a strict Habermasian view of action by bringing in an expressive/praxis model roughly consistent with Charles Taylor's work. While Habermas and Taylor frequently argue against each others' positions, Carspecken puts them together in a convincing manner. Taylor's emphasis on holistic modes of understanding and the act constitution that Carspecken employs make it possible to link the theory of communicative rationality to work on embodied meaning and the metaphoric basis of meaningful action. It also provides a means for synthesizing Giddens's ideas on part/whole relations, virtual structure, and act constitution with communicative rationality. This is another way in which Carspecken's work differs from Habermas and yet remains consistent with his theory and the internal link between meaning and validity.

## Recent Innovations in Critical Ethnography

In addition to Carspecken's brilliant insights into critically-grounded ethnography, the late 1990s have witnessed a proliferation of deconstructive approaches as well as reflexive approaches (this discussion is taken from Trueba and McLaren, in press). In her important book, *Fictions of Feminist Ethnography*, Kamala Visweswaran (1994) maintains that reflexive ethnography, like normative ethnography, rests on the "declarative mode" of imparting knowledge to a reader whose identity is anchored in a shared discourse. Deconstructive ethnography, in contrast, enacts the "interrogative mode" through a constant deferral or a refusal to explain or interpret. Within deconstructive ethnography, the identity of the reader with a unified subject of enunciation is discouraged. Whereas reflexive ethnography maintains that the ethnographer is not separate from the object of investigation, the ethnographer is still viewed as a unified subject of knowledge that can make hermeneuticic efforts to establish identification between the observer and the observed (as in modernist interpretive traditions). Deconstructive ethnography, in contrast, often disrupts such identification in favor of articulating a fractured, destabilized, multiply-positioned subjectivity (as in postmodernist interpretive traditions). Whereas reflexive ethnography questions its own authority, deconstructive ethnography forfeits its authority. Both approaches to critical ethnography can be used to uncover the clinging Eurocentric authority employed by ethnographers in the study of Latino/a populations. The goal of both these approaches is criticalist in nature: that is, to free the object of analysis from the tyranny of fixed, unassailable categories and to rethink subjectivity itself as a permanently unclosed, always partial, narrative engagement with text and context. Such an approach can help the ethnographer to caution against the damaging depictions propagated by Anglo observers about Mexican immigrants. As Ruth Behar (1993) notes: In classical sociological and ethnographic accounts of the Mexican and Mexican American family, stereotypes similar to those surrounding the black family perpetuated images of the authoritarian, oversexed, and macho husband and the meek and submissive wife surrounded by children who adore their good and suffering mother. These stereo-types have come under strong critique in the last few years, particularly by Chicana critics, who have sought to go beyond the various "deficiency theories" that con-tinue to mark the discussion of African-American and Latina/Latino family life. (p. 276)

The conception of culture advanced by critical ethnographers generally unpacks culture as a complex circuit of production that includes a myriad of dialectically re-initiating and mutually informing set of activities such as routines, rituals, action conditions, systems of intelligibility and meaning-making, conventions of interpretation, systems relations and conditions both external and internal to the social actor (Carspecken, 1996). In her recent ethnograghic study, *Critical Ethnology in Educational Research*, Kathleen Stewart (1996) cogently illustrates the ambivalent character of culture, as well as its fluidity and ungraspable multilayeredness when she remarks:

Culture, as it is seen through its productive forms and means of mediation, is not, then, reducible to a fixed body of social value and belief or a direct precipitant of lived experience in the world but grows into a space on the side of the road where stories weighted with sociality take on a life of their own. We "see" it . . . only by building up multilayered narratives of the poetic in the everyday life of things. We represent it only by roaming from one texted genre to another—romantic, realist, historical, fantastic, sociological, surreal. There is no final textual solution, no way of resolving the dialogic of the interpreter/interpreted or subject/object through efforts to "place" ourselves in the text, or to represent "the fieldwork experience" or to gather up the voices of the other as if they could speak for themselves. (p. 210)

According to E. San Juan (1996), a renewed understanding of culture—as both discursive and material—becomes the linchpin for any emancipatory politics. He writes that the idea of culture as social processes and practices that are thoroughly grounded in material social relations—in the systems of maintenance (economics), decision (politics), learning and communication (culture), and generation and nurture (the domain of social reproduction)—must be the grounding principle, or paradigm if you like, of any progressive and emancipatory approach (p. 177).

Rejecting the characterization of anthropologists as either "adaptational-ists" (e.g., Marvin Harris) or "ideationalists" (e.g., cognitivists, Levi-Straussian structuralists, Schneiderian symbolists, Geertzian interpretivists), E. Valentine Daniel (1996) has remarked in his new ethnography, *Charred Lullabies: Chapters in an Anthropology of Violence*, that culture is "no longer something out there to be discovered, described, and explained, but rather something into which the ethnographer, as interpreter, enter[s]" (p. 198). Culture, in other words, is co-created by the anthroplogist and informant through conversation. Yet even this semeiosic conceptualization of culture is not without it problems. As Daniel himself notes, even if one considers oneself to be a "culture comaking processualist" in contrast to a "culture-finding essentialist", one still has to recognize that he or she is working within a logocentric tradition that, to a greater or lesser extent, privileges words over actions.

Critical ethnography has benefited from this new understanding of culture and from the new hybridic possibilities for cultural critique that have been opened up by the current blurring and mixing of disciplinary genres—those that emphasize experience, subjectivity, reflexivity, and dialogical understanding. The advantage that follows such perspectives is that social life is not viewed as preontologically available for the researcher to study. It also follows that there is no perspective unspoiled by ideology from which to study social life in an antiseptically objective way. What is important to note here is the stress placed on the ideological situatedness of any descriptive or socioanalytical account of social life. Critical ethnographers such as John and Jean Camaroff (1992) have made a significant contribution to our understanding of the ways in which power is entailed in culture, leading to practices of domination and exploitation that have become naturalized in everyday social life. According to the Camaroffs (1992), hegemony refers to "that order of signs and practices, relations and distinctions, images and epistemologies—drawn from a historically situated cultural field—that come to be taken-for-granted as the natural and received shape of the world and everything that inhabits it" (p. 23). These axiomatic and yet ineffable discourses and practices that are presumptively shared become "ideological" precisely when their internal contradictions are revealed, uncovered, and viewed as arbitrary and negotiable. Ideology, then, refers to a highly articulated worldview, master narrative, or organizing scheme for collective symbolic production. The dominant ideology is the expression of the dominant social group.

Following this line of argument, hegemony "is nonnegotiable and therefore beyond direct argument" whereas ideology "is more susceptible to being perceived as a matter of inimical opinion and interest and therefore is open to contestation" (p. 24). Ideologies become the expressions of specific groups whereas hegemony refers to conventions and constructs that are shared and naturalized throughout a political community. Hegemony works both through silences and repetition in naturalizing the dominant worldview. There also may exist oppositional ideologies among subordinate or subaltern groups—whether well-formed or loosely articulated—that break free of hegemony. In this way hegemony is never total or complete; it is always porous.

## Conclusion: Critical Research in a Globalized, Privatized World

A critical postmodern research requires researchers to construct their perception of the world anew, not just in random ways but in a manner that undermines what appears natural, that opens to question what appears obvious (Slaughter 1989). Oppositional and insurgent researchers as maieutic agents must not confuse their research efforts with the textual suavities of an avant-garde academic posturing in which they are awarded the sinecure of representation for the oppressed without actually having to return to those working-class communities where their studies took place. Rather, they need to locate their work in a transformative praxis that leads to the alleviation of suffering and the overcoming of oppression. Rejecting the arrogant reading of metropolitan critics and their imperial mandates governing research, insurgent researchers ask questions about how what is has come to be, whose interests are served by particular institutional arrangements, and where our own frames of reference come from. Facts are no longer simply "what is"; the truth of beliefs is not simply testable by their correspondence to these facts. To engage in critical postmodern research is to take part in a process of critical world making, guided by the shadowed outline of a dream of a world less conditioned by misery, suffering, and the politics of deceit. It is, in short, a pragmatics of hope in an age of cynical reason. The obstacles that critical postmodern research has yet to overcome in terms of a frontal assault against the ravages of global capitalism and its devastation of the global working class has led McLaren (in press) to a more sustained and sympathetic engagement with Marx and the Marxist tradition.

The educational left in the United States has not been able to provide a counterforce to resist the ferocious orbit of capital and what we believe is the creation of a transnational global society in which the nation-state as the principal form of social organization has been superceded. We see as already underway an integration of all national markets into a single international market and division of labor and the erosion of national affiliations of capital (Robinson 1998). The transnationalism of labor and capital has brought about material shifts in cultural practices and the proliferation of new contradictions between capitalism and labor. The deepening instability following in the wake of global capitalism has been driven by overaccumulation, overinvestment, overcapacity, overproduction, and new developments in the theater of global finance. The bottom line is the production of goods must return a profit by selling at market prices. Despite efforts of working classes throughout the globe to resist capital's drive to exploit their labor, capitalism is able to dynamically and continuously reorganize and reengineer itself such that its drive to accumulate is unhampered. Efforts at regulating markets are not effective at overcoming capital's reign of global terror. What is called for is overturning the basic laws of capitalism and defeating the dominion of capital itself. Capitalism's concentration, centralization, and transnationalism have re-territorialized the laws of motion of capital. We need to view the phenomena of globalized capitalism not merely in terms of market competition but rather from the perspective of production. Since the logic of privatization and free trade—where social labor is the means and measure of value and surplus social labor lies at the heart of profit—now odiously shapes archetypes of citizenship, manages our perceptions of what should constitute the "good society," and creates ideological formations that produce necessary functions for capital in relation to labor, it stands to reason that new ethnographic research approaches must take global capitalism not as an end point of analysis, but as a starting-point. As schools are financed more by corporations that function as service industries for transnational capitalism, and as neo-liberal philosophy continues to guide educational policy and practice, the U.S. population faces a challenging educational reality (Kincheloe 1999). It is a reality that is witnessing the progressive merging of cultural pedagogy to the productive processes within advanced capitalism (McLaren 1997; Giroux and Searles 1996). While as researchers we may not be interested in global capitalism, we can be sure that it is interested in us.

Critical ethnography faces a daunting challenge in the years to come, especially since capitalism has been naturalized as commonsense reality—even as a part of nature itself—while the term "social class" has been replaced by the less antagonistic term "socioeconomic status." The focus of much recent postmodern ethnography is on asymmetrical gender and ethnic relations, and while this focus is important, class struggle has become an outdated issue (Kincheloe and Steinberg 1999). When social class is discussed, it is usually viewed as relational, not as oppositional. In the context of discussions of "social status" rather than "class struggle," postmodern ethnography has secured a privileged position that is functionally advantageous to the socially reproductive logic of entrepreneurial capitalism, private ownership, and the personal appropriation of social production (McLaren 1995). Critical research needs to address more than ever before, the objective, material conditions of the workplace and labor relations in order to prevent the further re-securing of the ideological hegemony of the neo-liberal corporatist state.

In many ways, the globalization process and the strengthening of the free market capitalism that accompanies it takes us back to the roots of critical research. As we have gained profound insights into the impact of the inscriptions of patriarchy, white supremacy, and class elitism on the consciousness of researchers operating under the banner of humanistic values, we also appreciate—mainly because it has profound implications for defeating the exploitation of human labor and the consolidation of a global ruling elite—critical insights into the domination of capital. In this context, we envision important new developments of Marxist ethnographic practices that both compliment and extend many of the exciting new approaches that we are witnessing within the precincts of postmodern and postcolonial ethnography. Future practitioners of critical research must take all of these crucial dynamics into account if their work is to help create a more just, democratic, and egalitarian world. The realm of the critical has yet to reach the potential it envisions. We hope this piece challenges its readers to engage in the hard work and research necessary to move critical praxis closer to its realization.

# References

Abdullah, J., and Stringer, E. "Indigenous Knowledge, Indigenous Learning, Indigenous Research." In L. Semali and J. Kincheloe, ed., *What Is Indigenous Knowledge? Voices from the Academy*. Bristol, Pa.: Falmer Press, 1999.

Abercrombie, N. "Authority and Consumer Society." In R. Keat, N. Whiteley, and N. Abercrombie, ed., *The Authority of the Consumer*. New York: Routledge, 1994.

Agger, B. *Critical Social Theories: An Introduction*. Boulder, Colo.: Westview, 1998.

Agger, B. *The Discourse of Domination: From the Frankfurt School to Postmodernism*. Evanston, Ill.: Northwestern University Press, 1992.

Alexnader, M., and Mohanty, C., ed. *Feminist Genealogies, Colonial Legacies, Democratic Futures*. New York: Routledge, 1997.

Alford, C. "Introduction to the Special Issue on Political Psychology and Political The-ory." *Political Psychology*, 14, no. 2 (1993): 199–208.

Alfino, M., J. Caputo, and R. Wynyard, ed. *McDonaldization Revisited: Critical Essays on Consumer and Culture*. Westport, Conn.: Praeger, 1998.

Allison, C. "Okie Narratives: Agency and Whiteness." In J. Kincheloe, S. Steinberg, N. Rodriguez, and R. Chennault, ed., *White Reign: Deploying Whiteness in America*. New York: St. Martin's, 1998.

Anijar, K. "Childhood and Caring: A Capitalist Taxonomy of the Mar(x)ket Place." In M. Hauser and J. Jipson, ed., *Intersections: Feminisms/Early Childhoods*. New York: Peter Lang, 1998.

Anderson, G. "Critical Ethnography in Education: Origins, Current Status, and New Directions." *Review of Educational Research*, 59 (1989): 249–70.

Apple, M. "Dominance and Dependency: Situating *The Bell Curve* within the Conserva-tive Restoration." In J. Kincheloe, S. Steinberg, and A. Gresson, ed., *Measured Lies: The Bell Curve Examined*. New York: St. Martin's, 1996.

Aronowitz, S., and Giroux, H. *Postmodern Education: Politics, Culture, and Social Criticism*. Minneapolis: University of Minnesota Press, 1991.

Ashcroft, B., G. Griffiths, and H. Tiffin, ed. *The Post-Colonial Studies Reader*. New York: Routledge, 1995.

Atwell-Vasey, W. "Psychoanalytic Feminism and the Powerful Teacher." In W. Pinar, ed., *Curriculum: Toward New Identities*. New York: Garland, 1998.

Bartolome, L. *The Misteaching of Academic Discourses: The Politics of Language in the Class-room*. Boulder, Colo.: Westview, 1998.

Barrows, A. "The Ecopsychology of Child Development." In T. Roszak, M. Gomes, and A. Kanner, ed., *Ecopsychology: Restoring the Earth, Healing the Mind*. San Francisco: Sierra Club Books, 1995.

Bauman, Z. *Life in Fragments: Essays in Postmodern Morality*. Cambridge, Mass.: Blackwell, 1995.

Behar, R. *Translated Woman: Crossing the Border with Esperanza's Story*. Boston: Beacon Press, 1993.

Behar, R., and D. Gordon, ed. *Women Writing Culture*. Berkeley: University of California Press, 1995.

Bell, D., and G. Valentine. *Consuming Geographics. We Are Where We Eat*. New York: Routledge, 1997.

Berger, A. *Cultural Criticism: A Primer of Key Concepts*. Thousand Oaks, Calif.: Sage, 1995.

Berry, K. "Nurturing the Imagination of Resistance: Young Adults as Creators of Knowl-edge." In J. Kincheloe and S. Steinberg, ed., *Unauthorized Methods: Strategies for Critic-ial Teaching*. New York: Routledge, 1998.

Bersani, L. "Loving Men." In M. Berger, B. Wallis, and S. Watson, ed., *Constructing Mas-culinity*. New York: Routledge, 1995.

Bertman, S. *Hyperculture: The Human Cost of Speed*. Westport, Conn.: Praeger, 1998.

Blades, D. *Procedures of Power and Curriculum Change: Foucault and the Quest for Possibilities in Science Education.* New York: Peter Lang, 1997.

Block, A. *Occupied Reading: Critical Foundations for an Ecological Theory.* New York: Garland, 1995.

Boon, J. *Other Tribes, Other Scribes: Symbolic Anthropology in the Comparative Study of Cultures, Histories, Religions, and Texts.* Cambridge: Cambridge University Press, 1982.

Bottomore, T. *The Frankfurt School.* London: TaviStock, 1984.

Bourdieu, P., and L. Wacquaat. *An Invitation to Reflexive Sociology.* Chicago: University of Chicago Press, 1992.

Boyles, D. *American Education and Corporations: The Free Market Goes to School.* New York: Garland, 1998.

Brents, B., and M. Monson. "Whitewashing the Strip: The Construction of Whiteness in Las Vegas." In J. Kincheloe, S. Steinberg, N. Rodriguez, and R. Chennault, ed., *White Reign: Deploying Whiteness in America.* New York: St. Martin's, 1998.

Britzman, D., and A. Pitt. "On Refusing One's Place: The Ditchdigger's Dream." In J. Kincheloe, S. Steinberg, and A. Gresson, ed., *Measured Lies: The Bell Curve Examined.* New York: St. Martin's, 1996.

Britzman, D. *Practice Makes Practice: A Critical Study of Learning to Teach.* Albany, N.Y.: State University of New York Press, 1991.

Britzman, D. "What Is This Thing Called Love?" *Taboo: The Journal of Culture and Education,* 1 (1995): 65–93.

Brock-Utne, B. "Reliability and Validity in Qualitative Research within Africa." *International Review of Education,* 42, no. 6 (1996): 605–21.

Brosio, R. *The Radical Democratic Critique of Capitalist Education.* New York: Peter Lang, 1994.

Buckingham, D. "Television Literacy: A Critique." *Radical Philosophy,* 51 (1989): 12–25.

Butler, M. "Negotiating Place: The Importance of Children's Realities." In J. Kincheloe and S. Steinberg, ed., *Students as Researchers: Creating Classrooms that Matter.* London: Falmer Press, 1998.

Camaroff, J., and J. Camaroff. *Ethnography and Historical Imagination.* Oxford: Westview, 1992.

Cannella, G. *Deconstructing Early Childhood Education: Social Justice and Revolution.* New York: Peter Lang, 1997.

Carlson, D., and M. Apple, ed. *Power/Knowledge/Pedagogy: The Meaning of Democratic Education in Unsettling Times.* Boulder, Colo.: Westview, 1998.

Carson, T., and D. Sumora. *Action Research as a Living Practice.* New York: Peter Lang, 1997.

Carspecken, P. *Critical Ethnography in Educational Research.* New York: Routledge, 1996.

Carspecken, P. *Power, Truth, and Method: Outline for a Critical Methodology.* Unpublished manuscript, 1993.

Carter, V. "Computer-Assisted Racism: Toward an Understanding of Cyber-Whiteness." In J. Kincheloe, S. Steinberg, N. Rodriguez, and R. Chennault, ed., *White Reign: Deploying whiteness in America.* New York: St. Martin's, 1998.

Cary, R. "I.Q. as Commodity: The 'New' Economics of Intelligence." In J. Kincheloe, S. Steinberg, and A. Gresson, ed., *Measured Lies: The Bell Curve Examined*. New York: St. Martin's, 1996.

Centre for Contemporary Culture Studies. *Women Take Issue: Aspects of Women's Subordination*. Birmingham, UK: University of Birmingham, Women's Studies Group, 1978.

Clatterbaugh, K. *Contemporary Perspectives on Masculinity: Men, Women, and Politics in Modern Society*. Boulder, Colo.: Westview, 1997.

Clifford, J. "Traveling Cultures." In L. Grossberg, C. Nelson, and P. A. Treichler, ed. *Cultural Studies*. New York: Routledge, 1992.

Clough, P. *Feminist Thought: Power, Desire and Academic Discourse*. Cambridge, UK: Blackwell, 1995.

Clough, P. T. *The End(s) of Ethnography: From Realism to Social Criticism*. New York: Peter Lang, 1998.

Coben, D. *Radical Heroes: Gramsci, Freire and the Politics of Adult Education*. New York: Garland, 1998.

Codd, J. "Introduction." In J. Codd, ed., *Philosophy, Common Sense, and Action in Educational Administration*. Victoria, Australia: Deakin University Press, 1984.

Collins, J. *Architectures of Excess: Cultural Life in the Information Age*. New York: Routledge, 1995.

Connor, S. *Theory and Cultural Value*. Cambridge, UK: Basil Blackwell, 1992.

Cooper, D. "Productive, Relational, and Everywhere? Conceptualizing Power and Resistance within Foucauldian Feminism." *Sociology*, 28, no.2 (1994): 435–54.

Corrigan, P. *Schooling the Smash Street Kids*. London: Macmillan, 1979.

Crapanzano, V. "Afterword." In M. Manganaro, ed. *Modernist Anthropology: From Fieldwork to Text*. Princeton: Princeton University Press, 1990.

Daniel, E. *Charred Lullabies: Chapters in an Anthropology of Violence*. Princeton: Princeton University Press, 1996.

Deetz, S. *Corporations, the Media, Industry, and Society: Ethical Imperatives and Responsibilities*. Paper presented to the International Communication Association, Washington, D.C., 1993.

Denzin, N. "The Art and Politics of Interpretation." In N. Denzin and Y. Lincolns, ed., *Handbook of Qualitative Research*. Thousand Oaks, Calif.: Sage Publications, 1994.

Denzin, N. *Symbolic Interactionism and Cultural Studies: The Politics of Interpretation*. Cambridge, Mass.: Blackwell, 1992.

Dewey, J. *Democracy and Education*. New York: The Free Press, 1916.

Douglas, S. *Where the Girls Are: Growing Up Female in the Mass Media*. New York: Times Books, 1994.

Drummond, L. *American Dreamtime: A Cultural Analysis of Popular Movies, and Their Implications for a Science of Humanity*. Lanham, Md.: Littlefield Adams, 1996.

Du gay, P., et al. *Doing Cultural Studies: The Story of the Sony Walkman*. London: Sage Publications, 1997.

Ebert, T. "Political Semiosis in/or American Cultural Studies." *American Journal of Semiotics*, 8, 113–35.

Elliot, A. *Psychoanalytic Theory: An Introduction*. Cambridge, Mass.: Blackwell, 1994.

Ellis, J. "Interpretive Inquiry as Student Research." In S. Steinberg and J. Kincheloe, ed., *Students as Researchers: Creating Classrooms that Matter*. Bristol, Pa.: Falmer, 1998.

Fehr, D. *Dogs Playing Cards: Powerbrokers of Prejudice in Education, Art, and Culture*. New York: Peter Lang, 1993.

Ferguson, M., and P. Golding, ed. *Cultural Studies in Question*. Thousand Oaks, Calif.: Sage Publications, 1997.

Finders, M. *Just Girls: Hidden Literacies and Life in Junior High*. New York: Teachers College Press, 1997.

Fine, M., L. Weis, L. Powell, and L. Wong. *Off White: Readings on Race, Power, and Society*. New York: Routledge, 1997.

Fiske, J. *Power Plays, Power Works*. New York: Verso, 1993.

Flossner, G., and H. Otto, ed. *Towards More Democracy in Social Services: Models of Culture and Welfare*. New York: de Gruyter, 1998.

Frankenberg, R. *The Social Construction of Whiteness: White Women, Race Matters*. Minneapolis: University of Minnesota Press, 1993.

Franz, C., and A. Stewart, ed. *Women Creating Lives*. Boulder, Colo.: Westview, 1994.

Fraser, N. "Politics, Culture, and the Public Sphere: Toward a Postmodern Conception." In L. Nicholson and S. Seidman, ed., *Social Postmodernism: Beyond Identity Politics*. New York: Cambridge University Press, 1995.

Freire, P. *The Politics of Education: Culture, Power, and Liberation*. South Hadley, Mass.: Bergin and Garvey, 1985.

Fuchs, M. "The Reversal of the Ethnological Perspective: Attempts at Objectifying One's Own Cultural Horizon. Dumont, Foucault, Bourdieu?" *Thesis Eleven*, 34 (1993): 104–25.

Gadamer, H. *Truth and Method*. Trans. J. Weinsheimer and D. Marshall. New York: Crossroads, 1989.

Gall, J., M. Gall, and W. Borg. *Applying Educational Research: A Practical Guide*. New York: Longman, 1999.

Gallagher, S. *Hermeneuticics and Education*. Albany, N.Y.: SUNY Press, 1992.

Garnham, N. "Political Economy and the Practice of Cultural Studies." In M. Ferguson and P. Golding, ed., *Cultural Studies in Question*. Thousand Oaks, Calif.: Sage Publications, 1997.

Gee, J. *Social Linguistics and Literacies: Ideology in Discourses*. 2nd ed. London: Taylor and Francis, 1996.

Gee, J., G. Hull, and C. Lankshear. *The New Work Order: Behind the Language of the New Capitalism*. Boulder, Colo.: Westview, 1996.

Gergen, K. *The Saturated Self: Dilemmas of Identity in Contemporary Life*. New York: Basic Books, 1991.

Gibson, R. *Critical Theory and Education*. London: Hodder and Stroughton, 1986.

Giroux, H. *Pedagogy and the Politics of Hope: Theory, Culture, and Schooling*. Boulder, Colo.: Westview, 1997.

Giroux, H. *Theory and Resistance in Education: A Pedagogy for the Opposition.* South Hadley, Mass.: Bergin and Garvey, 1983.

Giroux, H. "Critical Theory and the Politics of Culture and Voice: Rethinking the Discourse of Educational Research." In R. Sherman and R. Webb, ed., *Qualitative Research in Education: Focus and Methods.* New York: Falmer, 1988.

Giroux, H., and S. Searles. "The Bell Curve Debate and the Crisis of Public Intellectuals." In J. Kincheloe, S. Steinberg, and A. Gresson, ed., *Measured Lies: The Bell Curve Examined.* New York: St. Martin's Press, 1996.

Godzich, W. "Afterword: Reading Against Literacy." In J. F. Lyotard, *The Postmodern Explained.* Minneapolis: University of Minnesota Press, 1992.

Goldie, T. "The Representation of the Indigene." In B. Ashcroft, G. Griffiths, and H. Tiffin, ed., *The Post-Colonial Studies Reader.* New York: Routledge, 1995.

Goldman, R., and S. Papson. "The Postmodernism that Failed." In D. Dickens and A. Fontana, ed., *Postmodernism and Social Inquiry.* New York: Guilford Press, 1994.

Goodson, I. *The Changing Curriculum: Studies in Social Construction.* New York: Peter Lang, 1997.

Goodson, I., and J. Mangan. "Exploring Alternative Perspectives in Educational Research." *Interchange,* 27 (1): 41–59.

Griffin, C. *Typical Girls? Young Women from School to the Job Market.* London: Routledge and Kegan Paul, 1985.

Grondin, J. *Introduction to Philosophical Hermeneuticics.* New Haven, Conn.: Yale University Press, 1994.

Gross, A., and W. Keith, ed. *Rhetorical Hermeneuticics: Invention and Interpretation in the Age of Science.* Albany, NY: State University of New York Press, 1997.

Grossberg, L. *Bringing It All Back Home: Essays on Cultural Studies.* Durham, N.C.: Duke University Press, 1997.

Grossberg, L. "What's in a Name (One More Time)? *Taboo: The Journal of Culture and Education,* 1: 1–37.

Hall, S.,ed. *Representation: Cultural Representations and Signifying Practices.* Thousand Oaks, Calif.: Sage Publications, 1997.

Hall, S., and P. du Gay, ed. *Questions of Cultural Identity.* Thousand Oaks, Calif.: Sage Publications, 1996.

Hebdige, D. *Subculture: The Meaning of Style.* London: Methuen, 1979.

Hedley, M. "The Presentation of Gendered Conflict in Popular Movies: Affective Stereotypes, Cultural Sentiments, and Men's Motivation. *Sex Roles,* 31, nos. 11/12 (1994): 721–40.

Held, D. *Introduction to Critical Theory: Horkheimer to Habermas.* Berkeley: University of California Press, 1980.

Heshusius, L., and K. Ballard, ed. *From Positivism to Interpretivism and Beyond: Tales of Transformation in Educational and Social Research.* New York: Teachers College Press, 1996.

Hinchey, P. *Finding Freedom in the Classroom: A Practical Introduction to Critical Theory.* New York: Peter Lang, 1998.

Horkheimer, M. *Critical Theory*. New York: Seabury, 1972.

Howell, S. "The Learning Organization: Reproduction of Whiteness." In J. Kincheloe, S. Steinberg, N. Rodriquez, R. Chennault, ed., *White Reign: Deploying Whiteness in America*. New York: St. Martin's Press, 1998.

Jardine, D. *To Dwell with a Boundless Heart: Essays in Curriculum Theory, Hermeneuticics, and the Ecological Imagination*. New York: Peter Lang, 1998.

Jay, M. *The Dialectical Imagination: A History of the Frankfurt School and the Institute of Social Research 1923–1950*. Boston: Little, Brown, 1973.

Jipson, J., and N. Paley. *Daredevil Research: Recreating Analytic Practice*. New York: Lang, 1997.

Johnson, C. "Does Capitalism Really Need Patriarchy? Some Old Issues Reconsidered." *Women's Studies International Forum*, 19, no.3 (1996): 193–202.

Joyrich, L. *Reviewing Reception: Television, Gender, and Postmodern Culture*. Bloomington: University of Indiana Press, 1996.

Kellner, D. *Media Culture: Cultural Studies, Identity and Politics between the Modern and the Postmodern*. New York: Routledge, 1995.

Kellner, D., ed. *Baudrillard: A Critical Reader*. Cambridge, Mass.: Blackwell, 1994.

Kellner, D. *Critical Theory, Marxism, and Modernity*. Baltimore: Johns Hopkins University Press, 1989.

Kellogg, D. "Exploring Critical Distance in Science Education: Researching the Implications of Technological Embeddedness." In J. Kincheloe and S. Steinberg, ed., *Students as Researchers: Creating Classrooms that Matter*. London: Falmer, 1998.

Kelly, L. "When Does the Speaking Profit Us? Reflection on the Challenges of Developing Feminist Perspectives on Abuse and Violence by Women." In M. Hester, L. Kelly, and J. Radford, ed., *Women, Violence, and Male Power*. Bristol, Pa.: Open University Press, 1996.

Kincheloe, J. *Teachers as Researchers: Qualitative Paths to Empowerment*. London: Falmer, 1991.

Kincheloe, J. *Toward a Critical Politics of Teacher Thinking: Mapping the Postmodern*. Granby, Mass.: Bergin and Garvey, 1993.

Kincheloe, J. *Toil and Trouble: Good Work, Smart Workers, and the Integration of Academic and Vocational Education*. New York: Peter Lang, 1995.

Kincheloe, J. "Critical Research in Science Education." In B. Fraser and K Tobin, ed., *International Handbook of Science Education* (Part 2). Boston: Kluwer Academic Publishers, 1998.

Kincheloe, J. *How Do We Tell the Workers? The Socio-Education Foundations of Work and Vocational Education*. Boulder, Colo.: Westview, 1999.

Kincheloe, J., and W. Pinar. "Introduction." In J. Kincheloe and W. Pinar, eds., *Curriculum as Social Psychoanalysis: Essays on the Significance of Place*. Albany: State University of New York Press, 1991.

Kincheloe, J., and S. Steinberg. *Changing Multiculturalism: New Times, New Curriculum*. London: Open University Press, 1997.

Kincheloe, J., and S. Steinberg, ed. *Cutting Class: Essays on Socio-Economic Class and Pedagogy*. Lanham, Md.: Rowman & Littlefield, 1999.

Kincheloe, J., and S. Steinberg. "A Tentative Description of Post-Formal Thinking: The Critical Confrontation with Cognitive Theory." *Harvard Educational Review*, 63 (1993): 296–320.

Kincheloe, J., and S. Steinberg. *Students as Researchers*. London: Falmer Press, 1998.

Kincheloe, J., S. Steinberg, and P. Hinchey. *The Post-Formal Reader: Cognition and Education*. New York: Falmer Press, 1999.

Kincheloe, J., S. Steinberg, and D. Tippins. *The Stigma of Genius: Einstein and Beyond Modern Education*. New York: Peter Lang, 1999.

Kincheloe, J., S. Steinberg, N. Rodriquez, and R. Chennault. *White Reign: Deploying Whiteness in America*. New York: St. Martin's Press, 1998.

Kincheloe, J., S. Steinberg, and L. Villaverde, ed. *Rethinking Intelligence: Confronting Psychological Assumptions about Teaching and Learning*. New York: Routledge, 1999.

King, J. "Bad Luck, Bad Blood, Bad Faith: Ideological Hegemony and the Oppressive Language of Hoodoo Social Science." In J. Kincheloe, S. Steinberg, and A. Gresson, ed., *Measured Lies: The Bell Curve Examined*. New York: St. Martin's Press, 1996.

King, J., and C. Mitchell. *Black Mothers to Sons*. New York: Peter Lang, 1995.

Kogler, H. *The Power of Dialogue: Critical Hermeneuticics after Gadamer and Foucault*. Cambridge, Mass.: MIT Press, 1996.

Lacey, C. *Hightown Grammar: The School as a Social System*. London: Routledge and Kegan Paul, 1970.

Lash, S. "Learning from Leipzig . . . or Politics in the Semiotic Society." *Theory, Culture and Society*, 7, no. 4 (1990): 145–58.

Lather, P. "Fertile Obsession. Validity after Posststructuralism." *The Sociological Quarterly*, 34, no.4 (1993): 673–93.

Lather, P. *Getting Smart: Feminist Research and Pedagogy with/in the Postmodern*. New York: Routledge, 1991.

Leistyna, P., A. Woodrum, and S. Sherblom. *Breaking Free: The Transformative Power of Critical Pedagogy*. Cambridge, Mass.: Harvard Educational Review, 1996.

Lemke, J. "Analyzing Verbal Data: Principles, Methods, and Problems." In B. Fraser and K. Tobin, ed., *International Handbook of Science Education* (Part 2). Boston: Kluwer Academic Publishers, 1998.

Lemke, J. *Textual Politics: Discourse and Social Dynamics*. London: Taylor and Francis, 1995.

Lemke, J. "Discourse, Dynamics, and Social Change." *Cultural Dynamics*, 6, no.1 (1993): 243–75.

Lugg, C. "Attacking Affirmative Action: Social Darwinism as Public Policy." In J. Kincheloe, S. Steinberg, and A. Gresson, ed., *Measured Lies: The Bell Curve Examined*. New York: St. Martin's Press, 1996.

Lugones, M. "Playfulness, "World"-Traveling, and Loving Perception." *Hypatia*, 2, no.2 (1987): 3–19.

Luke, T. "Touring Hyperreality: Critical Theory Confronts Informational Society." In P. Wexler, ed., *Critical Theory Now*. New York: Falmer, 1991.

Lull, J. *Media, Communication, Culture: A Global Approach*. New York: Columbia University Press, 1995.

Macedo, D. *Literacies of Power: What Americans Are Not Allowed to Know*. Boulder, Colo.: Westview, 1994.

Maher, F., and M. Tetreault. *The Feminist Classroom: An Inside Look at How Professors and Students Are Transforming Higher Education for a Diverse Society*. New York: Basic Books, 1994.

Manganaro. M. "Textual Play, Power, and Cultural Critique: An Orientation to Modernist Anthropology." In M. Manganaro, ed., *Modernist Anthropology: From Fieldwork to Text*. Princeton: Princeton University Press, 1990.

Marcus, G., and M. Fischer. *Anthropology as Cultural Critique: An Experimental Moment in the Human Sciences*. Chicago: University of Chicago Press, 1986.

McGuigan, J. *Culture and the Public Sphere*. New York: Routledge, 1996.

McLaren, P., and R. Hammer. "Critical Pedagogy and the Postmodern Challenge." *Educational Foundations*, 3, no.3 (1989): 29–69.

McLaren, P. (1992a). "Collisions with Otherness: 'Traveling' Theory, Post-Colonial Criticism, and the Politics of Ethnographic Practice—the Mission of the Wounded Ethnographer." *Qualitative Studies in Education*, 5, 1 (1992): 77–92.

McLaren, P. (1992b). "Literacy Research and the Postmodern Turn: Cautions from the Margins." In R. Beach, J. Green, M. Kamil, and T. Shanahan, ed., *Multidisciplinary Perspectives on Research*. Urbana, Ill.: National Council of Teachers of English, 1992.

McLaren, P. (1995a). *Critical Pedagogy and Predatory Culture: Oppositional Politics in a Postmodern Era*. New York: Routledge, 1995.

McLaren, P. (1995b). *Life in Schools*. 3rd ed. New York: Longman, 1995.

McLaren, P., R. Hammer, S. Reilly, and D. Sholle. *Rethinking Media Literacy: A Critical Pedagogy of Representation*. New York: Peter Lang, 1995.

McLaren, P. *Revolutionary Multiculturalism: Pedagogies of Dissent for the New Millennium*. New York: Routledge, 1997.

McLaren, P. "Revolutionary Pedagogy in Post-Revolutionary Times: Rethinking the Political Economy of Critical Education." *Educational Theory*, 48, 4 (1998): 431–62.

McLaren, P. *Schooling as a Ritual Performance: Toward a Political Economy of Educational Symbols and Gestures*. 3rd ed. Lanham, Md.: Rowman & Littlefield, 1999.

McLaren, P. *Che Guevara and Paulo Freire: An Introduction to the Pedagogy of Revolution*. Lanham, Md.: Rowman & Littlefield, in press.

McWilliam, E., and P. Taylor, ed. *Pedagogy, Technology, and the Body*. New York: Peter Lang, 1996.

Miller, S., and J. Hodge. Phenomenology, Hermeneuticics, and Narrative Analysis: Some Unfinished Methodological Business. Unpublished, 1998.

Molnar, A. *Giving Kids the Business: The Commercialization of America's Schools*. Boulder, Colo.: Westview, 1996.

Morgan, W. "Personal Training: Discourses of (Self) Fashioning." In E. Mcwilliam and P. Taylor, ed., *Pedagogy, Technology, and the Body*. New York: Peter Lang, 1996.

Morley, D., and K. Chen, ed. *Stuart Hall: Critical Dialogues in Cultural Studies*. New York: Routledge, 1996.

Morrow, R. "Critical Theory, Gramsci and Cultural Studies: From Structuralism to Post-Structuralism." In P. Wexler, ed., *Critical Theory Now*. New York: Falmer, 1991.

Myrsiades, K., and L. Myrsiades, ed. *Race-ing Representation: Voice, History, and Sexuality*. Lanham, Md.: Rowman & Littlefield, 1998.

Newton, J., and J. Stacey. "Learning Not to Curse, or, Feminist Predicaments in Cultural Criticism by Men: Our Movie Date with James Clifford and Stephen Greenblatt." *Cultural Critique*, 2 (1992–1993): 51–82.

Nicholson, L., and S. Seidman, ed. *Social Postmodernism: Beyond Identity Politics*. New York: Cambridge University Press, 1995.

Pailliotet, A. "Deep Viewing: A Critical Look at Visual Texts." In J. Kincheloe and S. Steinberg, ed., *Unauthorized Methods: Strategies for Critical Teaching*. New York: Routledge, 1998.

Peters, M. Against Finkielkraut's la Defaite de la Pensee: Culture, Postmodernism and Education. Unpublished, 1993.

Peters, M., and C. Lankshear. "Education and Hermeneuticics: A Freirean Interpretation." In P. McLaren and C. Lankshear, ed., *Political Liberation: Paths from Freire*. New York: Routledge, 1994.

Pfeil, F. *White Guys: Studies in Postmodern Domination and Difference*. New York: Verso,1995.

Pieterse, J., and B. Parekh. "Shifting Imaginaries: Decolonization, Internal Decolonization, and Postcoloniality." In J. Pieterse and B. Parekh, ed., *The Decolonialization of Imagination: Culture, Knowledge, and Power*. Atlantic Highlands, N.J.: Zed Books, 1995.

Pinar, W. *Autobiography, Politics, and Sexuality: Essays in Curriculum Theory, 1972–1992*. New York: Peter Lang, 1994.

Pinar, W., ed. *Curriculum: Toward New Identities*. New York: Garland, 1998.

Pinar, W., W. Reynolds, P. Slattery, and P. Taubman. *Understanding Curriculum*. New York: Peter Lang, 1995.

Poster, M. *Critical Theory and Poststructuralism: In Search of a Context*. Ithaca, N.Y.: Cornell University Press, 1989.

Prakash, M., and G. Esteva. *Escaping Education: Living as Learning within Grassroots Cultures*. New York: Peter Lang, 1998.

Pruyn, M. "Becoming Subjects through Critical Practice: How Students in an Elementary Classroom Critically Read and Wrote Their World." *International Journal of Educational Reform*, 3, no.1 (1994): 37–50.

Quantz, R. A. "On Critical Ethnography (with Some Postmodern Considerations)." In M. D. LeCompte, W. L. Millroy, and J. Preissle, ed., *The Handbook of Qualitative Research in Education*. New York: Academic Press, 1992.

Rabinow, P. *Reflections on Fieldwork in Morocco*. Berkeley: University of California Press, 1977.

Rains, F. "Is the Benign Really Harmless: Deconstructing Some 'Benign' Manifestations of Operationalized White Privilege." In J. Kincheloe, S. Steinberg, N. Rodriguez, and R. Chennault, ed., *White Reign: Deploying Whiteness in America*. New York: St. Martin's Press, 1998.

Rand, E. *Barbie's Queer Accessories*. Durham, NC: Duke University Press, 1995.

Rapko, J. "Review of *The Power of Dialogue*: Critical Hermeneuticics after Gadamer and Foucault." *Criticism*, 40, 1 (1998): 133–38.

Robins, D., and P. Cohen. *Knuckle Sandwich: Growing Up in the Working-Class City*. Harmondsworth, UK: Penguin, 1978.

Robinson, William. "Beyond Nation-State Paradigms: Globalization, Sociology, and the Challenge of Transnational Studies." *Sociological Forum*, 13, no. 4 (1998): 561–94.

Rodriguez, N., and L. Villaverde. *Dismantling Whiteness*. New York: Peter Lang, 1999.

Roman, L., and L. Eyre, ed. *Dangerous Territories: Struggles for Difference and Equality in Education*. New York: Routledge, 1997.

Rosen, S. *Hermeneuticics as Politics*. New York: Oxford University Press, 1987.

Rosenau, P. M. *Post-Modernism and the Social Sciences: Insights, Inroads, and Intrusion*. Princeton: Princeton University Press, 1992.

Ruddick, S. "Material Thinking." *Feminist Studies*, 6 (1980): 342–67.

Samuels, A. *The Political Psyche*. New York: Routledge, 1993.

San Juan, E., Jr. *Articulations of Power in Ethnic and Racial Studies in the United States*. Atlantic Highlands, N.J.: Humanities Press, 1992.

San Juan, E., Jr. *Mediations: From a Filipino Perspective*. Pasig City, Philippines: Anvil Publishing, 1996.

Schurich, J., and M. Young. "Coloring Epistemologies: Are Our Research Epistemologies Racially Biased? *Educational Researcher*, 26, no. 4 (1997): 4–16.

Scott, J. W. "Experience." In J. Butler and J. W. Scott, ed., *Feminists Theorize the Political*. New York: Routledge, 1992.

Sedgwick, E. "Gosh, Boy George, You Must be Awfully Secure in Your Masculinity?" In M. Berger, B. Wallis, and S. Watson, ed., *Constructing Masculinity*. New York: Routledge, 1995.

Semali, L. "Still Crazy After All These Years: Teaching Critical Media Literacy." In J. Kincheloe and S. Steinberg, ed., *Unauthorized Methods: Strategies for Critical Teaching*. New York: Routledge, 1998.

Semali, L., and J. Kincheloe. *What Is Indigenous Knowledge? Voices from the Academy*. New York: Falmer, 1999.

Shelton, A. "The Ape's I.Q." In J. Kincheloe, S. Steinberg, and A. Gresson, ed., *Measured Lies: The Bell Curve Examined*. New York: St. Martin's Press, 1996.

Shelton, A., and J. Kincheloe. *The Shadow of the Golden Arches: A Cultural Study*. Boulder, Colo.: Westview, 1999.

Shohat, E., and R. Stam. *Unthinking Eurocentrism: Multiculturalism and the Media*. New York: Routledge, 1994.

Shor, I. *When Students Have Power: Negotiating Authority in a Critical Pedagogy*. Chicago: University of Chicago Press, 1996.

Silverman, E. K. "Clifford Geertz: Towards a More 'Thick' Understanding?" In C. Tilley, ed., *Reading Material Culture*. Cambridge, UK: Basil Blackwell, 1990.

Slattery, P. *Curriculum Development in the Postmodern Era*. New York: Garland, 1995.

Slattery, P., and J. Kincheloe. *Transformative Hermeneuticics: Interpretation in Research*. Forthcoming.

Slaughter, R. "Cultural Reconstruction in the Post-Modern World. *Journal of Curriculum Studies*, 3 (1989): 255–70.

Sleeter, C., and P. McLaren, ed. *Multicultural Education, Critical Pedagogy, and the Politics of Difference*. Albany, NY: State University of New York Press, 1995.

Smith, R., and P. Wexler, ed. *After Post-Modernism: Education, Politics, and Identity*. London: Falmer Press, 1995.

Soto, L. "Bilingual Education in America: In Search of Equity and Justice." In J. Kincheloe and S. Steinberg, ed., *Unauthorized Methods: Strategies for Critical Teaching*. New York: Routledge, 1998.

Stallabrass, J. *Gargantua: Manufactured Mass Culture*. London: Verso, 1996.

Steinberg, S. "The Bitch Who Has Everything." In S. Steinberg and J. Kincheloe, ed., *Kinderculture: The Corporate Construction of Childhood*. Boulder, Colo.: Westview, 1997.

Steinberg, S., and J. Kincheloe. *Students as Researchers: Creating Classrooms that Matter*. London: 1998.

Steinberg, S., and J. Kincheloe. *Kinderculture: Corporate Constructions of Childhood*. Boulder, Colo.: Westview, 1997.

Stewart, K. *A Space on the Side of the Road: Cultural Poetics in an "Other" America*. Princeton: Princeton University Press, 1996.

Sünker, H. "Welfare, Democracy, and Social Work." In G. Flosser and H. Otto, ed., *Towards More Democracy in Social Services: Models of Culture and Welfare*. New York: de Gruyter, 1998.

Surber, J. *Culture and Critique: An Introduction to the Critical Discourses of Cultural Studies*. Boulder, Colo.: Westview, 1998.

Swartz, E. "Using Dramaturgy in Educational Research." In S. Steinberg and J. Kincheloe, ed., *Students as Researchers: Creating Classrooms that Matter*. Bristol, Pa.: Falmer, 1998.

Tanaka, G. "Dygenesis and White Culture." In J. Kincheloe, S. Steinberg, and A. Gresson, ed., *Measured Lies: The Bell Curve Examined*. New York: St. Martin's Press, 1996.

Taussig, M. *Shamanism, Colonialism, and the Wild Man: A Study in Terror and Healing*. Chicago: University of Chicago Press, 1987.

Taylor, M., and E. Saarinen. *Imagologies: Media Philosophy*. New York: Routledge, 1994.

Thomas, S. "Dominance and Ideology in Cultural Studies." In M. Ferguson and P. Golding, ed., *Cultural Studies in Question*. Thousand Oaks, Calif.: Sage, 1997.

Trueba, E., and P. McLaren. "Critical Ethnography for the Study of Immigrants." In Henry Trueba and Lilia Bartomolme, ed. *Immigrant Voices: In Search of Pedagogical Reform*. Lanham, Md.: Rowman & Littlefield, in press.

Vattimo, G. *Beyond Interpretation: The Meaning of Hermeneuticics for Philosophy*. Stanford, Calif.: Stanford University Press, 1994.

Viergever, M. "Indigenous Knowledge: An Interpretation of Views from Indigenous Peoples." In L. Semali and J. Kincheloe, ed., *What Is Indigenous Knowledge: Voices from the Academy*. Bristol, Pa.: Falmer, 1999.

Villaverde, L., and J. Kincheloe. "Engaging Students as Researchers: Researching and Teaching Thanksgiving in the Elementary Classroom." In S. Steinberg and J. Kincheloe, ed., *Students as Researchers: Creating Classrooms that Matter*. Bristol, Pa.: Falmer, 1998.

Visweswaran, K. *Fictions of Feminist Ethnography*. Minneapolis: University of Minnesota Press, 1994.

Weil, D. *Towards a Critical Multi-Cultural Literacy: Theory and Practice for Education for Liberation*. New York: Peter Lang, 1998.

Weiler, K. *Women Teaching for Change: Gender, Class, and Power*. South Hadley, Mass.: Bergin and Garvey, 1988.

Welch, S. "An Ethic of Solidarity and Difference." In H. Giroux, ed., *Postmodernism, Feminism, and Cultural Politics: Redrawing Educational Boundaries*. Albany: State University of New York Press, 1991.

Weinstein, M. *Robot World: Education, Popular Culture, and Science*. New York: Peter Lang, 1998.

West, C. *Race Matters*. Boston: Beacon Press, 1993.

Wexler, P. "Preface." In P. Wexler, ed., *Critical Theory Now*. New York: Falmer, 1991.

Wexler, P. (1996a). *Critical Social Psychology*. New York: Peter Lang, 1996.

Wexler, P. (1996b). *Holy Sparks: Social Theory, Education and Religion*. New York: St. Martin's, 1996.

Wexler, P. Social Research in Education: Ethnography of Being. Paper presented at the International Conference, The Culture of Schooling, Halle, Germany, 1997.

Willis, P. *Learning to Labour: How Working Class Kids Get Working-Class Jobs*. Farnborough, England: Saxon House, 1977.

Woodward, K., ed. *Identity and Difference*. London: Sage, 1997.

Yates, T. Jacques Derrida: "There Is Nothing Outside of the Text." In C. Tilley, ed., *Reading Material Culture*. Cambridge, UK: Basil Blackwell, 1990.

Young, I. "The Ideal of Community and the Politics of Difference." In L. Nicholson, ed., *Feminism/Postmodernism*. New York: Routledge, 1990.

Zizek, S. *The Sublime Object of Ideology*. London: Verso, 1990.

# CHAPTER SIX

# Critical Ethnography in the Postcritical Moment

*Douglas E. Foley*

When I became an educational anthropologist in the mid-1960s, very few anthropologists thought of themselves as critical ethnographers. Early educational anthropologists like George Spindler, Solon Kimball, Elizabeth Eddy, Elenor Leacock, and many others were doing critical, practical studies of education. But very few American anthropologists of that era were doing what Marcus and Fischer (1986) call "cultural critiques" of the larger society. Avowed critical anthropological ethnographers in that era studied the political economies of tribal societies and the impact of colonialism on agricultural economies, not schools. From my perspective only Jules Henry and Margaret Mead were doing broad cultural critiques. Since they both had deep roots in psychological anthropology, neither deployed Marxist constructs, but I read Henry's *Culture against Man* (1960) as a "crypto- Marxist" critique of capitalist culture. His study highlighted how American culture and schools infused alienated youth with consumerism and competitive values.

Meanwhile, except for a few studies of the power elite and class privilege, positivist and functionalist thinkers dominated sociology of education. Most commentaries on critical educational ethnography (Karabel and Halsey 1977; Apple 1982; Anderson 1989; Apple and Roman 1990; Quantz 1992; Carspecken and Apple 1992; Kincheloe and McLaren 1994; Fine 1994; Levinson and Holland 1996) generally agree that a "new sociology of education" emerged in the early 1970s. This perspective was initially labeled "neo-Marxist" and was largely based on the sociology of Pierre Bourdieu and the sociolinguistics of Basil Bernstein (Karabel and Halsey 1977). The other critical perspective, which Marxists sought to discredit, emerged out of a tiny West Coast school of sociology called ethnomethodology (Mehan 1975). Outside an intriguing reader (Cicourel et. al 1974) and several excellent ethnographies (Mehan 1979; Mehan et al. 1986), this sociological version of phenomenology never really caught on in educational research circles. In retrospect, their fine-grained studies of policy makers, test takers, and teachers socially constructing reality through "ethno-practices" were an early version of what Allan Luke (1995–1996) calls poststructuralist "critical discourse" analysis.

Methodologically, most critical ethnographers, regardless of their theoretical orientation, still use the indepth research techniques of traditional ethnography. Like traditional ethnographers, they place a strong emphasis on doing prolonged, systematic fieldwork rooted in at least a year or two of participant-observation, key informants work, and extensive interviews. Unlike traditional ethnographers, however, they are less interested in producing holistic, universalizing portraits of whole cultures. They are more interested in producing focused, well-theorized ethnographies of societal institutions or subgroups. It is not enough to simply produce well-theorized accounts of a particular institution or subgroup, however. To use critical theorist Jurgen Habermas's (1971) apt phrase, knowledge production has to have an "emancipatory intent." Or to use postmodernist Pattie Lather's (1991) phraseology, critical ethnographies have to produce knowledge that has "catalytic validity" (i.e., that changes the status quo). Put succinctly, critical ethnography is a well-theorized empirical study with a serious political intent to change people's consciousness, if not their daily lives.

To fulfill these two goals, the critical ethnographer has to begin breaking with the conventional scientific ethnographic practice of being a detached, neutral observer. She has to openly collaborate with the oppressed. In the 1960s and 1970s the more activist style of collaborating was to work directly for and with oppressed groups to produce the types of studies they needed and valued. If they needed a study that would help them win legal battles, rent strikes, and various political actions, then the critical ethnographer was a pen for hire. The more academic style of collaboration was to write critiques of the capitalist production system and political power structure that demonstrated the systematic, oppressive character of capitalism. Such critical academic studies were supposed to reveal the hidden, systemic, oppressive reality of capitalism, thus raising the consciousness of the reader somewhat like Paulo Freire's cultural circles "concienticize" their participants.

By the late 1970s, leading Marxist educational theorists Mike Apple,

Henry Giroux, and others were championing a "cultural Marxist" perspective. It was their antidote for vulgar and economistic Marxism. Other American educational ethnographers were reformulating orthodox Marxist educational critiques with ideas from Frankfurt critical theory (Everhart 1983; Anyon 1981; Foley 1990). Meanwhile, within educational anthropology Enrique Trueba, Jeane Lave, Shirly Brice Heath, Luis Moll, Peter McLaren, John Ogbu, Harry Wolcott, and many others were also developing critical ethnographic perspectives rooted in a variety of non-Marxist frameworks. The range of these new perspectives, which utilize ideas from cognitive studies, ritual studies, sociolinguistics, and migration studies, is beyond this modest chapter. Put simply, the "new educational anthropology" of the 1980s and 1990s (Levinson and Holland 1996) was as dedicated to the study of inequality as the earlier psychological educational anthropology of Spindler, Henry, and Mead was.

But new players with other critical, non-Marxist perspectives were coming on the American anthropology/sociology of education scene. Sophia Villenas, Bradley Levinson, and I tell this story in two articles that highlight the contributions of feminist and ethnographers of color (Foley, Levinson, and Hurtig 2001; Villenas and Foley forthcoming). For example, Enrique Trueba's (1999) synthesis of Vygotsky's learning theory and Friere's critical pedagogy exemplifies the "new" psychological educational anthropology. Trueba's studies of Latino immigrants in the United States illustrate nicely how psychological anthropologists retooled with little recourse to Marxism or postmodernism. He advocates a critical, politicized form of ethnography that champions a "pedagogy of hope" for all progressive educators and oppressed communities.

During the late 1970s and early 1980s, new currents of continental philosophy also began challenging the foundational role of Marxist theory in critical educational ethnography. As early as the mid-1970s, progressive faculty at the University of Texas were reading French poststructuralists and deconstructionists like Foucault, Derrida, Baudrillard, and Lyotard. Initially, our study group thought the new "postmodern" perspective was interesting but lacked a transformative political agenda. Nevertheless, postmodernist's unrelenting skepticism forced us, many ex-1960s new leftists, to begin reconstructing our orthodox Marxist perspectives. Initially, we turned to the writings of Marxist revisionists such as the Frankfurt school and scholars at the University of Birmingham's Centre for Contemporary Cultural Studies (CCCS). At that time, CCCS scholars were busy interrogating the seminal work of Italian communist Antonio Gramsci, French structuralist Marxist

Luis Althusser, and British Marxist E. P. Thompson. In this regard, the early work of Paul Willis (1976, 1981) was seminal and provided cultural Marxists with what came to be known as a "cultural production" perspective (Lave 1995).

In retrospect, however, perhaps the leading figure in all this ferment became Jamacian Stuart Hall (Morely and Chen 1996). After Willis (1990) and many others left CCCS, Hall and his CCCS colleagues continued to engage postmodernism. The result, at least in Hall's later writings, was what Laclau and Mouffe (1985) call "post-Marxism." Some forms of post-Marxism do abandon the core assumptions of Marxian class theory, but I read Hall and various CCCS scholars as democratizing and expanding class theory. Put cryptically, Hall blends Gramsci, Foucault, and various postcolonial and feminist critiques into a multiple systems of dominance perspective. This perspective retains a Gramscian construct of social classes as historical blocs or class alliances. In his formulation, there is no progressive, unified proletariat that ushers in an inevitable socialist paradise. As Hall puts it, he subscribes to "a Marxism with no guarantees." In place of a unified proletariat is an ever changing historical bloc of stigmatized identity groups—racial, ethnic, gender, sexual identity, and physically disabled. These "new social movements" are precariously allied in their struggles for equality and democracy against objectifying, hegemonic discourses and unprogressive public policies.

Of late, various British and American Marxist educational theorists (Hill, McLaren, Cole, and Rikowski 1999) have begun representing post-Marxist scholarship as infected with postmodern relativism and lacking a political agenda. If you read the ethnographies of anthropologists working out of a post-Marxist/cultural production perspective (Foley and Moss 2000; Levinson and Holland 1996), you will almost certainly come to a more generous conclusion. Many cultural production/practice scholars still believe in studying an external reality of historical power structures, oppression, and poverty. They believe in giving authoritative accounts of how people resist ideological hegemony. Such cultural critiques are often based on Marxist theories of the state, ideology, alienation, and hegemony. Unconventional Marxist thinkers like Antonio Negri (1984) would argue that "cultural Marxist" studies extend the analysis of capital reproduction and class struggle into what he calls the "social factory," or what I call everyday cultural practices and communication (Foley 1990).

The rise of such studies in critical educational circles did not forestall, however, the rapid development of alternative poststructuralist and postmodern educational perspectives in the 1990s. Unfortunately, the postmodern intellectual movement is so eclectic and interdisciplinary that it is difficult to characterize, and the term is now in danger of becoming a meaningless slogan. Political theorist Pauline Rosenau (1992) provides a useful account of how various types of postmodernism have impacted on the social sciences. Some scholars conceptualize postmodernism as a new economic and cultural globalism marked by "flexible accumulation" strategies and time-space compressions. Others think of postmodernism as an aesthetic style that is replacing high modernism in architecture, literature, fine art, cinema, and fashion. Still others understand postmodernism as a new type of media-driven society marked by a kind of depthless, simulated, ahistorical sense of reality. Others argue that a postmodern society has new forms of power, surveillance, and governance founded upon discourses of the new social scientific disciplines. So what in this vast, sprawling perspective is of value for critical educational ethnographers?

The postmodern critique of advanced Western capitalist societies has some value, but their critique of science is particularly relevant for critical ethnographers. Postmodern thinkers generally argue that the eighteenth-century enlightenment and "reason" did little more than deliver Western civilization from the certainties of religion into the certainties of science and the scientific method. Their view has much in common with the Frankfurt critical theory critique of science, but postmodern deconstructionists advocate a particularly radical form of reflexivity. Various critical education theorists (Carspecken 1996; Popkewitz and Brennan 1996; Aronowitz and Giroux 1991; McLaren 1998; Carspecken and Apple 1992; Wexler 1992) have already engaged postmodernism as a philosophical perspective. Consequently, this chapter focuses more on its impact on the interpretive and narrative practices of critical ethnographers. To this end, I reviewed many postmodern and post-Marxist ethnographies (Foley 2000; Foley and Moss 2000) and eventually generated a revised version of George Marcus's (1998) typology of reflexive practices. In this chapter I use the following typology of reflexive practices to interrogate several key postmodern and cultural production/practice ethnographies. By contrasting these two different types of critical ethnographies, I hope to highlight some of the differences and similarities. Before presenting these textual readings, I would like to define and differentiate between the major types of reflexivity being advocated and practiced by ethnographers.

# The Reflexive Ideal and Its Many Guises

According to philosopher Hillary Lawson (1985), from the Greeks on, most thinkers have practiced some form of reflexivity. From the early 1900s through the 1950s, however, logical positivism and a particularly unreflexive style of social scientific research took root in the United States. A post-1960s explosion of philosophical relativism that takes too many forms to chronicle here began seeping into anthropology. The initial anthropological response was quite varied, but one influential special issue of *Semiotica* edited by Barbara Babcock (1980) is particularly noteworthy. The notion of reflexivity guiding that collection rests heavily on George Herbert Mead's modernist, symbolic interactionist perspective of mind, self, and society. For Babcock, reflexivity is the capacity of language and of thought—of any system of signification—to turn or bend back upon itself, thus becoming an object to itself. Directing one's gaze at one's own experience makes it possible to regard oneself as "other." Through a constant mirroring of the self, one eventually becomes reflexive about the situated, socially constructed nature of the self, and by extension, the other. In this formulation, the self is a multiple, constructed self that is always becoming and never quite fixed, and the ethnographic productions of such a self and the "cultural other" are always historically and culturally contingent.

Babcock warns her anthropological colleagues that such self-referential reflections tend to generate an "epistemological paradox." Turning in on ourselves in a critical manner tends to produce an awareness that there are no absolute distinctions between what is "real" and what is "fiction," between the "self" and the "other." Methodologically, this means that we are forced to explore the self-other relationships of fieldwork critically if we are to produce more discriminating, defensible interpretations. In Babcock's modernist formulation of reflexivity there remains a degree of optimism that the road to quasi-objective knowledge claims is through a reflexive, self-critical awareness of our limits as interpreters. It is only through being reflexive that we explode our fantasies about ethnographic texts being copies of reality. George Marcus labels this form of reflexivity "confessional," and in his recent book, *Ethnography through Thick and Thin* (1998), claims such practices have become fairly standard in contemporary American ethnography.

Barbara Tedlock (1991) notes that confessional reflexivity actually began before postmodernism with the publication of Malinowski's (1967) surprisingly frank diary. Many mini-diaries and personal journals (Spindler 1970; Golde 1970; Freilich 1970; Rabinow 1977; Dumont 1978; Dwyer 1982), and several important theoretical reflections quickly followed (Dwyer 1982; Crapanzano 1980; Fabian 1983). Important questions were raised about not only self-other field relationships but also ethical and political questions and the colonial nature of anthropological scholarship. During the 1970s and 1980s such confessional reflections were only permissible, however, after one had published a separate, formal scientific realist ethnography. Anthropologists of that era were essentially keeping two sets of books and writing in a somewhat schizophrenic manner.

As we moved into the postmodern era, feminist (Krieger 1991; Abu-Lughod 1991; Behar 1993, 1996; Behar and Gordon 1995) and native ethnographers (Hanyo 1979; Gwaltney 1980; Narayan 1993) boldly began incorporating such reflections into their formal ethnographies. Ethnographers that are reflexive in this sense generally make a serious effort to convey how their subjectivity may be affecting their interpretation. They seek to undermine grandiose authorial claims of speaking in a rational, value-free, objective, universalizing voice. The author as omniscient tape recorder and grand interpreter is replaced by the author as a living, contradictory, vulnerable, evolving multiple self who speaks in a partial, subjective, culture-bound voice. Some of my favorite confessional pieces are from the pens of Ruth Behar (1993, 1996), Susan Krieger (1991), Renato Rosaldo (1989), and Dorrine Kondo (1990).

Cuban American ethnographer Ruth Behar practices this form of reflexivity in a particularly intense, sophisticated manner. She says that "anthropology that does not break your heart is not worth doing" (Behar 1996). From her perspective ethnography is a long, irreversible voyage through a tunnel with no apparent exit. Hence, anyone presumptuous enough to witness and retell the stories about others must surrender "to the intractableness of reality." They must find a way of witnessing that is neither cold nor afraid to reveal what she calls "the hidden dialectic between connection and otherness that is at the center of all forms of historical and cultural representation" (Behar 1996). Behar insists that exploring the self-other tunnel has no easy exits and requires a great deal of emotional openness and honesty. Most scientific studies repress such emotion through distancing methodologies, theoretical discourses, and posturing as the invulnerable objective decoder of reality. In sharp contrast, Behar advocates "inscribing the self" into descriptive accounts of others through heartfelt autobiographic memories. She constantly foregrounds how her observations are filtered through her sorrow, shame, fear, loathing, guilt, vanity, and self-deception.

Behar highlights the autobiographical nature of her interpretation to demonstrate that a vulnerable, empathic, subjective observer is better able to see the intractability and inexplicability of life and people. Her ethnographic interpretation often uses analogies that she draws between her life and the other. Such simultaneous exploration of the self and other actually does more than simply confess her positionality, political ideology, and ethical foibles. The analogies she draws between the self and other function like literary metaphors. They are dramatic and poetic in a way that evokes a sense of verisimilitude or understanding rather than explain in the sense of scientific predictions. Such interpretive practices work against conventional gendered separations of the self into the rational and emotional as well. They do not privilege rational, scientific interpretation over evocative, poetic interpretation. In short, Behar pushes "confessional reflexivity," or what Michelle Fine (1994) aptly labels "working the hyphens," in some interesting new directions interpretively and narratively.

The second type of reflexivity highlighted in Marcus's (1994) typology is "intertextual reflexivity." Most ethnographies probably contain a degree of intertextuality, because a good ethnographer grounds her interpretations in previous studies of the same topic. But intertextual reflexivity goes well beyond a good comparative literature review. Such reflexive practices have been long advocated by sociology of knowledge practitioners. According to Steven Woolgar (1991), it behooves critical, reflexive ethnographers to make transparent how they, as members of a vast academic knowledge production process, produce truth claims and facts. Bourdieu calls this a "sociology of sociology" that uncovers or "objectivates" the effects of scientific "field" on interpretation (Bourdieu and Wacquant 1992). To produce such a local account of knowledge production, an ethnographer must pay particular attention to how the practices and discourses of their own discipline affects what and how they think and write.

To this end, Woolgar and Latour's (1986) exhaustive ethnographic study of a biotechnical laboratory is highly instructive. They demonstrate how deeply embedded the psychical scientists and the ethnographers are in the local relationships and politics of the laboratory and their disciplinary specialty. In this type of reflexivity, the author also consciously situates her representational practices among the representational practices of past and present researchers. Such an interpretive move makes transparent the socially constructed nature of the author's "facts," thus the partiality of the author's truth claims. A nice example of how an artist builds this type of reflexivity into their art is Francois Truffaut's *Day for Night*. The movie is about making a movie, thus it is a narrative that seeks to make its narrative practice transparent. It creates what deconstructionists call an "aporia," a gap or uncertainty that the movie is a copy of real life. Truffaut's reflexive movie, like Latour and Woolgar's highly intertextual account of the scientific laboratory, helps call into question fundamental assumptions about fact/ fiction, natural/constructed, truth/falsity.

Marcus's third and final notion of reflexivity, "theoretical reflexivity," distinguishes between the confessional (personal, emotional) and the theoretical (rational). He characterizes feminists as exemplars of the confessional and French sociologist Pierre Bourdieu as an exemplar of theoretical reflexivity. Bourdieu's own term is "epistemic reflexivity," and he goes to some lengths to distance himself from "confessional reflexivity," which he lumps in the impoverished category of postmodern "textual reflexivity" (Bourdieu and Wacquant 1992). Bourdieu's general project is to rescue sociological practice from Cartesian dualism and the epistemological extremes of objectivism and subjectivism. Put very simply, Bourdieu advocates a highly reflexive way of knowing that relentlessly tacks back and forth between social scientific metalanguages and the learned dispositions (habitas) of everyday actors in their constraining historical/cultural contexts (fields). The job of an ethnographer remains to produce as objective and authoritative account as possible of the cultural practices of people and sociologists. Using a Marxian aphorism, an ethnographer studies people making history (culture) out of what they have inherited.

Practice perspectives, like Marxist cultural production perspectives, are based on strong notions of agency (praxis) and structure (history) and focus on how people negotiate, assimilate, and transform their lived reality. This highly processual or dialectical way of conceptualizing the social order and actors uses contingent, conditional constructs of reality. The meaning of abstract concepts like a "class formation," a "taste culture," or an "ideological hegemony" are always contingent upon what Stuart Hall calls "articulations" within a given historical/cultural context. Knowing the lived reality of others can only happen by being highly reflexive (i.e., by engaging in a long, disciplined, systematic process of experiencing, recording, and critically reflecting upon lived reality). This abductive process that conjoins theory and empirical fieldwork eventually produces heuristic devices used for mapping and representing (objectivating) the taken-for-granted cultural and political practices observed. Social scientists map cultural space and practices in a manner somewhat similar to the way cartographers map physical space. Ideally, such mappings of cultural patterns produce useful, practical knowledge for understanding, navigating, critiquing, and transforming lived, inherited, and constructed social reality.

From a postmodern perspective, the aforementioned notions of "theoretical reflexivity" still do not break sufficiently with modernist epistemological assumptions and goals. Philosopher Hillary Lawson's (1985) discussion of antifoundational thinkers helps us imagine a more radical notion of epistemology. She demonstrates that Nietsche, Heidegger, Wittgenstein, and Derrida have initiated a full-scale attack on the modernist ideal of providing a reliable epistemology for the "factual" disciplines of social science and history. For many years antifoundationalists have argued that a scientific epistemology based on ordinary language is susceptible to what philosopher's call the "liar's paradox."

To illustrate the liar's paradox, Lawson tells the story of the Cretan prophet Epimenides who observed that "all Cretans are liars." Epimenides did so to demonstrate that categorical knowledge claims invariably falsify themselves. In this particular case, we have a Cretan asserting that it is true that all Cretans are liars. If all Cretans are liars, how is it possible that one Cretan can be telling the truth about all Cretans being liars? This truth claim, like all absolute truth claims, is based on an either/or logic that invariably degenerates into a paradoxical, contradictory knowledge claim.

Recent postmodern/deconstructionist thinkers like Derrida have restated this radical form of skepticism with theories of semiotics. He points out that all signification systems invariably generate such logical paradoxes. The moment we imagine ourselves representing external reality through purportedly rational constructs, we lose sight of these construct's commonsensical, metaphorical character. When we deconstruct our allegedly objective theoretical constructs (i.e., subject them to a rigorous rhetorical analysis), they turn out to be full of hierarchical preferences expressed through their either/or logic. Conceptual distinctions like bourgeois-proletariat, male-female, black-white inevitably "defer" or displace meaning (i.e., fix meaning in a way that is contrary to the way webs of signification work). Signification systems generate an endless, indeterminate play of signifiers that never produce one fixed meaning but rather analogic distinctions based on a paradoxical both/and logic.

Since our invented linguistic categories are always caught up in webs of signification and the ceaseless play of signifiers, our feeble attempts at logically, rationally stabilizing inherently unstable, ambiguous conceptual distinctions is doomed to fail. Postmodernists argue that our best hope may be to abandon our desire to know in any absolute sense and to make grand, foundational constructs and knowledge claims. According to deconstructionists, the best way out of this linguistic/semiotic quagmire is actually to embrace the paradoxical, analogic, both/and logic of signification systems. Consequently, postmodern ethnographers often advocate operating more like artists/poets than scientists (Tyler 1986). They replace the old positivist metaphors of "operationalizing" and "measuring" reality, and the newer post-positivist notions of "heuristically" mapping reality with the poetic ideals of "evoking" and "mirroring" reality. The ethnographic interpreter is no longer discovering facts and reality. She is no longer "translating" reality directly onto the pages of her ethnography. Instead, she is rendering impressionist portraits rather than discovering facts and reality. Consequently, when she tells admittedly impressionistic stories of her experience, she disrupts her authority to make sweeping, universalistic knowledge claims.

Pattie Lather (1998) conveys the more radical, antifoundational position of postmodern researchers in a particularly forceful manner. She stresses the need to open up rather than foreclose analytic categories and advocates exploring the aporias or indeterminate character of all representational attempts. She highlights the deep commitment of postmodern thinkers to indeterminate, evocative, poetic accounts of experience. As Lather puts it, being theoretical is about "getting lost" and building on the "ruins" of knowledge rather than assuredly mapping and discovering reality. To be "theoretically reflexive" in the deconstructive sense, is to be radically skeptical about the stability and utility of all theoretical constructs and metalanguages, thus all attempts at representation.

Such theoretical reflexivity manifests itself textually in a variety of ways. Some postmodern ethnographers may deconstruct/disrupt academic constructs through explicit technical discussions. Others deconstruct popular and academic constructs through texts that rely heavily on literary/poetic devices rather than explicit conceptual arguments. Such texts (Lather and Smithies 1997) simply refuse to explain their subject in authoritative ways. Instead, they use suggestive poetic metaphors, or they let the subject explain itself without any authorial explanation. Such texts lack the authoritative, rational authorial engine of modernist texts and a highly coherent, tightly theorized realist portrait of a particular cultural scene or phenomenon. Instead, they are often a pastiche of images and ideas in much the manner of surrealist painters. Their ambiguous, undertheorized ethnographic portraits leave much of the interpretive work to the reader.

Such texts are also bent on avoiding the familiar modernist trope of the heroic ethnographer. In this stock-story, an innocent, childlike, empathic ethnographer lands in an unfamiliar culture, and after extended fieldwork, metamorphizes into an all-knowing interpreter of that culture. Of course the analogue in critical ethnography is the noble humanist who metamorphizes into a brilliant social critic and/or dedicated political ally who rescues their downtrodden research subjects. The hubris in all these familiar postures is obvious, and it drives many postmodern ethnographers to uncommon lengths to disrupt, decenter, deconstruct their authorial authority and any notion of themselves as useful, benign social scientists. They fear that the scientist's will to know and explain may simply be a will to power laced with various forms of self-interest.

An ethnographer who has been deeply influenced by the aforementioned critique will be highly reflexive in a deconstructive sense. Or to use Pattie Lather's (1997) apt phrase, they will seek to "work the ruins" and "aporias" of conventional theories of reality for interesting, unexpected perspectives and insights. To break away from conventional, hierarchical system of signi-fications, Lather says that the ethnographic interpreter needs to get "lost" to find new ways of thinking about lived reality. Such a radical, antifounda-tional form of reflexivity should be apparent in the ethnographic practice and the texts of postmodern ethnographers. Ethnographic practitioners are an eclectic lot, and this either/or dichotomy, like all conceptual distinctions is hard-pressed to capture the both/and character of their ethnographic prac-tice. But as we shall see, this typology helps suggest some basic differences and similarities between the interpretive and narrative practices of postmod-ern and post-Marxist/cultural production ethnographers.

## Two Critical Ethnographies with Strong Postmodern Nuances

One way to gauge the influence of postmodernism on critical ethnographers is to take note of what exemplary cultural production/practice critical eth-nographers like Michelle Fine and Lois Weis are doing. Fine's "working the hyphens" article (1994) calls for a thorough interrogation of one's ethno-graphic practice: field relations; ethics; theoretical and interpretive con-structs; narrative and representational choices; political commitments. Their new book, The Unknown City (Fine and Weis 1998), is a powerful portrait of the urban poor that explores race, class, and gender differences in great and subtle detail. It chronicles the lives of young adults, their work, social rela-tionships, and families in an era of reactionary, racist, right-wing politics, deindustrialization, stepped-up state surveillance, and a public policy retreat of federal and state government agencies. The study is based on 165 indepth interviews or life stories in two different urban neighborhoods of two East Coast cities.

Philosophically, Fine and Weis restate all the political and ethical concerns we had in the 1960s. They frame their ethnographic work with what is basically a historical materialist perspective. The voices of the young urban poor are situated within the previously described political economic context. Fine and Weis describe themselves as "public intellectuals." The role of such intellectuals is to "give voice" to the urban underclass in the hopes of forcing liberal-minded policy makers and politicians to serve the poor more than they serve rich corporate interests. In the absence of a transformative progressive social movement, they see themselves helping to create an "imaginary space" of left, progressive thought. At the very least, they hope that the "uppity voices" in their text slows down the upsurge of reactionary, right-wing symbolic violence against the poor. Their emphasis on collaborating with the community being studied, taking accounts back to them, working for activist organizations is what early critical ethnographers called "activist anthropology" or "action research" (Hymes 1969).

Fine and Weis also represent a growing trend in critical ethnography toward more reflexive essays about one's fieldwork (Shacklock and Smythe 1998; Villenas 1996; Chaudhry 1997). Their latest qualitative study includes new postmodern concerns over representation, texts, and conceptual and epistemological issues. They agonize over selecting "treacherous" or "good" stories that feed or disrupt hegemonic discourses and representations. They advocate presenting a "quilt of stories" and a "cacophony of voices." By using a constant comparative frame, their narrative highlights both commonalties and subtle racial, class, and gender differences among the urban poor. Their representations clearly help disrupt or "deconstruct" the reader's common sense categories of these often stigmatized, stereotyped groups.

Narratively, the actual voices of different racial and gender sectors of the working class are sprinkled throughout the text. The narrative is organized like a series of documentary-style, realistic snapshots of specific groups and specific topics. It conveys a vivid, "I-was-there" sense of what it must be like to be trapped in declining urban areas. After presenting long, relatively unedited segments of interviews, the authors then interpret these testimonies and cite the relevant urban studies literature. They consciously foreground the voices of the poor and minimize extended theoretical discussions. This makes their text much more readable and accessible to a general audience, politicians, and public policy makers. Its poignant, realist style vignettes of individuals almost surely produces strong identifications with and admiration for the struggles of poor people. The authors generally appear in the texts as interviewers, data interpreters, and activists who collaborate with local activists and programs. Their formal ethnography, The Unknown City, incorporates few of their new reflexive practices. It presents little reflexive discussion of how the fieldwork was done, what it felt like, or who they are beyond demographic, "two liberal, Jewish, middle class white women" and catchy characterizations, two "Thelma and Louise feminist social scientists." Like earlier anthropologists, their more subjective reflections on field relations and ethics are published in separate articles and books (Weis and Fine 2000).

Although sensitive to postmodern concerns over essentializing cultural others, Fine and Weis opt for a narrative strategy that "strategically essentializes" (Spivak 1988) through what Abu-Lughod (1991) calls a "tactical humanist" account. In the face of elite domination of the media and popular press, academics who think of themselves as "public" or "organic intellectuals" feel a strong moral obligation to counter negative hegemonic discourses. Like most cultural production/practice ethnographers, they prefer to error on the side of positive othering or essentializing for political reasons. They are very explicit about the need to write against hegemonic right-wing discourses. Consequently, they produce a very positive, valorizing account of the urban poor, which is quite consistent with their philosophical perspective.

Another cultural production/practice critical ethnographer who has tried to incorporate postmodern reflexivity into his ethnographic practice is me. My latest ethnography, The Heartland Chronicles (Foley 1995), is the study of Indian-white relations in my hometown. I have described the reflexive elements of that text extensively elsewhere (Foley forthcoming) so will summarize briefly how that text blends postmodern reflexivity into a cultural Marxist theoretical perspective. My portrayal of Indian-white relations is structured around Gramscian and Foucaldian notions of a hegemonic discursive regime, which seeks to build a moral, ideological consensus that Indians must assimilate and become Whiteman. Academics, journalists, politicians, and local whites wield this pernicious, stigmatizing assimilationist discourse, both through written representations and through local storytelling. This discourse has provoked an intense, lively one-hundred-year political dialogue within the tribe over cultural assimilation. That dialogue has spawned a sustained counterhegemonic discourse against assimilation and for cultural survival that has been recently taken up by a small group of college-educated "organic intellectuals." These new Mesquaki voices are now writing their own representations in novels, history books, journalistic articles, and political cartoons.

The assimilationist discourse has also provoked daily racialized "discursive skirmishes" over white constructions of Indianness. My hometown is awash with white stories about Indians dying on train tracks, brawling in bars, sitting silent in schools, missing football practices, and keeping house poorly. Mesquakis challenge all these white constructions through counterstories that invert the negative white representations. In addition to the emphasis on cultural struggle, the text also portrays the rise of a post-1960s Mesquaki civil rights movement. Paralleling these discursive skirmishes are barroom fights, student walkouts, and courthouse demonstrations, and the development of a more autonomous tribal welfare state and a multi-million-dollar gambling casino. These more conventional forms of political struggle are conceptualized as a process of ethnogenesis led by a college-educated middle class. Although the tribe remains traditional spiritually, they are an emerging, assertive American "ethnic minority" with a progressive political and economic agenda.

None of my cultural Marxist conceptual framework is made explicit anywhere in the text, however, because I narrate in a highly personal, autobiographical voice. The text is full of Iowa humor, colloquialisms, and self-parodies to make it more accessible. It also uses racial memories allegorically to illustrate how many whites feel and relate to Mesquakis. I also portray my fieldwork encounters with key Mesquaki characters and the fieldnotes of previous anthropologists to explore self-other relationships and my biases. The encounters with a Mesquaki novelist, historian, and journalist generate "theories" of Mesquaki culture and politics that are foregrounded as authoritative explanations. The combination of autobiographical material and personal encounters gives the text a great deal of what Marcus calls "confessional reflexivity."

The text also incorporates "intertextual reflexivity" extensively. Its exhaustive account of how everyday popular talk, and local and national journalists and academics discursively construct the Indian cultural other spans fifty years and a variety of institutional sites of production. This long, complex portrayal of intertextual representations is used to foreground and call into question my own representations. Finally, all the key characters were asked to read and comment on the manuscript. Their responses are presented in an epilogue. The local commentary on my ethnographic representations points out how others and I have misrepresented Indians and whites. The local representation of my representations adds another layer of reflexivity to the manuscript.

My text, like Fine and Weis's text, also works hard to "deconstruct" popular images of cultural others—the poor, blacks, Latinos, Indians, "minority mothers." We both do this through a series of stories about cultural others that disrupt negative, one-dimensional caricatures of these marginalized cultural groups. Elsewhere, I have characterized this style of narrative as "reflexive realism" that "strategic essentializes" or valorizes oppressed cultural others (Foley forthcoming). Such ethnographies are more modernist in their interpretive and narrative style. The authors seek to make authoritative knowledge claims about cultural oppression and resistance. They still use constructs like heuristic devices to map a coherent, persuasive ethnographic story about patterns, social types, and structures. As we shall see, this type of interpretation and textual representation differs markedly from how most postmodernists and deconstructionists theorize their texts. Such texts tend to be theoretical in a disruptive rather than in a heuristic manner. Postmodern ethnographers often seem more interested in deconstructing their conceptual categories than in deconstructing the hegemonic ideologies of popular culture or academia. Consequently, they tend to eschew realist narrative styles and definitive representations of cultural others.

## Three Postmodern/Deconstructionist Ethnographies

Kirby Moss's (1998) ethnography of young poor whites is set in his hometown, a medium-sized, midwestern city. He follows a small group of poor whites into their school, work, and residential settings. Moss presents a series of vignettes that he claims "ironically juxtapose" what these youth talk about and do to how others imagine them. He shows us these young whites socializing across racial boundaries in unexpected ways and living in places that they are not supposed to live in. He shows these poor white youth clashing with upwardly mobile minorities and white preppies. We see the youth working out their self-images as privileged racial and class others in relation to various privileged others, including Moss himself, an educated, middle-class black ethnographer. Since his ethnographic representation of white privilege constantly shifts, the usual images of white racial and class privilege is disrupted or deconstructed. By zeroing in on the shifting, relative, context-bound character of white privilege, Moss is showing the limits of the race and class con-structs to explain and represent the everyday beliefs and behavior of these poor white youth.

Overall, the text's narrative is clearly an author-driven, linear, unitary narrative. It is written in a highly accessible, nontechnical manner that high-lights Moss's encounters with them and the voices of the youth. This is a "realist text" with, however, a deconstructionist logic and twist. Moss uses the narrative technique of "ironic juxtaposition" of his "realist" characters and "typical scenes" to force the character to question his or her sense of racial and class privilege. Consequently, his text is quite theoretically reflex-ive in the deconstructive sense without using explicit theoretical commen-tary in the text itself. The text is also reflexive in several other ways. Moss provides the reader with an extensive "intertextually reflexive" account of the local reality construction processes of poor whites and their cultural oth-ers. What he does not do, however, is contextualize this local reality process within larger academic and popular discourses about race and class. The text also explores the self-other relationship that literally coproduces these con-ceptual categories. His reflections on a privileged black ethnographer medi-ating these youth's construction of white privilege is particularly interesting. He works the hyphen in a manner that helps explore the construction of class and racial identities rather than explores his own subjectivity, bias, and vulnerability in a confessional manner.

Most cultural Marxists will appreciate how Moss disrupts negative images of poor whites and explores the subtleties of identity construction, but they will worry that his account does not strategically essentialize enough. They will also complain that Moss makes little or no effort to intervene in these people's lives or to empower community groups. Conversely, postmodernists may distrust his inclination to narrate in a humanist, realist style. They will question whether a text with one foot in modernist realism and one in deconstructionism is antirealist enough to produce an antiessentializing account. Moss's unusual synthesis is his search for a philosophical middle ground. He wants to produce more subtle, less fixed, essentializing represen-tations of cultural others that are both more accessible than jargon-filled, disruptive postmodernist accounts and more believable than the sweeping, sentimental, positive portraits of post-Marxist accounts.

Pattie Lather and Cris Smithies's (1996) *Troubling Angels: Women Living with HIV/AIDS* works hard to undermine any coherent explanation of these women's lives beyond what the women share. The authors use what they call a "split-level, hypertext," which highlights a series of focus group discussions with the women from three other distinct sections of the text written in different linguistic "registers": the author's methodological and ethical reflections, "factoids," and "angel texts." The author's reflections are explicit confessional statements at the bottom of the text. Factoids are carefully boxed information that claims to be the latest demographics and verifiable facts about AIDS and the AIDS crises. Angel texts are sections where Lather presents graphic representations and thoughts of various writers and artists about angels. They are Lather's poetic, metaphorical device that "evokes" the mystery and inexplicability of the AIDS crises rather than explaining it. The idea is to open up rather than foreclose critical reflection on the AIDS through a paradoxical, fertile image of angels. These narrative strategies are Lather's way of diminishing her own authorial authority as the grand interpreter.

Overall, the text is consciously organized as a disjointed jumble of factoids, angel texts, focus group discussions, and author reflections and confessions. The general aim here is to produce a text that is decidedly antirealist. No authorial engine or linear plot or conceptual framework organizes the fragments into a coherent whole. Nevertheless, the text contains a powerful residual realist style narrative. The documentary style presentation of women talking in focus groups ends up conveying a vivid "realist portrait" of the physical and psychological trials of being HIV positive. Despite Lather's passionate antirealist rhetoric, the women essentialize themselves as heroes and victims in much the same manner that post-Marxists authors essentialize stigmatized cultural others.

The focus group discussions also convey the psychological, racial, and class diversity among HIV-positive women powerfully. Some women are virtually abandoned by friends and family; others are embraced. Some face horrendous problems and are mercilessly stereotyped; others are not. The documentary style presentation of these women's voices produces a veritable cacophony of believable, realistic voices. It makes caricaturing HIV-positive women almost impossible. These unvarnished portrayals probably work like the staged interview testimonies of Fine and Weis and the ironic juxtapositions of Moss do to create reader empathy and disrupt stereotypes. It would seem that the narrative strategy of author absence and literally "giving voice" reintroduces a measure of realism into an avowedly antirealist text. Ultimately, the women's voices seem to be doing more of deconstructive work than the ambiguous angel texts, author asides, and factoids.

Overall, Lather's text is quite reflexive in at least two ways. First, by scrupulously avoiding authoritative explanations, she is actually being very theoretical in a deconstructive sense. Skeptical that she can empathically experience what these women are experiencing, she refuses to play the expert and explain their lives. Being suspicious of ethnographers who wear the heroic, empathic, sentimental humanist mask, she works hard to maintain a respectful, unsentimental, emotional distance from her subjects. Her coauthor Smithies, the practicing psychotherapist, seems to do more modernist explaining and empathizing than Lather does. Second, Lather also builds a good deal of intertextual reflexivity into her narrative. She makes little effort to provide a genealogy of the othering discourse on HIV-positive women, but one cannot read the women's passionate, painful accounts without understanding how they have been othered and stigmatized. To a degree, the factoids and the angel metaphor also provide a poetic, factual intertextual context for situating the images of these women.

On the other hand, neither she nor Smithies makes much effort to "work the hyphen" and explicate their personal relationships to the women or to each other in a confessional manner. The whole self-other process of power relationships and identification and misrecognition is never interrogated seriously. Lather seems to believe that such forms of reflexivity are the proverbial modernist wolf in sheep's clothing. Since Lather is bent on disrupting the realist trope of a heroic, empathic ethnographer on a knowledge quest, she avoids this kind of authorial "presence" like the plague. When she does appear, she is careful to represent herself as a rather cerebral, emotionally detached, unsentimental figure who is doing little interpretive work of any sort. Such a move strikes at the heart of a "good" modernist ethnography, which always has an author who is discovering, explaining, and giving a "deep reading" of her field experience. But it leaves Lather less inclined to work the hyphen the way many critical ethnographers are, which suits her fine philosophically.

A final, highly deconstructive, yet distinctly different postmodern ethnography is Kathleen Stewart's *Space on the Side of the Road* (1996), a study of poor whites in Appalachia. She characterizes her own narrative style of tacking between the local dialect and high theory as a "surreal space of intensification." She claims that such a text allows the reader to imagine the cultural other in something other than the "you-are-there," documentary style of realist ethnographies. Stewart piles one dense local narrative upon another to evoke the aporia she apparently felt during fieldwork. She then adds a theoretical exegesis of these stories that plies one academic construct upon another. A dizzying carnival of postmodern cultural critics—Barthes, Benjamin, Bahkthin, Jameson, Derrida, Taussig—step forward to give us suggestive meanings of the local talk she hears. No local story is too small, no theory is too grand for Stewart's montage of folk and academic discourse. At times these two distinct registers meld together into sentences that begin in obtuse jargon and end in colloquial Appalachian.

Stewart characterizes the poetics of local storytelling as a vast proliferation of signs, a "mimetic excess of remembering in the face of ruin and decline." The world and life represented in these stories is a world of place and people, a world "got down" (i.e., a world of spent mines, rusting automobiles, unpainted shacks, men bent from brute labor, and families living poor in piney wooded hollows). It is a world of restless, nervous storytelling that produce an endless stream of highly prosaic stories about aunt Ruth's pigs, Clem's car accident, and mines gone sour. The stories are so prosaic and concrete and referenced in recollections of local people and places, so excessively mimetic, that they evoke what Stewart calls of the "cultural real" of Appalachia like so many surrealistic paintings. Paradoxically, their prosaic, excessively mimetic character makes them profoundly poetic. Ultimately, they produce what Stewart calls a "space on the side of the road," a narrativized space that Appalachians create and inhabit, a space filled with desire, longing, memories, and mystery; a space where "other Americans," poor Americans, dwell.

She then deploys Roland Barthes's theory of semiology to conceptualize the folk's narrative poetics as a "first-order semiological system." This folk system has radically different epistemological practices than a second-order semiological system, which she calls the "bourgeois imaginary." In this system non-Appalachian bourgeois academics, journalists, policy makers, and bureaucrats ideologically represent Appalachians as an exotic, wild, depraved cultural other. This othering discourse is notable for its lack of connection to what she calls the "cultural real" of local narratives. If you want to know who Appalachians are, you must pay attention to their narrative self-representations rather than the ideological, othering discourse of the bourgeois imaginary. This will not magically provide one with a true account of Appalachian culture, but it at least evokes or mimics how they discursively produce their lived cultural reality.

So at the heart of this innovative postmodern ethnography lies an unconventional structuralist Marxist notion of social class. At times, Stewart represents this narratively produced space in a manner reminiscent of cultural production/practice ethnographies. She occasionally includes vignettes of tough back-talking women and sly tricksters challenging government bureaucrats. But most of the time she avoids portraying their storytelling as "back talk" (i.e., as explicit counterhegemonic discourses). Instead local storytelling is conceptualized as a "political unconscious" at work, which is marked by a distinct way of knowing or epistemology. Again, the folk are different because they know and discursively construct their world differently from bourgeois outsiders. This conceptual move seems a little like a postmodern analogue to Gramsci's notion that everyone is a philosopher. In this case, everyone is a poet who unconsciously constructs a habitable narrative space on the side of the road in a bourgeois society.

Having grasped and portrayed a cultural poetics of Appalachia, Stewart goes on to suggest that this discursively constructed space is actually a good metaphor for culture in general. She uses a deconstructionist metaphor to define culture as "the space in the gap between signifier and signified, the endless play of signifiers." The meaning of culture is as indeterminate as the play of signifiers, and like the folk tell her repeatedly, "It's just talk. It don't mean nothin' at all." As Stewart is fond of saying, culture is something that you "can't get right." She means that in the sense that it is a web of signification that never serves up a stable, fixed meaning. A cultural interpreter cannot simply scoop up the meaning of culture with her rational culture construct. The slippery reality of culture as narrative practice will slitter through any heuristic mapping device known to anthropologists. Earlier anthropological "theories" of culture are too static, deterministic, and fixed to capture the endless play of signifiers, the determinate yet indeterminate, real yet unreal, paradoxical character of human cultures.

Stewart's notion of folk narrativization as semiotic play with a class twist is an allegorical tale turned back upon anthropology itself. The way she narrates her "discovery" of this new metaphor for culture reminds me of how earlier cultural ethos theorists Margaret Mead and Ruth Bendict represented their cultural critiques. In this style of critique the anthropologist uses the trope of a journey to a distant, allegedly primitive culture to discover its civilizing lesson. The anthropologist then returns home to teach his fellow moderns more humane childrearing practices or a polymorphous sexuality. In this instance Stewart travels to an American backwater that is imagined to be savage and distant psychologically and socially. But Stewart finds that the so-called savages have a marvelously playful, indeterminate, poetic way of being in the world through language. This discovery should give the bourgeois mainstreamers pause for reflection. It should also teach fellow anthropologists how to think about the poetics of culture like a deconstructionist. But like any good deconstructionist, Stewart ultimately underplays her portrait of Appalacia as a true picture of the culture. Since no interpreter can "get culture right," that also applies to Stewart's account of Appalachian talk as well. She provides a striking poetic rendition of local poetics and nothing more. So sit back and enjoy the ordinary language poetics of the folks and Stewart's theoretical poetics because as she might say, "It's just talk. That's all it is."

On the other hand, Stewart's heavy emphasis on theory inadvertently reasserts her interpretive prominence and authority as an author. At times she appears in the text as the laid-back anthropologist rapping with and enjoying the folk, but mainly she appears as the social theorist who is reconceptualizing narrativization and the culture concept. Her incessant theorization of local practices makes it hard to read her representation as simply a poetic, mimetic representation of their cultural reality. Nowhere does she claim it is a true, scientific, objective account, but the heavy theorization of local poetics led me to read her account as a theory-driven academic ethnography that presents her "deep reading" or explanation of local narrative practices. Ultimately, her text seemed to be both a poetic postmodern narrative and a theory-driven modernist ethnography that produces an unbourgeois Appalacian cultural other.

In sharp contrast, Lather's narrative practices seem more consistently antimodernist. She avoids explicit theoretical discussions almost entirely and downplays her authorial authority more. She explicitly substitutes poetic angel texts, factoids, and the voices of her subjects for any formal theorizing. There is no way one can read Lather's text as her generalized portrait of a cultural other. The only portrait of the HIV-positive women that comes through is their self-portrait, which is quite varied and complex. The other postmodern ethnographer reviewed, Moss, also maintains his authorial prominence in a somewhat different manner. He is not in the text as a grand theorizer, but he is there as the omniscient narrator or authorial engine in the modernist sense. He organizes narratively a series of connected events and characters in ironic juxtapositions that deconstruct rather than theorize the class and race constructs. In the end, his portrait of the privilege of white working-class youth is decidedly mixed and complex but actually modernist and realist in style.

Both Lather and Stewart are experimenting with surrealistic narrative techniques of montage, pastiche, and juxtaposition to create an alternative to conventional ethnographic realist narratives. Both claim to be writing for the general public in an effort to disrupt their stereotypes of HIV-positive women and Appalachians. Lather in particular makes some spirited, empirically unsubstantiated claims for the effectiveness of her antirealist, surrealistic narrative style with ordinary readers. As I noted earlier, the realist voices of the HIV-positive women may actually be more disruptive of cultural othering than Lather's surrealist, poetic textual strategies. Stewart makes far fewer claims for her surrealist narrative style as an effective popular, accessible text, and she is clearly trying to write an exemplary methodological tale for her academic peers. Ultimately, neither text is an easy read nor particularly accessible except when the subjects tell their own stories. In contrast, Moss's text is a seamless, accessible, realist narrative with characters, events, and a "plot." In this case the idea that plots the narrative action is white youth constructing their white privilege through racial and class discourses. We see this happening in a documentary style in various work, play, school, and residential settings. The text is only disruptive in the sense that it disrupts popular, taken-for-granted ideas of poor whites and the privilege of whiteness. In sharp contrast, Lather and Stewart's texts are much more disruptive of conventional modernist, realist notions of narrative and story.

To sum up, first, all three of these postmodern ethnographers are quite theoretically reflexive (i.e., use theory to disrupt rather than to map reality). To this end, these postmodern authors deconstruct academic constructs and images of cultural others quite effectively. Lather is trying to be theoretically reflexive through a surrealistic narrative style and through her substitution of poetic, deconstructive angel texts for formal constructs. Moss unsettles anthropological constructs through the ironic juxtaposition of the stories about his subjects. Stewart's surrealistic narrative technique of piling one dense local narrative upon another evokes the paradoxical, ambiguous poetic quality of local narrative practices and ultimately suggests how to redefine the culture concept. Overall, all the author's accounts definitely question, disrupt, and renovate academic constructs in their own ways.

Second, none of the postmodern authors express much interest in working the self-other hyphen and representing themselves confessionally. None of the authors explores the vulnerabilities and complexities of self-other relationships in the manner that Behar, Krieger, and Fine and Weis do. Stewart sees this sort of textual experimentation as a lingering foundational search for a perfect textual solution to misrepresentation. Lather distrusts such reflexive textual practices as the vestiges of a modernist, authorial will to power to be the heroic, all-knowing, empathic ethnographer. Moss is generally more open to confessional reflexivity, and he explores the impact of his blackness on his poor white subjects to a point. But his explorations of self-other relationships are mainly used to disrupt and deconstruct the constructs of race and class rather than to explore his positionality or subjectivity in any depth.

Third, all three practice intertextual reflexivity to varying degrees. Lather and Moss tend to leave out of their texts an account of how they produced their "facts" or representations. On the other hand, both make an effort to situate their representations intertextually. In Lather's text the HIV-positive women convey vividly how they have been misrepresented, but she presents little systematic portrayal of how HIV-positive women have been misrepresented historically. Moss provides a few references to historical misrepresentations of poverty and class, but no sustained account. However, neither author provides a comprehensive intertextual account of how local and extra-local discourses produce the cultural other they strive to represent. In contrast, Stewart's account is unusually rich in intertextual reflexivity. She provides an extensive account of both how bourgeois outsiders misrepresent the region and its people and how locals narratively create their imaginary/real cultural space. She does little to situate herself in these historical representational processes, but she does ultimately underplay her own account as a true, scientific account.

Fourth, all these authors are also quite dedicated to combating the essentialization of cultural others. These postmodern ethnographers do not focus on the counterhegemonic discourses of subaltern groups, and they protest that they are not noble, heroic ethnographers "giving voice" to the subaltern. Nevertheless, they do tend to valorize oppressed cultural others by letting a little "strategic essentialism" slip back into their texts. It surfaces in Lather's text mainly through the women's representations of themselves. It is a by-product of Stewart's powerful portrayal of Appalachian narrativization that valorizes a working class "poetic cultural other." It is gently present in Moss's touching realist portraits of white welfare mothers and poor white youth. In this regard, all these postmodern texts seem to show some of the political work that cultural production/practice critical ethnographers do. These postmodern authors are less explicitly collaborative and directly involved in the local politics of their subjects, however, than Fine and Weis were. Postmodern ethnographers generally seem more interested in deconstructing reigning signification systems that in attacking the public policies of reigning political regimes. The political thrust of their ethnographic practice is more theoretical and academic than it is practical and public.

## Making Critical Ethnography More Reflexive

The postmodern critique of science generally suggests that we need a healthy dose of radical skepticism. Postmodernists implore us to live in a world of no epistemological and political guarantees. They demand that we be more critical of our personal, political, and ethical fieldwork practices, that we radically deconstruct our conceptual frameworks. We are implored to rethink how we interpret and write up our field experiences. Some observers like George Noblit call these recent developments the "postcritical moment" in critical educational ethnography. Whatever one calls the 1990s, many critical ethnographers now subscribe to a much less foundational notion of science. Their views are grounded in a variety of feminist, hermeneutic, postmodern, and post-Marxist perspectives. They no longer imagine themselves speaking from an objective interpretive position outside or above social reality. Many contemporary ethnographers are trying to "work the hyphens" (Fine 1994), but greater reflexivity will not turn out to be the silver bullet that slays the dragon of misrepresentation. Nor will greater reflexivity provide a firm, reliable foundation for an objective social sciences. As my postmodern colleague Katie Stewart is fond of saying, cultural analysis will never be a matter of "getting it right." But a more reflexive interpretive and narrative practice, although not a panacea, will help us produce more honest, believable stories.

I infuse reflexivity into my storytelling by using ordinary rather than technical language. I now write in a highly personal, autobiographical, nontechnical voice that foregrounds local characters and events and backgrounds theory. I also use various literary devices like irony, satire, puns, parodies, and metaphors rather than a flat, colorless, denotative scientific language style. An expressive, robust language style is much more accessible, engaging, and entertaining to read. Moreover, I still use a modified version of the realist narrative form. Unlike postmodern critics who flog realism mercilessly, I view modernism as having already produced reflexive forms of realist literature, drama, and cinema (Bradbury and McFarlaine 1972; Clifford 1988). Brechtian drama, neorealist cinema, literary magical realism, and many other forms can be used to enrich ethnographic storytelling.

My reasons for trying to create a more reflexive realist narrative style are mainly political. For better or worse, ordinary people understand, enjoy, and consume this deceptively simple, popular narrative style. Radically antirealist ethnographic texts (Lather and Smithies 1997; Stewart 1996) are interesting experiments, but they are not as clear and understandable as their authors' imagine. We should not abandon popular culture forms too quickly for more obscure avant-garde forms. We should learn to work through familiar narrative forms and everyday language to make our cultural critiques more accessible to ordinary readers.

Those of us still using modernist realist narratives must, however, heed the postmodern warning that realist texts are not carbon copies of reality. The old scientific realist ethnography was far too scientistic, authoritative, and official sounding (Marcus and Cushman 1982). If one heeds Foucault, such texts almost certainly help elevate the social science disciplines to a more prominent role in the new surveillance and governance systems of modern societies. Such texts glorify scientists and lead so-called intellectuals away from creating a more democratic, critical "public sphere" or civil society. Writing in a more reflexive realist style or a surrealist style will hardly arrest these broad political and cultural developments, but such texts may help teach people how to read all scientific and historical studies more critically. That would be an improvement over an academy that teaches people to consume scientific studies with little skepticism.

The postmodern critique that most representations of cultural others are essentializing has merit as well. Too many social scientific accounts of cultural others reinforce popular racial, class, gender, and sexual preference stereotypes. There is a great and continuing need to deconstruct the social sciences' role in producing these forms of symbolic violence against various identity groups. On the other hand, the post-Marxists are right that the representation scale is heavily tipped toward the ruling bloc. The ruling bloc and their academic and journalistic allies control and produce the discourses that stigmatize the less privileged. The privileged are constantly "normalizing" their identity and worldview through hegemonic discourses. Earlier scientific ethnographies often failed to actively counter popular and academic racist, sexist, classist, homophobic imagines that "essentialize" cultural groups negatively.

Academics who imagine themselves "public intellectuals," or "organic intellectuals," are forced to choose sides in a world of economic, political, and symbolic violence. Consequently, many contemporary critical ethnographers now use what Lila Abu-Lughod (1991) calls a "tactical humanist" narrative that "strategically essentializes" oppressed subalterns (Spivak 1988). Given the rise of ethnic, feminist, and gay/lesbian scholars who often think of themselves as the "organic intellectuals" of oppressed, stigmatized cultural groups, strategic essentializing has begun to displace negative essentializing. Scholars who strategically essentialize tend to tell stories about the ruling bloc's negative character, policy, and discourses, and the subaltern's positive character, agency, and resistance. They interrupt the ideological practices that systematically inflict symbolic violence upon ordinary people.

Critical ethnographers who are informed by deconstructionism will, however, also seek to avoid reproducing the either/or logic of metalanguages.

Such a logic leads too many well-intentioned authors to merely displace negative essentialist portraits with romantic positive ones. Instead, we must use analogic and dialectic logic to produce complex, contradictory, more believable representations of any and all cultural others. Such ethnographic texts will make strong political statements without romanticizing the downtrodden and caricaturing their oppressors. This may be a case of wanting my political cake and eating it too, but we must resist sweeping essentializations of others yet "strategically essentializing" the victims of symbolic violence.

Finally, a more reflexive ethnographic practice helps let some air out of the hubris of academics of all ideological persuasions. If an ethnographer really practices all varieties of reflexivity—from Behar to Bourdieu to Derrida—she will be forced to give up what Donna Haraway (1988) calls the "god-trick " of science and utopian thought. No matter how epistemologically reflexive and systematic our fieldwork is, we must still speak as mere mortals from various historical, culture-bound standpoints; we must still make limited, historically "situated knowledge claims." By claiming to be less rather than more, perhaps we can tell stories that nonacademics will find more believable and useful. This is what I take from postmodernism and feminism to make my critical ethnographies more critical.

## References

Abu-Lughod, L. "Writing Against Culture." Pp. 137–69 in Richard Fox, ed., *Recapturing Anthropology: Working in the Present*. Santa Fe, N.M.: School of American Research Press, 1991.

Anderson, G. "Critical Ethnography in Education: Origins, Current Status, and New Directions." *Review of Educational Research*, 59 (1989):249–70.

Anyon, J. "Social Class and School Knowledge." *Curriculum Inquiry*, 11, 1 (1981): 3–42.

Apple, M. *Education and Power*. New York: Routledge, 1982.

Apple, M, and L Roman. "Is Naturalism a Move Beyond Positivism." Pp. 38–73, Part I, Section 2 in E. Eisner and A. Peshkin, ed., *Qualitative Inquiry in Education*. New York: Teachers College Press, 1990.

Aronowitz, S, and H Giroux. *Postmodern Education: Politics, Culture and Social Criticism*. Minneapolis: University of Minnesota Press, 1991.

Babcock, B. "Reflexivity: Definitions and Discriminations." In *Semiotica*, 30 (1/2) (1980):1–14.

Behar, R. *Translated Woman: Crossing the Border with Esperanza's Story*. Boston: Beacon Press, 1993.

Behar, R. *The Vulnerable Observer: Anthropology that Breaks the Heart*. Boston: Beacon Press, 1996.

Behar, R., and D. Gordon, ed. *Women Writing Culture*. Berkeley: University of California Press. 1995.

Bourdieu, P., and L. J. D. Wacquant. *An Invitation to Reflexive Sociology*. Chicago: University of Chicago Press, 1992.

Bradbury, M., and J. McFarlane. *Modernism, 1890–1930*. New York: Doubleday Press, 1972.

Brecht, B. *Brecht on Theater: The Development of an Aesthetic*, John Willet, trans. New York: Hill and Wang, 1964.

Carspecken, P. *Critical Ethnography in Educational Research: A Theoretical and Practical Guide*. New York: Routledge, 1996.

Carspecken, P., and M. Apple. "Critical Qualitative Research: Theory, Methodology, and Practice." Pp. 507–53 in M. D. LeCompte, W. Millroy, and J. P. Goetz, ed., *The Handbook of Qualitative Research in Education*. San Diego: Academic Press, 1992.

Chaudhry, L. "Researching 'My People,' Researching Myself: Fragments of a Reflexive Tale." *Qualitative Studies in Education*, 10, 4 (1997): 441–53.

Cicourel, A, et al., ed. *Language Use and School Performance*. New York: Academic Press, 1974.

Clifford, J. *The Predicament of Culture: Twentieth Century Ethnography, Literature, and Art*. Cambridge, Mass.: Harvard University Press, 1988.

Clifford, J., and G. Marcus, ed. *Writing Culture: The Poetics and Politics of Ethnography*. Berkeley: University of California Press, 1986.

Crapanzano, V. *Tuhami: Portrait of a Moroccan*. Chicago: University of Chicago Press, 1980.

Dumont, R. *The Headhunter and I: Ambiguity and Ambivalence in the Fieldworking Experience*. Austin: University of Texas Press, 1978.

Dwyer, K. *Morrocan Dialogues: Anthropology in Question*. Baltimore: Johns Hopkins University Press, 1982.

Everhart, R. *Reading, Writing, and Resistance: Adolescence and Labor in a Junior High School*. London: Routledge and Kegan Paul, 1983.

Fabian, J. *Time and the Other: How Anthropology Makes Its Object*. New York: Columbia University Press, 1983.

Fine, M. "Working the Hyphens: Reinventing Self and Other in Qualitative Research." Pp. 70–82 in Y. Lincoln and N. Denzin, ed., *Handbook of Qualitative Research*. Thousand Oaks, Calif.: Sage, 1994.

Fine, M., and L. Weis. "Writing the 'Wrongs' of Fieldwork: Confronting Our Own Research/Writing Dilemmas in Urban Ethnographies." *Qualitative Inquiry*, 2, 3 (1996): 251–74.

Fine, M., and L. Weis. *The Unknown City: The Lives of Poor and Working-Class Young Adults*. Boston: Beacon Press, 1998.

Fine, M., L. Weis, S. Weseen, and L. Wong. "For Whom! Qualitative Research, Representations, and Social Responsibilities." Pp. 107–32 in Y. Lincoln and N. Denzin, ed., *Handbook for Qualitative Research*, 2nd ed. Thousand Oaks, Calif.: Sage, 1999.

Foley, D. "Critical Ethnography: The Reflexive Turn." In *Ethnography*. Thousand Oaks, Calif.: Sage Publications, forthcoming.

Foley, D. "On Writing Reflexive Realist Narratives." Pp. 110–29 in J. Shacklock and J. Smythe, ed., *Being Reflexive in Critical Educational and Social Research*. London: Falmer Press, 2000.

Foley, D. *The Heartland Chronicles*. Philadelphia: University of Pennsylvania Press, 1995.

Foley, D. *Learning Capitalist Culture: Deep in the Heart of Tejas*. Philadelphia: University of Pennsylvania Press, 1990.

Foley, D. *Philippine Rural Education: An Anthropological Perspective*. DeKalb: University of Northern Illinois Press, 1976.

Foley, D., B. Levinson, and J. Hurtig. "Anthropology Goes Inside: The New Educational Ethnography of Ethnicity and Gender." Pp. 37–98 in W. G. Secada, ed., *Review of Research in Education, 25, 2000–2001*. Washington, D.C.: American Educational Research Association, 2001.

Foley, D., and K. Moss. "Studying American Cultural Diversity: Some Non-Essentializing Perspectives." In I. Susser, ed., *Teaching Cultural Diversity*. Washington, D.C.: American Anthropological Association Publications, 2000.

Foley, D., with C. Mota, D. Post, and I. Lozano. *From Peones to Politicos: Class and Ethnicity in a South Texas Town, 1900–1989*. 2nd ed. Austin: University of Texas Press, 1989.

Freilich, M., ed. *Marginal Natives: Anthropologists at Work*. New York: Harper and Row, 1970.

Geertz, C. *Works and Lives: The Anthropologist as Author*. Stanford: Stanford University Press, 1988.

Golde, P., ed. *Woman in the Field: Anthropological Experiences*. Chicago: Aldine, 1970.

Gramsci, A. *Prison Notebooks*. New York: International Publishers, 1971.

Gwaltney, J. *Drylongso: A Self-Portrait of Black America*. New York: Vintage Press, 1980.

Habermas, J. *Knowledge and Human Interest*. Boston: Beacon Press, 1971.

Hall, S., C. Critcher, T. Jefferson, J. Clarke, and B. Roberts. *Policing the Crises: Mugging, the State, and Law and Order*. London: MacMillan Press, 1978.

Haraway, D. "Situated Knowledges: The Science Question in Feminism as a Site of Discourse on the Privilege of Partial Perspective." *Feminist Studies*, 14 (1988):575–99.

Hayano, D. "Auto-Ethnography: Paradigms, Problems, and Prospects." *Human Organization*, 38, 1 (1979):99–104.

Henry, J. *Culture Against Man*. New York: Vintage, 1960.

Hill, D., P. McLaren, M. Cole, and G. Rikowski, ed. *Postmodernism in Educational Theory: Education and the Politics of Human Resistance*. London: The Tufnell Press, 1999.

Hymes, D., ed. *Reinventing Anthropology*. New York: Vintage, 1969.

Karabel, J., and A. H. Halsey. "Educational Research: A Review and an Interpretation." Pp. 1–85 in J. Karabel and A. H. Halsey, ed., *Power and Ideology in Education*. New York: Oxford University Press, 1977.

Kincheloe, J., and P. L. McLaren. "Rethinking Critical Theory and Qualitative Research." In Y. Lincoln and N. Denzin, ed., *Handbook for Qualitative Research*. Thousand Oaks, Calif.: Sage, 1994.

Kondo, D. *Crafting Selves: Power, Gender, and Discourses of Identity in Japanese Workplace.* Chicago: University of Chicago Press, 1990.

Krieger, S. *Social Science and the Self: Personal Essays on an Art Form.* New Brunswick, N.J.: Rutgers University, 1991.

Laclau, E., and C. Mouffe. *Hegemony and Socialist Strategy: Towards a Radical Democratic Politics.* London: Verso, 1985.

Lather, P. *Getting Smart: Feminist Research and Pedagogy With/in the Postmodern.* London: Routledge, 1991.

Lather, P. "Troubling Clarity: The Politics of Assessable Language." *Harvard Educational Review,* 66, 3 (1996): 525–45.

Lather, P. "Drawing the Line at Angels: Working the Ruins of Feminist Ethnography." *International Journal of Qualitative Studies in Education,* 10, 3 (1998): 285–304.

Lather, P., and C. Smithies. *Troubling the Angels: Women Living with HIV/AIDS.* Boulder, Colo.: Westview Press, 1997.

Lave, J. "Contemporary Cultural Studies at Birmingham, England." *Annual Review of Anthropology,* 21: 257–82.

Lawson, H. *Reflexivity: The Postmodern Predicament.* La Salle, Ill.: Open Court, 1985.

Levinson, B., and D. Holland. "The Cultural Production of the Educated Person: An Introduction." Pp. 1–56 in B. Levinson, D. Foley, and D. Holland, ed., *The Cultural Production of the Educated Person: Critical Ethnographies of Schooling and Local Practice.* Albany: State University of New York Press, 1996.

Lukacs, G. *The Historical Novel.* London: Merlin Press, 1962.

Lukacs, G. *History and Class Consciousness.* London: Merlin Press, 1971.

Luke, A. "Text and Discourse in Education: An Introduction to Critical Discourse Analysis." *Review of Research in Education,* 21 (1995–6): 3–47.

Malinowski, B. *A Diary in the Strict Sense of the Term.* London: Routledge & Kegan Paul, 1967.

Marcus, G. "What Comes (Just) After 'Post'! The Case of Ethnography." Pp. 563–73 in Y. Lincoln and N. Denzin, ed., *Handbook of Qualitative Research.* Thousand Oaks, Calif.: Sage, 1994.

Marcus, G. *Ethnography through Thick and Thin.* Princeton, N.J.: Princeton University Press, 1998.

Marcus, G., and D. Cushman. "Ethnographies as Texts." *Annual Review of Anthropology,* 11 (1982):25–69.

Marcus, G., and M. Fischer. *Anthropology as Cultural Critique: An Experimental Moment in the Human Sciences.* Chicago: University of Chicago, 1986.

McCarthy, C. *The Use of Culture: Education and the Limits of Ethnic Affiliation.* New York and London: Routledge, 1997.

McLaren, P. "Revolutionary Pedagogy in Post-Revolutionary Times: Rethinking the Political Economy of Critical Education." *Education Theory,* 48, 4 (1998): 231–262.

Mehan, H. B. *Learning Lessons: The Social Organization of Classroom Instruction.* Cambridge, Mass.: Harvard University Press, 1979.

Mehan, H. B., and H. L. Wood. *The Reality of Ethnomethodology*. New York: Wiley, 1975.

Mehan, H. B., A. Hertweck, and J. L. Meihls. *Handicapping the Handicapped: Decision-Making in Students' Educational Careers*. Stanford: Stanford University Press, 1986.

Morely, D., and K.-H. Chen, ed. *Stuart Hall: Critical Dialogues in Cultural Studies*. London and New York: Routledge, 1996.

Moss, K. "Interrogating Images: Poor Whites and the Paradox of Privilege." Ph.D. Diss. University of Texas at Austin, 1998.

Narayan, K. "How Native Is a 'Native' Anthropologist?" *American Anthropologist*, 95, 3 (1993):28–29.

Negri, A. *Marx Beyond Marx: Lessons from the Gundrisse*. Mass.: Bergin and Garvey Publishers, Inc., 1984.

Noblit, G., ed. *The Playgrounds of Postcritical Ethnographies*, forthcoming .

Oakley, J., and H. Calloway, ed. *Anthropology and Autobiography*. New York and London: Routledge, 1992.

Popkewitz, T., and M. Brennan, ed. *Foucault's Challenge: Discourse, Knowledge, and Power in Education*. New York: Teachers College Press, 1996.

Quantz, R. "On Critical Ethnography (With Some Postmodern Considerations)." Pp. 447–506 in Margaret D. LeCompte, Wendy Millroy, and Judith Preissle Goetz, ed., *The Handbook of Qualitative Research in Education*. San Diego: Academic Press, 1992.

Rabinow, P. *Reflections on Fieldwork in Morocco*. Berkeley: University of California Press, 1977.

Roosens, E. *Creating Ethnicity. The Process of Ethnogenesis*. Thousand Oaks, Calif.: Sage, 1989.

Rosaldo, R. *Culture and Truth: The Remaking of Social Analysis*. Boston: Beacon Press, 1989.

Rosenau, P. *Post-Modernism and the Social Sciences: Insights, Inroads, and Intrusions*. Princeton, N.J: Princeton University Press, 1992.

Shacklock, J., and J. Smythe, ed. *Being Reflexive in Critical Educational and Social Research*. London: Falmer Press, 1998.

Spindler, G., ed. *Being an Anthropologist: Fieldwork in Eleven Cultures*. New York: Holt, Rinehart and Winston, 1970.

Spivak, G. *In Other Worlds: Essays in Cultural Politics*. New York: Methuen, 1988.

Stewart, K. *A Space on the Side of the Road: Cultural Poetics in an 'Other' America*. Princeton, N.J.: Princeton University Press, 1996.

Tedlock, B. "From Participant Observation to the Observation of Participation: The Emergence of Narrative Ethnography." *Journal of Anthropological Research*, 47, 1 (1991):69–94.

Trueba, E. *Latinos Unidos: From Cultural Diversity to the Politics of Solidarity*. New York: Rowman & Littlefield, 1999.

Tyler, S. "Postmodern Ethnography: From Document of the Occult to Occult Document." In J. Clifford and G. Marcus, ed., *Writing Culture: The Poetics and Politics of Ethnography*. Berkeley: University of California Press, 1986.

Van Mannen, J. *Tales of the Field: On Writing Ethnography*. Chicago: University of Chicago Press, 1988.

Villenas, S. "The Colonizer/Colonized Chicana Ethnographer: Identity, Marginalization, and Co-optation in the Field." *Harvard Educational Review*, 66, 4 (1996): 711–31.

Villenas, S., and D. Foley. "The Rise of Educational Ethnographers of Color and the New Latino/a Critique of Schooling." In Richard Valencia, ed. *Chicano Schooling*, 2nd ed. London: Falmer Press, forthcoming.

Weis, L., and M. Fine, ed. *Speed Bumps: A Student Friendly Guide to Qualitative Research*. New York: Teachers College Press, 2000.

Wexler, P. *Becoming Somebody*. Lews: Falmer Press, 1992.

White, Hn. *Metahistory: The Historical Imagination in Nineteenth-Century Europe*. Baltimore: Johns Hopkins University Press, 1973.

Willis, P. *Common Culture*. London: Open University Press, 1990.

Willis, P. *Learning to Labor: How Working Class Kids Get Working Class Jobs*. New York: Teacher's College Press, 1981.

Willis, P. *Profane Culture*. London: Saxon Press, 1976.

Woolgar, S. *Knowledge and Reflexivity: New Frontiers in the Sociology of Knowledge*. London: Routledge, 1991.

Woolgar, S., and B. Latour. *Laboratory Life: The Construction of Scientific Facts*. Princeton, N.J.: Princeton University Press, 1986.

⌐∾

# CHAPTER SEVEN

# The Challenge of Urban Ethnography

*David M. Smith*

## Prefatory Comments

Two considerations guide this chapter. First, although I had previously done some work in urban schools in Norfolk, Virginia, my formal introduction to doing urban ethnography came while I was serving as director of the Center for Urban Ethnography at the University of Pennsylvania. In the following presentation I will use as my point of departure the research we did at that time in West Philadelphia supported by grants from the now defunct National Institute of Education. I will also be using data from our experiences in working with Native American populations at the University of Alaska, with Aboriginal students at the Centre for Aboriginal Studies at Curtin University in Australia, and as a consultant on the middle schools mathematics project of the Institute for Research on Learning. Although the Philadelphia research was conducted in the 1980s, we encountered many of the continuing challenges to urban ethnography and some of the lessons we learned merit revisiting. Second, this chapter is data based, growing directly out of our research experiences and not heavily theoretical. These experiences should illustrate and provide a kind of lens for viewing the theoretical chapters in this volume.

## Introduction

The Center for Urban Ethnography (or CUE as I may refer to it) had its initial impetus in the urban riots of the 1960s. These upheavals caught much of the academic community, as well as the general public, by surprise. For the latter this may have been understandable but for the academic community it was embarrassing. Despite decades of study by social scientists, mainly sociologists, and the publication of reams of academic knowledge, the academic establishment realized that they had precious little understanding of inner-city, or "slum existence." It knew nothing of what it was meant to live, raise families, or go to school in North Philadelphia or Watts or much of Harlem, for example. Prevailing theories about the causes and meanings of poverty and about the nature of these invisible "others" who were popularly deemed to be like us but lazier or less intelligent or less educated were seriously confronted if not shattered.

It was out of this embarrassment that John Szwed, Erving Goffman, and Dell Hymes envisioned a research effort that would lead to a kind of understanding that eluded the positivist, hypothesis-testing approaches of the prevalent social science research of the day. With its roots in Boasian anthropology and descriptive linguistics, traditional ethnography, characterized by a commitment to holism, participant observation methodologies, the use of culture as its heuristic, and a largely inductive stance, claimed to be able to yield precisely the kinds of understandings urbanologists as well as the political leadership lacked. In its early days the Center, using researchers, mainly cultural anthropology, Goffman's sociology, and Szwed's folklore graduate students steeped in this perspective, undertook a wide range of urban studies.

Although this tradition in ethnography has frequently been criticized, and often rightly so, for being a handmaiden of colonial and other hegemonic agendas, it implicitly, in its insistence on relativism and its championing of cultural preservation, for example, nurtured the seeds of critical ethnography. Trueba and Zou have pointed out that, "its quintessential roots are in the seminal work of the early educational ethnographers such as George Spindler, Margaret Mead, Jules Henry and others" (Zou and Trueba 1998:19) Therefore, ironically, these characteristics of traditional ethnography continue to hold promise for ethnography to effectively illuminate contemporary urban issues and at the same time create some of its greatest challenges. Our experiences in the West Philadelphia project serve to illustrate this dilemma.

The research project I am referring to, "The Ethnographic Monitoring of Children's Acquisition of Reading/Language Arts Skills in and out of the Classroom," while conceived with this kind of traditional ethnography in mind was different in one important respect. (See Smith 1983 for a summary of this study.) Following Dell Hymes's published notion of ethnographic monitoring (Hymes 1979), we did not propose to do a traditional fully fledged, long-term comprehensive ethnography of a community. This has become the norm in ethnographic projects on schooling today, but was less so in the early eighties. Neither did we propose, strictly speaking, a problem-centered study. We were responding to the then—and still—strongly voiced concern that inner-city schools were not adequately preparing students in the area of what the educational establishment labeled "language arts skills." This, of course, basically meant that they were not testing as highly on reading and writing tests as parents and the educational community wished.

We proposed to look at unspecified issues surrounding the acquisition of language arts skills. To do this we placed researchers, operating from the perspective of traditional cultural anthropology, in the schools where they established relations with the teachers and students. From this they were able to gain insights first on what the teachers saw were the significant issues and ultimately, through extended dialog and through following these issues in the sub-rosa areas of the classroom as well as to the outside of school lives of the students and ultimately into their homes, to uncover dimensions of the issues that eluded teachers, students, and parents.

We had the good fortune to have secured a grant to fund our research rather than a contract. Furthermore, we happened to have as a project monitor a person who had a Ph.D. in sociolinguistics and an understanding of ethnographic research. This meant that we did not have to define a specific problem to investigate nor did we have to specify precisely what approach we would take, what the outcomes would be, or exactly what the final product would be. (I will come back to the importance of this freedom later.)

Despite having researchers on the project who were well read in traditional ethnography, mostly anthropological accounts of research in Third or Fourth World contexts, little of the literature dealt with the kind of urban school situation in which we were working and only one was an experienced fieldworker. In the tradition of cultural anthropology in which I was schooled, little attention was given to field research as a graduate student. Ethnography was what we read and what we were supposed to produce for a dissertation. How we did it was assumed to kind of take care of itself.

However, when I became director of the Center for Urban Ethnography and professor in the Graduate School of Education, my students and colleagues, who were enamored with ethnography, demanded more explicit guidelines on how to do it.

Having taught a number of ethnographic field methods courses to education graduate students, I had found it necessary to translate what to me were the essential characteristics of ethnography into a set of working principles. We used these to govern our approach. These principles are:

1. Hold in abeyance preconceived notions as to what what's happening, or not happening, means to participants.
2. Let the important questions to be addressed as well as the answers emerge from the context.
3. Do not view participants as subjects but as colearners with the investigator, each using the other to reach shared and ever-deepening understandings.
4. Take seriously the uniqueness of each setting and set of events.
5. Take as of primary importance relationships rather than *relata*.
6. Assume that people inevitably act to make sense of the world they are experiencing.
7. Assume that patterned behavior reflects the presence of underlying power relations.
8. Recognize that genuine understanding can only come through genuine participant observation.
9. Understand that ultimately the power to solve their problems, or even to determine what they are, rests with participants in an activity.
10. Change takes place when we hear another's "story"; it resonates with our own experience and we feel free to take from it for our particular uses.

It is apparent from these that this kind of traditional ethnography tacitly anticipated the more explicitly stated critical ethnography of today and that I approach ethnographic fieldwork much like that of Harry Wolcott—as an art (Wolcott 1998). I have always eschewed the cookbook approaches that have become so popular in the field of educational anthropology. To borrow the language of our measurement-oriented colleagues, the researcher is the research instrument and the techniques she uses must proceed naturally from the interaction between her and the field context in which she is working.

Following from this the training of ethnographers must concentrate upon getting the conceptual framework from which they will be operating straight rather than on merely developing facility with techniques that will largely take care of themselves. This can be discomfiting to researchers educated as teachers or traditional psychology-oriented educational researchers—as some of ours were—since attention to methods and techniques plays such an important role in their formation.

These principles, therefore, are precisely that—discovery principles that were meant to guide the development of the relationship between the field-worker and the people he is working with in the field and that serve as constant checks on the progress of the research. (This is not a chapter on ethnographic methodology and I will not spend time discussing the principles, their implications, and shortcomings here.) However, a quick perusal suggests several of the main challenges to urban ethnography—most of which are addressed from other perspectives in the accompanying theoretical chapters to follow.

The results of the West Philadelphia research project were generally well received by the scholarly community. We were able to help teachers and parents gain a better understanding of several issues of concern to them, shed some light on issues relating to the teaching and learning of literacy skills that helped the teachers in the project, and had some minor successes developing a reflective awareness of some of the oppressive hegemonic forces at work. Several graduate students were able to use their data to complete dissertations, the research generated several published articles, and the experience was partly responsible for launching the Penn Ethnography and Education Research Forum. At least one of the African American teachers who worked with us in the project enrolled in and finished a doctoral program at the University of Pennsylvania. (One of the African American parents was offered a scholarship at the University but turned it down because she felt out of place in the largely white environment.)

In spite of these "successes," I would do things differently today. Despite our best efforts to importantly involve school people in formulating the issues investigated, in participating in the research process, in taking ownership of the findings and responsibility for their implementation, and our insistence on providing them with remuneration; with one or two notable exceptions, the project did little to address the fundamental problems facing West Philadelphia's inner-city schools.

First of all, most of the project's "successes" accrued to us, the researchers, as faculty in the form of published articles and a record of grant-getting, and as graduate students, in the form of dissertations, research papers, and resume-enhancing experience. We were a group of mostly white, obviously privileged university researchers, working in schools with virtually all African American students and a mix of African American and white teachers most of whom lived outside of the district. We were closely allied with the white principals, one of whom was working on a doctorate at the university. Furthermore, in the political economy of American schooling, as university researchers we occupied a prestige status vis-à-vis the teachers. These inevitable status/power issues may well have undermined our attempts to address the hidden regimes of power at work in the schools and may have in fact reified them.

## The Challenges of Urban Ethnography

This experience, as viewed with the advantage of reflective hindsight and the illumination of subsequent experiences Perry Gilmore and I have had working with Native American and Australian Aboriginal populations, is largely consistent with the critique provided by critical ethnography. It also raises what I see as several important challenges to urban ethnography. I briefly discuss these.

### Locating the Problem
One of the major reasons for the somewhat limited success of the Philadelphia project in adding significantly to our understanding of the "problem" of language arts acquisition was that inevitably most of the issues the teachers and researchers identified were located in either the students themselves or the students' lives or some aspect of the pedagogy. Examples of these included, "the real problem is that parents don't care," "they don't pay attention," "these are low-track kids and they just don't write," or "the kids who don't do well just have an attitude."

We were able to look at these contentions in ways that helped us understand that parents really did care, it was just that the conditions under which they were forced to live precluded them from the behaviors that count as caring in school. We found that there are many ways of "attending" in addition to quietly doing the work teachers assign, that the low-track kids wrote all of the time—often even more than the good students but that teachers were either not aware of this or didn't count their writing as real writing, and what the teachers counted as attitude in low-achieving students was a normal and healthy response to a life context, behaviors that were given different and positive labels in students who were doing well.

Despite these and other insights it became clear that these were never the "problems." Suggestions as to what these were abound in our data and reports. We saw difference between African American teachers who had a stake in the community and the white teachers who did not. In several cases students in contexts outside of the classroom, or in sub-rosa spaces in the classroom, displayed the very skills they were deemed incapable of. We saw a principal who openly bargained with parents, promising them in return for effectively abandoning aspects of their own cultural lives their children's success in school and the chance to get into prestigious secondary schools. These were merely examples of data we uncovered to suggest that the problems we associated with the acquisition of language arts skills were not those of pedagogy and learning nor were they primarily located in the schools or homes of students.

Our research was not designed to pursue these leads into an investigation of the wider social issues of power and oppression. The funding agencies and the district policy makers were looking for answers that were both politically palatable and that admitted of solutions consistent with their technistic framework of schooling.

There were exceptions to this, one being the work of Gilmore on sub-rosa literacy that has been widely disseminated and quoted and has been expanded in subsequent work (Gilmore 1986).

While this research did not really explicate the underlying problems of schooling in West Philadelphia, this should not be taken as an indictment of ethnography—nor even of this project. Indeed quite to the contrary, I would argue that we were on the right track but just did not go far enough (I will return to this below). It is hard to imagine an approach to these kinds of issues, other than ethnography, that would have uncovered the kinds of leads we did nor that would have as pointedly suggested the more significant underlying political forces that were operating.

Indeed one of the strengths of ethnography, as embodied in the principles above, is that it provides a framework for allowing significant problems to arise from the context, to name them and then to locate them in their social context. This cannot be done a priori. To some extent we did this in the Philadelphia project. While the general topic we were to research was the acquisition of language arts, the specific issues we were to look at grew out of the research itself. The fieldworkers spent the first two weeks simply being in the classroom and hanging out in the neighborhood talking to the teachers and students about what they saw as the greatest problem in learning to read and write. As it turned out each of them came up with a different answer. These answers gave direction to the next steps in the research.

In retrospect, the disparate issues were not all that disparate. They all coded political and power concerns and reflect a common hegemonic view of schooling. A truly critical ethnography would, of course, have pursued these issues as a subject of the research.

I am concerned that much urban ethnography today, given the political and funding constraints under which it operates, is still not using enough rigor in locating the problems and issues that should be investigated. This leads to a second major challenge of urban ethnography.

### Finding Room to Pursue the Real Issues

Unlike the kind of traditional ethnography I did in Cameroun, in West Philadelphia we were limited by several constraints in pursuing the research to its appropriate conclusions. First we had limited time. Although we had more freedom than I have experienced in most of the funded research I have participated in and we were able to secure a second year's grant, we did have to turn in quarterly and final reports. Time pressures have always been a factor in ethnographic research and we all regret that we could not stay longer in the field, but they become particularly problematic in problem-centered research when the funding agency needs to demonstrate to the political establishment a reasonable return on its investment.

A more important constraint is the one anticipated by Laura Nader years ago; the propensity for anthropologists to inevitably study down (Nader 1972). It has been a well-noted practice in educational research of all types, to locate the problems in those who are powerless to resist, to the disenfranchised victims themselves (see Smith 1992). As an example, Alaska Natives have frequently been singled out as prone to fail both in K–12 schooling and in the university. Inevitably one of the reasons adduced is their lack of self-esteem. As a result myriad of programs have been developed to increase their self-esteem, programs that have done little to actually increase their rates of success. It doesn't take an astute observer, however, after spending time in the village to notice that village children are any thing but lacking in confidence. In fact one is struck by the respect and esteem in which Alaska Native children are held by their parents and other adults. The problem in school and the university is clearly the lack of esteem in which they are held by teachers and administrators. It would, however, be difficult indeed to get funding and permission to conduct an ethnographic study of the latter's attitudes.

To take another Alaskan example discussed in my chapter in Zou and Trueba (1998), the University of Alaska has offered to fund research that will result in the development of bridging programs, designed to remediate the weaknesses of Alaska Native students and to move them from what is seen as the periphery to the center. These programs have had some success but at the expense of reifying the conventional center-periphery configuration in ways that disadvantage the majority of Alaska Native people. It would be political suicide for the university to support research that suggests rather than bridging programs, the university and schools adopt pedagogies that build on Alaska Native pedagogies and emanate from Alaska Native cosmologies.

Two such projects are under way. One is directed by Raymond Barnhardt, Aanggayuquq Oscar Kawagley, and Frank Hill, *The Alaska Native Knowledge Network* (a National Science Foundation supported project at the University of Alaska, Fairbanks; for further information see http://www.ankn.uaf.edu). And the other is by Jerry Lipka on Yupiik pedagogy (see Lipka et al. 1998 for discussion of this research). However, both of these were funded externally without the university's blessing. Furthermore, talks with colleagues at the university suggest that it and the school districts are already posturing themselves, if not to discredit, at least to marginalize these efforts.

This leads to a further dimension of the challenge to find room in urban ethnography. As I indicated earlier, regarding the Philadelphia project, we were ready to take the step of working with the school community, several members of whom had signed on to expand and implement our findings, when a nasty school strike erupted. The principal we were primarily working with got beat up and was transferred. The teachers were confronted with picket lines and the community that had evolved largely dissipated. While in this case the strike was unrelated to our project and plans, as McDermott (1987) and others have pointed out, whenever threats to the entrenched power elites develop, the system quickly organizes itself to squelch them.

We were caught up in a particularly horrifying example of this at the University of Alaska in a controversy over grading Alaska Native students that Perry Gilmore, Larry Kairaiuak, and I analyzed in *Off White Readings on Society, Race and Culture* (1997). An expanded version of this analysis, replete with student voices, appears in Li (forthcoming).

I have suggested that "finding room," given the financial, political, and time constraints usually imposed on research, is a challenge to urban ethnography. However, this challenge is in some ways only apparent and assumes a particular model of ethnographic research, one in which trained ethnographers enter a social context to either describe and analyze culture or to investigate a perceived problem.

New models, faithful to the underlying perspectives of ethnography, need to be and are being created. Among these are various approaches to autoethnography (Reed-Danahay 1997), or the kinds of critical autobiographies Anzaldua (1987) and others have published. These models are neither constrained by funds nor the kinds of political realities more traditional models face. In school-based research teachers as researchers is another attempt to avoid some of these inherent constraints (See Cochran-Smith and Lytle 1992). While some of these efforts have provided us with strong voices that are seldom heard by policy makers and academics, others have turned out to be little more than more or less sophisticated informant accounts that do not reflect a consciousness that locates problems outside of the victims themselves. They also lack much of the holism and other characteristics of ethnography.

### Giving Voice to Narratives of Resistance and Resilience

This leads to a third challenge for urban ethnography, finding appropriate ways to give voice to narratives of resistance and resilience. The challenge is not just to find ways to surface these voices but to do so in formats and through vehicles where they cannot be ignored, where they are not filtered through researchers' dominant cultures or their theories, and where they promote movements of solidarity. Since publishing them in research reports or academic journals scarcely accomplishes these ends, if these are even viable, it is imperative that the authors themselves achieve positions of authority. Critical ethnography is uniquely suited to facilitating this process. It not only surfaces heretofore hidden underlying forces of oppression but also the cultural means of resistance.

A case from our work in Alaska immediately comes to mind. One of our undergraduate and graduate students at the University of Alaska, Fairbanks, Larry Kairaiuak, found himself embroiled in an ugly grading controversy at the university. He and others were forced to suffer immeasurable pain by the institution's actions in dealing with the issue. Despite serious threats of legal action from one of the most powerful members of the white university community, he courageously assumed a position of leadership in naming and confronting the atrocity. Later he worked with Perry Gilmore and myself to analyze and publish an account of the incident (Gilmore, Smith, and Kairaiuak 1997). While by no means the only factor, this experience gave him insights to the hidden agendas of power and oppression that, unknown to him, were at work in shaping his educational experiences. He was subsequently able to go on from this experience and assume an important leadership role in a powerful Bay Area community advocacy agency. (See the Gilmore chapter in this volume for further discussion of this issue.)

Another example is in the work of Stringer at the Center for Aboriginal Studies at Curtin University, Perth, Australia. During the fall of 1998, Perry

Gilmore and I had the privilege of working in this program with a cohort of Aboriginal graduate students, all of them using an action research model, working with stakeholders to surface and privilege narratives of repression by Australia's "lost generation" (see L. Smith 1999:127 for a summary of this program).

In summary, a challenge facing urban ethnography today is not only to surface the narratives of oppression, resistance, and resilience for the edification of the academic community but develop approaches that put these narratives to use in addressing the oppressive equations. It is not enough to uncover local "funds of Knowledge," to appropriate Luis Moll's term (Moll et al. 1992), nor to incorporate these into our pedagogical repertoire, but they must become the basis for a radical new pedagogy, one that is based on and privileges these narratives and local knowledge.

### How to Engage in Meaningful Participant Observation

No discussion of doing urban ethnography would be complete without reference to two of the traditional cornerstones of the approach—participant observation and holism. Many of the modern urban ethnographic accounts of schooling are based on quick in and out visits to a school or community, perhaps one day a week for a semester supplemented by an occasional weekend and heavily dependent upon information gleaned from focus groups.

For my money, good ethnography requires time and extended participant observation. It is important to hear accounts generated by focus group responses and even the reflective observations and unexpected insights that develop from such interactions. However, equally significant for the participants and fieldworkers is to have an account of how these values and beliefs play out in the mundane and crisis activities of daily life.

These understandings come from intensive interactions over long periods of time, interactions that lead to authentic human relationships. (Hopefully these interactions can be therapeutic—in the Spindler sense (Spindler and Spindler 1994)—providing opportunities to examine and share our various selves. Such relationships, while essential to an ethnography that will make a difference, are a challenge for urban ethnographers.

First, urban environments, including urban schools with commuting staff and students, don't easily foster intimate relationships.

Second, developing intimate, culturally therapeutic relationships carries ethical responsibilities and obligations that go beyond the research context. Colonizing methodologies are notorious for avoiding these responsibilities and obligations and for engendering unequal relationships.

A truly effective, critical urban ethnography will address the challenge of creating these participant observation–based relationships.

A postscript to the challenge of doing authentic participant observation is the effect on the ethnographer. It is axiomatic to cultural anthropology—an axiom often ignored—that ethnographic research should be as valuable in illuminating self-understanding and as critical to the researcher as to the people she is working with. In our haste to gain "understanding" of the other and to publish our findings, particularly in urban schooling contexts, we seem to have lost sight of this important facet of participant observation.

## Holism: Finding the Relevant Whole

Holism has been held up as another of the distinctives of cultural anthropology. I believe it is an important characteristic of effective ethnography in urban settings. However, it is often seen as a problem.

A holistic perspective is one of the reasons ethnography strives for understanding and not just knowledge generation. It is the recognition that culture is an intricate, abstract construct—no one part of which (language, technology, ideology, or the social system) may be understood—apart from the others. However, to say that ethnography is holistic is not to say that one must investigate everything to understand anything but that one must be willing to follow leads to what is the relevant whole for explicating issues. What it does not do is a priori define a whole, a universe to be researched.

To take just one small example, harking back to my original discussion of the Philadelphia language arts project, the relevant whole would not be limited to the culture of the school communities where we worked but the culture of testing—the ideological, political, social, linguistic, technological, and linguistic context in which it is embedded. I cannot conceive of an effective urban ethnography that is not holistic.

## Conclusion

I have chosen to discuss these five challenges to urban ethnography culled from our own experiences, almost willy nilly. There are others and other ways to dividing these up. After eight years of directing the Center for Urban Ethnography and an additional fifteen years of working with indigenous people, I would probably suggest that the charter of the Center be amended.

Instead of seeking to simply understand the inner city better so that we can address its needs, we need to recognize that it—and its problems—are simply parts of a larger whole, and that the real challenge is not to understand it but to understand ourselves and why we have created it the way it is.

# References

Anzaldua, G. Borderlands/La Frontera: The New Mesitza. San Francisco: Spinsters/Aunt Lute, 1987.

Cochran-Smith, M., and S. Lytle. "Communities for Teacher Research: From Fringe to Forefront?" The American Journal of Education, 100, 3 (1992):298–324.

Gilmore, P. "Sub-Rosa Literacy: Peers, Play and Ownership of Literacy." Pp. 15–168 in B. Schieffelin and P. Gilmore, ed., The Acquisition of Literacy: Ethnographic Perspectives. Norwood, N.J.: Ablex Publishing Co., 1986.

Gilmore, P., and D. M. Smith. "Identity, Resistance and Resilience: Counter Narratives and Subaltern Voices in Alaskan Higher Education." Pp. 103–34 in D. Li, ed., Discourses in Search of Members: In Honor of Ron Scollon. University Press of America, 2002.

Gilmore, P., D. Smith, and L. Kairaiuak. "Resisting Diversity: An Alaskan Case of Institutional Struggle." Pp. 90–99 in M. Fine et al., ed., Off White Readings on Society, Race and Culture. New York: Routledge, 1997.

Hymes, D. H. "Ethnographic Monitoring." In E. J. Briere, ed., Language Development in a Bilingual Society. Los Angeles: National Dissemination and Assessment Center, 1979.

Lipka, J., G. Mohatt, and the Chulistet Group. Transforming the Culture of Schools: Yup'ik Eskimo Examples. Mahwah, N.J.: Laurence Erlbaum Associates, 1998.

McDermott, R. P. "The Explanation of School Failure, Again." Anthropology and Education Quarterly, 4 (1987):300–11.

Moll, L. C., D. N. Amanti, and N. Gonzalez. "Funds of Knowledge for Teaching: Using a Qualitative Approach to Connect Homes and Classrooms." Theory into Practice, 31, 1(1992): 132–41.

Nader, L. "Up the Anthropologist." In D P. Hymes, ed., Reinventing Anthropology. New York: Pantheon, 1972.

Reed-Danahay, D. E. Auto/Ethnography: Rewriting the Self and the Social. New York: Berg, 1997.

Smith, D. M. "Ethnographic Monitoring of Children's Acquisition of Reading/Language Arts Skills In and Out of the Classroom: General Findings." The Generator. AERA (Winter 1983): 185–98.

Smith, D. M. "Anthropology of Education and Educational Research." Anthropology and Education Research, 3 (1992).

Smith, D. M. "Aspects of the Cultural Politics of Alaskan Education." Pp. 369–87 in Y. Zou and H. Trueba, ed., Ethnic Identity and Power: Cultural Contexts of Political Action in School and Society. Albany: SUNY Press, 1998.

Smith, L. Decolonizing Methodologies: Research and Indigenous Peoples. New York: Zed Books, 1999.

Spindler, G., and L. Spindler. *Pathways to Cultural Awareness: Cultural Therapy with Teachers and Students*. Thousand Oaks, Calif.: Corwin Press, 1994.

Wolcott, H. F. *The Art of Fieldwork*. Walnut Creek, Calif.: AltaMira Press, 1998.

Zou, Y., and H. Trueba, ed. "Introduction." Pp. 1–25 in *Ethnic Identity and Power: Cultural Contexts of Political Action in School and Society*. Albany: SUNY Press, 1998.

~

# CHAPTER EIGHT

# Methodological Challenges of Critical Ethnography: Insights from Collaborations on an Indigenous Counter Narrative

*Perry Gilmore*

Bakhtin has been described as continually finding unexpected ways to show that people never utter a final word, only a penultimate one. The opportunity therefore always remains for appending a qualification that may lead to yet another unanticipated dialogue (Morson 1981). In this chapter I hope to be able to accomplish this. I respond to the challenges of critical ethnography from a particular vantage point, drawing primarily on my last fifteen years of experience working with and learning from indigenous peoples, primarily Alaska Natives. I attempt to "people" the theoretical issues detailed in many of the chapters in this volume with a few examples taken from these experiences. Dominant in these examples are concerns about intellectual property rights, privacy issues, and project integrity.

Phillip Carspecken (in this volume) states that "More than anything else, the 'praxis epistemology' I have barely sketched in this chapter takes sameness and difference into account by always being open to new differences . . . and by requiring the voices of all people to be affected by a theory, to take part in the production of the theory, for it to be valid." While Carspecken and other critical ethnographers hold this openness and the participation of the "affected" people to be central to the conduct of this research and theory production, the possibility of achieving these goals in our present research community is thwarted at many levels. Closer scrutiny of the often subtle and always complex mechanisms that impede the well-intentioned goals of critical ethnography is necessary. In my view, the most powerful and productive critics of and resisters to this type of work have been the so-called affected people themselves, an emerging group of strong indigenous scholars.

For example, Linda Tuhaiwai Smith (1999) argues that indigenous peoples have been, in many ways, oppressed by theory and identifies research and theory as significant sites of struggle between the interests and ways of knowing of the West and the interests and ways of resisting of the Other. She declares that to "resist is to retrench in the margins, retrieve what we were and remake ourselves"(p.38).

As a Moari woman she writes, "From the vantage point of the colonized, a position from which I write, and chose to privilege, the term "research" is inextricably linked to European imperialism and colonialism. The word itself, "research", is probably one of the dirtiest words in the indigenous world's vocabulary" (p.1).

Kathy Irwin (as cited in Smith 1999), in an article entitled "Towards Theories of Moari Feminisms," urges "We don't need anyone else developing the tools which will help us to come to terms with who we are. We can and will do this work. Real power lies with those who design the tools—it always has. This power is ours." (p.38)

Thus while drawing on notions from critical and feminist theory (i.e., critique, resistance, struggle, and emancipation), critical theory and its methods have largely been seen as "failing" indigenous and other marginalized peoples. Certainly Willis's model and basic methodology as outlined by Carspecken (in his chapter in this volume) would be viewed as less than ideal for indigenous communities, where indigenous researchers are anxious to discover their own ways of naming and carrying out research, informed by and taking into account the legacies of previous research, but not being limited by it.

In our work in Alaska, David M. Smith and I became well aware of the rightful caution, suspicion, and historic anger with which indigenous Alaskans view "researchers" and "research" long before reading Linda Tuhaiwai Smith's words. Smith (in this volume) refers to some of our collaborative mentoring work with Alaska Native and Australian Aboriginal students (for further discussion of this work see Gilmore, Smith, and Kairaiuak 1997; Gilmore and Smith 2000). In these efforts we have attempted to become resources to our students as they develop "culturally safe" and appropriate localized research approaches and methods. We have documented with our students efforts to create academic narratives designed to counter the traditional and conventional discourse that shapes graduate education and characterizes much existing academic literature. With our students, we have explored deliberate resistance to established "grand and master narratives" and mainstream academic texts that frequently misrepresent, misinterpret, and stereotype indigenous populations. We have described ways in which students have adopted successful and creative ways to use counter narratives and other forms of expression that (1) more accurately and respectfully present indigenous knowledge, epistemologies, and worldviews, and (2) reflect presentations of self (both in style and content) more consistent with individual and community Aboriginal identities. These narratives attempt to both rewrite and reright existing academic research.

The literacy strategies we explore attempt to affirm subaltern knowledge, create "free spaces" for authentic voices, and provide access to power. Some of these efforts were highlighted in two summer research institutes I organized at the University of Alaska, Fairbanks, which focused on exploring a new vision of what research for a diverse society should and might look like.[1] A major aim of the project was to nurture a cohort of potential indigenous scholars who might not only see themselves as benefiting from the expanded knowledge they might gain but also see themselves as potential generators of new knowledge and meaningful research agendas for their own communities. These institutes provided opportunities for critical dialogue with a wide range of scholars and activists who had conducted a variety of ethnographic work. Indigenous researchers included Benjamin Barney, Walkie Charles, Beth Dementi Leonard, Phyllis Fast, Edna McClean, Oscar Qawagely, Verna St. Denis, and Miranda Wright. Other well-known researchers and ethnographers from a variety of disciplines who participated included David Bloome, Marilyn Cochran Smith, Concha Delgado-Gaitan, Lisa Delpit, Penelope Eckert, Michelle Fine, Shelley Goldman, Judith Greene, Richard Katz, Ray McDermott, Dan McLaughlin, and Henry Trueba. The interactions allowed for a localized discourse to develop with student participants that encouraged engagement and fostered relationships as well as research possibilities. Out of these experiences both indigenous researchers and professors and researchers from the mainstream Western dominant culture came to question what Maxine Greene (1988) describes as the "taken for granted" and look at things as if they could be otherwise.

One goal of the institute design was to provide a context where research and theory could be recontextualized in more of an informal setting where the oral/literate dichotomy was intentionally blurred. While academic literacy is often described as being engagement with "decontextualized" text, most published academics have actually met, interacted with, and know personally, and often intimately, those other scholars to whom they refer. They are more frequently involved in a more "oral" tradition centered around face-to-face meetings, conferences, visiting stints, and often lifelong friendships. Given the remoteness of the Alaskan interior and the prohibitive costs of travel to conferences and meetings in the "Lower 48," most of our indigenous students knew research and theory as something they read about, done by people "Outside" (a local expression referring to places outside Alaska).

By inviting scholars to visit, share personal life biographies, and spend social time with their own families and the families of the students, the format allowed students to be socialized into a dialogue with the visiting scholars who shared local foods like moose, caribou, salmon, and berries. At one session a student participant said to a visiting researcher, "I don't remember whether you said this or I read it but . . ." This statement captured the idea of a comfortable place on the oral/literate continuum where much of the dialogue took place.

Student participants initiated and developed their own research projects in this dialogic context. Early draft proposals received a range of feedback from the different visiting scholars. Students were encouraged to consider the different responses, suggestions, and information, using these editorial comments to strengthen their own sense of where they were going with their projects.

One of the research projects that took shape through the institutes was a language revitalization effort developed by Beth Dementi Leonard, an Athabascan linguist and my graduate student at the time. Dementi Leonard developed and modified her study through the institute process and ultimately used it as her master's project. Her work was an excellent example of resistance to mainstream academic theory and creative use of academic genre for generating new knowledge. Dementi Leonard's study is also an example of a "new" ethnographer's (see Trueba's chapter, this volume) response to the call for critical ethnography that rectifies the wrong cultural assumptions of past work, contributes to needed changes in the discourse of ethnography, and engineers social change in the service of equity and justice.

A community-based participatory language planning effort funded by an Administration for Native Americans Grant to the Tanana Chiefs Conference, a regional nonprofit tribal organization, the study documents the case of one particular grassroots language planning effort organized around a series of regional meetings, involving representatives from twenty villages in five traditional Athabascan language areas in western interior Alaska. The languages in this area include Deg Hit'an, Holikachuk, Koyukon, Upper Kuskokwim, and Lower Tanana. As a result of the aggressive American suppression of, and harsh position the schools and churches had taken toward indigenous languages, many of these languages have a only a few remaining speakers and of those remaining speakers most are over fifty years old. Community members from across the region who were participants repeatedly expressed strong concerns for the survival of these languages, a sense of urgency for the work on language and cultural regenisis, and a recognition of the need for educational and program support in these areas.[2]

As her graduate adviser, I participated throughout the process as Dementi Leonard developed, implemented, and wrote up her project for two distinct audiences. First she presented it as a grant report (1996) and second as a master's project (1997). Genre modifications were necessary in order to meet the needs and expectations of each audience. But a third reworking of the data required the most effort and ultimately provided some of the greatest professional reward.

Coincidently, soon after the work had been completed, I was contacted by Rosemary Henze, who was preparing a special theme issue on indigenous language revitalization for the *Anthropology and Education Quarterly*. She was looking for potential contributors. I suggested Dementi Leonard's work and with Henze's encouragement, I approached Dementi Leonard to see if she was interested in contributing. New to the field, and new to the ways of academic publishing, she agreed to contribute to the volume but rather than go "solo," she chose to coauthor with me. I share here some of our collaborative process because (1) it highlights the discourse struggles and methodological challenges that seem necessary for a critical ethnography and (2) as we have reflected on the process, we both found it to be enlightening professionally and personally.

Searching for an appropriate voice and platform from which to write presented particularly delicate choices and critical decisions that caused us both considerable doubt and confusion before we finished our final revision. We were concerned about many audiences and trying to be respectful of each while ferociously guarding the integrity of the project, the privacy of the communities, and the intellectual property rights of the indigenous peoples involved. Additionally we had to respond to editors' and reviewers' comments and suggestions that sometimes seemed at cross purposes.

We kept reminding ourselves that we didn't really have to publish the paper if "it didn't feel right" or if it wouldn't reflect the work or the community respectfully. At all steps of the conceiving, implementing, and writing up the research in this language planning project, community members, elders, and the sponsoring tribal corporation were closely involved. All quotes in the final write-up were carefully selected and used with community members' permission. Stories and anecdotes requested by the reviewers and editors to "enhance" the paper were deliberately resisted and excluded by us in order to protect the privacy and "safe space" the project had created for the community members.

But a major challenge for our collaborative analysis and presentation of the work was our different orientations and approaches to the use of theory in our presentation of the research. While I was more open to addressing and/or confronting relevant theoretical models, Dementi Leonard expressed resistance to reliance on outsiders' theoretical frameworks. One specific concern was in response to my urging that if we publish a paper on language revitalization we needed to cite and respond to Joshua Fishman's model of language shift. Dementi Leonard had problems with the model, pointing out that if we used Fishman's stages to describe the regional language situation it would present a dismal and misleading view that would publicly reinforce the obstacles facing the communities rather than highlighting the focus and determination of the people.

My response was supportive. We would take that position and then explain why. I suggested it would be an easy argument. It would go something like this: (1) Fishman has developed a typology of language stages in reversing language shift, (2) the interior Athabascan language situation would look dismal if we used his stages to assess the community language levels, and (3) since the language was systematically exterminated by outside Western colonizers through churches and schools in the first place, why use another outside dominant view (i.e., a Western theoretical model) to further demoralize and shame the communities that have decided to resist and reverse the language oppression at this point?

My colleague and coauthor didn't feel comfortable with the scenario. We can speculate that a public confrontation, especially in print, would not be considered appropriate or valued by the local indigenous community—even though it might be expected and desirable in an academic journal. But how could we possibly determine whether Dementi Leonard was uncomfortable *because* she was Athabascan? How could I determine that my lesser discomfort with the idea of confrontation was *because* I was not only an academic but also Jewish and from Philadelphia?

In addition, Dementi Leonard, as a relatively inexperienced unpublished researcher, might be reluctant to take on one of the icons in the discipline. I and many other more established researchers might well also have chosen other strategies in order to avoid confronting a leading scholar. (I have seen this repeatedly in academic life sometimes out of deference but more frequently motivated by career and/or political goals.)

Out of respect for Fishman and his elder status and stature in his field, it would seem somewhat disrespectful to contradict him.

We finally agreed not to confront his theory—but there was, I insisted, a need to at least cite him for what we both recognized would be respectfully acknowledging his standing in the field. We found something he said that Dementi Leonard felt was supportive of the type of effort we were documenting. We, however, never mentioned Fishman's model and we did not refer to his stages in describing the level of language uses in the communities we described.

Our coauthored struggle in this theoretical research site taught us both many valuable lessons and we were both pleased with the way we finally negotiated our final prose. This creolization blended features of traditional indigenous ways of knowing within the conventions of dominant culture academic writing. For example, in appropriate Athabascan protocol we introduced ourselves in the AEQ article, Dementi Leonard naming her place of birth in Shaguluk village on the Innoko River and naming her father, James Dementi. We also found a way to explain our resistance to theory and in doing so created an acceptable alternate construct. Our alternative view was expressed in the following way:

> This article celebrates the knowledge held in the small villages of Western Interior Alaska. We have chosen to organize and report our findings in ways that are consistent with that knowledge base and its epistemology. We therefore have chosen a more empirical, descriptive and less theoretical stance, documenting current practices and providing a public record as a resource. Additionally we have chosen to rely more heavily on local experts, their knowledge, interpretations and meanings, and less on scholarly outsiders' analysis and categorizations. As Fishman has recognized, in language and cultural renewal, revivalism and reversal efforts, community members are in the "process of re-establishing local options, local control, local hope and local meaning" (1991:35). Having outside experts determine the level or stage of success of these efforts or label the languages as dying or moribund can undermine the very notion of local control, local meaning and certainly, local hope. We have tried therefore to resist those categories and instead rely on a posture of possibility in describing events and activities, finding an enabling vocabu-

lary more suitable for capturing the self-determination, resistance and resilience
we found in the communities.

We used other academic conventions to mark and highlight and celebrate
the knowledge held in these small communities. In order to enhance the
status of the local experts we referred to, we reframed the ways in which we
referenced their knowledge and contributions so that they appear in the references as equivalent to academics rather than merely narrative mention of
them as "informants" in the body of the text or footnotes.

As coauthors, we were both pleased to note that Joshua Fishman (1999),
who, not surprisingly, was invited to respond to the collection of papers,
appeared himself to have no problem with his model not being the focus of
our analysis, making no mention of it in his commentary. Instead, however,
in his comments he specifically noted the solidarity, vigor, and strength of
the Athabascan community's resistance and resilience. These were the significant aspects of the project we indeed were emphasizing in our documentation.

Carspecken writes that "people continuously try to 'find themselves'
through expression toward audiences and this continuous effort is part of
what it means to be a person." He states the expressive and self-production
motivation complexes in people is what praxis theory is all about. These
words seem appropriate when I reflect on the collaborative experience
Dementi Leonard and I negotiated—this small example seems to capture a
snapshot of our continuous attempts to work together to deconstruct and
reconstruct our vision, our understandings, and our ways of knowing and
expressing that knowledge in the best interests of the local communities as
well as for the wider academic audience. These research collaborations with
our students, the "new" ethnographers, are sites for decolonizing and deconstructing past, often destructive research practices and theoretical frameworks. As mentoring professors and as researchers we have much to learn
from our students in these spaces in order to use research in the service of
equity and justice.

## Notes

1. Two Alaska Summer Educational Research Institutes (1997, 1998) were funded by
grants awarded to Perry Gilmore from the Alaska School Research Fund at the University
of Alaska, Fairbanks. Additional funds were awarded to Perry Gilmore and David M.

Smith for a public Colloquia Series "Dialogue on Diversity" by a University of Alaska President's Special Projects Fund in 1996.

2. A fuller documentation of the findings of this study can be found in B. Dementi Leonard, *ANA Planning Grant Reports*. Fairbanks, Alaska: Tanana Chiefs Conference, 1996.

# References

Fishman, J. *Reversing Language Shift: Theoretical and Empirical Foundations of Assistance to Threatened Languages*. Clevedon, U.K.: Multilingual Matters, 1991.

Fishman, J. "Comments." *Anthropology and Education Quarterly*, Special Theme Issue, Authenticity and Identity in Indigenous Language Revitalization, 30, 1 (1999): 116–24.

Gilmore, P., and D. M. Smith. "Identity, Resistance and Resilience: Counter Narratives and Subaltern Voices in Alaskan Higher Education." Pp. 103–34 in D. C. S. Li, ed., *Discourses in Search of Members: In Honor of Ron Scollon*. University Press of America, 2002.

Gilmore, P., D. M. Smith, and A. L. Kairaiuak. "Resisting Diversity: An Alaskan Case of Institutional Struggle." Pp. 90–99 in M. Fine, L. Weis, L. Powers, and L. M. Wong, ed., *Off-White: Readings on Race, Power, and Society*. New York: Routledge, 1997.

Greene, M. *The Dialectic of Freedom*. N.Y.: Teachers College Press, 1988.

Leonard, B., and P. Gilmore. "Language Revitalization and Identity in Social Context: A Community-Based Athabascan Language Preservation Project in Interior Alaska." *Anthropology and Education Quarterly*, Special Theme Issue, Authenticity and Identity in Indigenous Language Revitalization, 30, 1 (1999): 37–55.

Morson, G. S. "Preface: Perhaps Bakhtin." Pp. vii–xiii in G. S. Morson, ed., *Bakhtin: Essays and Dialogues on His Work*. Chicago: The University of Chicago Press, 1981.

Smith, L. T. *Decolonizing Methodologies: Research and Indigenous Peoples*. New York: St. Martins Press, 1999.

# CHAPTER NINE

# Adaptive Strategies of a Chinese Immigrant

## Yali Zou

Coming to the United States from mainland China is an experience that is only partially comprehensible to Westerners, and very confusing to immigrants themselves. Not only is the United States a radically different country, but the immigrant's inability to communicate in English can make this experience terrifying. Life in China is full of myths about this country as far away from the truth as Western beliefs about China are. Far from being a racially, socially, politically, economically, or ethnically homogeneous society, China is a complex nation with prevalent philosophies and traditions centered on the family and society.

The purpose of this chapter is to address significant theoretical issues related to my immigrant experiences both in China and the United States, issues of multiple identities, adaptive strategies, success, and resiliency of immigrants in America. I hypothesize that multiple identities allow immigrants to survive and function effectively in very different countries and societies. The questions that intrigue me are related to the formation of these identities and their functional value as adaptive strategies associated with my educational training, as often happens to other immigrants in the United States. My experiences may shed some light on complex problems of conflict in cultural values and its resolution. They are also related to the nature of academia and the dilemmas faced by researchers from ethnic backgrounds. I want to provide a theoretical perspective on multiple identities and the ethical and methodological challenges of conducting research as a member of a minority group. Second, I describe my experiences in China and put them in their historical and political context. Then I will relate my experiences in the United States and discuss how those experiences have influenced my research. The assumption that pre-arrival experiences shape immigrants' lives and worldview in the host country may find some support in this chapter. Also the contention that an ethnographer can function effectively in two cultures is made here.

## Immigrants' Adaptive Strategies

The researcher tends to make a leap by putting together all possible interpretations and assuming that they are an integrated whole reflecting a single identity of the person under study; that is, one story, one identity, one person. The reality is that both the persons under study and the researchers have many identities and many interpretations of human phenomena. Both identities and interpretations of daily life events are framed by contextual variables, including language, culture, social setting, and expectations. These identities, contrary to traditional belief, coexist within the same time period but become activated in different settings that are distinct and unique. Like linguistic code-switching and translating for other persons who ignore a given language and culture, so have identities a way of "naturally" fitting certain contexts.

Researchers deal with their own multiple and autonomous identities connected to a single consciousness, and obviously, they have more than one possible interpretation of events. In modern life, especially in countries with large rates of immigration from many countries, survival and success may depend on the ability of individuals to adopt many identities in order to understand and function in different cultural settings.

Immigration is an integral part of America's history in the last three hundred years. The new immigration, however, is unique:

> In 1945, just fifty years ago, the U.S. population was 87 percent white, 10 percent black, 2.5 percent Hispanic, and 0.5 percent Asian. Fifty years from now, in the year of 2050, demographic projections suggest a strikingly different population profile: 52.8 percent of the population will be white, 13.6 percent of the population will be black, 24.5 percent of the population will be Hispanic, and 8.2 percent of the population will be of Asian ancestry. (M. Suárez-Orozco 1998:5)

One in six children in the United States today lives in a household headed by immigrants. Immigrants are concentrated in California, New

York, Florida, Texas, and Illinois. In California, for example, about 20 percent of all school age children are immigrant. In New York City public schools today 48 percent of all children come from immigrant households speaking over 100 different languages. In contrast with previous decades, powerful new forms of transnationalism are shaping the immigration flood of the twenty-first century. Immigrants are culturally and racially heterogeneous and economically stratified. Some are rapidly achieving upward mobility, while many others, especially immigrants of color, find themselves isolated in semiskilled, low-paying service jobs. Finally, other immigrants inconspicuously disappear in mainstream middle-class institutions (Suárez-Orozco and Suárez-Orozco, 2000:17–35). The sheer volume of new immigrant children and their increasing access to technology leads to new social practices and cultural models.

In the past, psychologists viewed self-identity as a rigid and permanent state incompatible with alternative identities. Recent work, however, suggests that multiple identities are no longer seen as dysfunctional (along the old Freudian/Eriksonian model) (Suárez-Orozco and Suárez-Orozco 2000). To assume that each person has only one and a fixed identity relatively unchanged across the cultural and social experiences that differentiate individuals is simplistic and reductionistic. In fact, immigrants' success and resiliency, their powerful influence in mainstream society, all are related to their uncanny ability to become "others" in the appropriate contexts. To survive economically and psychologically, they must fulfill the expectations of employers, coworkers, social institutions, and government representatives. They must become "others" through the acquisition of communicative skills in another language and culture, but without depriving themselves of their quintessential selves and the security of the home culture, family, community, and their enduring self-identity.

Acculturation and assimilation are too simplistic, often contradicted by ongoing research and reality of social and economic enclaves of bilingual/bicultural immigrants in Europe and the United States. Furthermore, it seems as if recent young generations of immigrants see no conflict in retaining their ethnic identities while they prosper in the host country, learn a culture and language, and become proficient in a new cross-cultural lifestyle. The ability of immigrants to function effectively among members of mainstream society and to compete well with them in businesses, industry, and academia, far from signaling a surrender of their ethnic identity suggests that ethnic communities and ethnic identities make it possible for them to succeed. For example, young Asian Americans and Latinos (according to a recent study conducted with Spencer Foundation funds, see Trueba & Zou 1999, Annual Report; Trueba & Zou 2000, Annual Report; Zou 2002, Final Report) are proud to become both mainstream citizens, fully functional in modern America, aware of their new culture, and proud to participate fully in American institutions. And they take as much pride in remaining active members of their respective ethnic groups with fluency in Mandarin, Cantonese, Korean, Japanese, or Spanish.

Belonging to different ethnic and racial groups is something relatively new that occurs as a result of the increasing incidence of interracial and interethnic marriages. Thus, for example, immigrants who belong to a distinct racial group, blacks, but who come from different cultures (Black Africans, Black Latinos, Black Cubans, Caribbean Blacks, Mexican Blacks, etc.), can cross racial/ethnic boundaries comfortably. Another example, Indians from Mexico or Latin America and Indians from a variety of Native American groups in the United States associate without social penalties or discrimination. That is the case of Asians from the Pacific Islands and other Asians who have immigrated to the United States. Belonging to more than one ethnic/racial group comes naturally and at times is indispensable in order to practice a profession or succeed in a given career. Naturally, in order to cross boundaries individuals must become proficient in the communicative and interactional codes. The communication of biracial persons with their polarized groups (such as blacks and whites) presents unique challenges. For many years, interracial interaction was forbidden. The reality of mixed marriages and interracial unions has resulted in an open recognition of multiple types and shades of biracial constitutions. Black and white relatives are now in touch with each other, do associate with opposite groups, and seek membership in multiple groups, manage different linguistic codes (which is a unique asset), and understand interracial conflict well. In fact, these individuals view themselves and their generation as gifted and responsible for pioneering a new American society. As they learn the different communication styles and interactive patterns, they manage to imitate codes and patterns, and fit well in different groups with lesser penalties than *monoracial* persons suffer. There is no psychological dysfunctionality or cultural conflict in their daily interaction with opposite groups. Code switching and the assumption of different identities comes naturally and permits them to function in multiethnic and multicultural environments.

## Researchers Face Conflict in Modern
## Societies with Multiple Identities

Increasing intermarriage among ethnic and racial groups in modern societies may render opposed ethnic identities irrelevant and may stress social strata and economic hierarchies. Is it possible that traditional groupings along racial and ethnic lines with clear-cut oppositional political and cultural arenas cease to exist? What would a new multicultural and multilingual society look like? As taxonomic classification of racial types becomes useless or obsolete, what, if any, stratification will exist that marks clearly the predominance of economic power groups across shades of diverse racial types no longer clearly identified? Will the markers of new identities follow educational and economic lines? The answers to these hypothetical questions depend on the flow of immigration, and immigration waves in turn depend on political and economic forces around the world.

Looking at the demographic trends of the twenty-first century has produced frustration and anxiety. The projections of a rapidly increasing population of color in the country are indeed a reality in many of our cities. In fact, the future is here in Los Angeles, New York, Chicago, Houston, and other large cities, the diversity of student populations in the public schools has not only ended the predominance of "white" student populations, but it has established legitimate grounds for an ongoing interaction across ethnic and racial lines. This dominant pattern in voluntary associations, businesses, and industry is paving the way for a "new" American society. Have these trends solved the "race" problems in America? Of course not.

What lessons have we learned from the experience of inequity in academia? What are the consequences of closing the door to "ethnics" or to mistreating them? What is the role of ethnic academicians in the "conspiracy of silence" among colleagues, often observed by those who become victims? As we, ethnic academicians, examine the above accounts and recall a number of personal experiences, we might be tempted to view the academic world through the inequity lenses and maximize the "evil" nature of power holders. We should reflect on our own role and cooperation in the continuation of unfair treatment of women and "ethnics." But there is more to remember. We have a debt of gratitude to those who mentored us (very frequently, members of mainstream academia). For some of us who are immigrants, the opportunities and support given us in the United States would have never been available in our home countries. Yet, we must denounce inequity and unfairness in order to honor this country and to pursue seriously the "American Dream" of a democracy we could never enjoy in our countries of origin. The contributions of many "ethnic" scholars have been only possible under the mentorship and support of genuinely kind and compassionate mainstream mentors. When we look at the overall performance of mainstream academicians in support of ethnic, racial, and linguistic minority faculty we find a very positive picture. Another important reflection is that without the mentorship by mainstream scholars, many of us would have never been able to make a contribution in our fields. Ethnic scholars have been instrumental in enriching theoretical development and cross-cultural understandings of behavior. My own experiences opened up my mind to a better interpretation of academia and a deeper understanding of the role of researchers in cross-cultural areas.

## China in the Next Century

By the middle of the twenty-first century, China will have the most powerful economy in the world. The new generations in the post-Mao reform period will vigorously pursue personal wealth in contrast with the current groups of political leaders who fear change. China is, and will continue to be, one of the most complex countries in the world (Starr 1997). It is a country with many different ethnic groups, languages, traditions, and lifestyles. Even the physical appearance of many Chinese people breaks Western stereotypes. The challenge of understanding any of the many ethnic groups, or "nationalities," in China is compounded by the series of rapid demographic, social, economic, and political changes that have taken place in the last half century. Since the People's Republic of China was established, demographic changes have been dramatic. China had a relatively modest population of between fifty and one hundred million between the first and eighteenth centuries. During the Qing Dynasty (in the 1770s) the population was about one hundred million. By 1840 it had increased to four hundred million, and when China became the People's Republic of China on October 1, 1949, the population was five hundred million (Poston and Yaukey 1992:1). By 1990 the population had jumped to 1.13 billion people.

The ethnic, social, linguistic, and economic diversity of Chinese people is overwhelming and complicated. In 1951, China officially recognized fifty-six ethnic groups in China. Among these, the Han was considered the dominant group, both numerically and politically. The other fifty-five groups, the so-called minority groups or nationalities, had, according to the 1990 national census, a population of 91,200,314 people, which was 8 percent of the total population of China. Since 1982, when the Chinese census showed a population of 1,008,175,288 (Crespigny 1992:285), the policy of one child per family was adopted. The fifty-five ethnic minority groups, however, were exempted from this policy. (For a detailed listing of these groups and their geographic distribution, see Trueba and Zou 1994:61–70.) In 1990 the following five largest ethnic minority groups accounted for over 48 million people:

- the Zhuang in South Central China (with 15,489,630 people)
- the Manchu in the Northeast (with 9,821,180 people)
- the Hui in the Northwest (with 8,692,978 people)
- the Miao in the Southwest (with 7,398,035 people)
- the Uygur in the Northwest (with 7,214,431 people)

In China, 68 percent of the territory is primarily occupied by minority groups. China's borders with Russia, Mongolia, Korea, Pakistan, India, Vietnam, Laos, and Burma run through areas primarily occupied by minorities. These areas are relatively isolated. The privileges given to minority-dominated geographical areas (which constitute "autonomous regions") were granted by the central government in an effort to retain the affiliation of minority groups and the national unity, while at the same time holding onto the Han hegemony. Autonomous regions were offered administrative, legal, and resource control under specific parameters; in fact, the central government retained supervision and control of major resource allocations.

Ethnic and racial diversity in China has a history of confrontation and conflict. Ethnic intolerance, often associated with religious intolerance, for example anti-Manchu attitudes, are present along with preferences for skin color and other physical characteristics. In fact, there is documentation about racial wars at the turn of the nineteenth century that illustrates the practices of racial classifications and extinction (Dikötter 1992). Ethnic nationalism and religious differences clearly separate the Muslim Chinese (probably close to eighteen million of them live in the northwest part of the country—for a detailed discussion, see Gladney 1991).

Although my background and personal experiences in China are limited to Beijing, Shanghai, Jilin, and Changchun, I can understand the values and lifestyles of most Chinese. In order to appreciate the context of my narrative and my theoretical position, I will briefly describe my life in China, where I lived for about forty years. My intent is to give the reader an idea of how my experiences in China during the Cultural Revolution shaped my value system and educational philosophy. This is the China where I grew up, studied, and worked. My self-identity will forever be anchored in my experiences as a Chinese. Yet this is also the China that is furthest away from my daily life in the United States where I have lived for more than thirteen years.

## My Experiences in China

Perhaps no other experience in China had a greater impact on me than working in a rural village for two years during the Cultural Revolution. Being in that village changed my life completely. Although I suffered seriously physically and mentally, it nurtured my deep love for poor peasant children and helped me establish a very close relationship with my students' parents, which, in turn, laid the foundation for my future career. Beyond that, I learned how to face challenges and how to develop adaptation strategies. Leaving my comfortable family life in the city for the first time when I was seventeen years old, I was sent like millions of other educated young people to live in one of the poorest villages, where there was not enough food to eat (quite often chaff and wild herbs were the only food); there was no running water, electricity, or gas; and communication with the rest of the world was nonexistent. Every day I worked physically in an endless field, often for up to fourteen hours under the burning sun or in the freezing winter. In addition, I had to go to mountains to find tree branches for the evening fire and wild vegetables to supplement the regular meals. I was no different from the cow I had been working with. I was never prepared for this kind of life. I was depressed and felt like everything was hopeless. I did not know whether I had any future.

One day I was transplanting rice shoots in a rice field with cold water and had worked for four hours without a break. Suddenly I felt pain in my legs. When I looked at my legs, there were several leeches. I was terrified and fell into the water. I cried and sank into the muddy field. The villagers came to help me and were sympathetic; the leader of the village came to me and said, "Yali, I feel so sorry for you; tell me what we can do to help." "What can you do?" I said in despair, "Nothing, just let me die." I felt there was no way to escape from this life. He smiled and comforted me as he sat on the edge of the rice field and asked me, "Can you read?" "Of course," I answered. "Do you want to teach our children?" "Why?" I asked. He told me that no one in the village of 42 households with 286 people could read a single Chinese character. His dream was that the children in his village would read and write someday. I was shocked by this reality and told him I would like to try.

I started to use my simple living tent as a classroom to teach the village children to read, to write their names, to talk, and to express their feelings. The children looked so poor and hungry! Their faces were dirty, and their hair was very long and messy! I wrote to my father and asked him if he could bring a pair of scissors and hairclippers on his next visit to me. When he came with some little gifts and the scissors, I began to cut the hair of these poor children, hair full of lice and dirt. The lice would jump all over me! The children were happy to have their hair cut and their faces washed. They began to trust me and share everything with me. They told me about their families and invited me to visit them.

As I had the opportunity to get to know the parents of my pupils better, I noticed that many of them—although still young (some not yet thirty years old)—were suffering from pains in their joints, backs, and waists. Some had pains all over their bodies, perhaps as a result of arthritis or of physical injuries from the hard labor in the field. I realized that I might help them. Because I had serious migraine headaches quite often, I had brought an acupuncture book, some needles, and alcohol to the village in order to help get rid of my headaches. There were no doctors and no medicine at all in the village. I offered my help to the parents who suffered from pain, assuring them that although I did not know enough, I would do my best with acupuncture to help ease their pain. The needles became magical tools. Many parents recovered dramatically; they could move their hands and legs and walk without pain; many even started working in the fields again. Word of my skills passed from village to village. Many people began coming to me for help. They called me the "barefoot doctor," which in Chinese means a person who practices medicine without a formal education or a license.

Because of my excellent performance in the village as a teacher and a "doctor," I was transferred to an urban area, which at that time in China was considered a big promotion because leaving the countryside and going to work in a city was a great opportunity. I went to the Jilin Iron and Steel Plant where I became the inspector for quality control. The plant had 7,000 workers, 9 workshop divisions, and 1 research institute. The Jilin plant was one of the most important iron producers in China (about 60 percent of all iron produced in China came from there). It was managed directly by the Ministry of Metallurgic Industry. Each division had a number of open furnaces with unprotected laborers around who experienced extremely high temperatures and other hazardous working conditions. While I was there, I had the opportunity to talk to the workers and observe firsthand their difficulties. I was moved by their devotion to their work despite unbelievably difficult working conditions. I spoke on their behalf and asked leaders to improve their workplace.

In 1966, because of the Cultural Revolution, China's schools and universities were closed down. All former students and professors went to the countryside "to be re-educated by peasants" as Chairman Mao ordered. Eight years later, in 1972, China reopened the universities and began to recruit students from factories, plants, and villages. I was recommended for the Shanghai Foreign Language Institute; there I learned to speak Albanian and became a governmental interpreter. Later I worked in the Chang Chun Film Studio translating Albanian movies into Chinese. I met and was friends with writers, actors, and actresses from whom I learned about their concerns, ideas, and creativity. In 1985, I became a professor at the Chang Chun Architectural Institute, where I found that for over ten years the school had never changed textbooks. All the professors could recite the textbooks they used nearly verbatim. The schools suffered from a lack of both resources and new ideas. I started trying different textbooks and compiled readings that made my students very competitive in the provincial learning competitions. The quality of my teaching and the success I obtained in reforming the curriculum earned me provincial and national awards for teaching excellence in higher education.

## My Immigrant Experiences in the United States

With ambitious goals and rich life experiences in China, I came to the dreamed-of promised land—America. I was excited about my bright future in the United States because I believed that I had enough skills and guts to face the tough challenges ahead of me. However, when I came to the United States, I felt totally lost, incompetent, and dysfunctional. I lost my voice (because I could not speak English), my ideas, and even my thinking skills. I could not communicate with people, and I could not even order my food at McDonald's. People saw me as different, somebody unable to do anything. I was depressed and isolated myself from the outside world. I was afraid to meet people. The only way I could express my bitter feelings was by writing letters to my family and friends in China. I told them that "here is paradise because there is everything you want; but also here is hell because you suffer too much." I felt utterly hopeless. Near this time, one of my American friends, whom I had hired in China to teach English at the university, came to visit me. She introduced me to a professor at the University of California at Davis, who encouraged me to study. I did, but I traveled an extraordinarily difficult journey of psychological adjustment in doing so.

In order to support my study financially, I had to find a job. After competing with many applicants, I got a position as an instructor of Chinese at the University of California at Davis. It was my first time standing on the stage of an American institution, teaching American students the Chinese language. I was in a panic. Very soon, however, I discovered that I was considered an authority and the students respected me as a teacher with profound knowledge. In the evaluations of my course, students wrote the following: "Professor Zou is a very knowledgeable and effective instructor"; "She is humorous and resourceful"; "We learned a great deal from her." Teaching Chinese language instilled in me a sense of confidence and power that I needed badly. To be able to say what I wanted, to control the class, to become the professor, and to have Americans struggle to learn Chinese (as I was struggling to learn English) gave me interesting insights into the sort of dual personality I had begun to develop. On the one hand, I felt as if I was truly in control when I taught my Chinese class. On the other hand, when I was a student in the Division of Education, I felt, for the most part, patronized or neglected. The professors and students had trouble understanding me. They would speak to me slowly, masticating their words, as if I was stupid. I felt humiliated and depressed. For that reason I loved to teach my Chinese class. It gave me a sense of being myself again.

As a Chinese instructor I was a role model, a high-ranking member of the academic community, a person deserving of respect and admiration, a person with social responsibilities and the power to give grades to American students. Furthermore, I was opening a new world of sounds and ideas, of cultural traditions and practices, of history and philosophy for my students. I felt I was useful. I could contribute to the students' learning because I am a very good Chinese speaker, writer, and professor. But after I would finish my Chinese classes, I would start to worry about attending classes as a student myself. I felt confused, anxious, even stupid. In my classes the Americans looked so smart and competent. I felt I could never compete with them. Many times professors did not give me a chance to talk in public. When they did ask me questions, they were always very simple or just about China. One time in a class discussion it was my turn to discuss some issues about human learning development. The professor openly passed over to the student next to me. I felt embarrassed and humiliated. I raised my hand and requested that the professor give me a chance to talk. The professor did. This was the first time I felt better about myself because I got the chance to express my ideas. I got fair treatment. After the class many students told me how much they admired my courage. However, I had to accept the fact that, no matter how much I knew, I could not express myself well. I hated feeling that way, and feeling confused about the future! Later some professors who had faith in me helped me a great deal by giving me specific roles to perform and asking me to do research with them. Still, in my eyes, American students continued to look so eloquent, so articulate. I would tell myself, "I will never reach that level." My sense of self-confidence was shaken from time to time. I would tell myself, "How can I ever complete this assignment?" I was resolved to give all I had, my very best effort, but I was doing this in a language in which I could not express my most intimate thoughts, though one that I understood well enough to analyze meaning and nuances.

Gradually I began to realize that I benefited from knowing two languages and two cultures. This helped me to get deeper into the structure of the English language and analyze the content of texts better than some American students. That made me anxious to read more and to compare more. I found that comparing the two languages, the two cultures, and the two countries fascinated me and opened up a new world of knowledge to me. I realized I had found something I was really excited about. But I did not know exactly what it was.

One time in a class on ethnographic research, my professor asked me to tell the class about Chinese culture and how it differed from U.S. culture. This question was asked of me quite often when I came to this country. When I was in China no one asked me about this, and I never thought about my culture and how different I was from other people. This made me think about my identity more and about who I am. This reflection was very important for me to help characterize my life, the life of my daughter, and the lives of other Chinese immigrants I know: a predominant trait was resilience or the ability to endure hard labor, stress, and sacrifices, and to survive until one succeeds in a task. I spent long nights and many hours of work in the library, in my home, and everywhere I could have a minute to read, write, reflect, and comment. I realized I was passionate in my dedication to the completion of my work. I would go for many hours without food until I finished my job. Why did I do that? What prepared me to stand the stresses and the sacrifices and pursue the completion of my tasks at any cost? Perhaps it was my Chinese background, my philosophy of life, and my experience as a child and young adult, in which I had to endure many hardships in the fields as a laborer and from which I learned survival skills.

The work of John Ogbu (an immigrant from Africa) and his associates, which is highly respected, developed as an alternative theoretical approach to deficit theories, postulated that "caste-like" (or involuntary) minorities did not achieve academically because they became quintessentially handicapped. These involuntary (caste-like) minorities had undergone such primary cultural discontinuities (discontinuities ethnohistorically contracted prior to exposure to mainstream culture) as well as such secondary discontinuities (resulting from their oppression in contact with mainstream societies) that they formed an oppositional self-identity that led them to reject school achievement as a desirable goal (Ogbu 1974, 1978, 1982, 1983, 1987a, 1987b, 1989, 1991a, 1991b, 1992; Ogbu & Matute-Bianchi 1986; Gibson 1988; Gibson & Ogbu 1991). It is important to note that while the macro-sociological models of the 1960s and 1970s were seen as theoretical progress, other "ethnic" social scientists were concerned that such approaches would contribute to the stereotyping of minorities and would not explain their ability to succeed; in other words, an attempt to reject one type of determinism (genetic, biological, etc.) would end up taking us to another type of determinism (cultural). Trueba (1988) and Foley (1991) were clear in pointing at the potential risks of Ogbu's typology and theoretical premises. Valencia describes some of the historical currents that affected immigration policies in this country. The passing of the Immigration Act of 1924 followed years of debate and struggles to control European immigration currents from Italy, Russia, Poland, and Greece.

When John Ogbu began to write in the mid-1970s on the differential achievement levels of ethnolinguistic minorities, he combined a number of elements existing in anthropology, sociology, and psychology. His original typology (autonomous, immigrant, and caste-like groups) was already an effort to capitalize on the work of previous scholars. George DeVos had used extensively the "caste-like" concept; George Spindler had studied "cultural continuities and discontinuities" among Native Americans and other groups and had discussed their various adaptive strategies (nativistic, transitional, assimilated, bicultural, etc.). Ogbu capitalized on the sociological literature to recognize the social structural forces impacting behavior in ethnic groups, but goes on to capitalize also on psychological factors related to cultural continuities and discontinuities that affect the formation of self-identity. Thus, for example, among the caste-like (in contrast with immigrant and autonomous minorities which, in the end he labels "voluntary" as opposed to the caste-like labeled "involuntary") Ogbu theorizes that the explanation for their low achievement is not only the social constraints (segregation, job ceiling, etc.) but also their "oppositional self-identity" that makes them view school achievement as a "white" characteristic, and consequently one that persons of color ought to avoid if they want to remain consistent with their identity.

The very subtle relationship of self-identity to adaptive responses in the face of conflict is chosen as central to our understanding of the real or assumed failure of certain groups (Mexican American, black, Native Americans, etc.). But what this theory does not explain is the differential success of some members of these groups who are exposed to the same oppressive societal factors (segregation, poverty, job ceiling, etc.). It is in this context that we see the need to search for a more flexible and sophisticated model (such as that of Bourdieu) in search of special agencies and unique "fields" (economic, cultural, political, etc.) that affect individual's early socialization and self-identity formation, their "habitus," to use Bourdieu's terms, as a result of the continuous and dynamic interaction with special agents in each field. Furthermore, the complex relationship between fields, the relative autonomy of such fields, leaves enough room to explain differential performance of individuals in certain circumstances.

Bourdieu was well aware of the dangers involved in large macro-sociological or macro-psychological models (such as the cultural ecological theories postulated by Ogbu and associates); these macro models can take us directly to the kind of deterministic positions that Ogbu was originally battling against. As we all reject biological or genetic determinism on the basis of empirical data showing that socialization patterns, cultural influences, and other learned behavior can render genetic determinism false, especially if we compound concepts of determinism with racial typologies.

The significant degree of miscegenetion among all ethnic groups around the world, on the one hand, and the fundamental comparability of DNA structures across diverse ethnic groups around the world (for example in the study of diseases predominant in certain groups, like high blood pressure among blacks), shows that environmental influences, adaptive mechanisms, lifestyle, education, and other factors explain better the distribution of health conditions and risks than any fixed, racially structured model. South African blacks have one of the lowest incidences of high blood pressure. Chinese Americans, if compared with their siblings living in mainland China, develop high cholesterol and high blood pressure, in spite of sharing with their relatives the same genetic pool.

## Becoming an Ethnographer: My New Identity as a Scholar in the United States

After I took several courses on minority education and ethnographic research, I developed a great interest in minority students' academic motivations and their achievements. I am especially fascinated by the power of ethnographic research. My passion for the poor peasant children and my commitment to help those children led me to read about the Hmong people, who are refugees from Southeast Asia. Hmong people experience tremendous difficulties in adjusting to this new society. However, their children are doing extremely well both economically and academically. I admired their brave spirit and their hard work, and I wanted to know more about this group. Through researching the literature, I found that the ancestors of the Hmong people are the Miao people in China (see Trueba, Jacobs, and Kirton 1990).

After a long period of preparation in the United States, in 1992, my main professor and I began an ethnographic research project in China that focused on Miao university students. We did the study both in Beijing, at the Central University for Nationalities, in the heart of the capital of China, and at the Guizhou Institute for Nationalities located in the south central part of China. We selected fourteen Miao students for our study. Seven were from the Central University for Nationalities, and seven were from the Guizhou Institute for Nationalities. The Central University for Nationalities is affiliated directly with the State Educational Commission of China and was established in 1951. It has 2,300 faculty and staff (including maintenance personnel) and an enrollment of more than 7,000 students from all 56 ethnic groups. The Guizhou Institute for Nationalities was founded in 1951 under the leadership of the Educational Commission of Guizhou Province. It has 2,500 students from 18 different ethnic groups. The fourteen students we interviewed were all originally from rural areas. Their parents were mostly peasants, although a few were teachers, government officials, and village leaders. All of their families had very low annual incomes. However, the poorest Miao children, as university students and faculty, obtained high prestige as members of mainstream Chinese society and were recognized as leaders in their villages. How did this happen? Where did these poor children get the resources for their studies, and how did they succeed?

In order to conduct the ethnographic research project on the Miao, I obtained a postdoctoral fellowship at the University of Wisconsin at Madison. Being a native Chinese qualified me as an "insider" in China in the eyes of my professors because I was familiar with the Chinese culture and had the authority to interpret it to them. On the one hand, this perception was correct—I had spent forty years in China and knew the country fairly well (I thought). I had grown up in a Chinese middle-class family, and I knew mainstream ideology and lifestyle as a member of the Han people (the mainstream population that comprises 92 percent of the population of China or about 1.2 billion people). On the other hand, I was educated in the United States, I understood Western philosophy, I spoke English, and I dressed like an American. All this gave me the credentials to pass for an American in the eyes of the Chinese. Furthermore, I was armed with cultural ecological theories and ethnographic research methods, and, most importantly, I was funded by a U.S. university.

Before entering the research field, my professor and I reviewed the literature, developed a research design, articulated specific questions to be answered by the research, and carefully planned the implementation of the design through gradual strategic steps. In conducting the research, however, we had to wake up to the reality of our own social identities and cultural roles in China, at least as defined by the Miao people with whom we were working. Consequently, I became aware of my dual identity and was caught in a difficult position. I was both Chinese in the opinion of the Americans and an American in the eyes of the Chinese. But I knew I was neither, or perhaps I was both. That became a serious problem as I continued to reflect on my own identity, although during the research I did not have enough time to think seriously about it.

As I mentioned earlier, because I saw myself as a Chinese person who had lived in China most of my life, I was placed in the category of "insider" with regard to the Chinese culture. However, because I had come from the Han group, which is viewed as the mainstream cultural group and the "oppressor" or controlling group, I could not really claim to have the same way of thinking as those who are ethnically, socially, and economically different, as in the case of the Miao. They have constructed another set of values and perceptions or what is considered to be a "subculture" of Chinese society, and it is different from my own culture. Therefore, all I could do was describe my understanding of what I heard, what I saw, and what I felt in a way of thinking that I socially constructed in settings dominated by the Han people. Furthermore, I constructed these perceptual frames also from the perspective of Western academia. Indeed, the two cultures, the Han culture and Western academia, filtered my views. After five years of intensive study and training in the United States, I went back to China to conduct empowerment research with Miao students with whom I was unfamiliar. Therefore, my dual ideological identity placed me in an asymmetrical power relationship with the Miao students. They viewed me as an educated "Asian American" and consequently as an "outsider" and even "superior" or in a position of power.

When my professor, my American colleagues, and I went to the Central University for Nationalities in Beijing, we lived in a dormitory on the campus in order to be close to the students. Next to our rooms was the Foreign Affairs Office. All of our activities were under the officials' surveillance; they were responsible for approving who could come to see us, where we could go, and in what rooms we could meet. At the same time, however, the officials were eager to provide us with information after we told them we planned to write a book telling Americans about minorities in China. All the information the officials offered to us was official government policy or government propaganda material. We asked the foreign office for permission to meet with the Miao students. After some negotiations, we got the chance to interview and discuss our research project with some of the Miao students. Before we met them, we prepared a set of questions ranging from their personal backgrounds to their opinions about the government policies toward minorities.

The first meeting consisted of fifteen Miao students and two Miao professors. We started asking them questions about their experiences and their journeys from their home villages to the university. At first they kept silent, and they seemed to be anxious about the kinds of answers they could give to our questions. We felt a little embarrassed and did not know what we were supposed to do. Then their professor told us, "Don't feel bad. They didn't prepare for these questions, so they do not know how to answer them." After the meeting we learned that the foreign affairs officials had already prepared the students about what they should say to the Americans. At this time, only three years after the democracy rallies in Tiananmen Square, the Chinese government considered the United States an unfriendly power. Additionally, public expression of one's ideas was closely guarded. Students could not freely say what they wanted to say. In addition, when we arrived in Beijing the Chinese Communist Party Congress had just come to a close. The central theme of the conference was opposition to Chinese intellectual bourgeois liberalism, and the government was worried that students would once again stage demonstrations against the Chinese government. Therefore, the government kept a close watch on the students.

We remembered that on the day the conference ended, we went to Tiananmen Square and saw many military soldiers, policemen, and plainclothes public security personnel watching people's activities. So when we asked questions to the unprepared students, they hesitated in answering. The students did not know what they could tell foreigners and what might get them in trouble. The professor started to enlighten the students and told them in front of us, "You should not worry; you can say what you experienced. For example, you can tell them how the government cares about minority people and gives minorities preferential treatment, so you have a chance to enter college." Then the students started to recall their hardships both in their villages and in school. For example, Mr. Wang, a twenty-three-year-old student from the Guizhou Province, told us that his Han classmates laughed at his poor clothing and quite often he did not have money to buy food (Trueba and Zou 1994:88–91). As he talked about the hardships that he experienced and his family's difficult life, he began to cry. His story touched both the researchers and the professors.

On another day, a young Miao university professor invited us to observe his class. When he came to our dormitory to meet us, the gatekeeper (a government officer) stopped him and asked him whether he had reported his activity to the Foreign Affairs Office in advance, and the guard would not let him see us. When we came down to the door, we explained to the officer that we had asked the professor to come to discuss one of his courses and his pedagogy in the classroom. Similar red tape and bureaucratic inquiries occurred in situations when phone calls came from the outside, when unexpected students or other visitors attempted to talk to us, or when we tried to change our schedule.

In China, a discussion of oppression cannot be public because it would be considered antigovernment and would subject the participants to incarceration and other sanctions. For the Chinese students, however, the ideological position is that the government is always fair and nobody should view surveillance as oppressive. As we began to think about the consequences of asking people to cooperate with our research, we realized that there was an element of risk and uncertainty associated with critical ethnographic research in a specific context or situation, especially in the context of university students who are often penalized the most for their use of freedom of speech. As researchers, we had to keep in mind that our first responsibility was to the people we studied. Consequently, we had to accept the constraints of the cultural setting in which we functioned. In the end, we kept asking ourselves: How can we, as researchers in a foreign land, pursue our research agenda and still be responsible for the safety of the people we study?

Another dilemma was how as researchers we could best deal with our dominant cultural identity while working with ethnic minority persons. In critical ethnographic research sometimes we unconsciously recreate a context for dominance and tend to impose our values. When we began our research at the Central University for Nationalities, we identified a group of Miao students and professors and organized the schedule for individual and group interviews. We then proceeded to ask our questions regarding their rationales for leaving their villages and becoming university students and professors. We wanted to know how strongly they felt their identity as "Miao" and what roles this ethnic identity had in their motivation to achieve academically. We unconsciously conducted our research without reflecting on the automatic assumption about the "subjects" of our research as if they were "objects." This happened until we started to build rapport with the students and professors and heard the individual stories of poverty, struggle, and oppression that had characterized many of their lives. At that moment we turned our methodology around and began to investigate ways in which we could assist them. Gradually my professor and I were adopted as "honorary" members of their clan. It was only after we traveled 2,000 miles southwest to the Province of Guizhou and interviewed an entirely different group of Miao university students that we realized the fundamental differences between the two Miao student groups (the one from Beijing and the one from Guizhou).

We were interviewed first at length before we could even get to the points we were investigating. The students and professors in Guizhou demonstrated to us that they felt competent and in control of the situation. They described the Miao as a cosmological ethnic or racial group scattered throughout the entire world, and they interrogated us about the treatment of the Miao (Hmong) in the United States. They also gave us their long-term views of economic and industrial plans to move upwardly the entire Miao group around the world and wanted to know if we were ready to invest in such efforts. This experience made us aware that we had mistaken the first group of Miao students as objects of study, instead of as persons. We became humble on our visit to Guizhou, a province that has a high concentration of minority populations. As we turned the discussion to the Miao students' plans for the future, we realized that, instead of answering our questions, they would ask us what we thought they could do to help their own people in the future not only in China but throughout the world. Actually, they changed roles and became the researchers, using us as consultants. They were looking up to us for guidance and practical advice; and they were doing it with a unique global perspective and ambition, talking about the Miao being a cosmic group with a bright destiny and a significant international force. We felt obligated to tell them some success stories of minorities in the United States and how the Miao could use their knowledge to develop natural resources in their areas, to communicate with the outside world to attract investments from the Western world, and to participate actively in public events in order to make the Miao group more visible. They followed our thoughts and developed a lot of new ideas. Mr. Tao Wencen, an eighteen-year-old student, said that after he graduated he would organize county cooperatives and business firms, and later he would use the capital accumulated from the cooperatives to establish a Miao city with hotels, restaurants, and other tourist facilities. Mr. Xiaoping Tao said, "I want to help the Miao people become literate; collect and edit Miao folklore and publish a book; write a book on the history of my Miao village." Mr. Xiong Jianliang wanted to become a village leader and use his intelligence to develop his village (Trueba and Zou 1994: 99–100).

After we finished our research project and wrote a book about what we learned about Miao people, I went back to visit our informants several times. I found out not only that our research encouraged the students to pursue their dreams but that it also helped U.S. students get a better understanding of education. Some of the Miao students we studied now have become university professors and administrators. My American students were moved by the stories the Miao students told and this motivated them to achieve greater academic excellence.

Inequities, the formation of negative or oppositional identities in school (Davidson 1997), and the "subtractive" character of schooling (Valenzuela 1999) and the counter narratives that provide an ethnic perspective of historical and contemporary events, are all linked to the role of ethnic researchers. As Foley has pointed out (in press), the appearance of counter narratives written by ethnics follow a parallel trend. On the one hand, attempts are made at clarifying the grounds for rejection of deterministic notions of success or failure based on either genetic or cultural deficit models. These narratives that we mentioned at the beginning of this chapter have the virtue of giving a voice to the very people whose intellectual and academic demise was prematurely predicted by deficit models and who, by a rather unique paradoxical turn of events, are now excelling above any expectations. The challenge of explaining success among the poor and disenfranchised has forced reflection and redirection of theoretical explanations.

## Lessons Learned: Some Personal Thoughts

The immigration experience is a never-ending venture that continuously redefines one's life and self-concept. For me as a Chinese woman, becoming a permanent resident and getting to better know American society has given me a new view of life and a capability to see the world from different perspectives and in different dimensions. The Eastern and Western worlds are so vastly different and even opposed that a Chinese immigrant (from what I have experienced and seen in others) must make heroic efforts to become flexible, bicultural, and committed to learn every day many new and subtle nuances about the American culture and the English language. Perhaps much of the miscommunication between the East and the West has to do with the lack of ability to learn "new ways of life" and new cultural values. Raising my daughter in this country has opened my eyes to the profound differences in socialization patterns and to the dilemmas faced by Chinese parents in the United States. For me, being a Chinese immigrant is a continued intensive course in acculturation and self-redefinition that will last the rest of my life.

I believe that the foundation for genuine academic empowerment of children of immigrants is a solid self-identity and a clear concept of one's own ethnic community. My daughter and her friends not only are proud of being Chinese, but also are proud of understanding American culture and using English with a high level of proficiency. The Chinese community around us is very influential, and the competition for achievement is intense. One of the reasons why I have become very interested in self-identity and academic achievement is that I have lived through the pain of trying to compete with native English speakers, and I have seen my daughter work very hard to become a high achiever.

I go back to China every year in order to teach and conduct research among minority groups. This has been an opportunity to retain a profound adherence to my culture without losing my biculturalism; it has forced me to reflect on my own self-identity and has invited me to revisit some theoretical issues on the nature of the immigrant experience in the United States. For example, the complex issue of empowerment among Asian Americans and their need for liberation, voice, and appropriate space in the instructional process (see Freire 1973, 1995; Freire and Macedo 1996; Giroux and McLaren 1986, 1994; Gutierrez 1994; Gutierrez, Larson, and Kreuter 1995; and others). These issues are often misunderstood by teachers and academicians.

The new Asian Americans of my daughter's generation are not fighting to retain their own ethnic identity and to have a separate voice in schools. They are fighting to acquire an American identity and an equal voice along with other American youth. But they are well aware that they possess a new cultural capital by being bilingual, bicultural, and fully competent in modern societies. They will not abandon their own ethnic identity. Their vast networks and frequent communication with other children of immigrants will secure comfort in our own Asian community. But they do not want to be branded different, not even for the sake of recognizing their academic accomplishments.

Regarding the debate on the Asian American "model minorities" (see Ogbu 1974, 1978, 1992), achievement for us Asian Americans, as immigrants, and for our children has been far from easy. It has not been a rapid ascending line to success. On the contrary, we have failed many times but continued to fight. We have had to face our lack of knowledge and experience, but we continue to try because we are building the empowerment of the next generation. Our children struggle, and we encourage them to continue to try and make more serious efforts. It has not been easy! Specifically, as we try to adapt, along the lines of Gibson's (see 1988, 1997) model of accommodation not assimilation, we certainly retain the most important family values that brought us to this country: loyalty to our ethnic group and parents, commitment to help each other, commitment to always make the greatest possible effort to succeed, and resilience when we fail. The survival and adaptation of Asian Americans in this country is a complex process (see Kiang 1995, 1996; Trueba, Cheng, and Ima 1993). The drastic changes in our multiple identities (Trueba 2002) are directly and profoundly affected by the "transformations" and changes in the children of immigrants and their families (Suárez-Orozco and Suárez-Orozco 1995a, 1995b) and by the global economic and political currents accelerating migration waves (Suárez-Orozco and Suárez-Orozco 1991, 1998a, 1998b).

As a committed academician, my questions are the following: How can I deal with my multiple identities as I try to conduct objective research? How do my experiences, cultural capital, and ethnic identity impact the process and outcomes of my ethnographic research? What role should my identities play in ethnographic research? How can I turn my identity and experiences into assets? How should I deal with my own ethnic, cultural, and experiential biases? As have many other immigrants, I have had difficult moments adapting. Yet, in the end, I always come out convinced that my biculturalism has enriched my life. Becoming an immigrant often translates into painful experiences that require healing and understanding. In fact, one of my most recent and profound realizations is that I finally became convinced that often conflict across cultures can be resolved through the culture of therapy. I was feeling torn by two extremely different lifestyles and began to realize that I did not have to be both Chinese and American at the same time within the same cultural environment. My mind was opened when I read about cultural therapy as a means to increase our understanding of value conflicts and resolve such conflicts (Spindler and Spindler 1989, 1992a, 1992b, 1994; Trueba 1994).

In contrast with the philosophy of Paulo Freire, who sees education and the acquisition of knowledge as intrinsically political, the Spindlers feel that the acquisition obtained through anthropological knowledge about our personal ethnic, racial, and cultural identities is not necessarily political and leads to "cultural" reflection, a deeper understanding of value differences, and ultimately conflict resolution. Conscientization (or in the Spindlers' lexicon, cultural reflection) is a means to resolve personal and social problems associated with having the wrong cultural assumptions about other people and their perception of who we are. By learning about ourselves, our "enduring selves" and our "situated selves," and by reconciling them, we can prevent the painful experience of reaching an "endangered self" (confusion and uprootedness from our values). The central concepts of how the enduring self is deeply rooted in the first years of our cultural socialization within the family and community evokes many strong memories in my life. I cannot but accept the fact that my infancy and adolescence as directed by my parents and family left a profound mark on me. Therefore, at the heart of cultural therapy, as I understand it, is the ability to reflect on cultural values, traditions, and personal identity. As a Chinese immigrant, perhaps as many other immigrants have, I have become aware of the need to heal, to piece together my inner self, and to retain my cultural values of both Chinese and American origin (Zou 1998; Zou and Trueba 1998).

I assume that at the heart of cultural therapy as a healing process is the realization that there has to be an acceptance of the self based on a profound historical and cultural knowledge of one's own family. I am aware that in theory, cultural therapy does not assume that each member of humankind needs psychotherapy or that much of the sad state of affairs in the world today is related to social and cultural conflicts. The condition sine qua non for healing from hurts caused by prejudice or bigotry is the possession of a deep cultural knowledge and understanding of human groups and their culturally determined behaviors, as well as an understanding of the mediating role played by language and culture in the acquisition of new knowledge (Trueba 1994: viii–ix). To the extent that I know the nature of my biculturalism and that I use effectively the Mandarin and English languages, I feel at peace, confident, and competent. But the price of this peace has been a great deal of work and persistence to survive failure, to stand up and try again.

# References

Crespigny, R. de. *China This Century*. New York: Oxford University Press, 1992.

Davidson, A. L. "Marbella Sanches: On Marginalization and Silencing." Pp. 15–44 in M. Seller and L. Weis, ed., *Beyond Black and White: New Faces and Voices in U.S. Schools*. New York: SUNY Press, 1997.

Dikötter, F. *The Discourse of Race in Modern China*. Stanford: Stanford University Press, 1992.

Foley, D. "Reconsidering Anthropological Explanations of Ethnic School Failure." *Anthropology and Educational Quarterly*, 22 (1991):60–86.

Foley, D. *Reconceptualizing Ethnicity and School Achievement: The Rise of Ethnic Ethnographers*. Austin: University of Texas, in press.

Freire, P. *Pedagogy of the Oppressed*. New York: Seabury, 1973.

Freire, P. *Pedagogy of Hope: Reliving Pedagogy of the Oppressed*. New York: Contnuum, 1995.

Freire, P., and D. Macedo. "A Dialogue: Culture, Language, and Race." Pp. 199–228 in P. Leistyna, A. Woodrum, and S. A. Sherbloom, ed., *Breaking Free: The Transformative Power of Critical Pedagogy*, Theme Issue. Harvard Education Review, Reprint Series 27, 1996.

Gibson, M. *Accommodation without Assimilation: Sikh Immigrants in an American High School*. Ithaca, N.Y.: Cornell University Press, 1988.

Gibson, M., ed. "Ethnicity and School Performance: Complicating the Immigrant/Involuntary Minority Typology." *Anthropology and Education Quarterly*, 28 (1997):315–462.

Gibson, M., and J. Ogbu, ed. *Minority Status and Schooling: A Comparative Study of Immigrant and Involuntary Minorities*. New York: Garland Publishing, 1991.

Giroux, H., and P. McLaren. "Teacher Education and the Politics of Engagement: The Case for Democratic Schooling." *Harvard Educational Review*, 26, 3 (1986):213–38.

Gladney, C. C. *Muslim Chinese: Ethnic Nationalism in the People's Republic*, Council on East Asian Studies, Harvard East Asian Monographs. Cambridge, Mass.: Harvard University Press, 1991.

Gutierrez, K. "How Talk, Context, and Script Shape Context for Learning: A Cross-Case Comparison of Journal Sharing." *Linguistics and Education*, 5 (1994):335–65.

Gutierrez, K., J. Larson, and B. Kreuter. "Cultural Tensions in the Scripted Classroom: The Value of the Subjugated Perspective." *Urban Education*, 29, 4 (1995):410–42.

Kiang, P. "Bicultural Strengths and Struggles of Southeast Asian American Students." Pp. 201–25 in Antonia Darder, ed., *Culture and Difference: Critical Perspectives on the Bicultural Experiences in the United States*. New York: Bergin and Garvey, 1995.

Kiang, P. "Persistence Stories and Survival Strategies of Cambodian Americans in College." *Journal of Narrative and Life History*, 6, 1 (1996):39–64.

Ogbu, J. *The Next Generation: An Ethnography of Education in an Urban Neighborhood.* New York: Academic Press, 1974.

Ogbu, J. "Cultural Discontinuities and Schooling." *Anthropology and Education Quarterly*, 13, 4 (1982):290–307.

Ogbu, J. "Minority Status and Schooling in Plural Societies." *Comparative Education Review*, 2, 2 (1983):168–90.

Ogbu, J. "Variability in Minority Responses to Schooling: Nonimmigrants vs. Immigrants." Pp. 255–78 in G. Spindler and L. Spindler, ed., *Interpretive Ethnography of Education: At Home and Abroad.* Hillsdale, N.J.: Lawrence Erlbaum Associates, 1987a.

Ogbu, J. "Variability in Minority School Performance: A Problem in Search of an Explanation." *Anthropology and Education Quarterly*, 18, 4 (1987b):312–34.

Ogbu, J. "The Individual in Collective Adaptation: A Framework for Focusing on Academic Underperformance and Dropping Out among Involuntary Minorities." Pp. 181–204 in L. Weis, E. Farrar, and H. Petrie, ed., *Dropouts from School: Issues, Dilemmas, and Solutions.* Albany: State University of New York Press, 1989.

Ogbu, J. "Immigrant and Involuntary Minorities in Comparative Perspective." Pp. 3–33 in M. Gibson, and J. Ogbu, ed., *Minority Status and Schooling: A Comparative Study of Immigrant and Involuntary Minorities.* New York: Garland Publishing, Inc., 1991a..

Ogbu, J. "Low School Performance as an Adaptation: The Case of Blacks in Stockton, California." Pp. 249–85 in M. Gibson, and J. Ogbu, ed., *Minority Status and Schooling: A Comparative Study of Immigrant and Involuntary Minorities.* New York: Garland Publishing, Inc., 1991b.

Ogbu, J. "Understanding Cultural Diversity." *Educational Researcher*, 21, 8 (1992):5–24.

Ogbu, J. *Minority Education and Caste: The American System in Cross-Cultural Perspective.* New York: Academic Press, 1978.

Ogbu, J., and M. E. Matute-Bianchi. "Understanding Sociocultural Factors: Knowledge, Identity and School Adjustment." Pp. 73–142 in *Beyond Language: Social and Cultural Factors in Schooling Language Minority Students.* Sacramento, Calif.: Bilingual Education Office, California State Department of Education, 1986.

Spindler, G., and L. Spindler. "Instrumental Competence, Self-Efficacy, Linguistic Minorities, and Cultural Therapy: A Preliminary Attempt at Integration." *Anthropology and Education Quarterly*, 10 (1989): 36–50.

Spindler, G., and L. Spindler. "The Enduring, Situated, and Endangered Self in Fieldwork: A Personal Account." Pp. 23–28 in L. B. Boyer and R. Boyer, ed., *The Psychoanalytic Study of Society. Volume 17: Essays in Honor of George D. and Louise A. Spindler.* Hillsdale, N.J.: Analytic Press, 1992a.

Spindler, G., and L. Spindler. "The Lives of George and Louise Spindler." Pp. 1–22 in L. B. Boyer and R. Boyer, ed., *The Psychoanalytic Study of Society. Volume 17: Essays in Honor of George D. and Louise A. Spindler.* Hillsdale, N.J.: Analytic Press, 1992b.

Spindler, G., and L. Spindler, ed. *Pathways to Cultural Awareness: Cultural Therapy for Teachers and Students.* Newbury Park, Calif.: Corwin Press, 1994.

Starr, J. B. *Understanding China: A Guide to China's Economy, History, and Political Structure*. New York: Hill and Wang, 1997.

Suárez-Orozco, C., and M. M. Suárez-Orozco. *Transformations: Immigration, Family Life and Achievement Motivation among Latino Adolescents*. Stanford: Stanford University Press, 1995a.

Suárez-Orozco, C., and M. M. Suárez-Orozco. "Migration: Generational Discontinuities and the Making of Latino Identities." Pp. 321–47 in L. Romanucci-Ross and G. DeVos, ed., *Ethnic Identity: Creation, Conflict, and Accommodation*, 3rd ed. Walnut Creek, Calif.: AltaMira Press, 1995b.

Suárez-Orozco, C., and M. M. Suárez-Orozco. "Introduction." Pp. 5–50 in M. M. Suárez-Orozco, ed., *Crossings: Mexican Immigration in Interdisciplinary Perspectives*. Cambridge, Mass.: David Rockefeller Center for Latin American Studies and Harvard University Press, 1998a.

Suárez-Orozco, C., and M. M. Suárez-Orozco. "State Terrors: Immigrants and Refugees in the Post-National Space." Pp. 283–319 in Y. Zou and H. T. Trueba, ed., *Ethnic Identity and Power: Cultural Contexts of Political Action in School and Society*. New York: State University of New York Press, 1998b.

Suárez-Orozco, C., and M. M. Suárez-Orozco. "Migration, Minority Status, and Education: European Dilemmas and Responses in the 1990s." *Anthropology and Education Quarterly*, 22 (1991): 99–120.

Suárez-Orozco, M. Marcelo, ed. *Crossings: Mexican Immigration in Interdisciplinary Perspectives*. Cambridge, Mass.: Harvard University Press and D. Rockefeller Center for Latin American Studies, 1998.

Suárez-Orozco, M., and C. Suárez-Orozco. "Some Conceptual Consideration in the Interdisciplinary Study of Immigrant Children." Pp. 17–35 in H. Trueba and L. Bartolomé, ed. *Immigrant Voices in Search of Pedagogical Reform*. Lanham, Md.: Rowman & Littlefield, 2000.

Tamayo Lott, J. *Asian Americans: From Racial Category to Multiple Identities*. Critical Perspectives on Asian Pacific Americans Series. Walnut Creek, Calif.: AltaMira Press, 1998.

Tharp, R. G., and R. Gallimore. *Rousing Minds to Life: Teaching, Learning, and Schooling in Social Context*. Cambridge, Mass.: Cambridge University Press, 1998.

Trueba, H. T. "Culturally-Based Explanations of Minority Students' Academic Achievement." *Anthropology and Education Quarterly*, 19, 3 (1988): 270–87.

Trueba, H. T. "Linkages of Macro-Micro Analytical Levels." *Journal of Psychohistory*, 18, 4 (1991):457–68.

Trueba, H. T. "Foreword." Pp. vii–xi in George Spindler and Louise Spindler, ed., *Pathways to Cultural Awareness: Cultural Therapy for Teachers and Students*, Newbury Park, Calif.: Corwin Press, 1994.

Trueba, H. T. "Interpreting Menchú's Account: Sociocultural and Linguistic Contexts." *Qualitative Studies in Education*, 13, 2 (2000):115–29.

Trueba, H. T. "Multiple Ethnic, Racial, and Cultural Identities in Action: From Marginality to a New Cultural Capital in Modern Society." *Journal of Latinos and Education*, I, 1 (2002):7–28.

Trueba, H. T., L. Cheng, and K. Ima. *Myth or Reality: Adaptive Strategies of Asian Americans in California*. London: Falmer Press, 1993.

Trueba, H. T., L. Jacobs, and E. Kirton. *Cultural Conflict and Adaptation: The Case of the Hmong Children in American Society*. London: Falmer Press, 1990.

Trueba, H. T., and Y. Zou. *Power in Education: The Case of Miao University Students and Its Significance for American Culture*. London: Falmer Press, 1994.

Trueba, H. T., and Y. Zou. Report for the Grant of National Ethnographic Research Conference to the Spencer Foundation. Unpublished document, 1999.

Trueba, H. T., and Y. Zou. Annual Report for the Research Grant to the Spencer Foundation. Unpublished document, 2000.

Valenzuela, A. *Subtractive Schooling: U.S.–Mexican Youth and the Politics of Caring*. New York: SUNY Press, 1999.

Zou, Y. "Dilemmas Faced by Critical Ethnographers in China." Pp. 389–409 in Y. Zou and H. T. Trueba., ed., *Ethnic Identity and Power: Cultural Contexts of Political Action in School and Society*. New York: State University of New York Press, 1998.

Zou, Y. Final Report for the Research Grant to the Spencer Foundation. Unpublished document, 2002.

Zou, Y., and H. T. Trueba, ed. *Ethnic Identity and Power: Cultural Contexts of Political Action in School and Society*. New York: State University of New York Press, 1998.

# CHAPTER TEN

# Stories and Structures of Persistence: Ethnographic Learning through Research and Practice in Asian American Studies

*Peter Kiang*

## Introduction

In its long-awaited 1999 report, *Reaching the Top*, the College Board's National Task Force on Minority High Achievement called for comprehensive, targeted support for African American, Latino, and Native American students from pre-K through higher education. Whites and Asians, the report asserted, are succeeding academically and, therefore, do not need comparable attention or interventions.

Upon learning of the report's assumptions and conclusions—first through national media coverage of its release and then directly through hard copy—my thoughts turned quickly to what I know about my own community and school contexts. Here in Boston, a city renowned for its universities, it is true that 32 percent of the adult Asian American population hold a bachelor's degree or higher, compared to 37 percent of the white population and only 14 percent of the black population. But an even higher percentage of the Asian American adult population (38 percent) has less than a twelfth-grade education, compared with 19 percent of the white population and 33 percent of the black population (Watanabe 1996). The distribution of Asian

American professionals and workers locally and nationally is strikingly bimodal.

Asian immigrants also show wide differences in educational achievement that reflects the filters of U.S. immigration preferences and the structure of the U.S. postindustrial economy. Nationally among Asian immigrants aged sixteen and older, for example, one out of four Filipinos and one out of five Indians have undergraduate degrees, compared with only one out of eleven Vietnamese, one out of forty Cambodians, and one out of eighty-five Hmong.[1]

If College Board researchers had disaggregated their statistical data or simply visited my urban, public university, they would have discovered that Southeast Asian American[2] students and many urban Asian American students of various nationalities do not have high educational achievement levels. Ironically, in a separate report also commissioned by the College Board's National Task Force on Minority High Achievement, Patricia Gándara, a highly esteemed scholar of educational policy and Chicano student achievement, critically explains:

> Data are not disaggregated by the College Board for Asian groups; indeed the College Board lumps all Asians with Pacific Islanders, and this obscures wide differences within the group. The typical standard deviation for SAT scores of Asian students is almost one-fourth of a standard deviation larger than for whites and about one-fifth of a standard deviation greater than for other minority groups, suggesting that some Asian students are performing much higher than others. (Gándara 1999:9)

The College Board's commitment to enhance African American, Latino, and Native American student achievement is urgent and righteous. Its inadequate analysis, however, distorts the diverse realities of Asian American students, families, and communities. Gándara's candid critique regarding the validity of using Asian American aggregate data echoes numerous warnings that appear in every major study or literature review on Asian American educational issues produced for more than two decades (Park and Chi 1999; Cheng and Pang 1998; Weinberg 1997; Lee 1996; Nakanishi and Nishida 1995; Kiang and Lee 1993; Trueba, Cheng, and Ima 1993; Suzuki 1977, 1989; Chun 1980). It is remarkable that research of the scale and significance of the College Board's National Task Force could ignore such longstanding and clearly articulated concerns.

Furthermore, the College Board's powerful, institutional influence triggers a cascade of similarly flawed decisions by national, state, and local funders, government agencies, and schools that target resources, policies, and services for specific student populations—and neglect those who share comparably low levels of academic achievement but are hidden within the Asian American aggregate category. This current dismissal of the realities of Southeast Asian American students belies a continuing weakness in educational research that reminds me of a period ten years ago when I first realized that mainstream analyses of college student achievement and persistence had completely ignored the strengths and survival strategies employed by Southeast Asian refugee students at my working-class university.

Much of my own agenda as a biracial, Chinese American teacher/ researcher and organizer/advocate working at the intersections between the fields of education and Asian American Studies,[3] therefore, has focused on documenting and analyzing the voices, strengths, and needs of Vietnamese and Cambodian immigrant/refugee students, precisely because of the failure of educational institutions to support or even acknowledge them. Inspired by those same students, I have also explored how specific curricular and pedagogical commitments in Asian American studies can serve as models of transformative practice for U.S. higher education.

This chapter seeks to connect various phases of applied research and reflection over the past decade focusing on questions of pedagogy, student learning, and persistence within the structure and culture of Asian American studies classrooms at one urban public university. Though not originally designed to be ethnographic, this evolving body of research shares much in its intentions, methods, and implications with educational ethnography. Moreover, it suggests that an alignment of educational ethnographers with ethnic studies classrooms, programs, and practitioners has rich possibilities for advancing critical research across many relevant areas.

## Phase I: Intuitive Analysis and Early Grounded Theory

I have written at length in recent years about the challenge facing the Asian American studies field to reconceptualize its curricular content and pedagogy in order to be meaningful to working-class, immigrant/refugee students (Kiang 1998, 1997, 1989). Such a vision of curriculum and program development, however, is only viable if grounded in the experiences and perspectives of those students. For faculty like myself who are typically not Southeast Asian Americans, this necessitates a learning process much like the practices of ethnographic participant observation and teacher research.

My entry to Southeast Asian American educational research began when many second wave[4] Cambodian, Vietnamese, and Chinese Vietnamese refugee students enrolled in my initial Asian American studies classes at University of Massachusetts (UMass) Boston in 1987. Their interests and needs led me to develop a new course focusing specifically on the migration, resettlement, and adjustment experiences of refugees from Vietnam, Laos, and Cambodia in the United States. At that time in 1989, "Southeast Asians in America" was one of only four such courses in the country and the only one offered at a university outside of California. In reviewing potential readings for the course, I found most of the available literature to be rooted in dominant, uncritical paradigms of cultural assimilation and client/ provider social services. My critique of the dominant literature was twofold. First, it was breathtakingly blind to or silent about the asymmetrical power dynamics inherent in its assumptions. Second, it ignored the realities of racism that were deeply implicated in both the involvement of the United States in Southeast Asia (del Rosario 1999; Kiang 1991a) and in the subsequent dispersal of Southeast Asian refugees enacted through federal resettlement policy (Kiang 1997). I refused to center my course on those distorted perspectives in the literature, and began searching for alternative frameworks.

Thankfully, my instincts as a student-centered teacher and curriculum designer led me to listen, observe, and engage with students in my own classrooms as a way of generating new theory. A crucial breakthrough occurred one day in 1989 when a student mentioned to me after class, "Mai's not acting like herself lately." I had noticed it, too. Mai[5] had been quiet and unengaged in class all week long. She was usually one of the most dynamic students in the room—voicing ideas and experiences more readily than others who shared her background as a second wave Vietnamese refugee.

Later, when I asked Mai privately how she was doing, she revealed with a mixture of sadness, frustration, and anger, "My family's car was burned, right on the street in front of our house! I don't know why. But I couldn't study. Just keep thinking about it. So depressed . . . I didn't tell anybody." As she disclosed her story in fuller detail, I realized that she had felt helpless *as a new immigrant* after the incident because she did not know how to handle it—how to call or communicate with the police or fire department at the time. She had internalized the problem *as a Vietnamese*—not telling people outside the family about what had happened. Furthermore, the actual arson of the car had triggered memories of the war in Vietnam that depressed her even more—reflecting her experience *as a refugee*. Yet, whether or not she realized it, the source of the problem was racial conflict in the neighborhood—reflecting her reality *as a racial minority*.

Recognizing each of these distinct dimensions of Mai's identity enabled me to understand more clearly why her participation had changed in class, and, more importantly, how I could better respond to her situation. Viewing her as "not acting like herself" was incorrect. In fact, Mai was being herself—a fully bicultural individual within a complex, multifaceted social context. We needed to see who she really was.

My understanding of Mai's story led me to conceptualize a multidimensional, theoretical framework that integrated various aspects of the Southeast Asian refugee experience and that suggested coherent ways to recognize their strengths and struggles in school. I defined these background characteristics along four distinct dimensions (Kiang 1995, 1991a, 1991b):

- as Southeast Asians with distinct linguistic, cultural, and historical characteristics determined by growing up in their home countries and, to some extent, maintained by their continuing integration in their basic family and community structure in the United States;
- as refugees with survival skills and psychologies adapted to war, famine, flight and forced migration, loss of family members, secondary trauma from refugee camp, and resettlement;
- as immigrants in America adjusting to drastic changes in status, opportunity, living conditions, climate, and other aspects of daily life, especially in relation to culture and language;
- as racial minorities facing discrimination, disenfranchisement, racism, and violence as social, economic, and political realities in the United States.

*As Southeast Asians*, students' expectations, learning styles, and performance in school reflected traditional values and educational practices of their homelands. Differences, as well as similarities, between each country and between regions within a single country in culture, language, history, religion, and geopolitical development were important to consider. For example, pursuit of higher education was especially important for Vietnamese and ethnic Chinese influenced by the standards of Confucian society. Along this dimension, Southeast Asian students experienced problems related to cultural dislocation, but also were able to draw from traditions and cultural values to achieve in school.

Having fled their home countries *as refugees*, Southeast Asian students

revealed through life history narratives and their own writings common stories of war, rape, escape, and victimization together with themes of guilt,
survival, loneliness, family loyalty, and hope for the future. While facing
experiences of loss—loss of family, friends, and social networks; loss of homeland, property, and culture; loss of identity, security, and self-esteem, they
also demonstrated strengths—strengths of survival and sacrifice; strengths of
shared support and loyalty; and strengths of values, especially with regard to
education. The tragedy of the refugee experience may have limited some in
their pursuit of higher education, and motivated others to do so with even
greater determination. Southeast Asian refugee students faced a variety of
mental health issues arising from their past experience of trauma and loss
along this dimension, but their strengths, if recognized and engaged, could
also enable refugees to overcome their difficulties.

Over time, Southeast Asian refugees were reconstructing new lives *as
immigrants*—maintaining aspects of traditional identity while integrating
into U.S. society. Themes for students also especially concerned intergenera-
tional conflict with parents and the importance of education to the family.
Though "immigrant drive" may have accounted for certain achievement patterns observed among Southeast Asians in school that paralleled those of
Jewish and Japanese immigrants, immigrant family responsibilities and
expectations also intensified the problems and pressures faced by many
Southeast Asian students.

Southeast Asians were also facing a distinct racial dynamic in U.S. society
not experienced by European ethnic immigrant groups. *As racial minorities*,
Southeast Asian students confronted social conditions and institutional categories that situated them in a racialized category as Asian American minorities. Social-psychological problems of Southeast Asian students were
exacerbated by growing anti-Asian sentiment and racial violence on campuses and in neighborhoods throughout the country. At the same time,
minority student support services and pan-Asian student advocacy enhanced
the persistence of Southeast Asian refugee students in school. Group mobili-
zation and coalition-building provided vehicles with which to gain greater
access to resources and to demand political power.

Individually, each of these dimensions foregrounded a distinct set of issues
facing Southeast Asian American students and pointed to specific directions
for intervention and further research. When integrated together, as shown
by Mai's story, they illustrated multidimensional obstacles and possibilities
for strength that Southeast Asian students were bringing to the university.
Developing this framework created an alternative to the dominant, assimila-

tionist paradigms that defined majority writings about Southeast Asian Americans during that period. Furthermore, it offered a model for analyzing parallel, multidimensional backgrounds of other nonwhite refugee/immigrant populations such as Salvadorans and Haitians who were also entering schools in growing numbers at that time (Suarez-Orozco 1989). Most importantly, though, it enabled me to move beyond simply understanding the backgrounds of Southeast Asian refugee/immigrant students to consider their actual status and needs within the university.

## Phase II: Mapping Stories of Persistence

At this point, I moved to explore the mainstream literature on college student attrition and persistence—hoping to find some theories or models to help me make sense of how Southeast Asian American students were struggling and surviving in school. Once again, however, the dominant analyses seemed to discount the realities with which I was most familiar. Mainstream studies concluded, for example, that student degree completion was more likely at private versus public institutions and at residential versus commuter campuses, but said nothing about how students actually did persist at public, commuter institutions like UMass Boston.

The most influential work at that time was sociologist Vince Tinto's *Leaving College* (1987). College student persistence, according to Tinto, "entails the incorporation, that is integration, of the individual as a competent member in the social and intellectual communities of the college. . . . Student institutional departure is as much a reflection of the attributes of those communities, and therefore of the institution, as it is of the students who enter that institution. . . . Thus the term membership may be taken as connoting the perception on the part of the individual of having become a competent member of an academic or social community within the college" (1987:126–27).

Tinto found that faculty contact was the most important predictor of student persistence, and that its impact was heightened for minority and working-class students and for older students who have families or other external demands—the typical profile of students from UMass Boston. Tinto also emphasized that possibilities for persistence were substantially enhanced if student integration were taking place both academically and socially within the institution. These ideas seemed compelling and theoretically compatible with the community development strategies and sensibilities that I had brought to my own teaching, but I questioned whether Southeast Asian

American students' persistence stories matched Tinto's model. This led me to look and listen even more carefully for my own students' perspectives about surviving in school.

Through two years of indepth research based on student life history narratives, structured student interviews, participant observation as a teacher/advisor, and formal/informal student writings, my grounded theory of Southeast Asian American student persistence emerged with three major findings (Kiang 1996, 1991a, 1991b):

- Southeast Asian American students, including those who persisted, were not integrated either academically or socially within the university;
- Southeast Asian American students' motivation to persist in college was based on reference points outside of the university;
- Asian American Studies classrooms provided Southeast Asian American students with a university context in which to experience academic and social integration.

The following subsections illustrate each of these points in greater depth.

## 1. Stories of Academic and Social Isolation

*"On My Own" Stories*
In their school experiences, Southeast Asian American students described receiving little direct assistance from family members, friends, or school personnel. Students typically defined their approach to dealing with difficulties in terms of being "on my own" or "by myself." Sokal, a Cambodian male, lamented, "You have no guideline, you know. Your parents doesn't know really what they want you to be. And you lost, you know, searching for it by yourself." At the same time, he felt, "there was nobody in school to talk to, you know . . . seem not to find anybody."[5]

Students also made decisions not to ask for help. Khamkeaw, a Chinese Cambodian, who first escaped to Laos with his family before coming to the United States at age seventeen, admitted, "since I came to this school I never tried to look for any help. Everything I do is on my own." Sounthara, a young Lao woman agreed, "it's like you're kind of on your own. Yeah, professors seem like they don't care . . . you on your own." Sokal added, "Always on my own. . . . I rarely go see professors or TAs. . . . Most of the time I can figure it out. If I can't, just do the best I can and pass it in. And sometimes when the grade comes back, there's writing on the bottom—'Why didn't you come for help?', you know. I've seen many of those . . . I don't think I have any teacher ever follow up, say, you have to come see me or you got a problem right now."

None of the students gave examples of seeking help from or being assisted by university personnel in any consistent manner. For example, Sok, who came to the United States from Cambodia with her family at age thirteen, reported, "Since I have been in college I had never used the support from school service. When I have problem with school I would talk to my friends or solve it myself." The isolation perceived and experienced by Southeast Asian American students within the university's academic domain, particularly in terms of student-faculty relations and utilization of academic support services, was striking. "On My Own" stories and strategies—defined in relation to classroom dynamics as well as issues such as course selection, academic advising, career preparation, and major choices—expressed not only how students viewed their reality within the university, but also how they attempted to survive academically within it.

Students' feelings of social isolation, both in school and the larger society, were equally striking. Danielle, a Chinese Vietnamese woman, noted about school, "In the classes, like most of the American students, they don't like to be your friend . . . even when you walk in the hall, you see them, they don't even say hi. Or probably they don't recognize me, I don't know."

Similarly, but with reference to the larger social environment, Chanda wrote poignantly, "The more I absorb the environment I live in, the more I have a better sense of real life. I continue to see things that divide me from American society. But I could not recognize what it is and why? Everyday living just puts a lot of pressure on me, the anger and struggle I am facing are never overcome. It is crying inside me. No one wants to hear or even cares and I have no one to turn to."

These students were clearly not integrated academically or socially within the university. Though some relied on other Asian students for friendship and support, such informal friendship networks provided only limited assistance in terms of dealing with difficulties in school. "On My Own" stories dominated their discourse and their reality in very concrete ways at particular times, such as during the process of choosing majors.

*Major Stories and Dropping Out Stories*
Related to feeling "on my own," especially academically, many Southeast Asian American students described themselves as "lost"—not knowing how

to take care of problems or where to get good advice and not feeling able to "speak up" or ask questions. Furthermore, feeling "lost" had real meaning for them, given their refugee experiences. Recalling his family's escape across the Mekong River, for example, Khamkeaw vividly remembered feeling "like you don't know where you going." Similarly, Seng recalled, after finally reaching the refugee camp in Thailand, the anxiety of having, "no idea where we going, what we are going to do."

Pathways through the university curriculum, though far safer than the jungle, were no easier to find or negotiate. Sokal recalled, "I take different courses and I was lost. I do not know what I want to study. I keep looking for it, and searching for it. And I missed one whole year just looking for what I want to do."

In the face of these difficulties, Phat, a Chinese Vietnamese refugee man, concluded, "We can't rely on whatever the major we're interested in, but we have to go from the major whichever is easiest for us to accomplish." Chanda initially followed advice from an admissions counselor who told her that Asian students are good in math. When she failed her first math class, Chanda recalled feeling, "depressed, cry many times that I could not make it. And never think I would graduate."

Sokal's major story (Bagasao 1989) was also dramatic and revealing, "I was watching the film on [public television]. They do it on Southeast Asians, on rice . . . all this genetics, I mean biologists and biochemistry, they always studying how to find a better way to grow rice, you know. Cambodia, once, was exporting rice. Now they couldn't find enough rice to feed the people. There's something wrong, you know. And I say, well, I want to go in that field and study. . . . I did not consult anybody at all. Just based on my decision. I didn't even talk to my mother or anybody."

A television program, rather than the university curriculum or advising system, directed him to choose chemistry as his major. But, frustration, stress, and resignation, rather than satisfaction, then followed as consequences of his choice, "Once I made the decision, it's too late to turn back because it's my second or third year. . . . I have to go back to review all the science courses that I haven't had for a long time. . . . I forgot everything. . . . I fail every test I took in Physics. . . . I got a D+, which is the worst grade I ever get in my school career. . . . I'm not that happy with my major, but I have to find something, you know . . . so there's no turning back. If I can't make it, I drop out of school."

Not surprisingly, given their "On My Own" stories of isolation and confusion, many students like Sokal considered dropping out as an alternative, "I thought about it many times, and say, why am I doing this, you know. Go to school and working. And my family is having a tough time financially. Should I drop out a couple of years, and work outside and then help support the family and then come back? I think about it and say, well, you heard your parents' conversation. They say over and over again, 'go to school,' you know . . . I see my friends, a couple of friends gone. Disappear. You see your friends working, buying brand new car, sports car. It's tempting, you know. But then I say, no it's not worth it. That's not my goal."

He went on to describe the situations of friends, "Nothing you can do about it. . . . Two or three of them dropped out. And I thought they'd take a semester or two off, but they never come back. . . . Financially they couldn't do it and they dropped out, get married. . . . And then having children, you know, couldn't come back. Another friend of mine dropped out a year ago. He say he'll come back when he gets older. I say, yeah, right."

Like Sokal, Phat also referred to friends who left, "A lot of students dropped out because they don't know where to go . . . there was nobody to help them."

Chanda, who during her first year thought she would never graduate, agreed. "The Southeast Asian students, particularly the Cambodian students, it's just hard, it's very tough for them. The first year I came here, we have four or five Cambodian students, but I'm the only one who stick with school . . . they all drop out from university because they could not handle it, and no one really guide them or help them throughout the difficult time."

Dropping out stories documented both the substantial obstacles facing Southeast Asian American students and the failure of college personnel to guide those students appropriately. Given students' pervasive lack of integration academically as well as socially, the odds of Southeast Asian American student persistence—especially at an urban, public, commuter institution—seemed terribly slim.

Nevertheless, Chanda, Mai, Khamkeaw, Danielle, Phat, Sokal, and others successfully graduated—making their stories all the more significant to learn from. Clearly, their college experiences, like much of the rest of their lives, were characterized by struggle and survival. Rooted in their family contexts and background dimensions as refugees, immigrants, and racial minorities, Southeast Asian American students turned to reference points outside of the university for powerful sources of motivation and direction. These reference points, described in stories of refugee flight, family life, and race/gender discrimination, enabled them to persist in college, despite their marginal relationships to the academic and social domains of the university.

## 2. Recognizing Reference Points of Persistence Outside of the University

*Refugee Stories as Reference Points*

Students' experiences and status as refugees—reflected in both chilling and inspiring stories of survival—shaped their views of getting through college. Khamkeaw was separated from his family by the Khmer Rouge when he was nine years old and evacuated to a labor camp where he was forced to work eighteen to twenty hours each day. He whispered in an interview, "You never stop. . . . 365 days a year . . . I almost died a couple of times over there." Sokal added, "You never had a childhood life, so you never dreamed what you want to be when you grow up, you know . . . more important things to think about, survival."

Mental health issues resulting from trauma and family separation confounded the difficulties confronted by many students in school. Post-Traumatic Stress Disorder (PTSD) and related symptoms of depression, guilt, anxiety, and anger marked the continuing effects of their traumatic experiences (Ascher 1984; Herman 1991; Nidorf 1985; Welaratna 1993). Yet students' refugee stories also provided powerful reference points of resilience and determination that inspired persistence in school. Recognizing his own PTSD, Hai, a Vietnamese man, noted, "Sometimes I thought, just a couple of times, I'm crazy. But I'm strong. My spirit is strong enough to fight." Referring to her major story, Minh, a Vietnamese woman, agreed. "I'm a survivor. I mean, I don't have to do things I want to do or are interested to do. But I have to do things I have to do." Seng added, "I think I am a strong person, you know. I have gone through a lot of things during Khmer Rouge; the day I escaped from Cambodia; I lived in the camp. Over there I faced so many things . . . the experience I'd gone through before and my family in Cambodia, all those things is just in my mind. It always pushes me to work hard, to get a good education, to get more money and try to survive. Another thing I want to go back to see my people, to see my homeland, to see my friends in Cambodia. All of those things push me."

Students' refugee stories resonated deeply as motivating forces for persistence within the university. Seng's memories of and commitments to his family in Cambodia also served as significant reference points for his continued survival as a college student.

*Family Stories as Reference Points*

The context of family had significant meaning for Southeast Asian American students in relation to their responsibilities, expectations, and roles as the first generation in their families to go to college in the United States. Sok, for example, described her family's expectations as follows, "I do a little housework, I cook when no one is home. I help my sisters with math, English. Sometimes I have to take care of the bills for my family contribution. In addition, well, my parents expect something from me which they never told me what. However, I knew what they are expecting. They expect me to finish school."

Students shouldered major responsibilities to provide financial support for their families. Sokal, for example, worked twenty to twenty-five hours each week during the school year and three jobs during the summer in order to "help with everything that I can . . . every dime I make, I give to my mother." This led to a confrontation with the financial aid office over his earnings from three jobs, "They say, what you do with this money, you know? And I say, I help my family. And he said, what?! You know, they don't understand that. Usually they hear the parents helping the students. Instead, it's the reverse. And it's tough."

Students also served as the interpreters and intermediaries between their families and U.S. society. Khamkeaw described his duties as: "translate problems and reading English writing, go to hospital, pay the bill, writing letter, making phone calls, communicating with outside." Students played essential roles in enabling their families to survive in this country. But their studies suffered as a result. Exhausted from her daily schedule, Sok sighed, "I return home around nine o'clock, take a shower and do my homework until four o'clock in the morning. I never have enough time for sleep, I go to bed at three or four in the morning and get up a few hours after at seven or seven-thirty." Sokal also complained, "I can't study at home. I have room to study but when I get home, your sister tell you about this happened, your mother says, well, you have to do this, all the oil is gone, you know, the boiler is not working. There's so many things going wrong, and you say, well, I got to do this, I got to do that, and I can't study."

Although students identified strong family expectations that motivated them to persevere in college, those expectations were not accompanied in any tangible way by direct family involvement. This further contributed to the isolation experienced by students and contradicted studies of first wave refugees and other Asian immigrant groups who have class and educational advantages that support strong family involvement in students' schooling and educational achievement (Caplan, Whitmore, and Choy 1989). Sokal argued convincingly, for example, that he would do better in school if he did not live with his family, "I can handle myself [in school] if I live alone. I can take care of it. I can do pretty well, but I got to help my family. That affects a lot, take a lot out of you. Mentally you're not concentrating. Something always happen. If I'm alone, I'll probably do better."

Furthermore, many students did not have intact families in this country. Though separated by distance, if not death, family expectations still motivated student achievement by exerting powerful influences through guilt, grief, and pride. Recalling his escape story, Seng sighed, "When I left my family, I feel really bad, I don't know what to do. But try to survive, you know. Just keep thinking that someday, someday I will see them if they still alive." Sokal agreed, reflecting on his family's survival story and his deceased father's continuing influence, "I look through my past, you know. I say, well, I've been through this and I've seen many things. I've been through a lot of stuff that, you know, I thought I never come out of it alive. And then, you know, here's my father who brought me here . . . he want you to get through education and he struggle to get here, and, you know, you don't want to disappoint your parents. It really motivates you, you know. Psychologically, that's what I live by."

Although she lost her entire family and lived by herself, Chanda concluded, "I am on my own, but I live to the expectation of the culture. I just try to do well and prove to them that I can do it. . . . The only thing is I have to struggle."

*Race/Gender Discrimination Stories as Reference Points*
As with their refugee stories, many students shared discrimination stories that illustrated their own and their families' experiences as urban, racial minorities and low-wage, immigrant/refugee workers. Racism, especially in the workplace, acted as a powerful motivating force for students to complete their higher education. Lien recounted the sentiments of her parents' generation, which served as reference points for her own educational persistence.

"They all complain that they were treated like a stupid person. And they said if they were in Vietnam, probably not the same here. Because some of them, they were teachers or dentists or somebody in Vietnam. But they went here. They was nothing. Just do something, wash dishes, something like that. Because they didn't pass the test for the dentist or something like that. And they feel terrible."

Chanda bitterly recalled from her own life, "When I first came to America, I work in a cleaning company in a nursing home. They treated me very badly, the boss. They pay me less than other people and some people that were hired at that time, in a later period, they got higher wage than I did. The way they treated me like in a very cruel behavior . . . sometimes I want to kill them. . . . I cannot live in a society that put you down because you are an ethnic group. And without education, you are nothing. So that's why, you know, I think no matter how hard it is, I have to struggle in school. I have to have education so people would not treat me that bad."

Chanda also linked her motivation to persist in school with gender discrimination and feudal attitudes in her own community. She explained, "Since I am a woman, you know, my people tend to think that women cannot do anything as good as men. So, by having a degree to prove it, that I have achieved, then probably they take me a little bit seriously." The shifts in expectations and gender roles resulting from women gaining higher education, however, made this a complex and difficult process. Chanda continued, "From school I learn a lot. And I want to share those things with my people, with the community. But the question is how? They would not allow me. It so hard just to be part of the community. If you are there, you do what they tell you to do. You act very submissive, always take the orders, then it's fine. But if you gain your voice, you try to suggest things—what should be done, what should not be done—then, forget it. They don't like you."

Mai's description of gender dynamics in the Vietnamese community was strikingly similar, "It's very hard for us [women pursuing higher education], you know, some of us have this idea we can do something—men can do something, so women can do something. But it hard for us 'cause only few of us. . . . We need to do something. We have to help the community . . . women are the ones who recognize all this stuff, all these issues that we have to deal with. But men, they kind of, they just want to keep, you know, controlling power. They always look back to go back there [to Vietnam]. But, you know, now we live here. We have to deal with things here."

Though entering school and the workforce out of socioeconomic necessity, Southeast Asian immigrant/refugee women, nevertheless, experienced a resulting expansion of opportunities that sharply contrasted with the concomitant decline in status and options for men who lost their traditional social roles. Seng, a Cambodian man, also noted the strains of changing gender roles within the community, albeit with ambivalence, "Women change faster than men . . . like men, because they don't want to change anything. They like the way it is. But women, they want to change because they want the equality, they want the freedom, they want to be independent. They want to show men how strong they are. They want to be aggressive. Right now in the Cambodian community, girls seem to be more succeed than men. A lot of girls stay in college. . . . Men care too much about money, they care too much about what's going on in family economics, what's going on in the family. They decide to give up school to go to work because they want to support the family economics. And girls, they just want to be in school, to get ahead. I see a lot of girls, a lot of women work in the offices, stay in school while men are out working in the factories somewhere else."

While becoming increasingly acculturated to notions of women's equality and economic independence, Chanda's experiences of social alienation and racial discrimination also intensified, and her critique of U.S. society deepened: "I'm happier here in a way because I can look for a better future. But in spirit, no. In Cambodia, I would feel shoulder to shoulder with the people. Even if I were a farmer, I would be proud; I would be qualified. Here, I feel so bad spiritually." Reflecting on these seemingly contradictory tendencies, she explained, "When I first came, I just want everything just imitate American way. Everything Western way is just great, civilized! But when I grow older, I think how important my culture, the heritage. I realize how much I miss, I lose, and feel so sad, feel like why all this time I deny it? I deny it, I just think even being a Cambodian or anything part of Cambodian is just come from a Third World country, is just so bad! Now I feel like nothing should be ashamed of it. I should keep it and maintain it because it's something I can identify with . . . not just for myself, but for my children, for the Cambodian population here. It's so important since the refugees, especially the Cambodians, are not treated as equals, are not treated as part of the mainstream. Why deny our own and want something that never, never accept me? Before I never think that Cambodian is good, the language. But now I suddenly just think it is so important and I try to learn more. Even write in Cambodian. I never wore a traditional Cambodian dress, I just hate it! It's too feminine to me. But now, you know, I love it. I even imagine to see if I have a wedding I would wear it. It's just beautiful! [laughs]."

Interestingly, while developing her sense of gender consciousness as an outspoken, college-educated, Cambodian American woman, Chanda's awareness of racism and inequality reawakened her love of her heritage and returned her to her community. In identifying more closely with her traditional culture, however, Chanda continued to advocate critically for women to look and move beyond the community in order to gain higher education, "My dream is like to play a role model, to tell them how much education is important. Without it, they cannot move up. To tell many young women there that life is not only married and have children . . . life has to have some education."

Mai attributed similar meaning to the effects of her college education on her racial, ethnic, and gender identity, noting on one hand that, "dealing with my father, I used to be quiet, not saying things back to him . . . so now I change, well, now I argue with him, but before I just listen." On the other hand—and also paralleling Chanda's expression of love for her traditional aesthetics and values—Mai explained, "I cannot say I'm Vietnamese, but I'm saying I'm Vietnamese American because I keep some and I, because I'm exposed to this society, to this custom, so I'm not being completely Vietnamese. I'm not being completely American. . . . But I still leave my hair long [laughs]."[6]

By articulating fully with their own reference points of persistence outside of the university—as expressed through stories of refugee survival, family commitments, racism in the workplace, and gender inequality in the community—Chanda and Mai transformed themselves from lost first-year students who were failing math and nursing to graduating seniors who completed majors in women's studies and sociology. With an emerging sense of herself as a role model, Chanda realized that she could construct and represent new reference points of persistence for others. Like Chanda, Mai also recognized that her own process of transformation provided her with experience and a vision to construct new reference points of educational persistence and community empowerment that could benefit others, "My dream is just to help the new people be aware of what is going on here in this society. They need to get involved in fighting for their beliefs, I mean what they think is right for justice and equality. You know, set up the program or help the younger generation to go on, like get higher education and help their people. That's all I can do."

Beyond their inspiring stories of struggle and persistence, Mai, Chanda, and others also highlighted the important role of Asian American studies classrooms in which they were able to experience academic and social integration at the university, and where they not only survived, but thrived. This emerged as a third key finding from this phase of research.

### 3. Asian American Studies as a Context for Persistence

Recalling the frustration of her earlier years in not having clear direction, Chanda emphasized the impact of Asian American studies courses in guiding her to change her major from math and science to sociology and women's studies, "Even when I was here two years, I still did not know what I really want, did not know what I'm good in. . . . But when I took the Asian American Studies courses, then it's like a light come in to define what really I am and what I want . . . for so long I did not know that I would fight for justice. . . . But when I learn, when I see those things that say that's it! That I want to help society to change. . . . After that, it [my education] improved. You know, I took something that I enjoy and that I learn . . . if I do not take [the Asian American Studies] course, probably I will never, never understand or know who I really am or what I want to do in the future."

Mai described the effect of taking her first Asian American studies course in much the same way: "That [first] class show me the experience of Asian Americans, that changed me since that time . . . after that, I have a clear direction. I can do things. I can graduate."

While course content was important, students also emphasized the classroom environment—expressing motivation and appreciation because their voices were encouraged and their experiences were shared by both the teacher and their peers. A Vietnamese student noted, "half of the class are already Asian whose background are similar to mine, including the professor. This way we can be more open to share our problems and experiences because no one would laugh." Sokal, one of the most active participants in an Asian American studies course, reported being unable to speak up in other classes, "There's a lot of Asians in there, and they probably have the same basic experience. We're together . . . similar problems, accents, pronunciation. . . . I always have an opinion, something to say. But somehow, the class also help the fear inside, don't be afraid, you know. Have question, ask. But somehow, after that class, I go into the same pattern again, you know. Not asking questions."

He then described his view of Asian American studies classes compared to other courses in terms of death and life—concepts with which he was intimately familiar. "In science course, you go there, listen, sit back and write down all the notes or record it, come back and write it down. . . . I come from there, I saw it change so quick, you know. Get out of [the Asian American Studies] class, you go to another course, sit back and, you know, just write down notes. And then when you get out of from that class, go to another one, same thing. Next day, before you come to [the Asian American Studies] class, you go another class, like you're dead. And then, all of a sudden, you come alive, you know. Full of life!"

Lien similarly described the significance of her Asian American studies class in relation to her memories of Vietnam, "When I talk, I felt like somebody listen to me. . . . I feel like the old times in Vietnam—have a teacher who is concerned about, have friends to share with . . . you feel like at home

. . . look like everybody is happy. So I thought I wish I had more classes like that."

In effect, students in Asian American studies courses functioned as competent members of classroom communities supported by both the course content and learning environment. The combination of a critical mass of Asian students and an Asian American teacher engaged together with a relevant curriculum enabled students to "come alive" in sharing ideas and experiences with their peers, thus breaking down both the academic and social isolation that they faced on their own in other settings of the university.

By mapping their persistence stories, this phase of research showed—contrary to traditional models of college student persistence—a) that Southeast Asian American students were not integrated in either the academic or social domains of college and b) that reference points motivating them to persist in college against formidable odds were family and community-centered rather than college-related. Asian American studies courses, however, served to establish viable reference points within the university's curriculum, student-faculty relations, and student peer relations that explicitly recognized and directly reinforced those external reference points of refugee stories, family stories, and race/gender discrimination stories which were motivating Southeast Asian American students' educational persistence.

As a curricular and pedagogical intervention, then, the praxis of Asian American studies itself deserved further research and grounded theoretical development. This became a major commitment in my evolving research agenda as I moved to consider more systematically the institutional structures that hindered or supported Southeast Asian American students' persistence. In the following section, I offer brief examples of how the research agenda of Phase III evolved during the 1990s, moving beyond thick description and grounded theory to address critical issues of impact in three important ways—institutionally, comparatively, and longitudinally.

## Phase III: Toward Systemic, Comparative, Long-Term Perspectives

During Phase II, Southeast Asian American students engaged in research around issues of their own and their peers' persistence in college. This process not only generated important stories, themes, and challenges to dominant paradigms, it also influenced students' own views and subsequent actions. The research interviews served not only as sources for data collection, but also as interventions in students' lives. Hung, for example, a Vietnamese student who was on academic probation after failing a course, but had not told any of his family members about his difficulties, stated at the conclusion of his interview, "This is the first time I sharing my experience. I never talk to anybody [laughs]. Before, my English teacher told me to see the psychiatrist, you know, talk about it, try to open more. I said, well, I don't think so. . . . You want to know more about the difficulties of Asian people who are trying in university, who have problems with it, so I think that's good for me. So I said okay, I'll share my experience [in this interview]."

Mai similarly noted at the end of her interview, "Yeah, I never thought of these questions . . . we never have a chance to talk like people asking questions to feed back and forth, but it's in your mind. I see myself different than before. But when you don't talk about it, you don't have the language to describe." Mai also highlighted the peer support and development engendered through the research process (student focus groups, students interviewing students, etc.), "I feel that I'm not the only one who face those problems . . . then you feel more comfortable with working in school, like explaining your points because you have, you get support from other people."

Donna, a Chinese Vietnamese refugee, similarly recognized the need to share her experiences with younger students so that they would not have to face so many difficulties on their own, "The freshmen or sophomores, they're very lucky because we giving them a lot of advice. I hope someone help me before when I got here . . . I told them what to take and shouldn't take. Yeah. I told them that."

Beyond these types of individual effects and interventions within informal networks, however, students also identified larger institutional barriers that needed change in the university.

### 1. Challenging Institutionalized Anguish as a Second Language[7]

Among the obstacles forcing some students to stop/drop out, for example, was an English writing proficiency graduation requirement that became the target of student advocacy and a new focus of applied research described briefly here and documented in detail elsewhere (Kiang 1993).

Minh, for example, an early participant and peer facilitator in a Southeast Asian student oral history project that I directed during Phase I, emerged as one of the campus student leaders who filed a formal Title VI complaint with the U.S. Department of Education Office for Civil Rights (OCR), alleging that the university's graduation requirement of a writing proficiency exam (WPE) had disparate negative impact against minority students. Indeed, anecdotal evidence had always suggested such a reality, but the university had never released data about who passed and who failed the WPE until the OCR's investigation required it to do so. The results confirmed students' impressions.

The data, based on records for all students taking the WPE from 1981 to 1987, showed that 29 percent of all black students, 23 percent of all Hispanic students, and 24 percent of all Asian students had not passed the WPE after three or more attempts. In sharp contrast, only 7 percent of white students similarly failed the exam after three or more tries. When students' grade point averages were controlled, students of color still failed the WPE at disproportionately higher rates. Other data offered disturbingly corroboratory evidence. During the same 1981–1987 period, Asian students had a higher retention rate than all other student racial groups during their first four semesters—the critical period according to mainstream studies of student attrition—followed by a dramatic and continued decline after their sixth semester when passing the WPE became mandatory.

Following release of the institutional data, Minh, Mai, Chanda, Seng, and other Southeast Asian American students involved in Phase I and Phase II organized, wrote, and spoke for institutional policy changes. In a scathing, emotional commentary for the student newspaper that was also reprinted on hundreds of flyers distributed across the campus, a Vietnamese refugee student asserted, "UMass/Boston is the only four-year college that is accessible and affordable for us. This is the only place we have a chance to get a college education. But if we spend four years here and then you kick us out because our writing is not what the school wants, then the school has wasted our time. You have to realize, we Asian students are starting from scratch, trying to build new lives in this country. We don't have any time to waste. . . . Don't bring us out into the middle of the ocean and leave us there. We have already been there once before" (comment by a student).

From follow-up student research projects in Asian American studies classes and my own interviews, we pieced together a critical analysis of the issue to complement the statistical data. For example, a Chinese Vietnamese refugee student complained bitterly about a WPE essay question focusing on Mozart and the Hollywood film, *Amadeus*, which he knew nothing about. Chanda directly faulted the director of the WPE, "She gives you pressure, and says you have to pass the exam or else you'll be expelled from school. Her attitude is not to help you." Other informants noted that many Vietnamese students were enrolling in the two-year engineering program so that they could transfer to another school before their junior year when they would be required to take the WPE. Extending the "major stories" documented in Phase II, these Phase III findings similarly suggested that students may not have been so committed to engineering as a field, but chose to major in it as a sad but shrewd survival strategy to avoid being forced out of school by the WPE.

Stories and critical insights generated from the Phase III research bolstered students' civil rights complaint against the university. By the conclusion of OCR's investigation several years later, a wide range of WPE policy reforms had been implemented, including the crafting of less Eurocentric readings and essay questions, the reassignment of the WPE director, and the development of a writing portfolio option as an alternative to the timed, essay examination format. Through this process, Southeast Asian American students directly participated in advocacy research that positively impacted the institution.

Furthermore, their work inspired other students to critically examine parallel struggles of Southeast Asian American students at the K–12 level. Though not described in detail here, other examples of research designed to document and challenge systemic inequity in schools during Phase III included a project I designed with two former undergraduate students—one of whom had become a Vietnamese bilingual teacher in Boston and the other who was a graduate student in Special Education—to capture how recently arrived Vietnamese elementary students in a fourth-grade bilingual classroom were making sense of the daily racial conflicts they experienced or witnessed at school and in their neighborhoods (Kiang, Nguyen, and Sheehan 1995). The project grew out of concerns expressed by Nguyen Ngoc-Lan, a first-year Vietnamese American teacher who observed her students being harassed frequently. I still recall the afternoon when she first came to see me in frustration, "Some of my kids just got into a fight with older boys who were harassing a younger Vietnamese student on the way home from school. It happens every day and I get so angry. People need to know about it. Sometimes I just want to shout, 'Don't ignore it!' to the school and the community."

Two years earlier, Ngoc-Lan was struggling with the WPE at UMass Boston herself. Having failed the exam, she agreed to try the alternative portfolio option. With support from another student majoring in Asian American studies, she eventually passed—but not without facing significant anguish. Like many other immigrant/refugee students, Ngoc-Lan experienced failure and discouragement within those educational environments where her linguistic and cultural backgrounds were viewed as deficits. But within the fourth-grade bilingual classroom where she taught professionally, Ngoc-Lan was successful, motivated, and respected by students, parents, and school colleagues. In turn, she affirmed and reinforced those same strengths for the newcomer children she served.

Ngoc-Lan had also always achieved at high levels in her Asian American studies classes. She had often shared her desire to become an elementary school teacher—a dream she had carried from childhood in Vietnam. Asian American studies not only provided a learning environment in college where Ngoc-Lan's linguistic and cultural backgrounds represented valuable assets, but also served as a continuing structure of support that sustained her visions as a critical, bilingual educator following her graduation. Ngoc-Lan's example inspired me to wonder, both as a teacher and researcher, what kinds of impact and meaning our courses could have in the lives of our students and alumni over the long term.

## 2. Comparative Perspectives on Long-Term Curricular Impact

As the primary faculty member responsible for the first decade of teaching and course development in Asian American Studies at UMass Boston between 1987 to 1997, I knew that evaluation forms and informal feedback from students indicated year after year that the courses were effective and meaningful at the time of instruction. However, we knew little about what difference our Asian American studies courses made over time. This emerged as a second important commitment of the research agenda during Phase III.

In 1997, I launched a two-year Asian American Studies alumni research project in conjunction with a campus diversity research initiative funded by the Ford Foundation (Center for Improvement of Teaching 1999). Utilizing both quantitative and qualitative methods[8] to reach alumni who had taken at least one Asian American studies course prior to graduating between 1987 and 1999, the study found that the greatest effects reported by alumni were increased understanding of the immigrant experience, greater awareness of racial stereotypes, increased clarity about their own identities in U.S. society, and enhanced abilities to interact comfortably with Asian Americans. For example, 91 percent of survey respondents specifically indicated that their Asian American studies courses had much or very much increased their understanding of the immigrant experience; 86 percent stated that their learning had much or very much raised their awareness of racial stereotypes. Seven out of ten respondents (70 percent) noted that the courses had much or very much enabled them to make friends with people different from their own backgrounds. Eight out of ten (83 percent) indicated that the courses had much or very much helped them to interact more comfortably with Asian Americans. For nonresidential university settings in which the development of student attitudes and competencies related to diversity were largely limited to what happens in the classroom, these were powerful effects (Kiang 2000).

The alumni research focus in Phase III also provided a qualitative way to explore comparative perspectives with those former students of non-Asian backgrounds who had taken Asian American studies courses. Marisol, for example, a Latina who graduated in 1996 and was working as a job developer for low-income communities while raising her one-year-old child at the time of the interview, recalled, "I learned that I have a lot more in common with the Asian community. . . . I found a lot of pieces of my identity with my friends of countries like China, Korea, Japan, etc. . . . I felt connected and it was very exciting to feel and know that I had friends who are Asian American who really care for me. . . . I can communicate and relate to people when I have knowledge of their history and struggles as well as achievements. This is what I learned and pass on to others."

Tanisha, an African American alumna who graduated in 1990, was teaching social studies in an elementary school at the time of her interview. Like Marisol, Tanisha was one of many informants who described the significance of cross-racial learning facilitated by the courses, "As a black person, I hate to be stereotyped, and I'm sure that Asians feel the same way. . . . When people of different races have an opportunity to interact and get to know each other, they often like each other. Like I meet many people I probably would have never had the opportunity to meet and get to know (from the courses). I learned that I liked them and respected them as people."

The important professional teaching roles played by graduates like Tanisha and Tara, a white alumna who graduated in 1989, further illustrated the long-term effects of Asian American Studies in reaching new generations. Tara asserted, "I finally decided to become a teacher of English as a second language, and I am sure that the Asian American course had some effect on that decision, partly by giving me a stronger sense of empathy for the immigrants' experience and at the same time giving me a greater sense of respect.

Tanisha further explained, "I have a few Chinese students, a Cambodian student, a Vietnamese student, and a student from Thailand. My Chinese students were shocked. The AAS courses I took definitely had an impact on my ability to interact with my students and their families when I brought issues of Sampan [a bilingual Chinese newspaper from Boston] in for them to read."

We also focused qualitatively on the experiences of alumni with learning disabilities who had taken Asian American studies courses. Interview find-ings clearly suggested how targeted course advising could be linked effec-tively with classroom pedagogy in Asian American studies courses to address the needs of students with learning disabilities. Crystal, a white alumna who graduated in 1997, for example, recalled, "The advisor would tell LD [learn-ing disabled] students to take these [Asian American studies] courses because the professors accept these kind of students. They make them feel at home as they do with immigrants." She then added,

> I was probably one out of six white Caucasian people in the class and there were about 30 of us . . . and the other white students in the class were learning disability students and this is because [the advisor] always suggested that we take that class because there's a good teacher. . . . When she suggested that to me, I was like, 'what are you crazy? I'm not going to take a class like that. You must be crazy!' I took it and I'm like, oh God, this class is going to be awful but I really enjoyed it . . . after the first few classes, it was really interesting. . . . And I loved it through the end.

Informants highlighted important connections they had recognized and shared between their own struggles with learning disabilities and the strug-gles of Asian Americans that they witnessed through their classroom interac-tions and course work. Carl, a white alumnus who graduated in 1996, for example, described his integrative learning, "You find out how to take [care] of these problems easier. And it's like adjusting to the picture and the people adjust to the problem of your learning disability or adjust to the problem that you're Asian American."

Echoing the "On My Own" stories of Southeast Asian American students several years earlier, Crystal agreed: "When you're an immigrant or a person with LD you can find yourself lost, find yourself needing help most of the time."

Philosophically, Asian American studies at UMass Boston were never intended to serve only Asian American students. The comparative foci in our Phase III alumni research, however, empirically showed how a curricu-lum and learning environment designed explicitly to support Asian immi-grant/refugee students could also be empowering for other marginalized populations. Findings from this type of comparative diversity research deserve much more attention.

## 3. The Research Process as a Structure for Persistence

In addition to the data and findings, however, the alumni research project of Phase III also focused on collaborative learning, research training, and community-building processes for those students who were directly involved in the research process. This emphasis on process reflected a commitment of the university's Diversity Research Initiative (DRI), funded by the Ford Foundation with the premise that students at an urban commuter institution like UMass Boston could become more effectively integrated in university life by participating for credit with a team of peers and a faculty facilitator in meaningful research about a significant issue inside the institution itself (Center for the Improvement of Teaching 1999).

Through an independent study course with me in spring 1997, seven students agreed to work together to assess the long-term impact of our courses through research with Asian American studies alumni. Our goals to build an affirming learning community for students while training them in research methods and conducting meaningful research all during the same semester were a challenge to achieve. In the end, each team member's reflections clearly touched each of the goals we had articulated for our work. Naoki,[9] for example, explained in his evaluation memo how the team provided collective support to complete the research: "For me, this experience is first research class, so I had some confusion or hesitation. Every time I met my team mates in the school, I said first, 'How is your research?' They also asked me, 'How about yours?' . . . I was really encouraged from my team mates because everybody were struggling and trying hard."

HyunJung recalled the impact of the group's shared learning from each other, "Yes, the findings of a research project are very important and also the gaining of knowledge and research method skill. However, to me, reflections and insights from each group member are much more valuable and meaningful because it is alive information and can't get from anywhere, even textbooks."

Albert revealed some of his own growth as a researcher, "Personally, I am still learning how to do the analysis. I am confused about how to interpret and analyze the quotes from the interviews. I feel like my analysis is not in-depth enough. . . . When reading the transcript, I need to read carefully and think about what the person was trying to tell me."

Yen, a Chinese Vietnamese refugee student, noted her appreciation for the social role of research:

> I remember at different times during this research project, I have wondered about 'Why are we taking so many little steps in this gathering of data? It's such a

waste of time!' I thought we could just do the interview and pick out lines or quotes that are important to answering the questions we were asking. But now that we are at the end of the semester, I realize that all those steps were important because we are not the only people working with the data, and that people from other semesters might be looking at these also [as the research continues]. I feel now that I was somewhat selfish before; I didn't think about who else might benefit from the hard work we have done to find out all this information. Now that I realize this, I feel that all the different steps we took to get to this point have not been wasted, and it was very important to everyone.

Finally, from participating in the research process, Yuko concluded, "I feel that I have found a niche for myself in school."

With this simple but profound reflection, Yuko-chan confirmed that student-faculty collaborative research focusing on Asian American studies at the university could not only generate useful data, but could also provide a structure of persistence—the constructing of a niche—for urban, commuter students.

## Phase IV: Follow the Life Stories

### Toward Longitudinal Research and Southeast Asian American Life Stories

When interviewed for the alumni research project in Phase III, many former students like Marisol and Tanisha also spoke about applying their learning from Asian American studies courses in their roles as parents. For example, Kunthea, a Cambodian interviewee who took one Asian American studies course in 1989 and was raising two children at the time of her interview, stated, "(the course) will have an effect on my way of raising my children. I will raise my children to be aware of their parents' root and to respect others, regardless of race, class, and gender. . . . I gain a lot of knowledge from Asian American Studies courses and it will always stay with me."

At an Asian American studies alumni gathering in fall 1999, Lien and Mai each came with two children. When asked about her seven-year-old daughter's experiences in elementary school, Lien replied, "I know it's tough for her sometimes, being a minority. I always tell her to hang in there and tell me whenever she has problems." Listening to her closely, I remembered that Lien had used the exact same phrase, "hang in there," to describe the essence of her own approach to persist in college ten years earlier. Since then, I have often wondered how the survival strategies and motivating reference points of persistence utilized by Southeast Asian American students in college continue to be adapted and applied developmentally throughout their lives.

Seng also attended the fall 1999 alumni gathering. Working as a class-room ESL teacher at an urban middle school, Seng sounded a familiar theme—being "on his own" as the only Cambodian and only refugee among the school's adult staff. While connecting intimately with the strengths and struggles of students from Haiti, Bosnia, Korea, Vietnam, and elsewhere around the world in his own classroom, he found his white colleagues to be profoundly disconnected and ineffective. Recalling their reactions to the 1999 school shootings in Littleton, Colorado, Seng recounted, "They just sat in the teachers room talking about it, like what if it happened at our school and they got trapped inside. They were so scared, they had no idea what to do. I just said, 'Look, just open that window and jump down to the roof and climb down from there. Can't you see that?!!'"

From these recent perspectives offered by former students like Lien and Seng, I continue to feel passionately that Southeast Asian American stories of survival, struggle, and persistence are important to share. In Phase IV and beyond, I hope to reconnect periodically with the core informants from Phase I and II in order to craft developmental and longitudinal portraits of their lives.

With this in mind, I also recognize that research on college student persis-tence has advanced in recent years. In *Answers in the Tool Box*, for example, Cliff Adelman (1999), offers a sophisticated and highly original statistical analysis of what contributes most to bachelor's degree completion, and con-cludes, in part, that studies on higher education persistence need to "follow the student" rather than the institution. Although methodologically I choose to invest my own researcher resources in qualitative approaches such as grounded theory and portraiture (Lawrence-Lightfoot and Davis 1997) within specific institutional or community settings, I greatly appreciate Adel-man's long-standing contributions to educational research and policy in the United States. By invoking Adelman's work here in relation to studies of Southeast Asian American persistence over time, I am similarly suggesting the value of "following the life story."

## Conclusions

Looking back at my research agenda during the past dozen years, I realize that much of it took shape in response to my frustrations with dominant paradigms. Although presented here as "phases" based loosely on a chronology of research/advocacy projects, the insights and interventions represented in the design and development of each of the discrete projects have never been linear in their trajectories or conceptualizations. Indeed, the student and community populations served by urban public universities are so diverse and dynamic that—to work effectively with and for them—teachers, researchers, curriculum developers, service providers, and organizers must constantly intuit, map, and reground theories (Phase I and II) in order to revitalize commitments, systemically assess impact, and sustain comparative, longer-term connections (Phase III).

The various phases of research described in this chapter have, over time, documented Southeast Asian American student stories, generated alternative theories of college persistence at urban commuter universities, and influenced the reform of specific campus-based policies and the design of curriculum and pedagogy for the Asian American studies program. But, as Harry Wolcott might ask, *is it ethnography?*

Frankly, this question has not concerned me at all during these past ten years. Still, many of the attributes of ethnographic research that Wolcott and others might highlight, such as being conducted in natural settings based on intimate experience over a long-term period, and being flexible, holistic, and comparative, are identifiable here. These commitments are organic and will continue.

One afternoon recently while completing this chapter, I took a break from writing in my cluttered, windowless office and went outside to get some air and sun. Tram, a recent immigrant from Vietnam and an outstanding student in my "Southeast Asians in America" course two years ago, was sitting alone on a bench and greeted me. I've learned over the years how important these spontaneous moments can be in reinforcing connections with students outside of the classroom, especially at an urban, commuter school, so I quickly asked Tram some "catching up" questions about school, work, family, and future plans while she waited for her boyfriend to pick her up. Among her responses, she revealed, "I'll be graduating next year, but I'm really bored now with my major. I don't like the computer field. I'd rather be out in the field, you know, in the community, talking with people. I really like that. I'm thinking about maybe studying another major like sociology."

Like Lien's cross-generational echo of "hang in there," Tram's insight triggered my memories of students like Sokal who told me ten years earlier: "I don't like chemistry, you know, that much at all. I kinda like political science and English." Given political reforms in their homelands, dramatic demographic and policy shifts in the United States, and enhanced diasporic contact through telecommunications and the Internet during that same ten-year period, the contemporary context for Southeast Asian American students differs markedly from the time when I first began mapping their stories of persistence. Nevertheless, the continuities of meaning and urgency conveyed by students' current stories of struggle and survival still demand attention, whether or not they are validated by mainstream educational research or institutions such as the College Board.

This chapter is adapted from a presentation at *The Role of Educational Ethnography in Pedagogy: Critical Ethnography in a Global and Interdisciplinary Perspective* sponsored by the University of Houston Asian American Studies Center and the Spencer Foundation in February 2000.

# Notes

1. U.S. Bureau of the Census, 1990 Census, PUMS File (5 percent sample).

2. Here, Southeast Asian American populations refer to Cambodian, ethnic Chinese, Vietnamese, Hmong, Lao, Mien, and other individuals and communities residing in the United States with origins from the countries of Cambodia, Laos, Vietnam, and migration histories associated with (though not limited to) refugee flight and resettlement. This definition differs from that of the Southeast Asian *area* studies field, which is based principally on geography and also includes, for example, Indonesia, Malaysia, Myanmar, the Philippines, and so on.

3. Asian American Studies is an interdisciplinary academic field dedicated to the documentation and interpretation of the history, identity, social formation, contributions, and contemporary concerns of Asian and Pacific Americans and their communities. Asian American Studies has evolved nationally from both the campus ethnic studies movements of the late 1960s and the sweeping demographic changes of the 1980s and 1990s.

4. The second wave of Southeast Asian refugee resettlement refers to the period from roughly 1979 to 1983 when massive flows of refugees sought escape by boat from Vietnam and by land from Cambodia and Laos to refugee camps where they awaited resettlement in third countries. Roughly 400,000 Southeast Asian refugees entered the United States during this period. Unlike the first wave of 125,000 refugees who constituted the elites of their countries and were resettled in the United States in 1975, the second wave was far more diverse in terms of socioeconomic status, education level, and ethnic/linguistic background.

5. Unless otherwise noted, all names used in this chapter are pseudonyms.

6. Interview quotes and excerpts from student writing are presented in the students'

words, including errors in spelling, word selection, and grammar. A string of ". . ." indicates omission of nonessential material.

7. Women in Vietnam traditionally wore long hair as a symbol of beauty and femininity.

8. Thanks to esteemed UMass Boston colleague, Vivian Zamel, for her phrase, "anguish as a second language."

9. Survey questionnaires (n = 88), individual interviews (n = 70), focus group interviews, and alumni writings were the principal sources of data we collected and analyzed.

10. Student names in this subsection are real and used with permission.

# References

Adelman, C. *Answers in the Tool Box: Academic Intensity, Attendance Patters, and Bachelor's Degree Attainment.* Washington, D.C.: U.S. Department of Education Office of Educational Research and Improvement, June 1999.

Ascher, C. "The Social and Psychological Adjustment of Southeast Asian Refugees." *ERIC/CUE Digest*, 21, (1984).

Bagasao, P. Y. "Student Voices Breaking the Silence: The Asian and Pacific American Experience." *Change* (November/December 1989): 28–37.

Caplan, N., J. K. Whitmore, and M. H. Choy. *The Boat People and Achievement in America.* Ann Arbor: University of Michigan Press, 1989.

Center for the Improvement of Teaching. *Diversity Research at an Urban Commuter University.* Boston: UMass Boston,1999.

Cheng, L. R. L., and V. O. Pang, ed. *Struggling to be Heard: The Unmet Needs of Asian Pacific American Children.* Albany, NY: SUNY Press, 1998.

Chun, K. T. "The Myth of Asian American Success and Its Educational Ramifications." *IRCD Bulletin*, Teachers College, 15, 1/2 (1980):1–12.

Cochran-Smith, M., and S. L. Lytle. *Inside Outside: Teacher Research and Knowledge.* New York: Teachers College Press, 1993.

Del Rosario, C. A. *A Different Battle: Stories of Asian Pacific American Veterans.* Seattle: Wing Luke Museum, 1999.

Gándara, P. *Priming the Pump: Strategies for Increasing the Achievement of Underrepresented Minority Undergraduates.* Washington, D.C.: The College Board, 1999.

Herman, J. L. *Trauma and Recovery.* New York: Basic Books, 1991.

Kiang, P. N. "Long-Term Effects of Diversity in the Curriculum: Analyzing the Impact of Asian American Studies in the Lives of Alumni from an Urban Commuter University." Pp. 23–25 in *Diversity on Campus: Reports from the Field.* Washington, D.C.: NASPA: Student Affairs Administrators in Higher Education, 2000.

Kiang, P. N. "After the Initiative: Envisioning Diversity Research Sustainability." Pp. 85–104 in *Diversity Research at an Urban Commuter University.* Boston: UMass Boston Center for the Improvement of Teaching, 1999.

Kiang, P. N. "Writing from the Past, Writing for the Future: Healing Effects of Asian

American Studies in the Curriculum." *Transformations: A Resource for Curriculum Transformation and Scholarship*, 9, 2 (Fall 1998):132–49.

Kiang, P. N. "Pedagogies of Life and Death: Transforming Immigrant/Refugee Students and Asian American Studies." *Positions*, Duke University Press, 5, 2 (1997):529–55.

Kiang, P. N. "Persistence Stories and Survival Strategies of Cambodian Americans in College." *Journal of Narrative and Life History*, 6, 1 (1996): 39–64.

Kiang, P. N. "Bicultural Strengths and Struggles of Southeast Asian American Students." Pp. 201–25 in Antonia Darder, ed., *Culture and Difference: Critical Perspectives on the Bicultural Experience in the United States*. New York: Bergin & Garvey, 1995.

Kiang, P. N. "Stratification of Public Higher Education." Pp. 233–45 in L. A. Revilla, G. M. Nomura, S. Wong, and S. Hune, ed., *Bearing Dreams, Shaping Visions*. Pullman: Washington State University Press, 1993.

Kiang, P. N. "Issues of Curriculum and Community for First-Generation Asian Americans in College." Pp. 97–112 in H.d B. London, and L. S. Zwerling, ed., *First-Generation Students Confronting the Cultural Issues*, New Directions for Community Colleges, no. 80. New York: Jossey-Bass, 1992.

Kiang, P. N. "About Face: Recognizing Asian & Pacific American Vietnam Veterans in Asian American Studies." *Amerasia Journal*, 17, 3 (1991a): 22–40.

Kiang, P. N. "New Roots and Voices: The Education of Southeast Asian Students at an Urban Public University." Ed.D. diss., Harvard Graduate School of Education,1991b.

Kiang, P. N. "Bringing it All Back Home: New Views of Asian American Studies and the Community." Pp. 305–14 in G. M. Nomura, R. Endo, S. H. Sumida, and R. C. Leong, ed. *Frontiers of Asian American Studies*. Pullman: Washington State University Press, 1989.

Kiang, P. N., and V. W. Lee. "Exclusion or Contribution: Education K-12 Policy." Pp. 25–48 in *The State of Asian Pacific America*. Los Angeles: LEAP Asian Pacific American Public Policy Institute and UCLA Asian American Studies Center, 1993.

Kiang, P. N., N. L. Nguyen, and R. L. Sheehan. "Don't Ignore It!: Documenting Racial Harassment in a Fourth-Grade Vietnamese Bilingual Classroom." *Equity and Excellence in Education*, 28, 1 (1995): 31–35.

Lawrence-Lightfoot, S., and J. H. Davis. *The Art and Science of Portraiture*. San Francisco: Jossey-Bass, 1997.

Lee, S. J. *Unraveling the "Model Minority" Stereotype*. New York: Teachers College Press, 1996.

Nakanishi, D. T., and T. Y. Nishida. *The Asian American Educational Experience*. New York: Routledge, 1995.

National Task Force on Minority High Achievement. *Reaching the Top*. Washington, D.C.: The College Board, 1999.

Nidorf, J. F. "Mental Health and Refugee Youths: A Model for Diagnostic Training." Pp. 391–429 in T. C. Owan, ed., *Southeast Asian Mental Health: Treatment, Prevention, Services, and Research*. Bethesda, Md.: National Institute of Mental Health.

Park, C., and M. M. Y. Chi. *Asian-American Education: Prospects and Challenges*. Westport, Conn.: Bergin & Garvey, 1999.

Suarez-Orozco, M. M. *Central American Refugees and U.S. High Schools*. Stanford: Stanford University Press, 1989.

Suzuki, B. H. "Asian Americans as the 'Model Minority.'" *Change* (November/December1989): 13–19.

Suzuki, B. H. "Education and Socialization of Asian Americans: A Revisionist Analysis of the 'Model Minority' Thesis." *Amerasia Journal*, 4, 2 (1977): 23–51.

Tinto, V. *Leaving College: Rethinking the Causes and Cures of Student Attrition*. Chicago: University of Chicago Press, 1987.

Trueba, H. T., L. L. R. Cheng, and K. Ima. *Myth or Reality: Adaptive Strategies of Asian Americans in California*. London: Falmer Press, 1993.

Watanabe, P. *A Dream Deferred: Changing Demographics, Challenges, & New Opportunities for Boston*. Boston: Institute for Asian American Studies and the Boston Foundation, 1996.

Weinberg, M. *Asian-American Education: Historical Background and Current Realities*. Mahwah, N.J.: Lawrence Erlbaum, 1997.

Welaratna, U. *Beyond the Killing Fields*. Palo Alto: Stanford University Press, 1993.

# CHAPTER ELEVEN

# The Class Clown: A School Liminar

*Judy Radigan*

I meet Pete, the teacher in this study, in the hallway on the way to his room. Even though this is the fifth period of the day, he is walking with his usual bounce and gives his quick, impish "hee-hee" giggle as we pass. As I enter the door of the classroom, Jerry, a boy in camouflage pants with his jelled hair devilishly carved into two spikes skids past me in time to catch the whizzing pass of a rubber chicken from Mike. Jerry neatly tucks the captured chicken into the mouth of a waiting, three-foot, paper-machéd dinosaur wearing a sailing cap with a jaunty air. The chicken-stuffed dinosaur swaggers precariously on two filing cabinets. This is the beginning of my observations of an energy-filled social studies high school classroom. Pete walks into the room as the pass receiver hastily returns the chicken to its place in the wire container in front of the teacher's desk that also seems to be the depository for boys' hats. So ends an example of McLaren's (1986) street corner state, the exuberant, physical world of the teenager.

The room turns into an educational habitat with Pete's entrance. This teacher's entrance signals the beginning of McLaren's (1986) student state where these adolescents become subservient to the norms of traditional classroom behavior. The pencil sharpener whirrs as students slip into their chairs at their tables. Although the students in this room sit at tables, most students in this lower-middle-class, suburban school spend much of their classroom time sitting in neatly arranged rows of desks listening to a teacher's lecture or completing a textbook-centered worksheet. This world geography class opens with a vocabulary assignment written on the classroom's front board. Pete looks quietly around the room as he makes note of absences on the daily role sheet. The academic work that now fills the classroom trans-forms this initial funhouse into a place of order and ritual. The roles of the spiked-haired class clown, Jerry, and his quarterback passer, Mike, will be important for this study's analysis of epistemological beliefs and their justifi-cation and for the humor and inversion of the reasoning process the class clown brings to this process. The intrusion of this trickster uncovers tacit and controversial epistemological claims for investigation in this study.

Defining epistemology and its principal tenets facilitates discrimination of tacit and explicit epistemological statements from other assertions in the classroom. Epistemology is the nature of knowledge and the justification of knowledge claims (Fenstermacher 1994). Current cognitivist research includes two specific epistemological elements that help limit the nature of knowledge to the source of knowledge and the certainty of knowledge (and King and Kitchener 1994; Kuhn 1991; Schommer 1994). The source of knowledge moves on a continuum from one, absolute source to the evalua-tion of multiple sources. Certainty of knowledge moves from unchanging to evolving. A person may say, "I know it is true because I read it in a book," and her epistemological claim is that knowledge comes from one source that is unchanging. The justification of knowledge involves the stating of a posi-tion and defending that position with reasons (Kuhn 1991).

McLaren's (1986, 1993) resistance theory, Bakhtin's (1973, 1984) concept of carnival and the clown with the contributions of Turner's (1969) liminar and Fernandez's (1986) shape-shifting trickster assault this epistemological framework of a social studies class with the role of the spiked-haired class clown Jerry, and his sidekick, Mike, whom you met in the first paragraph. Habermas's (1981) theory of cultural rationalization and Carspecken's (1996) reconstructive analysis offer a framework for analysis of the objective asser-tions of academic knowledge beliefs, of the classroom and cultural norms, and the subjective needs of the students and teacher. Greene (1994) pro-poses that this interest in situated or embodied knowledge is important to the educational researcher for its attention to a plurality of views and for the resultant pedagogy that can inform the practice of education.

## Method of Analysis

Subjects of this three-month's study included a third-year teacher of a world geography class and his thirty students. Of these students, seven were special education, and two were Limited English Proficient (LEP). There were five additional Latino students and one African American student in the class.

The rest of the students were white. I used pseudonyms for the teacher and his students in this case study.

The method of investigation included seven ethnographic observations during which I took field notes on students' and teacher's reactions to each other during class work and lessons. Five of these lessons were also tape recorded and transcribed. Four observations were compiled with field notes incorporated into the transcribed text of the audiotaped class sessions. One lesson was videotaped for recall sessions with the teacher and students, separately and jointly, during which the parties viewed the tape and reflected on what they saw in interviews with me.

The transcribed tapes were analyzed using Carspecken's (1996) reconstructive analysis including coding for major themes, role analysis, meaning field possibilities, validity horizon reconstruction, and interactive sequence investigation. The interactive sequence investigation was important for discovery of the negotiations of epistemological beliefs and for the role of the clown exposing what Fernandez (1986) calls the "inchoate" or the ambiguous area where contradictions and paradoxes dance. The teacher or student offers the "setting" or what Carspecken (1996) describes as the topic, mood, and/or tone in an interactive sequence. As the interchange continues, the teacher and/or a student can offer a bid to change the setting, that is, a setting shift bid. When a setting shift bid is made and accepted by another, a negotiation takes place. The negotiations in this study offer clown challenges and epistemological discoveries. A volunteer group of students were also interviewed using a protocol that asked questions about the students' epistemological beliefs concerning controversial issues and their reactions to the controversial elements of their unit of study on the Middle East that included a lesson on terrorism, the centerpiece of this chapter. The teacher participated in a similar interview. The interviews also included checks for the validity of the reconstructive analysis of the classroom interaction. In the next sections the role of the clown in its changing forms will be viewed under Bakhtin's (1973) carnival banner with contributions from McLaren's (1985, 1986) resistance theory, Fernandez's shape-shifting trickster and Turner's (1969) liminar.

### The Class Clown

In his study, McLaren (1985,1986) sees the clown as one who mocks the teacher, fellow students, classroom procedures, current topics, and classwork; but McLaren argues that the clown is "the arbiter of passive resistance" (1986: 160). He claims that most students passively accept the packaged information they receive from teachers putting these students on the level of King and Kitchener's (1994) prereflective thinkers and Kuhn's (1991) absolutists. Passive resistance comes in the form of leaning back on chairs, tapping pencils, throwing paper, passing notes, facial expressions of disgust, and daydreaming. Resistance, active and passive, contests the classroom rituals and the instructional process. The class clown mediates between passive and active resistance as he crashes into overt resistance with a humorous inversion of classroom instruction or rituals. His clown, Vinnie, parodied the students and the teacher and the schoolwork they seemed to take seriously. Vinnie would roll a baseball across the floor as students worked, or he would fold his hands in mock prayer as his index finger explored the inside of a single nostril.

McLaren sees clowns who resist the authoritarian hold of the school and its teacher representatives as liminars, a term introduced by Turner (1969). Liminars introduce a moment that takes the traditional structure out of interaction as they unwittingly challenge norms that people take for granted. Liminars may bridge the movement from ordinary social life to that at a higher status of awareness, unintentionally and unknowingly. In this chapter Jerry is the liminar who facilitates the discussion of epistemological beliefs and the possible underlying normative claims that cause seeming contradictions.

Turner (1969) explains that liminality is the middle phase, a betwixt and between state, of a rite of passage or transition in life. The first phase is separation from society, the second, transition or liminality where the initiate lives with others who share his position, and the third, reaggregation into society. Liminality introduces a period of antistructure where societal norms and rules are suspended and the participants interact in a spirit of equality. Turner (1969) calls this sharing of unequal participants "communitas" because it operates organically without the rules of a community. Liminality in its strict sense is a part of tribal societies, but Turner (1979) sees "liminal" moments in postindustrial cultures where the social structure, normal routines, and inequitable rules are challenged.

Anfara (1999) claims that the high school can be a liminal place where students can critically examine, challenge, and possibly change the social structure of the society that the school replicates. This requires teacher recognition that the students are in this liminal space between childhood dependency and adult independence. A class clown may facilitate this realization in a nonthreatening way with his equalizing antics that level the playing field between the teacher and his students.

The reasoning process supports expression of knowledge beliefs and is part of the definition of epistemology that Fenstermacher (1994) offers. In the interchange below this liminous clown challenged the linear progression of a logical scenario of work in a dictatorial regime manned by terrorists. This shapes-shifting trickster (Fernandez 1986) turned the teacher's story frame in on itself. Jerry, the class clown, inverted the teacher's words and ideas, and contradicted the teacher and himself. His nonlinear fun-making stopped the work scenario the teacher constructed. For a moment the clown unwittingly exposed the class and the teacher to another liminal moment that allowed the breakdown of a logical construction. With the breakdown came the realization that reasoning may not always be on one level and semantic relationships of "working outside," "you wouldn't have to work," and "working already" point to the complexities that underlie what is taken for granted to be a natural progression (Spradley 1979).

Field Note Excerpt: Interactive Sequence on Work Scenario in Pete's Class
[In this sequence, Pete attempts to offer a scenario of what would happen if the Karankawa Indians came back to the Houston, Texas, area to reclaim their land, just as the Israelis came back to claim their land from the Palestinians.]
[375] F : "Hold on, hold on. You can't, you can't have a job except jobs that are between eight o'clock in the morning and four o'clock in the afternoon. And you cannot have a job if you are in air conditioning. You have to work outside."
[Pete is offering a setting bid for work parameters in his terrorist setting.]
[376] "Jerry: I did, I did—"
[Jerry says he worked outside in rejection of the scenario framework in this setting shift.]
[377] F: "Hold on, hold on. I'm telling you something. Shhh, shh."
[378] Mike: "Hold it."
[Mike tries to assist Pete in reclaiming the original bid, but Jerry remains determined.]
[379] Jerry: "And you wouldn't have to work."
[Now Jerry seems to accept the setting shift bid and maintains a person wouldn't have to work since he wouldn't work outside.]
[380] F: "Shh, shh."
[381] Jerry: "So you wouldn't have to work."
[382] F: "And you wouldn't have to eat because you'd probably starve to death."
[Pete believes Jerry has accepted the bid and shows Jerry the error of his judgment.]
[383] Jerry: "Well, I work already."
[Jerry stops the scenario with his return to a contradictory setting of working outside, you, not having to work, and already having a job.]

The discourse above carried a sing-song rhythm reflective of children's nursery rhymes and interchanges like that at "A Mad Tea-Party" in Lewis

Carroll's (1960) *Alice's Adventures in Wonderland*. The ambiguous use of "I" and "you" followed a similar pattern as those in these same children's works. It reflected a child's difficulty with the proper use of these personal pronouns. Fernandez (1986) maintains that the roles people play in society are multiple and conflicting and that they can be reflected in the duplicitous use of "I" and "you" in a confusing interplay of message and code. Fernandez asserts that the interchangeable use of "I" and "you" is an example of shape-shifting. In the clown's discourse above, the "I" and "you" could refer to the interchangeable roles of student and teacher.

Besides playing with the roles of teacher and student with these two personal pronouns, Jerry may have intensified the role shift with a context shift. Jerry framed his challenge to Pete's work scenario with an "I did" and "I work already" in a rejection of the rule of working outside in the scenario. The middle section reinforced Jerry's rejection of the forced working outside scenario with the repetition of "You wouldn't have to work." Couched in the playful interchange and shape-shifting of "I" and "you" by Jerry as he contradicted Pete's "You'll starve" with "I work already" was a challenge to the hierarchical role of teacher and the student's obligation to accept the parameters of a teacher's scenario. Because Pete could not stop Jerry's "I/you" wordplay, Pete threw up his hands and gave up this section of his terrorist scenario. Jerry shifted the shape of the scenario and the shape of his role with his teacher. The teacher and class were left with the taste of an illogical reasoning process marked with contradictions. The flavor of the challenge to a teacher's hierarchical role and to a teacher's ability to define the parameters of class work underlay the fun-making taste and signals a concern students may have with classroom inequity. This is an example of how the clown can participate in class discussion and shift the teacher's plan with seemingly illogical reasoning. When a clown can create liminal moments like the one above, he does it with humor and that humor wears the cloak of Bakhtin's (1973) carnival.

Bakhtin finds in the wavy mirror of carnival, with its irreverent exuberance and laughter, the seeds for change in society's official order, in its institutions. He traces carnival back to the folk culture of the Romans and forward through the Middle Ages and the Renaissance where the oppressed displayed a free society in direct opposition to church and state. Carnival continues in modern society in what Quantz and O'Conner (1988) call "carnivalesque moments." Bakhtin embraces carnival for its exposure of nonlegitimate voices in cultural contexts.

While he stresses the complex character of carnival, Bakhtin offers four categories of attitude that find a place in this study of a classroom's epistemological negotiations and the role of the class clown. The first category is the releasing of the prohibitions, restrictions, and laws that govern daily life. In this study the class clown challenges classroom norms by resisting both the classroom normative claim that students should sit in desks and that they cannot pray in schools.

In the scene below, L. D., a Special Education student with a noticeable limp, has just fallen to the floor after leaning sideways in his chair. Jerry, the clown, provides a quick cover for L. D.'s embarrassment by making a setting shift bid (Carspecken 1996). He moves the teacher's concern for L. D.'s fall on the floor to a bid for the floor as a good place for all students to sit.

Field Note Excerpt: Interactive Sequence in Pete's Class

[119] P: "... L.D.!"

[Observer Comment (O. C.): As if concerned and surprised by L. D.'s fall. Some student laughter follows.]

[120] Jerry: "I wish we could all sit on the floor."

[Jerry offers the setting shift bid of sitting on the floor.]

[121] P: "Yeah, well, it would be comfortable. Heh, heh. It's a rather dirty floor! Now if we had carpet here, we'd push, we'd push the chairs to the walls and we'd sit here and we'd play Duck-Duck-Goose."

[Pete accepts Jerry's bid with reservations. He notices the floor is dirtier than the chairs. He also makes reference here to a kindergarten game, "Duck-Duck-Goose." Pete seems to suggest that sitting on the floor would be a return to elementary school routines.]

[122] Emma: "We could meditate."

[O. C.: As if she is sincerely interested in sitting on the floor.]

[Emma is a usually quiet student who is a friend of Jerry's. She reinforces the original setting shift and brings the value of sitting on the floor back to a high school level activity.]

[123] P: "And meditate. . . . Yes, but we can't meditate because that's a form of prayer and we can't do that here at school. So . . ."

[O. C.: As if he catches himself and corrects his words. Prayer is taboo in public schools.]

[The mention of "meditation" forces Pete to resume his professional teacher role and offer another setting shift bid with his admonition of no school prayer.]

[124] Josh: "Don't they do that at football games?"

[Josh accepts the bid and offers his own observation.]

[125] L. D.: "Yeah. I heard about that. That lady that made that a rule, she disappeared."

[O.C.: L. D.'s response, now that he and his chair are upright, is referring to the disappearance of Madeleine Murray O'Hare.]

[L. D. has not only recovered, he offers a historical perspective to the issue of school prayer as he participates in the new setting.]

In this instance, Jerry offered a new way to sit in the classroom in response to the fall of a physically challenged Special Education student, but his statement also stimulated another suggestion from Emma about meditation. Before the ideas about floor sitting and meditation were dismissed as inappropriate and unlawful (unlawful raises the colorful flag of carnival and liminality), students and teachers had a moment to see this inversion of a classroom ritual, sitting on the floor as opposed to sitting in desks. There is no action taken, but a challenge is made to a tacit claim of same level seating for teacher and students that could offer change and more equality for teachers and students. A discussion of classroom beliefs, meditation and prayer in schools, and/or the opinion of O'Hare on school prayer could have exposed epistemological beliefs and promoted negotiations for reasons and evidence to support those beliefs.

In the second category, the clown frees the language, gestures, and behavior of all participants from the hierarchy of status, rank, and age. Jerry and his sidekick, Mike, bring McLaren's (1986) street state that shows the exuberant antics of students at play in the streets as opposed to students working in the classroom. The scene that began this chapter introduced the comic duo, Jerry and Mike. These two marginal students, Jerry and Mike, outside of the popular high school jock culture (Eckert 1989; Foley 1990), performed a carnival mockery of the most popular game in Texas. The quarterback pass of the rubber chicken to the wide receiver running for the touchdown of placing the chicken in the mouth of the paper-machéd dinosaur turns this most popular game in high school, football, "wrongside out." The teacher facilitates this school parody as the rubber chicken is also the hall pass, and the three-foot dinosaur is the class mascot. In most classes the hall pass is a written permission slip and a class mascot is some appropriate animal or minority group. In this room, students and teacher challenge the normative claim that a school's identity lies in its football team and its school mascot. The teacher adds his own challenge to the school claim that a student must have a pass to go to the restroom by making his classroom pass the comic, dead and defeathered, rubber chicken. This rubber remnant of vaudeville humor reflects the teacher's contribution of an atmosphere that allows the students to gain some equity in the classroom. A discussion of the importance of football in high school or of the necessity of a pass for the bathroom would offer opportunity for the interaction of epistemological beliefs that may spark the interest of a student.

With the third aspect of Bakhtin's carnival, anything that has been iso-lated, separated, or sanctified is open to contact with carnival. The fourth and final category embodies a whole system of parody and blasphemy of everything the culture holds sacred with particular emphasis on the repro-ductive system and the church. The third and fourth aspects of carnival find expression in the two major themes resulting from the coding of class obser-vations and interviews, sex and violence. The clown touches these themes with parody and blasphemy.

*Sex and Violence*
The adolescent claims using sex and violence in a bid for power, when ado-lescent claims are often minimized, come as the culture compartmentalizes these natural parts of the bipolar cycle of life and death. Sex and the repro-ductive system are life giving whereas death often comes violently in nature and natural death of a loved one can have violent effects on the person's inner life of those left behind. Culture establishes laws, tacit rules, and overt prohibitions as sex and violence are secreted into enclosed compartments and sanitized, segregated from their natural role in life's death and rebirth cycle. Society's controls that separate, analyze, and sanitize these natural phenomena backfire with the media's entrance to satisfy the adolescents' interests.

Tacit assertions that sex and violence offer power and voice to the disen-franchised is disguised by the media in songs, story lines, and commercials. These media reflections arise in opposition to societal attempts to set limits, impose rules, and compartmentalize activities that have a natural role in the life and death cycle. Tacit claims receive expression in media representation as the enticement of the forbidden fruit of sex and the defensive aggression of violence. These paradoxical expressions of sex and violence as sterile, private functions with sensual power are promoted in idealized contexts created by the media makers of television, movies, musical recordings, and print. The natural cultural context is removed, glamorized, or sensationalized tacitly while society explicitly attempts to sanitize and hide these controversial topics.

The combination of explicit societal prohibitions and media exploitation of implicit cultural norms gives added enticement to the use of sex and vio-lence as they become independent, ambiguous entities that can create their own content and context. Sex and violence become targets for power claims by disempowered individuals seeking voice and equality in the culture. These voices are often those of teenagers.

Creating these societal entities opens the gates of vocalization in the classroom for Bakhtin's carnival and the class clown who is fearless in his desire to violate the official order of restrained response. The clown consciously uses these topics to make exuberant power claims. Jerry gains the spotlight when he plunges in with words and phrases like "menstrual cycle" that bring student laughter and challenges the teacher's control of the class.

Interview Excerpt of Judy and Jerry about Sexual Topics in the Classroom

[102] Jerry: "Uh, I was telling them the other day. Uh, we was like talking about women's menstrual cycle and stuff. And I was like, I was wondering some stuff about it, you know, and instead of just like going up and asking, you know, I just asked plain out what it was. And like the kids started laughing at me, and it was a serious question. She thought I was joking around and so."

[103] J: "But she didn't answer."

[104] Jerry: "She answered, but she just thought I was trying to make people laugh by the question."

[105] J: "Now, you know that if you say the word 'menstrual' in a classroom because you've been around."

[106] Jerry: "I know."

[107] J: "You know that people are going to laugh."

[108] Jerry: "Yes, a lot of times I will say things like that to make people laugh. But then I'll ask a question, and I'll be serious, and she'll think I'm joking around or something."

[113] J: "Can you think of any . . . controversial issue that you've discussed in class where people have opinions on both sides of it, like abortion?"

[114] Jerry: "Abortion."

[115] J: "In class."

[116] Jerry: "Yeah, I've discussed that. I was in speech class and we were suppose to give a speech. . . . And, uh, I went up there and we started talking about abortion because we were just suppose to come up and talk about anything. And I started talking about abortion. And people on this side of the classroom were yelling at people on this side about they agree and they disagree. . . . And then eventually the teacher was like, 'You need to go down. You're starting too big of an argument,' and stuff."

The normative claims that underlie students' views of sex and violence are not discussed in the classroom. Instead teachers and students use sex and violence in innuendos, jokes, and caustic remarks that offer no opportunity for the communicative act that encourages consensus building in dealing with these controversial topics. Jerry's description of the abortion yellathon is an example of what happens when the volcanic dome of this controversial topic explodes into the classroom. Teacher refereed discussions that facilitate the orderly expression of multiple viewpoints on the abortion issue would provide an opportunity for an epistemological discussion.

Presentation of sex and violence in school is limited to carefully controlled assemblies, film documentaries, and tightly orchestrated student workshops. A dialectic is rarely a part of these activities. Class discussion does not center on the themes of violence and sex in natural contexts because a teacher wants to uphold his image as the person in control of his classroom who promotes restrained, well-behaved students. The clown puts the spotlight on topics that live in the underbelly of students' lives.

The clownish exuberance of Jerry reaches its height as a class discussion of terrorism begins. Jerry pulls up an imaginary machine gun and shouts, "Boom!" and he continues to fire his imaginary gun with its accompanying gunfire until the end of the lesson. This class clown breaks the protective covering of the normative issue of violence so it becomes a part of the communicative act. In the next interactive sequence, the class clown uses his brash, uncompromising humor to punctuate, question, and expose tacit claims and dangers about violence. Nothing is solved in this interactive sequence but the covert epistemological claim that an omniscient authority is the source of knowledge receives a booming challenge. This section begins with a meaning field range and a validity horizon reconstruction that look at possible implicit, intersubjective (from the point of view of the speaker) interpretations of the explicit statements in the interaction, and at the broad spectrum of Habermas's (1981) possible objective, subjective, and normative claims. The normative power claim with its grotesque connection of violence and sex in the validity horizon below reflects carnival's ribald blasphemy.

Field Note Excerpt: An Interactive Sequence on Terrorism in Pete's Class with Meaning Fields and a Validity Horizon Reconstruction

[53]Pete: "We had three short, simple words to define, and the reason I want you to keep those kind of under you hat. You're going to use those again today and again on your test. But, uh, primarily what I want to talk about today is terrorism."

[Meaning Field: "I'm transitioning into the lesson for today," AND/OR "It's time to get down to business."]

[54] Jerry: "Boom!"

[O. C.: Stands to shoot his imaginary machine gun, as if excited by this topic.]

[M. F.: "This is my favorite topic," AND/OR "This is my time to shine." AND/OR "Am I funny or what?" AND/OR "I really like guns," AND/OR "I'd like to shoot some people."]

[55] Pete: "Now, you've seen it in the news . . ."
[56] Jerry: "Boom!"
[O. C.: Repeats previous gesture. This prompts responses from around the room. Darla and Annie fulfill their roles of classroom monitors with *Shh!* and *Quiet!* respectively. Pete smiles and waits patiently for silence.]
[M.F.: "Did anybody hear me? (AND/OR) "One more time should draw a reaction," (AND/OR) "It is really fun to do this!"]

---

Horizon Analysis of Jerry's "Boom!" with its accompanying mimed machine gun action

---

**Possible objective claims**
*Quite foregrounded, quite immediate*
"Terrorists shoot guns."
*Less foregrounded, less immediate*
"I know a lot about guns."
*Highly backgrounded, remote, taken-for-granted*
"Guns are an integral part of our culture's history."

**Possible subjective claims**
*Foregrounded, immediate*
"I feel good when I shoot a gun."
*Less foregrounded, less immediate*
"I'm in the spotlight when I shoot this gun."
*Highly backgrounded, remote, taken-for-granted*
"I need to shoot a gun to prove that I exist."

**Possible normative claims**
*Quite foregrounded, quite immediate*
"Shouting a gun is good because it gives a person power."
*Less foregrounded, less immediate*
"Shouting a gun is the sign of a real man."
*Highly backgrounded, remote, taken-for-granted*
"A gun is good because it is an extension of a man's penis."

---

As the sequence continues, the reactions to Jerry's power claim vary. Initially Pete, the teacher, sits Jerry down in his chair asking for silence. This teacher response echoes the teachers' reactions McLaren (1985, 1986) found in his clown, Vinnie. His friend, Emma, sitting across from him responds with quiet sarcasm: "You're scaring me." Jerry draws laughter from the entire class in his duet with Chris of the theme from the television show, "Love Boat," that is interrupted and terminated with his BOOMing reprise. The class joins the clown in a moment of Turner's *communitatus* as the room is drawn into this liminal moment. This ludic reaction highlights this liminar's unconscious ability to plunge the class into aporia of contradictions that underlies the system man creates to order his life (McLaren 1986). Fernandez (1982) calls this the "inchoate," the darkness at the top or bottom of the stairs. Fernandez explains that the way the inchoate finds its expression is in metaphor. Here, the safe, secure, and idealistic world of man-finds-woman on the Love Boat sinks repeatedly with the class clown's BOOMing reprise. When an ideal is challenged, an ideal of romantic love in this case, the possibility of verbalizing that ideal and questioning its knowledge beliefs exists (Freire 1993).

Two times in the scenario Pete tries to convince Jerry that when he retaliates with gunfire he accomplishes little and may hurt an innocent bystander. To that last possibility, Jerry responds, "Oh, people at the wrong place at the wrong time." Mike laughs at the flippant irony that may be a substitute for his challenge of the teacher as a source of knowledge. As Pete describes a specific act of terrorism, the demolition of a 747-passenger jet in the air, Jerry makes his final "BOOM!" Pete replies, "Big boom! Multimillion-dollar plane falls. Everybody on board dies."

As the lesson on terrorism moves to its conclusion, Pete questions Jerry, "So you think that violence is an acceptable solution to not being heard?" Jerry thematizes, makes explicit, the tacit subjective and normative claim he has been making throughout the lesson with his response. "It's about the only way to be heard." Jerry reinforces this normative claim that worries school authorities with his final sally as the lesson draws to a close. The clown's declaration that the shooting of a gun is "the only way to be heard" echoes into the disturbing violence of Columbine and other schools throughout the United States in the past few years. Discussion has focused on eliminating guns, but not why students need to use guns, need to kill others to be heard. Open discussion of controversial topics like violence may allow students to be heard, expose epistemological beliefs, and lead to rewarding epistemological negotiations.

Field Note Excerpt: The End to the Interactive Sequence on Terrorism in Pete's Class
[697] Pete: "By the way how can you stop the violence in the Middle East?"
[698] Jerry: "Nuke 'em."
[699] Pete: "How, how do you know—"
[700] Jerry: "Shoot 'em all."
[701] Mike: "Oh, yeah!"
[O. C.: Said as if to make fun of Jerry's responses, in a strong Texas accent.]

This ending to the lesson on terrorism punctuates the fatalistic view that some teenagers take in this either/or world of black and white, life or death beliefs that needs the gray area of possibilities teased apart through opportunities for extended communication. Violence is an emotion-ridden topic with strong validity claims like the ones in the interchange above that fuse normative and subjective assertions making the development of the communicative act difficult. Pete, the teacher, never denies Jerry's power claim. He questions it, mocks it, but always allows its exposure. This gun-festering sore in the side of the class on terrorism challenges the teacher's epistemological claim to be the source of knowledge and offers confirmation that violence is a complex subject that needs more democratic discussion in the classroom. These violence power claims entice marginalized students like Jerry and serve as an invitation for further dialogue to thematize normative validity claims of adolescents and separate them from subjective claims to encourage students' development of the communicative act.

In the next section, a discussion about the Karankowa Indians in Texas leads to a full interactive epistemological claim/challenge sequence on the certainty of knowledge and the source of knowledge. The class clown, Jerry, and his sidekick, Mike, are the principal participants together with their teacher, Pete. Habermas's (1981) theory of cultural rationality gives clarity to the reconstruction of the sequence as it thematizes, makes explicit, the tacit claims or assertions of the participants.

## Habermas's Theory of Rationality, Meaning Fields, and Validity Horizon Analysis

Students and teachers make epistemological assertions with claims of objective fact, for example, "Indians were the first U. S. citizens," or normative claims, for instance, "the death penalty is bad." If a discussant adds information to verify one of these assertions or questions the assertion an epistemological negotiation begins. This section introduces an epistemological discussion of constructed knowledge that follows a claim/challenge pattern. This interactive sequence that is the subject of the remainder of this chapter actually occurred as the teacher allowed his students to get him off track when both teacher and student questioned the accuracy of Texas's and the United States' historical facts. Discovery and analysis of the sequence could not have occurred without an understanding of the types of claims that shape the communicative act. Habermas's (1981) theory of rationality encompasses a person's objective, normative, and subjective domains, and the validity claims, assertions of truth, that a person makes regarding those worlds. When an individual considers knowledge, he faces the influences of his

country, his community, his family, and, in the case of a student, the influence of a school and its teachers. Just as a student deals with the epistemological beliefs of the teacher and his classmates in the classroom, he also faces
his own beliefs in the subjective world, in the objective world of facts, and in
the normative world of society's traditional beliefs. This theory of rationality
exposes the embedded, nested, and tacit beliefs that often lead to misunder-
standing and negative reactions in everyday conversation. To understand the
implicit, tacit validity claims, the ethnographer and the person participating
in the dialogue must put herself intersubjectively into the other person's position and think as that individual thinks. It is this intersubjective recognition
(the understanding of the other's objective, normative, and subjective
claims) of each other's perspectives that allows nested epistemology to be
productive. The ethnographer can glean a range of meanings for each statement in an interaction by position-taking with a subject and writing other
assertions that restate the original claim and allow the ethnographer to
determine the tacit claims underlying the explicit statement or action. The
original claim and the other possible interpretations make up the meaning
field. These meaning fields (Carspecken 1996) become more explicit as they
give way to validity horizon reconstructions. The excerpted classroom interchange from the social studies class below will be used to examine meaning
fields and the objective, normative, and subjective claims of the participants.
These claims, both tacit and explicit, compose a layered validity horizon
with claims in the foreground, middle ground, and background (Carspecken
1996).

Field Note Excerpt: Interactive Sequence about Indians as Cannibals in Pete's
Class with Horizontal and Vertical Validity Reconstructions
[Pete is trying to establish a parallel between the hypothetical return of the Karankawa Indians to Texas to reclaim their homeland as the Jews returned to
demand their homeland from the Egyptians and Palestinians.]
[307] P: "Okay. Who originally lived here? Before Europeans and Asians and Africans came."
[Meaning Field (M.F.): "Who were the indigenous people?" (AND/OR) "Who
holds original claim to this land?" (OR) "What did you learn in Texas history?"]
[308] Mike: "Indians."
[309] Josh: "Americans."
[308] P: "Native Americans. Indians. What tribes?"
[M.F.: "Both answers are good." (AND) "Let's combine the two answers." (AND/
OR) "Let's be specific."]

[309] Jerry: "Woowoowooaah" (Indian war whoop)

[M.F.: "I don't know the answer, but I want in on this." (AND/OR) "I know the sound they make." (AND/OR) "I'm a good sound effects man."]

[310] Mike: "On the-the-"

[311] Darla: "Cherokees."

[312] Mike: "The Karankawa. Or what are they called?"

[313] Pete: "The Cherokees lived over there. We made them go this way."

[O.C.: Pete is using the diagram on the board to explain the location.]

[M.F.: "The Cherokees is a close answer." (AND) "Here, let me show where they live."]

[315] P: Karankawa.

[316] Mike: "They were cannibals, weren't they?"

[M.F.: "Cannibals are bad because they eat people." (AND/OR) "I learned that in my junior high Texas history class." (AND/OR) "I feel good that I remember something about these Indians."]

---

Horizon Analysis of Mike's Statement: *They were cannibals, weren't they?*

---

**Possible objective claims**
*Quite foregrounded, quite immediate*
"Cannibals eat people."
*Less foregrounded, less immediate*
"I learned that in my junior high Texas history class."
*Highly backgrounded, remote, taken-for-granted*
"I learned this from my teacher and textbook. They are both experts that know."

**Possible subjective claims**
*Foregrounded, immediate*
"I feel good that I remember something about these Indians."
*Less foregrounded, less immediate*
"I need to say this to show my intelligence" or "I want you to accept me as a student who knows."

**Possible normative claims**
*Quite foregrounded, quite immediate*
"Cannibals are bad because they eat people."
*Less foregrounded, less immediate*
"Indians are bad because they are not civilized."
*Highly backgrounded, remote, taken-for-granted*
"White people should be the most civilized people."
"I need to believe the Indian is beneath me to strengthen my good feeling about myself."

There is an extra clownish punch that comes with the normative claim that these Karankowa Indians are uncivilized Indians who are not as good as white people. With this normative assertion, Mike, who is Jerry's sidekick, questions Pete's tacit, normative claim of reverence for the Native American Indians. This reverence is explicit in Pete's final statement of this interactive sequence as he explains the white man's contribution to the demise of the

Karankowa. A challenge to the sacredness of the Karankowas could upset the balance Pete is trying to set up between the white settlers and the indigenous landholders claim to Texas as a parallel scenario to the Palestinian and Israeli claim to the same land.

Pete may consciously or unconsciously realize that challenge to his scenario because his response is to the tacit normative claims in the interchange below. When a teacher responds to a tacit claim of the student after taking the subjective stance of the student, the intersubjectivity of the interchange between teacher and student facilitates an epistemological negotiation. Notice the teacher response to, "They were cannibals, weren't they?"

Field Note Excerpt about Junior High School Teachers with Mike, Pete, and Jerry

[317] P: "No, they were not. In fact, you probably have some junior high teacher who told you they were. That teacher was incorrect."

[318] J: "Those morons."

[319] P: "They were not . . . they were not cannibals. In fact, they told you that just to make you interested in them. You know what they . . . they really didn't—"

[320] M: "They lied."

[321] P: "Yeah. They didn't lie. They exaggerated."

There are two interrelated structures here. One is Pete's challenge to the epistemological claim that knowledge is certain with his assertion about junior high teachers' inaccuracy. The other is Mike's clownish, normative challenge to Pete that his reverence for the Native American Indian is ill-founded. In the first concern for junior high teachers and their competency, "some junior high teacher who told you they were," Jerry and Mike add their chorus of censorial judgments. They quickly position-take and grab the tacit normative validity claim, "Junior high teachers are not doing a competent job," and add their chorus of comments: "Those morons" and "They lied." The teacher's view that junior high teachers are not as good as high school teachers is suggested by Pete's interview observation, "Their teachers have spoon-fed everything to them (the students)." Pete appears to espouse the Freirian (1993) view that teachers are not infallible experts who deposit irrefutable information into students' brains, yet he replaces the authority of the junior high teachers exposing an educator's hierarchy.

Despite the moments of contradiction in the interactive sequence, the epistemological challenge of the validity of prior information continues throughout this interchange with an opportunity for students and teacher to question other information they have received. Before this sequence considers another challenge to the certainty of knowledge, Pete answers Mike's clownish, resistant challenge to the normative claim about the Native American's sacredness.

Field Note Excerpt with Pete's Explanation of Karankowas
[323] P: "For example, they didn't munch on the flesh of their victims okay. What they did . . . if I wanted to terrorize this guy before they really died and I had them tied up around a tree, I'd cut off a piece of his body and pretend I was eating it just to tick him off."

The irony is that Pete is taking the criticalist view in this lesson as he encourages students to question dominant ideologies about Native Americans. So perhaps Mike's clownish resistance comes in the form of conservatism and its negative view of culture that challenges the premises of its dominant ideology.

After Pete explains how students receive false information in their junior high Texas history class about the Karakawa Indians, Jerry decides to test other historical facts he has learned. In the interchange below, our class clown attempts to interject the historical use of marijuana, the drug of choice at this high school, but a taboo in class discussion or expressions. Jerry facetiously raises the epistemological claim that valid knowledge is found in books. Then he continues his ironic plunge into the epistemological framework by challenging the knowledge claim that knowledge comes with rational discourse. (Carnival rears its ironic head.) The sequence moves toward its conclusion with a question about Santa Ana's supposed sexual exploits on the day of his defeat at the Battle of San Jacinto.

Field Note Excerpt: Interactive Sequence on Revisionist History in Pete's Class
[This sequence continues where the validity horizon excerpt ended with the discussion of the Karankowa Indians. Pete is discussing one of the most common misconceptions in American history.]
[323] Pete: "It's like the story of George Washington cutting down the cherry tree. That was impossible. There weren't cherry trees grown in that part of the United States until like 1890. So . . ."
[324] Jerry: "You know he had weed back then."
[Jerry makes a bid to introduce a controversial topic, one that brings snickers, marijuana, and its early use in American history. Pete accepts.]
[325] Pete: "Pot."
[326] Jerry: "Yes, he did. I read it in a book."

[Jerry makes the tacit epistemological claim that valid knowledge is found in books.]

[327] Pete: "Oh, you did. Is that a book that wants to legalize hemp?"

[328] Jerry: "Yes."

[329] Pete: "Thought so. People make up facts they want you to believe."

[Pete again challenges the epistemological claim that knowledge is certain with the challenge that people construct knowledge.]

[330] Jerry: "No, he deed."

[Jerry makes a bid for illogical reasoning as he plays with the word *did*, rhyming *deed* with *weed* in the same way Pete plays with words as he presents a lesson.]

[331] Pete: "No, he deedn't. (Students laugh.) Oh, yeah, and Thomas Jefferson was sleeping back on opiates."

[Pete accepts the bid and carries the illogical reasoning forward with his *reductio ad absurdum* strategy.]

[332] Jerry: "How'd you know?"

[333] Pete: "And Alexander Hamilton was shooting up."

[334] Jerry: "Cool!"

[335] Pete: "That's the reason the constitution's the way it is. No folks, that's wrong. Number 1, people believe what they want to, and what you're looking at is revisionist history."

[Pete again challenges the certainty of knowledge epistemological claim with the assertion that people interpret knowledge.]

[336] Jerry: "Well, if that wasn't true, tell me if this was true. When Sam Houston got Santa Ana, what was Santa Ana doing?"

[Now Jerry introduces a question that involves revisionist history created to elevate the heroes of the Texas Revolution over the lascivious Mexican villains.]

[337] Pete: "He was entertaining a mulatto woman."

[338] Jerry: "Okay. So that is true. That's what they say."

[339] Mike: "He had some fun."

[O.C.: Annie and Darla are laughing.]

[This is a popular legend that gave rise to the Texas song, "The Yellow Rose of Texas." I had recently attended a Mexican-American Studies Conference at the University of Houston where the harmful effects of this story were discussed. I was unable to remain quiet.]

[340] J: "No, it isn't."

[341] Pete: "The mulatto story is not true. I've got a published version."

[Pete makes the same epistemological claim Jerry offered earlier that knowledge is valid if it is in a book.]

[342] J: "It was done to denigrate the Mexican."

[I challenge this claim with the statement that knowledge is interpreted.]

[343] Pete: "Upp, it is! It's not true."

[344] J: "No, it isn't."

[345] Pete: "No, it isn't. He wasn't entertaining a mulatto."

[346] Jerry: "Whoaaa."

[350] Pete: *Thank you, Ms. Radigan.*

[Perhaps my response to the Santa Ana misconception prompts Pete to shift the setting and respond to Mike's tacit claim that white people are better than Indians.]

[352] Pete: "By the way that story about the Karankowas being cannibals was something the Anglos cooked up so they could systematically murder what was left of the Karankowas after the disease took the rest."

[Pete now solidifies my challenge with his criticalist example of the extinction of the minority for the greater good of the dominant group.]

[353] Mike: "Really?"

[354] Pete: "Yes, in fact, we've got stories of settlers, Stephen F. Austin and a whole bunch of people who came down here. And they, they brag about, 'I saw what I thought was a Karankowa, so I shot him.' And they bragged about it. They thought it was the neatest thing in the world. They would kill these . . . these indigenous people. Now, right now, there is probably no Karankawa, full-blooded left."

This interactive sequence on revisionist history begins with a challenge to a misconception that students had about a minority group and ends with the normative claim that some misconceptions are fostered to denigrate the minority and secure the majority position of superiority. The sequence has a carnivalesque epistemological moment when Jerry challenges rational discourse and Pete follows him with his *reductio de absurdum* strategy. Jerry's own epistemological development level is still prereflective or absolutist, reflected by his response to questions in his personal interview, yet he challenges assumptions about rational discourse, introduces contradictory knowledge claims, and questions current knowledge claims that facilitate the discovery of the teacher's contradictory epistemological belief structures.

This three-part claim/challenge sequence is an example of epistemological negotiation on the topic of revisionist history. A fun-making subtext supported and played throughout the main epistemological claim/challenge sequence. Pete initiated the fun with the Karankowa example of bone knawing for fun of scaring enemies. Jerry's claim that the American heroes used drugs played with the revisionist history theme as did his "deed" and "weed" rhyming so that he could continue to have fun with this topic. When Jerry asked about Santa Ana's actions, he already knew about the supposed sexual liaison and just wanted to hear it discussed again in class. In keeping with Giddens's (1994) assertion that humor like this is used to show skepticism of the "official" view of society, Jerry jabbed his fun-making punches at junior high school teachers and infallible national heroes throughout the sequence.

## A Closing and an Opening for the Value of a Class Clown

The class clown in this study carries Bakhtin's (1973) flag of carnival as he challenges the high school prohibition of sitting on the floor and meditating, the status of high school football players with a chicken game, the isolated norms of sex and violence, and the sacred value of teacher as lecturer. A prereflective absolutist (King and Kitchener 1994; Kuhn 1991), Jerry, the clown, also shakes the epistemological tree of interaction with his questions about historical drug use and illicit sex. His assertions and questions made him the catalyst for the negotiation of epistemological claims in this study.

Jerry's impudent remarks could easily be discarded by the teacher as attention-getting, but the clown's antics and remarks may be a barometer of the class reaction to a lesson or to the oppressive hand of a teacher or school community. Rather than viewing the clown as someone to be controlled a teacher should consider allowing his voice to be heard as Pete did because the clown may broach topics and asks questions his classmates find intimidating because of the oppressive nature of a classroom controlled by a teacher (Freire 1993).

The fact that a student who has the lowest level of epistemological development can facilitate a discussion about knowledge beliefs on the topic of revisionist history has implications for the way teachers view students. A student does not need high grades to participate in an epistemological negotiation. A student does not need to be regarded as intelligent or as a critical thinker to lead or facilitate epistemological interaction. Discussions that lead to an exploration of meaning and foundations of knowledge beliefs are possible with all students.

The contributions of this class clown extend beyond his epistemological involvement. He functions as the class liminar who cuts fissure in the school's routines and exposes the underbelly of student interests in free class movement, sitting on the floor, meditating, and desiring equity in classroom participation. In one instance, Jerry took away the logic of a work scenario and his position in it with his contradictory responses that he already works outside, a reversal by saying he doesn't have to work, and a return to his original position of already having a job. Jerry allowed the students and the teacher the experience of a liminal moment (Turner 1969, 1974, 1979) betwixt and between the cultural construction of a logical scenario. This brief moment of wordplay with the work scenario exposed the accepted linear model of logical consequences for not following work rules in a contextual environment for what it was. It was a fallible man-made model that expected people to fit generic labels. Linear logic, the reasoning process of assertion plus evidence plus awareness of counterevidence that is part of epistemology's definition may not work perfectly in epistemological negotiations. The role of subjective claims, the needs and feelings, of the individual as well as the normative claims of cultural differences may disrupt common assumptions about the reasoning process. The multiple domains of claims, objective, subjective, and normative, may cause the reasoning process to operate on multiple levels at one time. This possibility was exposed with Jerry's facetious wordplay.

In the mocking shape of a terrorist, when Jerry pulls up an imaginary machine gun and shouts "Boom!", he begins an action that will become a disturbing reprise in this classroom and in schools throughout the United States. It is the school, a common shared structure of knowledge exportation for teachers and students, that Jerry, the clown, challenges. Jerry's challenge throws the class into Turner's (1969) antistructural world of liminality or Fernandez's (1986) inchoate darkness where students sit on floors and meditate, play football games with rubber chickens, discuss sex and violence openly in a classroom with booming gunshot reprises, challenge the linear order of a work scenario, and question George Washington's and the Founding Fathers' use of drugs in the United States. Rather than viewing this clown as a ludic menace to be controlled, further research needs to investigate the possibility that this clown is actually a barometer for school reform and the challenger for equity between teacher and students.

# References

Anfara, V. A. "Urban Schools and Liminality." *National Forum Journals*, 10 (1999):1–7.

Bakhtin, Mikhail. *Problems of Dostoevsky's Poetics*. R. W. Rotsel, trans. New York: Ardis, 1973.

Bakhtin, Mikhail. *Rabelais and His World*. H. Iswolsky, trans. Bloomington: Indiana University Press, 1984.

Carspecken, P. F. *Critical Ethnography in Educational Research*. New York: Routledge, 1996.

Eckert, P. *Jocks and Burnouts: Social Categories and Identity in the High School*. New York: Teachers College Press, 1989.

Fenstermacher, G. D. "The Knower and the Known: The Nature of Knowledge in Research on Teaching." *Review of Research in Education*, 20 (1994):3–56.

Fernandez, J. W. *Persuasions and Performances: The Play of Tropes in Culture*. Bloomington: Indiana University Press, 1986.

Foley, D. E. *Learning Deep in the Capitalist Heart of Tejas Culture*. Philadelphia: University of Pennsylvania Press, 1990.

Freire, P. *Pedagogy of the Oppressed*. M. B. Ramos, trans. New York: Continuum, 1993.

Giddens, A. *Central Problems in Social Theory: Action, Structure and Contradiction in Social Analysis*. Berkeley: University of California Press, 1994.

Greene, M. "Epistemology and Educational Research: The Influence of Recent Approaches to Knowledge." *Review of Research in Education*, 20 (1994):423–64.

Habermas, Jurgen. *The Theory of Communication Action. Vol.1: Reason and the Rationalization of Society*. T. McCarthy, trans. Boston: Beacon Press, 1981.

Habermas, Jurgen. *The Theory of Communication Action. Vol.2: Lifeworld and System: A Critique of Functionalist Reason*. T. McCarthy, trans. Boston: Beacon Press,1987.

King, P., and K. S. Kitchener. *Developing Reflective Judgment*. San Francisco: Jossey-Bass, 1994.

Kuhn, D. *The Skills of Argument*. Cambridge: Cambridge University Press, 1991.

McLaren, P. L. "The Ritual Dimensions of Resistance: Clowning and Symbolic Inversion." *Journal of Education*, 167 (1985):84–97.

McLaren, P. *Schooling as a Ritual Performance*. New York: Routledge, 1986.

Quantz, R. A., and T. W. O'Conner. "Writing Critical Ethnography: Dialogue, Multivoicedness, and Carnival in Cultural Texts." *Educational Theory*, 38 (1988):95–109.

Schommer, M. "Synthesizing Epistemological Belief Research: Tentative Understandings and Provocative Confusions." *Educational Psychology Review*, 6 (1994):293–319.

Spradley, J. P. *The Ethnographic Interview*. Forth Worth, Tex.: Harcourt Brace Jovanovich College Publishers, 1979.

Turner, V. *The Ritual Process: Structure and Anti-Structure*. Chicago: Aldine, 1969.

Turner, V. *Dramas, Fields, and Metaphors: Symbolic Action in Human Society*. Ithaca, N.Y.: Cornell University Press, 1974.

Turner, V. *Process, Performance and Pilgrimage*. New Delhi, India: Concept Publishing Co., 1979.

# CHAPTER TWELVE

# Critical Ethnography and Community Change

*Miguel A. Guajardo and Francisco J. Guajardo*

## Context

I remember several years ago sitting in the doctor's office. My wife and I had taken our children for a routine check-up. Javier was about to turn four and Emiliano was seven. As the nurse, a Mexican American, checked all their vitals signs and measured their head, height, and weight, I remember asking myself, *"Is this what anthropologists used to do to measure the intelligence of people?"* This raised my anxiety a little as I thought their answers would reflect on me as a parent and teacher. But curiously and quietly, I observed. As the process moved along, the nurse asked Emiliano to jump across a tablet as the doctor checked Javier's ears, nose, and throat. Along with the measurements, the nurse asked the boys some questions. The question that caught my attention was the following: "What do you do when you are cold?" Emiliano, who was the first to get the inquiry, appropriately replied by making a shivering and shaking motion. The nurse agreeably and predictably gave him a positive reinforcement, "You are so smart." Then Javier followed doing everything the nurse asked of him. Then the question came: "What do you do when you are cold?" Javier quickly replied, "I get a *colchita*" (I get a little blanket). The nurse reacted with a surprised look; with a blank face, she pondered for several seconds, and after noticing that we had noticed her blankness and surprise, she broke into a big smile. Immediately, she and Javier rejoined us. Upon her return, I asked her, "What reaction would Javier have gotten had the nurse not been bilingual?" She was puzzled by the question and said, "I do not know. I had not thought of that." But indeed, she unconsciously knew what not to say. Javier did not get the same "You're so smart" response.

Emiliano knows the same language as Javier, and he could have responded to the question in the same manner, but he is much more socialized to the expectations of the popular culture. He understands that in this office you speak English, and the mixing of languages would confuse people. But Javier, being younger, more innocent and naïve, did not make that connection; his response came from "home." Indeed, Javier's response is much less "packaged" and much closer to the heart than Emiliano's. In my eyes, it is much more organic. Unfortunately the nurse, who unknowingly granted the label of smartness to my children, was in a position of power and felt at ease ascribing intelligence, a position many of us as ethnographers frequently find ourselves in.

I share this story because it begins to ground this chapter and place a context to an issue that is by design a topic that is well packaged and usually discussed in university campuses and/or professional conferences. Critical ethnography is an issue that is privileged by well-trained and very polished graduate students and academicians. But as the story above illustrates, the authors of this chapter are committed to taking us out of this safe terrain. And as my little boy did, we will share with you a reality that will disrupt the status quo, and will paint a picture of young people and old people alike practicing the art of ethnography. Indeed, it is this practice of critical ethnography that has allowed us to live life on the margins as we learn, teach, and practice the art of knowing, the science of asking, and the reality of being. But because we are less trained, and much less socialized to the traditional practices and disciplines, we mix epistemologies as we do language, we blend techniques, we confuse traditional researchers, we create new realities, and thus, we create new knowledge. By including those who have not had a voice in the past, we begin to privilege new information that is grounded on a different ontological reality, just as Javier did. Thus, in mixing these realities, techniques, and epistemologies, we use not only the written word as a vehicle for expression, but we use audio, video, music, and performance art as means for sharing the story and painting the picture of our community. To be sure, we are all at different points in our careers and we are at different places academically and intellectually. This chapter is grounded where we and other intellectuals of color find ourselves. We are intent and excited about looking at critical ethnography and its role in community change.

Clearly, the literature on critical ethnography positions itself as the voice and vehicle for challenging the power structures and working to equalize power dynamics. This does not mean that the research and its integrity are compromised, but it does challenge the illusion of objectivity.

In the spirit of critical ethnography and community change, the rest of this chapter will be developed in two ways. The first message is that the method of delivery will be critical in nature and will work to disrupt the isolation and inaccessibility of traditional academia. The second is that this document will use research as praxis (Freire 1993; Lather 1991). We attempt to connect critical ethnography with the impact it has had on community change. The structure of the document will be grounded in practice, yet informed by theory and reflective in nature. The emphasis on community change will be delivered in three different aspects. First, we emphasize the value of giving people "voice." Second, we shift from the micro to the macro in an attempt to give the reader some of the thinking and strategies that are used on a daily basis. Then we present the impact that critical ethnography can have on researchers and communities who have been traditionally marginalized. Last, we close by posing some challenges for the future. But first, we begin with a description of some theoretical points.

## Theoretical Issues

Qualitative research and critical ethnography in particular creates an opportunity for academicians and common people alike to put forth the stories of people, cultures, and communities. The role tradition of ethnography has been rooted and practiced by anthropologists, but quickly adopted and practiced by other disciplines such as education, business, and other professional schools. But in spite of these cross-discipline practices, the common practice of the ethnographer telling the story is constant. And it is on this front that we want to deviate from the traditional critical ethnographers. Indeed, as Foley so aptly quotes Behar as writing, "anthropology that does not break the heart is not worth doing." Clearly, this forces the practice of critical ethnography to a deeper level. This level is traditionally interpreted as reflexivity. A practice that Marcuse writes about and anthropologists like Foley, Trueba, and Behar have perfected. We propose that there is a different interpretation to Behar's quote, which to us espouses an even more effective method for implementing a strategy and process that creates an anthropology that breaks the heart. Indeed, the context is one where Behar pushes the issue on making our selves vulnerable as Rosaldo (1989) did in his book *Cul-*

*ture and Truth* and as Behar does in *The Vulnerable Observer*. But it is here where we want to deviate and propose that Behar used her statement as a metaphor. To us this is a metaphor for breaking the mold. In our minds this mold is the traditional way of seeing life, people, and culture. In short, it is a different way of doing ethnography. The old has been constructed and maintained by white males. We propose that a new way of doing critical ethnography can and should be part of the discourse. In short, we propose that when the observed becomes part of the process of observing, the reality and story of people, cultures, and communities will be told in a very different way, with different vigor, indeed, with a different voice. This in turn surfaces and creates a different power dynamic.

It is this different way of painting the picture of people that we want to develop further in this document. It is clear in our minds that if critical ethnography is to live up to the values and principle of traditionally marginalized people, resist oppression, and become a counterhegemonic tool, it must continue to develop a message that not only talks the talk, but also walks the walk. It is clear to us that critical ethnography is not just about giving people a voice, which in and of itself puts forth a traditional power dynamic; but it should be about giving people skills, allowing people to create their knowledge, and in the process sharing and co-creating the power. In short, critical ethnography can be pedagogical in theory and in practice.

But to do this we cannot follow the prevailing discursive regimes; indeed, it is up to those of us who come to academia from the margins to push the envelope not only on developing a new language (one that is accessible to people), but is also on developing and practicing a different method of critical ethnography. It is imperative for us to continue to struggle with what Villenas (1996) posits in *The Colonizer/Colonized Chicana Ethnographer* in order for us to reflect on the work we do and how we do it. This is critical as we attempt to live in the multiple worlds that Holland (1999) writes about, and it is at the core of Ladson-Billings and Tate's (1995) and other critical race theorists' argument that people and their characteristics are not property to be commodified.

So it is on these theoretical grounds that we propose a hybrid version of critical ethnography that is true to the principle/criteria for a good ethnography outlined by Spindler and Spindler (1987), yet propose a pedagogical strategy for including common people in the process of observing and painting their own picture. This frames a dynamic that needs to see the community participants as partners and not "informants," and the ethnography must go beyond being the "Professional Stranger." We must respect relationships, and we must understand how they are built.

Below, we provide an example of how some of this work has been done on a daily basis. It is a process developed and implemented by organic intellectuals who range from fourteen to seventy years of age. It has been the beginning of a new ethnography that is described above and it has given birth to a new intellectual whose talents have been latent during this past century. Thus, as we paint the picture of a people and their community, we have given them a brush to paint with us as we simultaneously legitimize their knowledge that in turn creates power. Next we provide some snapshots of this reality.

## A Case Study: *The Llano Grande Center*

The Llano Grande Center for Research & Development, a school- and community-based nonprofit organization, is located at Edcouch–Elsa High School (E–E H.S.) in Elsa, Texas, fifteen miles north of the Texas–Mexico border in the Rio Grande Valley. The Center was born out of numerous conversations that some of us from the rural communities of Edcouch and Elsa had during a period of several decades, spanning from the time when we were students at E–E H.S. until the time when some of us joined the faculty of the same high school in the early 1990s.

A number of sources have inspired the creation and development of the Llano Grande Center. We were inspired by the stories our elders told us, just as we were inspired by the immense talent and potential of our youth, which typically goes uncultivated by an increasingly standardized system of public education. Singular acts have also inspired us. Take, for example, an instance in 1992 when a Mexican American high school student posed the question, "Were Mexican people around in 1776 when Thomas Jefferson was crafting the Declaration of Independence?" and followed with the statement, "We're nowhere in the history books." That question, along with the wisdom of our elders, and our growing disaffection with public schooling, inspired us to seek alternative paths for schooling. The Llano Grande Center was born out of that energy.

Initially, the Center took shape as an ambitious oral history project supported by an Annenberg Foundation Rural Challenge grant. Through the oral history project, we promised to confront the traditional method by which history was taught in our schools, where 99 percent of the student body was of Mexican ancestry, but where every state adopted textbook E–E

H.S. used blatantly disregarded the experience of Mexican people in the making of Texas. Indeed, we were nowhere in the history books.

We addressed the issue by convening community people with teachers and students to develop a plan of action. The history of rural south Texas, we contended, was yet to be told. We began the oral history project out of Edcouch–Elsa and La Villa High Schools in the summer of 1997; three years and several hundred oral histories later, the project has been a source for the profound transformation of people, institutions, and even a community.

## From Deficit Model to an Assets-Based Approach

The prevailing paradigm that influenced many of us growing up in the latter part of the twentieth century is distinctly rooted in a needs-based, or deficit-driven, model (Valencia 1997). Community development initiatives typically begin with the question, "What does this town need," and civic leaders react to the identified needs. The teaching profession similarly is guided by the needs of children, although today's needs are increasingly identified in the context of what a child needs to pass the state-mandated test. Growing up in a community where half the population participates in the migrant farm working stream, a place where annual unemployment rates hover around the 30 percent mark and where most of our parents did not attain a high level of formal schooling, our region was easy to describe as an area with high needs, a region with pronounced deficits. For decades the pitiful indicators of high poverty, high unemployment, and low levels of educational attainment have defined our south Texas communities. Not surprisingly, educational and other public policy makers characteristically respond to the needs.

While the Llano Grande Center is acutely conscious of the needs of our youth, our schools, and our community, the needs approach is not what defines the core of our philosophy. To the contrary, the Center has deliberately departed from the traditional deficit-driven model to education and community development by creating an aggressive assets-based approach (Kretzmann and McKnight 1996). The conventional approach suggests that because the majority of people in our community do not speak, read, or write English, they are deficient. On the other hand, our students and staff believe that we have extraordinary assets in our community because many of our residents are very proficient in Spanish. Because we have used this approach, we are in the process of developing various microenterprises, including the Llano Grande Spanish Language Immersion Institute; we recently received a $50,000 grant from the Kellogg Foundation to launch such an enterprise. The community-based research work of the Center has revealed abundant assets within our towns; our researchers, in fact, utilize research data to engage the community in development initiatives (Lather 1991).[1] The Center's purpose for conducting youth development programming, community-based research, and a school reform initiative is primarily focused on creating positive social, cultural, and institutional change (Lather 1991; Trueba 1999). Youth, teachers, and a wide range of community members who participate in the Center's ongoing research work drive much of what is created; they are the ones who emerge as the experts of our schools, our community, and our history—as we continue to grow together as researchers, educators, and agents of change (Scheurich and Imber 1997).[2] In short, we utilize a wide variety of assets, including our young researchers, our wise elders, and the distinct assets-based approach to development.

## Impact of the Assets-Based Model on Youth and Raising Expectations

The pitiful indicators would suggest that our students would be dropping out of school, working in the fields, and standing on the welfare lines. But ask our sixty students—all Mexican American, all poor (meaning working class)—who have gained acceptance into Ivy League universities since 1993,[3] when we began to dream and imagine that a kid like Delia Pérez, whose father worked in the fields and whose mother was a housewife, could go to a place like Yale University. Or a kid like Blanca Rojas, who didn't have indoor running water until she was in high school, who attended Brown University.[4] Or Mónica Marroquín, who lives in an isolated *colonia*, who attended Harvard and then medical school. Or Carlos García, who grew up in federal housing in Edcouch and whose mother earns $4,000 per year cleaning houses, who is paying $33,000 per year to attend Yale. We imagined that José Luis DeLeon, a lifelong farmworker, could leave his family working in the fields of Wisconsin, hop on an airplane at O'Hare Airport in Chicago en route to Cambridge, Massachusetts, where he would enroll in MIT in August of 1993. He did, and he graduated from the Sloan School of Management in 1997.

After Yale, Delia returned to Edcouch–Elsa to teach and has since enrolled at the LBJ School of Public Affairs.[5] Blanca graduated from Brown and returned to teach, just as Ernesto Ayala also graduated from Brown and returned to develop a community-based research program with the Llano Grande Center. Karina Cardoza graduated from Columbia and will soon be joining our community development efforts, just as Modesto Hernandez who graduated from Brown has returned to help develop our Geographic Information System research project. José Salívar, who graduates from Stanford next year, will return as well . . . and the list goes on.[6]

## A Sampling of Stories and Voices

### José Isabel Gutiérrez

When we embarked on our oral history project, one of the first people we interviewed was ninety-seven-year-old José Isabel Gutiérrez, known by many in the community as don Chavelo. Don Chavelo came to Texas from Guanajuato as a young man, landing in Edcouch before the town was sold in land tracts in 1926. "Yo soy uno de los fundadores de Edcouch" ("I am one of the founders of Edcouch"), don Chavelo proclaimed to the interview team as he stiffened his small body for emphasis. "How can that be, don Isabel?" one interviewer retorted. Don Chavelo's comment puzzled the interview team, particularly because during the previous forty-five minutes of conversation, he had described himself as a lifelong laborer, and even as one of the thousands of Mexican men and women who cleared the thick south Texas brush to make way for the establishment of towns such as Edcouch. Very deliberately, but with terrific resolve, don Chavelo posed a question to the inquiring interviewer: "Have you ever drunk Edcouch water?" "Yes, I have," said the young interviewer. "Well," said don Chavelo, "you can thank me for that, because in the late 1920s I was one of the men who dug up the ditches to install the water pipes. You drink water because of the work that people like me did. I am a founder of Edcouch" (*Llano Grande Journal* 1997–1998). With that, and with dozens of other stories, don Chavelo established himself as an invaluable character in the creation and development of the community. As he did so, he also challenged young people to question their own paradigms. Who really are the founders, builders, and heroes of our communities?

The Center published don Chavelo's story in the *Llano Grande Journal*, and we have archived and digitized it (*Llano Grande Journal* 1997–1998). His story will live forever. But while don Chavelo lived—he died during the spring of 2000—his story validated the great value of his life. During the last five years of his life, don Chavelo attended the Blue Bonnet Adult Day Care Center, where daily he drank coffee, played cards, and exchanged stories with several dozen other local elders. We received a telephone call at the Llano Grande Center one morning from don Chavelo. We were surprised to get such a call. As we had gotten to know don Chavelo, we understood that he did not own a phone, nor was he known to speak on the phone with any regularity. It must have been important, we thought. And it was. Don Chavelo called to request thirty copies of the *Llano Grande Journal*, because his friends at the Blue Bonnet were interested in seeing him "en el libro." Immediately, we dispatched a team of researchers to the Blue Bonnet, whereupon we proceeded to hand out copies of the *Journal* to a couple of dozen eager elders. After a few minutes of observation, the director of the Blue Bonnet approached one of our young researchers and confided, "Do you know that at least half of those people who are reading the journal are actually illiterate?" Indeed, the power of the oral history, don Chavelo's story, and the publication began the process of transforming many of us. We began to redefine literacy, education, stories, and numerous other concepts deeply imbedded within our minds and in our souls.

### Santos Layton

When high school students interviewed seventy-six-year-old Santos Layton, they quickly learned what master storytelling is about. La señora Layton told the joyful story of when she raised her children in Elsa during the greater part of each year and in the fields in west Texas as the family followed the crops every summer. Uplifting anecdotes characterize narrative, until she told the story of Pablito. Early one morning in the mid-1950s Pablito was out delivering newspapers on his bicycle as part of his daily routine when a car fatally hit him. The entire Mexican side of Elsa mourned the death of the youngster, and a traumatized señora Layton was devastated. Shortly after the death, and against the wishes of la señora Layton, el señor Layton bought an accordion and a guitar for the four remaining children. The event would forever change the Layton family, just as it would change the cultural complexion of the entire community. Today, Los Hermanos Layton stand as an important institution in the music industry of south Texas. They have been featured at the Smithsonian Institution and have played an integral role in the formation of Tejano music in the Rio Grande Valley (Llano Grande 1998).

The Layton oral history has been presented in the classrooms at Edcouch–Elsa High School and in numerous other classrooms across the country. La señora Layton's interview is part of a collection of stories from rural America that is used in some 600 rural schools across the nation. At E–E H.S., her story resonates particularly well. When several freshman students debated the merits of a literary selection last year in a freshman English class, a fifteen-year-old female student emphatically pounded her fist on her desk and declared, "No, that's not what my grandmother meant in that paragraph!" The student? La señora Layton's granddaughter. At E–E H.S., Santos Layton has become an important part of the literary canon.

### Olga Solis

Through our work this past year, as well as with the changes we have seen, we have learned invaluable lessons. We have learned how using the wisdom of people from our community and the relationships we have built can be adopted for creative development. Indeed, the oral history process has guided us as we continue to create the direction for community development. Take, for example, the development implications of the oral history we conducted with Olga Solis.

In a recent oral history, a team of a teacher and students conducted an oral history with eighty-four-year-old Elsa resident Olga Solis. As usual, it was an inspiring and enlightening house visit. Doña Olga Solis, the interviewee, taught us about life in the community years ago. As she shared her experiences and wisdom, we once again observed the intellectual, spiritual, and historical values embodied in our elders.

But Doña Olga went way beyond these aspects. As she shared the stories of her children, she especially focused on her daughter Mary. In 1942, when Mary was six years old, Doña Olga took little Mary to the Edcouch Elementary School, whereupon superintendent White, who stood on the front door steps of the all-Anglo elementary school, met mother and daughter.

"Mrs. Solis," the superintendent said. "I'm sorry, Mary cannot come to this school. There is another school for her on the other side of the tracks."

Mrs. Solis responded, "Mr. White, I've trained Mary from day one so that she could come to this school. She knows English, she knows how to read, and she is ready to go to school."

But superintendent White reiterated that school policy called for segregation. Mrs. Solis conceded, for the moment. That very day, however, Mrs. Solis drafted a letter to Franklin Delano Roosevelt, urging the president to intervene on the side of justice.

Two months later, the White House delivered a directive to do what was right. The school district responded by instituting a literacy test for Mexican children. Mary took the test, passed it, and integrated Edcouch Elementary School. Mary graduated from Edcouch–Elsa in 1954, left Elsa in 1955, and has seldom been heard from again in our community. But her story intrigued us, and we decided to seek her out.[7]

Through Doña Olga, we made contact with Mary and quickly found that she was owner and president of a survey research operation in a large city. We also learned she was on the board of directors of major corporations and foundations. She flew down to Elsa one weekend to visit with a team of students and teachers for an oral history. After an hour's worth of conversation/interview, we asked Mary about her business. She described to us the survey research work she conducts and offered to mentor us in learning the research techniques and methods she used. We have since formed a strong relationship with her, and she has played an integral role in helping launch the Llano Grande Center's community-based research work.

Through this research work, we have transformed curricula. Researchers have become transformed because of the power of people's stories, and we have begun to create the infrastructure for a new economy—an economy based on the spirit, will, and the stories of our people.

## A Theory in Practice

The work we have engaged in is pedagogical and relational at the core, and because we have consciously begun with the relational, we have put youth, parents, teachers, and community members at the forefront of our efforts. We are committed to deviating from the traditional mode of programming dictating practice; on the contrary, people will dictate programming. Additionally, we have developed programs with the assets of people in mind. Consistent with the writings in *Latino Cultural Citizenship* (Flores and Benmayor 1997), we have developed a proactive and assets-based model (Kretzmann and McKnight 1996). Our communities are full of assets, yet traditional practices and funding organizations (foundations, government programs, and bureaucracies) force us to continue to label people as poor, deficient, and helpless. This many times puts service deliverers, schools, and institutions of higher education in the role of the "grand savior" and expert. But Macedo has found a more appropriate label, considering the self-serving and negative practices of many of these institutions. He boldly refers to them as "poverty pimps" (1994). This has created multiple victimizations of our communities: first by the historical racists' social structures; second, by a paternalistic top-down school system that excludes many of our citizens from participation in the process and reaping its benefits; and third, by institutions who receive resources to "save or fix" our community, yet little is done.

These are bold words, but we must be conscious of the history and traditional practices that have gotten us here if we are to prevent this cycle from continuing. We can easily say that since most of us involved in this effort are local and sensitive to these practices, this will prevent the replication of these structures. But history has shown us otherwise. This same behavior is obvious during the last twenty-five years while local Chicanos have been in leadership roles. Some of us would make the argument that it has taken us thirty years to see the benefit of people ruling themselves. Essentially it has taken a generation to begin decolonizing our community. During the last twenty to thirty years our ancestors' only knowledge of leadership was that of the white dominant power structures. It has taken some of us leaving the area to see the damages as we begin to train ourselves and create alternative yet native theories of thought and practice. It is this transition that we see before our eyes that raises the importance of documenting our reality.

Our theory is a hybrid. One that takes from critic pedagogical writings of Freire (1993), Trueba (1999), and Giroux (1996), while also building on Moll et al.'s (1992) funds of knowledge, Reyes (1999) High Performing Hispanic learning communities, and the loving caring schools Scheurich (1998) writes about. Additionally, as we build on our knowledge and assets, we have worked to enhance our theories by adapting and adopting Pittman's (1996) community youth development model. Our youth are not only our future leaders; they are also our present shining stars. They are the reason why 5,000 people congregate at the Friday night football games, and it is in their educational interest that our public funds and institutions provide employment for many of our community's residents during a time when private-sector industry has abandoned us. Additionally, if there is any expert in what youth need, it is youths themselves. Thus, it is by developing a mutually beneficial partnership that we can collectively begin to tend to our past pain, present needs, and future concerns while working on building our local assets. Young people must understand the past and be active participants and partners as we deal with local community issues (Giroux 1996) if we are to prepare healthy citizens of all ages.

So, as we engage our youth, we develop our own epistemology based on family (Hidalgo 1998), and as we begin to better understand the past, we build our resistance against many of the dominant forces. Simultaneously, we become more resilient (Trueba 1999). And as we become stronger, we begin to dream and develop a pedagogy of hope (Freire 1993; Trueba 1999) that our community and institutions desperately need if we are to resist and survive the effects of the racist epistemologies (Scheurich and Young 1997) that the dominant research practices use as they research us and not research with us. It is this emancipatory tactic that we are committed to developing with our community partners. As Habermas (1972) writes, as we research, we are committed to developing the instrumental knowledge, relational knowledge, and the critical knowledge. Thus, as we research, we have built our own capacity to deal with the issues like education, economic, and spirituality of our community. Certainly these three components overlap, but I have delineated them because they are the most pressing issues I have identified that presently need our attention. A number of other stories need to be told and are being chronicled, but consistent with the need for our research to be grounded in practice and responsive to our community needs and assets, it is critical that this story be captured. Because once documented, it will further expand the discourse; and to an extent, we agree with Wolcott (1994) when he raises the point that it is much more important to be provocative than right.

## Some Strategies of the Process

McClelland's (1985) theory of needs puts forth the ideas that people have three major needs if their lives are to be meaningful. He writes that we all have the need for achievement, affiliation, and power. This theory of needs helps us outline the responsiveness that we are committed to delivering to the youth, families, and professionals in our community. These needs are thus articulated, implemented, and practiced in a variety of ways. The youth and adults are part of the learning community, and every opportunity is a teachable moment. The Center's director, employees, and students decide the management, resources allocation, and daily operations. The outreach and resources development duties are shared between all of the above, with those who have more contacts and access to resources making more of the public presentation. The structure and mode of operation is very horizontal and based in a democratic value. The daily work is intense; adults who are outnumbered by youth are always in a teaching and learning mode. The strategies used to weave the theory of needs with practice are the following: 1) every child needs a safe place, 2) every child needs a positive relationship with an adult, 3) every child needs to learn skills, 4) every child needs a safe place to apply these skills, and 5) we must celebrate our victories.

## Developing a Safe Place

In developing this safe structure it is critical that we go beyond looking at safety as only a physical issue. This safe place must be a place that nurtures and stimulates the thought process of children, youth, and adults. It is a place where young people feel safe to take intellectual risks, and it is a place where youth feel safe enough to share their dreams, hopes, and expectations. It is also a place where we develop and practice a high quality standard, and a culturally relevant process that rids itself of the symbolic violence that many of our children of color experience too frequently.

## Creating Positive Relationships

We firmly believe that youth must have a safe and positive relationship with an adult in their life. The adult can be a parent, relative, friend, teacher, or administrator. However, in case the youth we work with do not have any of the above, we see it as our responsibility to develop these relationships with youth when they are with us. These relationships will look like a mentorship relationship at the surface, but I would propose that these relationships are at another level. Mentorships many times imply a unilateral relationship where knowledge is given from the adult to the youth, but the process we practice is reciprocal. The youth and adults are simultaneously both the teachers and the learners. This relationship is pedagogical and democratic in nature. Further, from the exchange between the learners and the teachers, new knowledge is created (Giroux 1992). This new knowledge must be acknowledged, shared, and utilized to expand the learning process for the community.

## Learning of Skills

It is critical that all youth leave school with the needed skills to live a productive life. But it is just as important to value, respect, and build on the skills that youth bring with them to school. This is congruent with critical pedagogy thinkers, and essentially presents a neo-Vygotskian perspective to his concept of the zone of proximal development (1978). Consistent with this practice, Giroux (1996) writes that the skills youth learn must be relevant to their daily lives. Also, Levy and Murnane (1996) in their book *Teaching the New Basic Skills* argue that if the information youth are learning does not equate to a future livable wage, we must question the information they are being taught. In short, the education youth obtain must be relevant, stimulating, and applicable.

## Creating Opportunities to Apply Skills

We see the extracurricular activities as one of the vehicles where youth apply the skills they learn; however, these avenues become problematic when only a small number of young people can participate in these events. An alternative opportunity we have developed for youth to apply the skills they have learned in school is to expand the school environment beyond the traditional four walls. Essentially, the community becomes the classroom. These venues might include performing service-learning projects, working in internships, training of other youth, doing history research, making public presentations, writing grants, participating in conferences, hosting and planning conferences, participating in teacher trainings, and the list can continue. But the participation in these activities alone is not the answer; the participation must be accompanied with a strong reflexive and evaluation process with adults and peers. This practice then presents education in very familiar and practical context for the learners and teachers.

### Celebrating Our Victories

Acknowledging and celebrating our accomplishments is critical to us. The spirit of people must be energized and their hard work must be acknowledged. The constant celebrations allow for people to associate, celebrate our accomplishments, and reenergize the power we have collectively created; we also acknowledge the importance of breaking bread together.

## Developing a Framework

These very basic strategies and values mentioned above in turn connect the three defining initiatives of the Llano Grande Center: 1) Policy and Education Reform, 2) Education, Training, and Leadership Development, and 3) Research and Development and Publications. These three foci in a very aggressive way inform our sustainable community and economic development initiatives. Through this initiative we then begin to define what the role of schools and education is in creating a sustainable and healthy community. Additionally, the rest of this chapter articulates the work we have done to impact the education, economy, and the spirituality of our community. To be clear, I define spirituality, in a broad sense, as that which relates to the nature of relationships with people, the environment, and ones past and future.

Our work with Llano Grande is a neo-Vygotskian (Moll 1990) approach to youth development and education. We are committed to working with youths', teachers', and families' local environments and ecology to develop an alternative way of creating new knowledge, or as appropriate in this case, surfacing latent knowledge. Education must be relevant to youth's reality if it is to be effective and significant. So, in response to the local needs and to building on our local assets, we have developed a place-based curriculum. A process that has included local research, rewriting curriculum, and recruitment of teachers who have been willing to engage in this process. The principles and values of our Pedagogy of Place curriculum guide are the following: environment, history, economy, spirituality, and politics. Additionally, our students have become researchers and are collecting and telling their relatives' stories as they go home and interview their *pardes, abuelos, tios,* and *tias.* So needless to say, a new local history is surfacing and now it is Don Chavelo who claims it was he and not Ed Couch who found the *pueblo* of Edcouch. Also, it is not uncommon to see fierce debate in the classroom as fifteen- and sixteen-year-old students debate about what their grandparents meant by the language they used in their published oral history.

This stimulating environment is created and replicated as we use multiple strategies to document our local histories. Oral histories are always videotaped and audio recorded, pictures are scanned, and these histories are transcribed and published in our locally founded *Llano Grande Journal.* As Giroux writes (1996), students should be researchers, and their findings should be documented in "free presses." The *Llano Grande Journal* is our version of a free press. We will not stand for others to decide and judge if our stories are fit for publications; we will publish our own history.

Additionally, we use research as praxis (Lather 1991; Freire 1993) as our research is used for educational purposes and consistent with participatory action researchers it is also used to democratize information, thus making it an emancipatory strategy, for we consider information a form of obtaining power.

The educational practices we have embraced are diverse and our local community has become our classroom. Thus, our teachers are the local *veteranos* who were in the battlefields of Europe during World War II, and those who returned to share their stories from the Vietnam conflict. The primary sources they provide for student learning are invaluable. Their data has helped the students construct their own Vietnam Memorial as we honor the local *Raza* who didn't make it back. Also, the English curriculum has been augmented and strengthened by a writer in residence program we have sustained during the last two years. Local writer David Rice (1996) helps students develop their stories so they can be published in our journal or the local newspaper. David and our media expert Lauriano Aguirre are now helping students produce their own films.

So the educational experience we have introduced is holistic, diverse, and grounded in reality. Our community education strategy has been developmental at the core as youth share their research and the knowledge they created with the local school board and city officials to impact public policy. Our youth are learning and applying their skills as they become learners, teachers, and active participants in the development of their local community. Youth have embraced their birthright as citizens in their community and their country. They have become change agents as they engage in challenging the traditional practices and outdated public policies. Also, as we expand the definition of education and redefine the size and possibilities of a greater classroom, we have invited many of our community partners to be part of the education of their children and themselves. One strategy we have adopted and modified is the concept of community learning teams (Senge 1990). Recently we secured resources for the creation of ten community teams with each team having at least ten members. Every team consisted of both youth and adults, and after participating in six training sessions, they became eligible for $15,000 per team to implement a community project of their choice. This has produced a local youth run radio station, a publishing center, several community centers for neighboring communities, and a comprehensive database. We have consciously invited the community to be partners in the their children's learning, for as Secretary of Education Richard Riley says, "If the school is the center of the community, then learning is at the center of the community" (1999).

## Community Economics

Since the late 1960s our country's public policy has embraced the human capital theory (Ghez and Becker 1975; Marshall and Tucker 1992), which in brief says that the more you invest in the educational development of people, the higher the economic return. Additionally, the traditional market-driven economy is based on three major assumptions: 1) people make rational choices, and they categorize and order these choices, 2) these decisions are transitive, and 3) the consumer always wants more than less of the goods. These policies and assumptions of the traditional market economy are very problematic because most of the assumptions and applications do not consider race, education, or other discriminatory practices, and they are developed from values that are incongruent with those of our community (Clark 1995). Thus, this scenario puts forward a political economy that, based on its values and assumptions, eliminates many of our communities that differ on these values. For even the most liberal of policies, affirmative action is intended to benefit individuals as opposed to strengthening communities. In short, it is consistent with the Euro-American individualistic value system instead of valuing the collective. Additionally, in a market economy, the only currency is money and we have begun to define our currency in multiple forms, which includes money. Some of our other currencies are funds of knowledge (Moll 1992), strong values and commitment to the collective/ community, the community assets of young people, and the philanthropic spirit (Campoamor, Diaz, & Ramos 1999) of giving resources, time, ideas, and energy for supporting our neighbors and youth during times of need. In short, we have decided that in our work there are multiple bottom lines. Certainly, we understand the need for creating jobs and becoming active in our rapidly changing economy, but our values must be established if we are to develop a viable and sustainable alternative to the existing amoral market economy that has gotten us to this point of poverty and disenfranchisement. The only invisible hand we are familiar with is the one that has marginalized us and excluded us from the process. In this context, Wheatley (1992) aptly quotes Einstein: "No problem can be solved from the same consciousness that created it." I propose that it is time for a new consciousness that is based on our community's common sense to surface if the strategies for educating our future generations are to be congruent with the values, beliefs, and cultural practices of our community.

We believe that a healthy local economy can only be created and nurtured if developed along with our education and based on our local assets, but we must be aware of the traditional discriminatory practices and other pitfalls that have stagnated us in the past. It is then when we can begin to establish our political will and our economic power and begin to establish a "healthier" political economy that benefits the many in our community not only the few. As we work to develop the political economy, we have accepted the responsibility of creating the conditions that nurture the investment of resources into the area that will help us create new jobs. It is not just about creating new jobs, but it's about creating new jobs that are congruent with the "new economy," based on knowledge and skills not the traditional jobs that nurtured the old economy, and based on manual backbreaking labor. In creating new jobs we are committed to starting the conversation at the livable wage level—not minimum wages. We believe that as one nurtures these values and develops new jobs, our youth will want to come back home. During the last three years, we have secured over 2.5 million dollars and have created new employment for people who would have found employment elsewhere. We are committed to developing the supply of labor and the demand.

Further, as we continue to establish credible outcomes and significant impacts in this community, we begin to role model a different process of education and community and economic development.

This new process is pedagogical in nature and based on our local assets and common sense. This democratic framework has begun to demonstrate positive alternative modes of operation and viable opportunities that will navigate us toward a sustainable community development model. This model will move away from focusing on a single bottom line to a multiple bottom line where we respect the economy, environment, ecology, and human needs of our community.

## Spirituality

As we develop a new knowledge base by both retelling our local stories that had been excluded from our educational system and augmenting them with the lessons and knowledge we bring back from our national and international travels and university experiences, we are creating a new spirit. This spirit is grounded in our local values and a language and theory that is global in nature. We are committed to developing a spirit that is respectful of who we are as a people. This spirit acknowledges, respects, and celebrates our *viegitos* for the strong cultural grounding and the identity they have endowed us with; as important, we are committed to developing a politic that rids itself of the patron democracy that has controlled our reality during this century. This politic we have nurtured and practiced and are laboring to evangelize is based on our community values of trust, respect, honesty, and security. For when we develop these basic and essential elements then we create the safe environments and conditions that allow us to dialogue about issues of race, gender, politics, economy, ecology, and values that must take place if we are to continue developing a new spirit of participation.

The spirit of our community will continue to be developed as we include the young and the old in our conversations. These discussions will then continue to inform the development of our community including our education and economy. These discussions have also rekindled the spirit of hope in our community that used to only be obvious during pep rallies and Friday night football games. Our spiritual practices and commitment to our youth have increased the participation of youth that have been traditionally disengaged. Thus, our commitment to our spirituality goes beyond the traditional religious practices. It is relational at the core. Ideas, dreams, and experiences fuel it. The diverse thoughts and experiences our partners bring with them make our community stronger. It is this diversity and spirituality that has helped us develop and begin to manifest a new leadership. This leadership is grounded in community and interdependence, inclusive, participatory, and transformational,. This practice and value along with our strategies of development have nurtured and created the conditions that have surfaced in new organic public intellectuals (Simon 1991) who embody, live, and evangelize this spirituality that is a hybrid of the local and the global. Thus, Delia Perez, Raul Valdez, Ernesto Ayala, Blanca Rojas, Jose Saldívar, and many colleagues who are teenagers or in their early twenties are our new local heroes, role models, spokespersons, and change agents.

## Impact of This Practice

There have been some significant impacts in the local community from our work. Some of the most celebrated accomplishments have been the thirty-six students from our community we have helped get into Ivy League schools. This has taken place in the span of the six years since we began this work. Certainly many other students have attended local and state universities, but it is these thirty-six students who come from one of the poorest areas in the country, and the second poorest school district in the state, who have helped put our work in the public eye. This impact has gained us credibility. Six years ago when we shared some of our ideas with local leaders and teachers they laughed, but now people believe they can make a difference in their community. We have nurtured a new hope; but the best, however, is yet to come, as is reflected by how many of our talented youth are returning to south Texas to participate in community development.

## Future Challenges

Certainly we have many challenges before us, but our evangelizing has created disciples, and thus there are many more of us carrying the metaphoric cross. One of the challenges we see is our ability to train more teachers who are willing to try different strategies for educating our youth. The greatest challenges are not the youth, but our adults who have been institutionalized and some that are tired of the work they do. Because of this we must continue to tap our assets and help them shine. We have many assets in our community, and we must create the vehicles and space for them to share their stories of success and challenges. For as we begin tell our stories, we begin to document our community change, and community change begins with people sharing their stories, with people sharing their vulnerabilities publicly. But we have learned much from our short experience and we are aware we will continue to face many of the same challenges we have faced historically, including the racism and patron democracy that has prevented our communities from healing. However, we are a little older and a little wiser as we include more of our community in the process. This inclusion will continue to convey the stories of our elders and the spirit and innocence of our youth. Thus, as we collectively struggle with very painful issues, we will then begin to heal cognitively, economically, and spiritually. Further the inclusion of young people in this process will also help us prepare for our future, and we know that our future is now!

An additional challenge from the field of research is to see if the existing structures and practice will allow those of us to form the margins in. This is of interest because as researchers at the Llano Grande Center define critical ethnography consistent with other practitioners, the ontological reality we bring as ethnic minority and organic intellectuals thus delineates a practice defined by its ecology. Indeed, knowing, understanding, deconstructing, building, and learning how to use and how to share power are concepts that are at the core of our work. We hope we have laid out a clear picture on how we live this idea while also painting the picture of our community.

## Notes

1. For a published discussion on the Llano Grande Seminar Series see "State Farm Partners with Llano Grande Center to Grow with Prosperity," *South Texas Star*, 6, 10 (October 2000):13–14.

2. Unlike the Johnsonville reform experience that Scheurich and Imber 1997 discuss, the work of the Llano Grande Center is radically different. The process of local elites playing traditional local elite roles has been kept in check, at least in the case of the Llano Grande Center's development and influence. That reality can be explained, to a large degree, because those who lead the work of the Center were raised with or around school board members and other influential administrators and have long-lasting relationships with them. The leaders of the Center and those who evangelize the philosophy, spirit, and mission of the Center are primarily youths, teachers, and the elderly.

3. Ample published information tells at least part of this story: "Small Town, Big Dreams," *South Texas Star*, 6, 10 (October 2000); "Battling Modest Dreams: Valley Students Go to Ivy League, then Return to Make a Difference," *Austin American Stateman* cover story, October 8, 2000; "Why Frank Guajardo Went Home: A Texas Ex Makes a Real Difference in a Poor South Texas Community," *Texas Alcalde*, January/February 2000; "Mentorship at Its Best" from the *National Research Center on the Gifted and Talented*

Newsletter, Spring 1999; Standing Up for Community and School: Rural People Tell Their Stories; "Francisco Guajardo and the Llano Grande Center," published by the Rural School and Community Trust, by Bradwell Scott, Spring 1999; Francisco Guajardo, essay published in Public School Standards: Discussing the Case for Community Control, a symposium hosted by the Annenberg Foundation's Rural Challenge, Burlington, Vermont, January 1999.

4. David Ruben, "Great Expectations," Brown Alumni Magazine, August 1999.

5. "Something in Return: Valley Natives Who Left for College Return Home to Pursue Their Careers," The Monitor, December 6, 1998, cover story.

6. "South Texas Teacher Inspires Students to Walls of Ivy," Associated Press article, October 1997.

7. Llano Grande Center Oral History Collection, Edcouch, Texas.

# References

Behar, Ruth. The Vulnerable Observer: Anthropology That Breaks Your Heart. Boston: Beacon Press, 1996.

Bourdieu, Pierre, and Loic J. D. Wacquant. An Invitation to Reflexive Sociology. Chicago: University of Chicago Press, 1992.

Bowles, Samuel, and Herbert Gintis. Schooling in Capitalist America: Educational Reform and the Contradictions of Economic Life. New York: Basic Books, 1976.

Campoamor, D., W. Diaz, and H. Ramos, ed. Nuevos Senderos: Reflections on Hispanics and Philanthropy. Houston: Arte Publico Press, 1999.

Clark, Mary. "Changes in Euro-American Values Needed for Sustainability." Journal of Social Issues, 51, 4 (Winter 1995).

Flores, W. V., and R. Benmayor, ed. Latino Cultural Citizenship: Claiming Identity, Space, and Rights. Boston: Beacon Press, 1997.

Freire, Paulo. Pedagogy of the Oppressed. Rev. 20th-anniversary ed. New York: Continuum, 1993.

Freire, Paulo. Pedagogy of Hope: Reliving Pedagogy of the Oppressed. New York: Continuum Publishing Co., 1996.

Ghez, Gilbert, and Gary Becker. Allocation of Time and Goods over the Life Cycle. Studies in Human Behavior and Social Institutions. National Bureau of Economic Research, 1975.

Giroux, H. "Educational Leadership and the Crisis of Democratic Government." Educational Researcher, 21, 4 (1992):4–11.

Giroux, H. A. Fugitive Cultures: Race, Violence, and Youth. New York: Routledge, 1996.

Habermas, Jurgen. Knowledge and Human Interest. London: Heinemann Educational, 1972.

Hidalgo, N. M. "Toward a Definition of a Latino Family Research Paradigm." International Journal of Qualitative Studies in Education, 11, 1 (1998):103–20.

Holland, D., et al. *Identity and Agency in Cultural Worlds*. Cambridge, Mass.: Harvard University Press, 1998.

Kretzmann, J., and J. P. McKnight. "Assets-Based Community Development." *National Civic Review*, 85 (1996):23–30.

Ladson-Billings, G., and W. Tate, IV. "Towards a Critical Race Theory." *Teachers College Record*, 97 (1995):47–68.

Lather, P. A. *Getting Smart: Feminist Research and Pedagogy With/in the Postmodern*. New York: Routledge, 1991.

Levy, F., and R. Murnane. *Teaching the New Basic Skills: Principles for Educating Children to Thrive in a Changing Economy*. New York: Free Press, 1996.

*Llano Grande Journal*. Llano Grande Oral History Project. Edcouch, Tex.: Llano Grande Publications, 1997–1998.

Macedo, Donaldo. *Literacies of Power: What Americans Are Not Allowed to Know*. Boulder, Colo.: Westview Press, 1994.

Marshall, R. F., and M. Tucker. *Thinking for a Living: Education and the Wealth of Nations*. New York: Basic Books, 1992.

McClelland, D. C. *Human Motivation*. Glenview, Ill.: Scott, Foresman,1985.

Moll, L., ed. *Vygotsky and Education: Instructional Implications and Applications of Sociohistorical Psychology*. Cambridge: Cambridge University Press, 1990.

Moll, L. C., C. Amanti, D. Neff, and N. Gonzalez. "Funds of Knowledge for Teaching: A Qualitative Approach to Connect Households and Classrooms." *Theory into Practice*, 31, 2 (1992): 132–44.

Piñon, F. *Patron Democracy*. Mexico: Contraste, 1985.

Pittman, K. J. "Community, Youth, Development: Three Goals in Search of Connection." *New Designs for Youth Development*. National Network for Youth (Winter 1996).

Pizarro, M. "Chicano/a Power: Epistemology and Methodology for Social Justice and Empowerment in Chicana/o Communities." *International Journal of Qualitative Studies in Education*, 11, 1 (1998):57–80.

Reyes, P., J. D. Scribner, and A. Paredes-Scribner, ed. *Lessons from High-Performing Hispanic Schools: Creating Learning Communities*. New York: Teachers College Press, 1999.

Rice, D. *Give the Pig a Chance and Other Stories*. Tempe, Ariz.: Bilingual Press, 1996.

Riley, R. Schools as Community Centers. Remarks presented to American Institute of Architects, 1999.

Rosaldo, R. *Culture and Truth*. Boston, Mass.: Beacon Press, 1989.

Scheurich, J. J., and M. Imber. "Educational Reforms Can Reproduce Societal Inequities: A Case Study." Pp. 8–28 in Jim Scheurich, ed., *Research Method in the Postmodern*. London: Falmer Press, 1997.

Scheurich, J., and M. Young. "Coloring Epistemology." Pp.132–58 in Jim Scheurich, ed., *Research Method in the Postmodern*. London: Falmer Press, 1997.

Scheurich, J. "Highly Successful and Loving, Public, Pre-K–5 School Populated Mainly by Low SES Children of Color: Core Beliefs and Cultural Characteristics." *Urban Education*, 33, 4 (1998): 451–91.

Senge, P. M. The Fifth Discipline: The Art & Practice of the Learning Organization. New York: Currency, 1990.

Simon, R. Gramsci's Political Thought: An Introduction. London: Lawrence & Wishart, 1991.

Spindler, G., and L. Spindler, ed. The Interpretive Ethnography of Education: At Home and Abroad. Hillsdale, N.J.: Lawrence Erlbaum Associates, 1987.

Trueba, H. Latinos Unidos: From Cultural Diversity to the Politics of Solidarity. Lanham, Md.: Rowman & Littlefield, 1999.

Valencia, R, ed. Contemporary Deficit Thinking. London: Falmer Press, 1996.

Valencia, R, ed. The Evolution of Deficit Thinking: Educational Thought and Practice. London: Falmer Press, 1997.

Villenas, S. "The Colonizaer/Colonized Chicana Ethnographer: Identity, Marginalization and Co-optation in the Field." Harvard Educational Review, 66, 4 (Winter 1996):711–31.

Vygotsky, L. S. Mind in Society: The Development of Higher Psychological Processes. M. Cole, V. John-Teiner, S. Scribner, and E. Souberman, ed. Cambridge: Harvard University Press, 1978.

Wheatley, M. J. Leadership and the New Science: Discovering Order in a Chaotic World. San Francisco: Berrett-Koehler Publishers, 1999.

Wolcott, H. F. Transforming Qualitative Data: Description, Analysis, and Interpretation. Thousand Oaks, Calif.: Sage Publications, 1994.

# Index

305